Anonymous

The Clergy of America:

Anecdotes illustrative of the character of ministers of religion in the United States

Anonymous

The Clergy of America:
Anecdotes illustrative of the character of ministers of religion in the United States

ISBN/EAN: 9783337718800

Printed in Europe, USA, Canada, Australia, Japan

Cover: Foto ©Lupo / pixelio.de

More available books at **www.hansebooks.com**

THE
CLERGY OF AMERICA:

ANECDOTES

ILLUSTRATIVE OF THE CHARACTER OF MINISTERS OF
RELIGION IN THE UNITED STATES.

PHILADELPHIA:
J. B. LIPPINCOTT & CO.
1869.

PREFACE.

The facts placed before the reader of this volume, are not only pleasing to the fancy, and interesting as calling up many delightful and solemn reminiscences, but they are important as materials of History. They show the character of the age, illustrate nature and religion, and supply those details of knowledge which cherish the habits of induction: without these there can be no certain philosophy.

In the compilation of this work, far more labour and pains have been expended than the vast majority of its readers would suppose; but its editor has been well repaid by the happiness he has enjoyed in going through the biography of so many eminent men, at once ornaments to the church and blessings to the world. No part of the globe has furnished brighter specimens of what Christian ministers should be, than these United States.

It is scarcely necessary to say much either of the materials of which the volume is composed, or the manner in which they are classified. The former, the editor believes, are all true; and, as to the latter, he has done what he could so to arrange the facts as to please and to profit his readers. At all events, here is a volume perfectly *unique*—unlike every thing else in the language.

In carrying out his design, the editor has found materials accumulate on his hands far beyond the capabilities of a single volume. Whether the other collections shall see the light, remains in a very great degree for the readers of this volume to decide. He has contemplated somewhat even beyond this, and would be happy to furnish one or two volumes of important and valuable specimens of American pulpit eloquence. Time will decide as to whether these projected volumes may hereafter be called for and published.

The Editor has now only to commend his volume to the blessing of God and the friendship of the Reader.

CONTENTS.

PREPARATION OF THE CLERGY FOR PUBLIC DUTIES.

	PAGE
Rev. William Robinson,	17
Rev. Hugh Knox,	18
Rev. Mr. A.	22
Rev. Mr. Ravencross,	22
A New England Divine,	23
Two Clergymen,	25
An Able Minister,	27
Six Young Ministers,	28
Several Young Ministers,	30
Rev. J. W. James,	33
A Young Clergyman,	34
A New England Clergyman,	35
Rev. Mr. Polk,	36
Rev. S. Nightingale,	37
Rev. S. Stoddard,	38
Rev. Dr. M'Cartee,	38
A Pious Bishop,	40
A Zealous Minister,	40
Rev. W. Cooper,	41
A New England Minister,	42
Rev. Dr. West,	42
An Old Clergyman,	44
The Beecher Family,	44
Rev. Joseph Eastburn,	46
Rev. Mr. C.,	47
Rev. President Edwards,	48
Rev. Dr. Dwight,	48
Several Young Clergymen,	49
Rev. Mr. Japhet,	53
Rev. Dr. Patten,	54
Rev. W. Tennent,	54
Rev. S. Blythe,	57
An Indian Preacher,	58
Rev. Charles Beatty,	59

Rev. President Davies, ... 60
Rev. Dr. Rodgers, ... 61
Rev. Dr. Harris, ... 63
Rev. Dr. King, ... 64
Rev. Dr. King and Rev. H. Lyman, . . . 65
A Clergyman, ... 68
An Indian Missionary, ... 69
Several Clergymen, ... 71
A Young Minister, ... 71
Rev. Mr. Willey, ... 72
Rev. Dr. Griffin, ... 73
Several Eminent Clergymen, ... 74
Rev. E. T. Taylor, ... 76
Rev. Dr. Payson, ... 78
Rev. Dr. Strong, ... 79

INCIDENTS CONNECTED WITH THE PULPIT LABOURS OF THE CLERGY.

Rev. Dr. Rodgers, ... 83
Rev. Mr. S., ... 87
A Clergyman in Indiana, ... 88
Rev. J. Kennaday, ... 89
Rev. Dr. Griffin, ... 90
Rev. W. Robinson, ... 94
A Clergyman in Maine, ... 95
An Indian Missionary, ... 96
An Impressive Preacher, ... 103
Rev. Dr. Payson, ... 104
Rev. E. T. Taylor, ... 106
Rev. Sylvester Larned, ... 107
Rev. Dr. Fisk, ... 108
Two Clergymen, ... 109
Rev. Dr. Bedell, ... 109
Rev. Dr. Miller, ... 111
Rev. T. Hooker, ... 111
A Forcible Preacher, ... 112
Rev. Dr. Staughton, ... 113
Rev. Dr. Humphrey, ... 115
A Faithful Minister, ... 116
Rev. W. Tennent, ... 117
Rev. Bradford Homer, ... 120
Rev. Mr. Howe, ... 122
Rev. Dr. Lathrop, ... 122
Rev. Dr. Beecher, ... 123
An Effective Clergyman, ... 124
Rev. Dr. Mercer, ... 125
A New England Clergyman, ... 130
Rev. T. Porter, ... 130
Rev. Mr. Rawson, ... 131

CONTENTS.

Rev. Dr. Welsh,	131
An Aged Clergyman,	133
Rev. John Sunday,	134
Rev. George Whitefield,	135
Rev. Mr. Bennett,	145
Rev. Dr. Hitchcock,	145
A Minister in New England,	148
Rev. Mr. S.,	148
Rev. Dr. Stillman,	149
An Eminent Clergyman,	150
Rev. Mr. Gillespie,	151
Rev. Mr. Moody,	152
Rev. Mr. Willard,	154
Rev. Mr. Truair,	155
Rev. Dr. Waddell,	155
Peter, the Indian Preacher,	159
Rev. Z. Adams,	160
A Clergyman in Massachusetts,	161
A Good Preacher,	161
Rev. Mr. S.,	162
Rev. President Edwards,	163
A Methodist Clergyman,	165
An Eccentric Clergyman,	166
Rev. President Davies,	166
Rev. Benjamin Harvey,	167
A New England Clergyman,	169
Colored Preachers,	171
Rev. Dr. J. M. Mason,	172
Rev. Dr. F.,	172
Rev. Mr. Stevens,	173
Rev. B. Standford,	175
Several Clergymen,	175
Rev. Professor Sheppard,	177
Rev. Dr. Stanford,	177
A Universalist Minister,	178
Rev. John Eliot,	178
Rev. John Gano,	180
A Clergyman,	181
A Practical Preacher,	181
Rev. Luther Rice,	182
Rev. John Summerfield,	184
A Young Clergyman,	185

DEVOTEDNESS OF CLERGYMEN TO THEIR LABOURS.

Rev. John Brock,	189
Rev. President Davies,	190
Bishop Griswold,	191
A Missionary in New York,	192

CONTENTS.

Rev. S. Stoddard,	195
Rev. S. H. Stearns,	195
Rev. G. Whitefield,	196
A City Minister,	197
Rev. S. Allen,	200
Rev. Dr. J. M. Mason,	200
Rev. President Edwards,	201
Rev. John Eliot,	202
Rev. Dr. Rodgers,	202
Rev. Dr. Manning,	203
Rev. D. Tinsley,	204
Rev. Dr. Coke,	204
Rev. Dr. Chaplin,	205
Rev. Dr. Rice,	206
Rev. Dr. Payson,	206
Rev. John Shepherd,	207
Rev. Dr. Byles,	207
Rev. Dr. Dwight,	208
Rev. Dr. Nott,	208
A Popular Minister,	209
Rev. Dr. Porter,	210
A Missionary to the Indians,	210
Rev. Dr. Beecher,	211
A Devoted Pastor,	213
Rev. Dr. Mather,	215
Rev. Mr. Bailey,	217
Rev. Mr. Backus,	217
Rev. Dr. Mercer,	218
Bishop Asbury,	219

INTERCOURSE OF THE CLERGY WITH EACH OTHER.

Rev. Dr. Rodgers,	223
Thoughtless Ministers,	224
Rev. Dr. Stanford,	225
Rev. Dr. Harris,	225
A Minister in New Hampshire,	226
Rev. Gideon Hawley,	227
A Minister,	228
Rev. Joseph Craig,	229
A Universalist Preacher,	229
Rev. Dr. Livingston,	230
Two Clergymen,	231
A Baptist Clergyman,	231
Rev. Dr. Emmons,	232
Rev. Dr. Dwight,	235
Rev. Dr. Scudder,	235
Rev. Thomas Brown,	235
Rev. Dr. Taylor,	237

Rev. Lemuel Haynes,	238
Rev. Dr. Nettleton,	241
Aged Clergymen,	244
Two Clergymen,	245
Rev. Dr. Furman,	246
Rev. Dr. Pond,	247
Rev. Drs. Cooper and Chauncey,	248
Two Ministers,	249
Rev. Dr. Staughton,	250
Rev. Dr. Payson,	252
Rev. John Eliot,	254
Rev. Dr. Lathrop,	255
A Persecuting Clergyman,	256
Bishop George,	257
Two Young Ministers,	262
Rev. Dr. Bellamy,	263
Two Clergymen,	264
Rev. George Whitefield,	264
Several Clergymen,	266
Rev. John Leland,	267
Rev. Dr. Mercer,	268
Rev. Caleb Blood,	269

INTERCOURSE OF THE CLERGY WITH SOCIETY.

Bishop Chase,	273
A Faithful Minister,	276
Travelling Clergymen,	277
Rev. Dr. Armstrong,	280
A Young Minister in the West,	282
A Colored Preacher,	283
Rev. Mr. Moody,	285
An Unsuccessful Minister,	286
Rev. Thomas Brown,	287
An African Preacher,	289
Rev. Dr. Staughton,	290
A Presbyterian Clergyman,	290
A Delighted Minister,	292
A Wise Pastor,	292
A Clergyman in Virginia,	293
Rev. Dr. Nettleton,	296
A Baptist Minister,	311
A Poor Minister,	312
A Courteous Clergyman,	312
Rev. Joseph Eastburn,	313
Rev. John Wesley,	315
Rev. Dr. Spring,	316
Rev. Mr. Clap,	317
Rev. Dr. Waddell,	317

Rev. Mr. Spencer,	321
Rev. Bela Jacobs,	322
Rev. Mr. Estabrook,	323
An Anxious Pastor,	324
A Clergyman,	325
Rev. Dr. Judson,	325
A Good Pastor,	326
A Minister in New York,	326
Bishop Griswold,	327
A New England Clergyman,	328
Rev. Dr. Mercer,	329
A Clergyman in Philadelphia,	331
Rev. Mr. F.,	334
A Faithful Minister,	335
A Minister in Boston,	336
Two Clergymen,	336
Rev. John Gano,	337
Rev. T. P. Benedict,	338
An Unknown Preacher,	338
Rev. Samuel Harris,	339
Rev. Dr. Laidlie,	340
An Aged Minister,	340
Rev. Dr. Stanford,	341
A Village Clergyman,	346
A Travelling Minister,	347
Rev. Mr. Grafton,	348
Rev. Calvin Colton,	348
Rev. Dr. Beecher,	350
Rev. Dr. C.,	351
Rev. Mr. Coley,	352
A Clergyman in New York,	354
Rev. E. Byne,	355
Rev. Mr. Baker,	356
Rev. Dr. Todd,	357
A Clergyman in Tennessee,	358
Rev. W. Tennent,	360
An Aged Clergyman,	362
Rev. Dr. Harris,	362
Rev. Mr. Hyde,	366
Several Clergymen,	367
A New England Minister,	375
Rev. Dr. Griffin,	377
A Penitent Minister,	377
A Universalist Minister,	378
A Methodist Clergyman,	379
A New England Clergyman,	383
Rev. Dr. Witherspoon,	383
A Good Preacher,	384
Rev. Dr. Baldwin,	385

CONTENTS.

Rev. Mr. Bushnel,	386
Rev. Mr. Walker,	387
A Clergyman in Virginia,	388
Rev. John Cotton,	389
Rev. Dr. Coke,	389
Rev. Mr. Cross,	391
Rev. Dr. C. Mather,	392
An Aged Clergyman,	395
Rev. Mr. Bennett,	396
Rev. Dr. L.,	397
A Wise Clergyman,	398
Rev. Mr. Hull,	400
Rev. John Summerfield,	400
Rev. Dr. J. M. Mason,	402
Rev. Mr. Worcester,	408
Rev. J. Armstrong,	409
A Clergyman at New Orleans,	410
Rev. Mr. Case,	411
Rev. Dr. Lathrop,	412
Rev. T. Hooker,	412
Rev. Mr. C.,	413
A Pastor,	414
Rev. Dr. Livingston,	415
Rev. Dr. John H. Rice,	415
Rev. Dr. Payson,	417
A Minister in New York,	424
A Clergyman at St. Louis,	424
Rev. Dr. Henry,	425
Rev. Mr. Trefit,	426
A Shrewd Minister,	427
A Travelling Clergyman,	427

SUCCESS AND ENCOURAGEMENT OF THE CLERGY.

Rev. President Edwards,	431
Rev. Mr. S.,	431
Rev. Dr. Rodgers,	432
A Universalist Minister,	432
Rev. John Bailey,	433
An Aged Minister,	434
Several Pastors,	435
American Missionaries,	437
The Puritan Ministers,	437
Rev. Dr. L. Beecher,	438
Rev. Dr. Hopkins,	439
Rev. J. Patterson,	441
Rev. Mr. M.,	411
A Clergyman in New York,	413
A New England Minister,	444

Rev. Mr. Prince,	444
Bishop M‘Ilvaine,	446
A Minister among the Cherokees,	447
A Preacher from England,	448
Rev. G. Whitefield,	449
A Mistaken Minister,	450
Rev. David Brainerd,	451
Rev. President Davies,	452
Rev. Gilbert Tennent,	453
Rev. Dr. B.,	454
Rev. Dr. Backus,	455
A Home Missionary,	455
A Minister in New York,	457
Rev. Mr. Massey,	458
A Discouraged Young Minister,	459
Rev. Dr. Stanford,	460
A New England Minister,	461
A Southern Clergyman,	462
Rev. Joseph Smith,	463
A Missionary among the Indians,	466
Moravian Missionaries,	467
A Discouraged Pastor,	468
Rev. Sylvester Larned,	469
A Clergyman,	469

PREPARATION OF THE CLERGY FOR PUBLIC DUTIES.

THE AMERICAN CLERGY.

REV. WILLIAM ROBINSON.

ONE of the most eminent Christian ministers of the South n the last century was the Rev. W. Robinson, whose conversion was exceedingly striking. He was the son of a wealthy Quaker in England. Being permitted to pay a visit of a few weeks to an aunt in the city of London, from whom he had considerable expectations, he greatly overstayed the time which had been allowed him; and becoming deeply involved in dissipation, he incurred large debts, which he knew his father would never pay, and which his aunt refused to discharge. In this situation, fearing to return home, and unable to remain long in London, he determined to quit his native country, and seek his fortune in America. In this determination his aunt reluctantly acquiesced, and furnished him with a small sum of money for that purpose. Soon after his arrival in America, he had recourse, for subsistence, to teaching a school in New Jersey, within the bounds of the Presbytery of New Brunswick. He had been for some time engaged in this business, without any practical sense of religion, when it pleased God to bring him to a knowledge of himself, and of the way of salvation, in a remarkable manner. He was riding at a late hour, one evening, when the moon and stars shone with unusual brightness, and when every thing around him was adapted to excite reflection. While he was meditating on the beauty and grandeur of the scene which the firmament presented, and was saying to himself, "How transcendently glorious must be the Author of all this beauty and grandeur!" the thought struck him with the sadness and the force of lightning, "But what do I know of this God? Have I ever sought his favor, or made him my friend?" This happy impression, which proved, by its permanency and its effects, to have come from the best of all sources, never left him until he took refuge in Christ as the hope and life of his soul. He soon resolved to devote himself to the work of the gospel ministry; completed his academical education, and studied theology, while he went on with his school; and was, in due time, licensed and ordained by the Presbytery of New Brunswick. He was remarkable for the native vigor of his mind, and still more for the fervour of his piety. Wherever he went, it pleased God to grant him some precious fruits of his ministry. He died at St. George's, in Delaware, April, 1746.

REV. HUGH KNOX.

Mr. Hugh Knox, a native of Ireland, came to America when quite a young man, about 1753 or 1754. He immediately waited on his countryman, the Rev. Dr. Francis Allison, then residing at New London, Penna., to whom he had letters, and in whose academy he hoped to find employment as a teacher. Dr. Allison, not being able to give him a place in his seminary, furnished him with a letter to Mr. Rodgers, requesting his good offices in endeavouring to procure a grammar school for the young stranger, within the bounds of his parish. Mr. Rodgers soon succeeded in forming a respectable school, at the

Head of Bohemia, about ten miles from St. George's, as master of which Mr. Knox was comfortably placed. He continued to preside over this school for more than a year; and having received a good classical education in his own country, being remarkably prepossessing in his personal appearance and manners, and attending with great assiduity to the duties of his station, he soon became much esteemed by his employers; and was considered as most agreeably settled. He attended public worship, with great punctuality, at Mr. Rodgers's Lower or Forest church, near Middletown, and looked up to the pastor as his patron and friend. Things had been going on in this happy and promising manner for a number of months, when a sudden reverse occurred. Mr. Knox, though a respectable attendant on public worship, and a young man, hitherto, of decent morals, had manifested nothing like real piety. He was accustomed, every Saturday afternoon, to meet some gay companions at the tavern of a Mr. Witherspoon, near the place of his residence, with whom he passed several hours, at first with decency and temperance; but, after a while, not so entirely in this manner as could have been wished. On a certain Saturday afternoon, when Knox and his companions had been diverting themselves in their usual way, some of the company said to him, "Come, parson," (a title they gave to him on account of his being the most grave of their number, and a great admirer of Mr. Rodgers,) "Come, parson, give us a sermon." He declined. They urged him. He still resisted. At length, however, overcome by their importunity, and probably excited, in some degree, by liquor, he said, "Well, come, I will give you the sermon which Mr. Rodgers preached last Sunday.' Mr. Rodgers had preached, on the preceding Sabbath, from 2 Cor. v. 20, and had given an unusually solemn and excellent discourse. Mr. Knox, having a good memory, a flexible voice, and great powers of imitation, was enabled, not only to recollect and repeat the substance of the discourse, as he heard it delivered, but also to copy the voice and manner of Mr. Rodgers so closely, that Mr. Witherspoon, who heard it all from an adjoining apartment, declared that, if he had not known to the contrary, he should really have supposed it was Mr. Rodgers himself preaching. In short, he was carried beyond himself, and spoke so much like a man preaching the gospel in good earnest, that his profane hearers were deeply affected, and when the discourse was ended, one after another silently withdrew. But what is still more remarkable, Mr. Knox himself was solemnly impressed by his own mock preaching, especially as he drew towards the close of the discourse; and when it was finished, he sat down with mingled emotions of shame and horror at the profane mockery of which he had been guilty, and deep conviction of the important doctrines he had been delivering in application to himself. So strong, indeed, were these impressions, that he could not bear the thought of looking Mr. Rodgers, or any of his other pious patrons, in the face, after such conduct: and accordingly, early the next morning, without waiting to collect any of his dues, or to adjust his affairs, he precipitately quitted that part of the country, and was not heard of for a number of months.

The next autumn, when Mr. Rodgers attended the commencement of the college of New Jersey, which was then seated at Newark, he was surprised to find Mr. Knox at the house of the Rev. Mr. Burr, the president of the college. The young fugitive had applied to Mr. Burr, soon after his retreat from Bohemia, for admission into one of the classes of the college; but having informed him that his last residence had been in the neighbourhood of Mr. Rodgers, and being unable to produce testimonials from that place of his good moral character, Mr. Burr advised him to wait in Newark until the commencement, when he expected to have an opportunity of seeing Mr. Rodgers, and of conversing with him on the subject. Mr. Knox, upon first meeting his old pastor, was much agitated, and, as soon as possible, took him aside; acknowledged his unworthy conduct, with every appearance of humiliation; implored his pardon for the offence committed against himself, in turning his sermon into profane mockery; and informed him of the situation in which he stood with regard to his expected admission into the college. Mr. Rodgers promised to speak as favourably of him to Mr. Burr as truth would permit, and not to disclose the conduct which led to his elopement from Bohemia, unless it should be drawn from him by unavoidable questions; and, with these promises, left him in the most painful anxiety.

Here Mr. Rodgers learned from young Knox, that the serious impressions made on his mind by the sermon which he had so profanely repeated had never been eradicated; that his wickedness had been overruled, as he hoped, for his eternal good; that he had for some time cherished a hope concerning himself, as a real Christian; and that his earnest desire was to complete his education at the college with a view to the gospel ministry.

Happily, president Burr, in the hurry of the commencement, only asked Mr. Rodgers whether he knew Mr. Knox; and whether he would advise that he should be admitted into the college. To both these questions Mr. Rodgers answered promptly in the affirmative. The young man was admitted; passed through the college, and his subsequent theological studies, with reputation; and, after receiving many testimonials of sincere and active friendship from his old pastor at St. George's, entered on the work of the gospel ministry, and became equally honoured and useful in his profession.

REV. MR. A.

The Rev. Mr. A—, of B—, Mass., some time since publicly stated that when a student of law in the vicinity of B—, and in the midst of fatal error, he became desirous of knowing more about religious truth. He went to B—, and searched through all the book-stores of that city, asking for a copy of *Baxter's Saints Rest*, of which he had heard in his youth. At last he found an old, mutilated copy, with a green morocco cover, in Bumstead's second-hand book-store. He seized it as though it were a treasure, and bore it home; "and now," said Mr. A., "if I ever attain to the 'saints' everlasting rest,' I owe it, under God, to that old book." He became one of the most evangelical and useful ministers in New England.

REV. MR. RAVENCROSS.

Mr. Ravencross was a slave-holder in Virginia, and reputed a hard master. His poor distressed slaves were in the habit of meeting at night in a distant hut, for the purpose of worshipping God. He was informed of this, and at the same time put on his guard, as it was suspected their motives for meeting were different from what they held out, and that an insurrection might be the consequence. Under this impression, he determined to prevent their assembling in future, chastised the promoters of this work, and gave positive orders, under the most serious penalty, that they should never assemble again under any pretence whatever. A short time after he was told they had been seen going in a body into the hut. Much displeased at their disobedience, and resolving that night to put a stop to their proceedings, he approached the hut with all the feelings of an offended master. When he reached the door, it was partly open. He looked in; they were on their knees. He listened; there was a venerable old man, who had been long in his service, pouring out his soul in prayer to God. The first words which caught his ear were, "Merciful God, turn my poor massa's heart: make him merciful, that he may obtain mercy; make him good, that he may inherit the kingdom of heaven." He heard no more, but fainted. Upon coming to himself, he wept; went into the sacred hut, knelt by the side of his old slave, and prayed also! From this period he became a true penitent, studied the Scriptures, took orders, and became a shining light. He preached at the general convention of the Episcopal church, in the city of Philadelphia, before more than two hundred of the clergy, in the year 1820.

A NEW ENGLAND DIVINE.

A clergyman in New England, thus addressed his congregation:—

I once knew a young man, who was a student in one of our universities, who, by reading the works of Combe, and others of similar character, had become very skeptical on such points as prayer, the total depravity of man, regeneration, and the influence of the Holy Spirit. Though he professed religion and was studying for the ministry, he had lost all religious enjoyment, and was fast going down an inclined plane into the abyss of infidelity. During a vacation in mid-winter, he was travelling on business among the Germans in the interior of

Pennsylvania, when he was laid on his bed with a dangerous disease—hundreds of miles from home, "a stranger in a strange land." When he began to think of dying, he found himself entirely unprepared. His new sentiments hovered like dismal clouds around his sick-bed, so that not a star of hope shone through. There was little time for logic then : but one short mode of reasoning swept away his skeptical notions like chaff. He thus reasoned from effect to cause :—Embracing these new sentiments has evidently brought my mind into this wretched condition ; and as the fruit is bad, the tree must be bad also. He that followeth me, says Christ, "shall not walk in darkness;" therefore, as I am walking in darkness, it must be because I have been led astray from him. These new opinions must, therefore, be erroneous. I will renounce them forever, and embrace, in all humility and simplicity, the truths of the Gospel, as I embraced them at first. Speedily did he put his resolutions into action, and he soon found his way back to the fold of Christ, to the Shepherd and Bishop of souls. He recovered from his sickness, and returned home, rejoicing to tell his friends what great things God had done for him. And that young man, my hearers, is preaching to you to-day! I have many blessings for which to thank God, for he has strewn my way with the gifts of his providence ; but for the blessing of that affliction, I sometimes feel that I ought to praise him most. And if I am ever so happy as to get to heaven, I shall remember that affliction with gratitude still.

TWO CLERGYMEN

The following interesting statement of facts was written by Bishop M'Ilvaine.

It is now nearly thirteen years since a very remarkable work of grace occurred in the Military Academy of the United States. During a condition of almost universal indifference to religion, and of wide-spread infidelity, against which the efforts of the ministry of one man, set for the defence of the gospel, seemed for a long time to make not the least way, suddenly almost, in a very few days, many minds, without communication with one another, and without personal intercourse with the minister, appeared deeply, and almost simultaneously interested in the great matters of eternal life. Officers as well as cadets participated in this, and to such an extent, that the minister's study was soon occupied every evening with assemblies, composed of both, for prayer and the exposition of the word of God; and a serious impression, more or less deep and abiding, was spread over a large part of the whole military community. Several became at that period very decided soldiers of Christ. Many others received the seed of the word, in whom, though it seemed to die, it has since, under the continued influence of the Spirit, sprung up and brought forth fruit. Some are still in military life. Others have been, long since, adorning the Christian profession in the ministry of the gospel.

The very first appearance of this work of grace, so remarkably and singularly the work of God, was the coming of a cadet, alone and most unexpectedly, to introduce himself to the chaplain, and unburden the sorrows of a contrite heart. All around him was coldness and skepticism. To speak decidedly in favour of religion was then so unusual in the academy, that it made one singular. To converse with the chaplain on that subject had not been ventured by any, except out of opposition to the truth. That any one would appear there seriously seeking eternal life, even the chaplain was afraid to hope. A cadet, however, did venture to come, in open day, to the chaplain's study, too deeply concerned to heed what would be said of him. He was personally unknown to the chaplain. His message he tried to utter, but could not. Again he tried, and again; but his heart was too full for speech. At length he said, "Tell me what I must do; I have come about my soul. I know not what I want; I am entirely in the dark. What must I seek? where must I go? Such was the first declaration of one who, for some days, had been awakened under the preaching and reading of the truth. A sermon preached on the Scriptures, and a tract, sent at a venture from the chaplain's study, to whomsoever it might meet, had been blessed to his soul.

Doubts and cavils were all abandoned. Implicit submission seemed his engrossing principle. From that moment the young man appeared to take up the cross, and to stand decidedly and boldly on the Lord's side. The singular and very prominent evidence of the hand of God in this case, was very greatly blessed to others. After graduating at that institution, and leaving the army, he passed through a regular course of study for the holy ministry, and was successively ordained deacon and presbyter. Many years have since elapsed. The chaplain has since been called to a higher order in the ministry, and more enlarged responsibilities in the church. The cadet, meanwhile, after many vicissitudes of active duty and of disabling ill health, supposed he had settled himself for the rest of his life as a preacher and pastor to an humble and obscure congregation of negroes, whom he had collected together from neighbouring plantations; to whom, living entirely upon his own pecuniary means, he appropriated a part of his own house for a church and to whose eternal interests he had chosen cheerfully and happily to devote himself, as their spiritual father, with no emolument but their salvation. But such was just the true spirit for the highest of all vocations in the church. To be a servant of servants is the very school in which to prepare for the chief ministry under Him who "took upon himself the form of a servrnt." The church needed a missionary bishop for a vast field, for great self-denial, for untiring patience, for courageous enterprise. Her eye was directed to the self-appointed pastor of that humble congregation. With most impressive unanimity did she call him away to a work, not indeed of more dignified duty, but of more eminent responsibility, not indeed of more exquisite satisfaction to a Christian heart, (for what can give a true Christian heart more exquisite satisfaction than to lead such of the poor to Christ?) but of severer trials, and vastly greater difficulties and hardships. Counting the cost, he has not dared to decline it. Regarding the call as of God, he has embraced the promised grace, and is now ready to be offered. And thus the chaplain has here met the beloved cadet again, seeing and adoring the end of the Lord in that remarkable beginning.

AN ABLE MINISTER.

A YOUNG man, who had graduated at one of the first colleges in America, and was celebrated for his literary attainments, particularly his knowledge of mathematics, settled in a village where a faithful minister of the gospel was stationed. It was not long before the clergyman met with him in one of his evening walks, and after some conversation, as they were about to part, addressed him as follows :—" I have heard you are celebrated for your mathematical skill ; I have a problem which I wish you to solve." "What is it?" eagerly inquired the young man. The clergyman answered, with a solemn tone of voice, "What shall it profit a man, if he shall gain the whole world, and lose his own soul?" The youth returned home, and endeavoured to shake off the impression fastened on him by the problem proposed to him, but in vain. In the giddy round of pleasure, in his business, and in his studies, that question still forcibly returned to him, "What will a man profit, if he shall gain the whole world, and lose his own soul?" It finally resulted in his conversion, and he became an able advocate and preacher of that gospel which he once rejected.

SIX YOUNG MINISTERS.

There is something in the following narrative eminently illustrative of the vitality of the gospel, and adapted to encourage the heart of the Christian minister amidst every discouragement.

About half a century since a Christian church was organized in Virginia. For some years it eminently flourished, but after a while the pastor died, some of the members removed to different parts of the country, and others returned into the world. The house of worship fell into decay, the doors were broken from their hinges, and the birds of the air built their nests upon the deserted walls. The pulpit bowed to its fall, and utter desolation reigned where once the praises of Zion's King had resounded. Close by arose a grog-shop, and it soon became the Sunday resort of the young and old in the vicinity. In that neighbourhood lived a wealthy gentleman, who had on-son, a youth of great promise. This youth was in the practice of spending his Sabbaths with other young men at the grog-shop above named, though it had not been said that he ever was guilty of any outbreaking immorality. One Sabbath, as he was going to the general place of rendezvous, when passing the old meeting-house, he turned his head and saw an old gray-headed negro sitting on one of the benches. A degree of superstitious fear came over his mind, and an impression was produced which rendered the society at the grog-shop irksome, and he soon returned to his father's. On the next Sabbath, as he was again passing the old house, he saw the old negro again, seated on a bench, leaning his head on the top of his staff. Riding up to the window, he inquired of the old man what he was doing there. "Get down, young master, and come and sit down, and I will tell you," was the reply. He accordingly went in and took his seat by the side of the old man, whom by this time he recognised as the aged servant of a neighbouring planter.

"Thirty years ago," proceeded the old man, with deep emotion, "I used to come to this house of a Sunday to meet God and his people. And precious times we have had here. This house used to be filled with professed Christians, engaged in the service of God, and anxious sinners inquiring the way to be saved. In that old pulpit, now leaning ready to fall, used to stand the servant of God, telling us the precious truths of the gospel of Jesus. Now he is dead; some of the members have moved away, some gone back to the world, and some are dead, while the old house is ready to fall. Young master, I used in those days to come here to meet God. I have come here to-day to meet him in this house, and he has met with me. He is here now." The aged man then respectfully, yet earnestly, pressed upon the youth the importance of religion, and the danger of neglect. "Young master, you see my head, it is white. I was once young like you. I am now old and

3*

shall soon die. And you will die too. Are you prepared?" The young man wept, and the old Christian proposed that they should kneel down and pray for the salvation of his soul. They knelt down, and God *was there.* During the ensuing week the young man was greatly distressed, and early the next Sabbath morning repaired to the old church to meet the old negro, who preached Jesus to him as the way, the truth, and the life. In a few days the young man obtained a hope, and by his exertions, and the blessing of God's grace, an extensive revival of religion very soon commenced. A new church was soon organized, the old house was repaired, a minister settled, and many were converted to the faith as it is in Jesus. As one of the fruits of that revival, six individuals from that neighbourhood entered upon the work of the ministry, and the Lord greatly blessed their labours. One person converted at this time became afterwards the governor of a state, and died, after a life of usefulness, as the righteous die. These facts were communicated to the writer since by a person who received them from some who were themselves the subjects of the revival.

SEVERAL YOUNG MINISTERS.

As the following facts connect themselves, as it will be seen, with the conversion of more than one minister; they are here narrated, on the authority of a pious pastor. An old man called his children around his dying-bed, and entreated their attention to a narrative :—

When young, I enjoyed religious privileges, and was the subject of occasional serious reflection. When just entering my sixteenth year, religious impressions were made on my mind with unusual force. I seemed to hear a voice continually saying to me, *Seek religion now!* I was unhappy; my former amusements lost their relish. Still, I was not willing wholly to relinquish them, and obey the voice which urged me to seek religion immediately. One day, after much reflection, I deliberately promised to God, that as soon as the season of youthful amusement was past, I would give myself to religious pursuits. My anxieties immediately left me; I returned to my amusements, and the whole subject was soon forgotten.

When at thirty-five, the monitory voice returned, reminded me of my promise, and again pressed upon me the importance of eternal things. Though I had not thought of my promise for years, I acknowledged its obligations, but an immediate fulfilment seemed more impracticable than it did nineteen years before.

I vowed with increased solemnity, that when the cares of a rising family should subside, I would certainly attend to the concerns of religion.

Again I applied myself to worldly avocations, and soon buried all thoughts of the admonition I had received. At fifty, when you, my children, were diminishing, instead of increasing my cares, this heavenly monitor returned. "Fulfil your promise; seek religion now;" was continually pressing upon my mind. I knew that I had made such a promise, but I felt dissatisfied that its fulfilment should be claimed so soon. I regretted that I had not attended to the subject before, when I could have done it with less difficulty; but such was the extent and pressure of my business, that to do it then seemed impossible. The subject made me unhappy, and after much deliberation, I sought relief to my troubled feelings by most solemnly renewing my promise to God. When, I said, the pressure of business is past, I will devote my whole attention to a preparation for eternity.

No sooner had I fixed my mind on this course, than my anxieties left me—the strivings of the Spirit ceased in my bosom, and ceased for ever. When sickness warned me of approaching death, I sought to fix my feelings on this subject, but it was in vain. There was a gloom and terror drawn around religion, at which my soul shuddered. I felt that I was forsaken of God, but it did not move me. I had no love to God, no repentance for sin, nor wish to forsake it. I felt nothing but the sullen gloom of despair—I knew I was in the hands of a justly offended God, from whom I expected no mercy, and could ask none. With these feelings I am now about to enter the eternal world. To you, my children, I can only say—Profit by my example; quench not the Spirit; seek religion now, if you would avoid a miserable eternity—put not off the concerns of your soul till——The sentence died upon his lips; his strength, which had been all summoned to make this last effort, suddenly failed—he fell back upon his bed, and with a groan that seemed to speak the pains of another world, the immortal spirit took its flight from that body which it had inhabited nearly fourscore years, to receive according to that it had done.

This little narrative I had from a grandson of the old man, who stood by his dying bed. He was a minister of the gospel, and dated his first permanent conviction from the solemnities of that awful scene. The descendants of the old man were numerous, most of whom became hopefully pious. Two, who are now preachers, and several others, were first awakened by his dying charge.

REV. J. W. JAMES.

In a lecture to Sunday-school teachers, a few years since, the Rev. J. W. James, of Philadelphia, related the following narrative:—

A young man who had been piously educated, and whose religious impressions in early life had been strong, while at college mingled with worldly and gay companions; so that in a short time he ceased to be serious or prayerful. He graduated as worldly and careless as his classmates, and removed to a distant city. Ambitious of eminence in the profession he had chosen, he secluded himself from society, not from fear of its contamination, but to preserve his time from unnecessary waste. While thus engaged, he became acquainted with the pious superintendent of a Sabbath-school, whom he was not long after invited to succeed. After much persuasion he reluctantly consented, but was unacquainted with the duties of the school. On finding that he must open the school with prayer, he started and turned pale. He had formerly been taught by his mother to pray, but he had now forgotten how to address the Author of his mercies. By the aid of the prayer-book he succeeded, but his conscience allowed him no rest. He could not retire from the work. For some weeks he endured the lashes of an awakened and guilty conscience, until at length, by the assistance of the Holy Spirit, he was enabled to give up all for Christ. He retained his office of superintendent for more than a year: then, at length, after a course of theology, was settled as a Christian pastor in one of the Atlantic cities, where he was engaged in winning souls to Christianity; "and now," he added,—and his face grew pale, and his limbs trembled with emotion as he spoke—" and now, he has the satisfaction of addressing this assemblage of superintendents and teachers."

A YOUNG CLERGYMAN.

A young licentiate, after throwing off a highly wrought, and, as he thought, eloquent gospel sermon in the pulpit, in the presence of a venerable pastor, solicited of his experienced friend the benefit of his criticisms upon the performance.

"I have but just one remark to make," was his reply, "and that is, to request you to pray that sermon."

"What do you mean, sir?"

"I mean literally just what I say; pray it, if you can, and you will find the attempt a better criticism than any I can make upon it."

The request still puzzled the young man beyond measure; the idea of praying a sermon was a thing he never heard or conceived of; and the singularity of the suggestion wrought powerfully on his imagination and feelings. He resolved to attempt the task. He laid his manuscript before him, and on his knees before God, undertook to make it into a prayer. But it would not pray; the spirit of prayer was not in it, and that, for the very good reason—as he then clearly saw for the first time—that the spirit of prayer and piety did not compose it. For the first time he saw that his heart was not right with God; and this conviction left him no peace until he had "Christ formed in him the hope of glory." With a renewed heart, he applied himself anew to the work of composing sermons for the pulpit; preached again in the presence of the pious pastor who had given such timely advice; and again solicited the benefit of his critical remarks.

"I have no remarks to make," was his complacent reply, "you can pray that sermon."

A NEW ENGLAND CLERGYMAN.

A few years ago, a gay lady in New England had occasion to go to a neighbouring town, where she had often been before. In the immediate vicinity was a stream which she had to go near, and which at this period was high. With a view of showing her courage to a young person whom she had taken with her as a companion, she went into the stream with her horse, and in a very little time was thrown into the water,—had already sunk once or twice to the bottom, and felt that she was within a few moments of an eternal world, without being prepared for so great a change.

It so happened, that a young man in another neighbouring town had felt a powerful impression on his mind that morning, that he should visit the same place. He had no business to transact; but, being forcibly impressed with the importance of going thither, he invited a young man to accompany him. Arriving at the side of the stream just as the young ladies were about to cross it, they saw it was improbable that they could ford it; yet, as the ladies went, they determined to follow.

By the time the young lady was thrown from her horse, the others had nearly reached the opposite shore; but, perceiving her danger, one of them immediately followed her on his horse, and in the last moment of life, as it then appeared, she caught hold of the horse's leg; he thus secured her, and snatching hold of the other drowning young lady, she was saved also. After the use of proper remedies, they recovered; and the young gentlemen, believing that the design of their coming from home was now answered, returned back.

The impressions made on the mind of this young lady were permanent, and she was led to reflect on the sins she had committed against God, to pray for the pardon of her guilt, and to devote herself to the Divine service. She embraced the mercy of the Lord, believing in the Redeemer, who alone saves from the wrath to come.

In the same town with herself lived a young gentleman, who had often spent his hours in vain conversation with her. On her return home, he went to congratulate her on her escape, and to his surprise, found she attributed her deliverance to the power of God, and urged him to seek that grace which they had both neglected. Her serious conversation was blessed to his conversion, and he became a faithful minister of Jesus Christ.

REV. MR. POLK.

The Rev. Mr. Polk, at a general meeting of the Religious Tract Society, in London, stated, that he had a right to speak of the value of tracts, because, under God, he was indebted for all he knew of Christianity to a tract. In an institution for the education of young men, in his own country, out of two hundred and fifty individuals, there was not one who was a Christian; and though the minister laboured among them with great zeal, he seemed to labour in vain. At last, he got a young man to go through the building, and distribute some religious tracts. He left a tract on infidelity in one of the rooms, where two young men lodged together, one of whom was apparently of doubtful principles. The other, however, got hold of it, and read it. It arrested his attention, and set his mind on inquiring; and he afterwards fell in with Dr. Olinthus Gregory's "Letters," which led him to procure a Bible. The truths of that blessed book were brought home to his mind with great power, and he became a converted man. And his conversion was the beginning of a revival of religion in that place, during which twenty other young men, and some of the professors, became converted to Christ.

REV. S. NIGHTINGALE.

In the beginning of 1845, at a union prayer-meeting in Philadelphia, the Rev. S. Nightingale, a Baptist minister from Montgomery county, was present by invitation, and at the close of an exhortation related the following anecdote:

"About twenty years ago, there was a wild and daring lad in the city, who feared neither God nor man. One day he was thrown accidentally into the company of a clergyman, who had some serious conversation with him on religion. Among other things, he told him that it was his opinion, that in after life he would either join the army or become a minister of the Gospel. A few years after this conversation, that boy made a profession of religion and entered the ministry. I," added he, "am that individual; and," pointing to Dr. Ely, who sat on the platform beside him, "this is the minister who held the conversation with me when a boy."

The congregation appeared electrified; and Dr. Ely, who had forgotten the boy in the person of the speaker, now recollecting the circumstance, started from his chair, and embraced

REV. S. STODDARD.

The Rev. Solomon Stoddard, of Northampton, the predecessor of the far-famed President Edwards, was engaged by his people on an emergency. They soon found themselves disappointed, for he gave no indications of a renewed and serious mind. In this difficulty their resource was prayer. They agreed to set apart a day for special fasting and prayer, in reference to their pastor. Many of the persons meeting for this purpose, had necessarily to pass the door of the minister. Mr. S. hailed a plain man whom he knew, and addressed him, "What is all this! What is doing to-day?" The reply was, "The people, sir, are meeting to pray for your conversion." It sunk into his heart. He exclaimed to himself, "Then it is time I prayed for myself!" He was not seen that day. He was seeking in solitude what they were asking in company; and "while they were yet speaking," they were heard and answered. The pastor gave unquestionable evidence of the change; he laboured amongst a beloved and devoted people for nearly half a century; and was, for that period, deservedly ranked among the most able and useful of Christian ministers.

REV. DR. M'CARTEE.

The Rev. Dr. M'Cartee, of New York, in delivering an address at a tract meeting in Philadelphia, related the following anecdote:—

The mention of two of the publications of the American

Tract Society, in your report, sir, has excited emotions in my own mind which I cannot repress. I well remember when two young lawyers, both far from God, and engaged in the pursuit of the honours and wealth of this world, met in the city of New York, when, as one took some legal documents from his pocket, the other, to his surprise, discovered among them 'DODDRIDGE'S RISE AND PROGRESS OF RELIGION.' Nor was the surprise of the first at all less, when he discovered lying on the table, at the hand of his fellow, 'BAXTER'S SAINTS' REST.' Each appeared at first confused and ashamed at the discovery, for they had not yet learned to glory in the cross. But a few moments, however, had elapsed, when they mutually found that the attention of each had been powerfully arrested by those volumes, and that each was deeply anxious for the salvation of his soul. Together they sought the Lord; and, agonizing to enter into the kingdom, they both, about the same time, were enabled to hope in the mercy of Jesus Christ for eternal life. One of them, having fought the good fight, and kept the faith, has long since gone upward, I doubt not, to rest in the bosom of the Saviour he loved and served. The other, called, as he believes, of God, became a preacher of the Gospel of Christ, and still lives to proclaim to dying sinners, in his native city, salvation through the blood and righteousness of the blessed Redeemer; and now, when he finds your society engaged in sending forth, among your other valuable publications, these two precious volumes, he (referring to himself) presents himself before you to add, this evening, his feeble, but heartfelt testimony to the excellence of the Tract Society.

A PIOUS BISHOP.

A worthy and excellent bishop of the Episcopal church, was in early life an immoral and dissipated man. Dining one evening with a party of gentlemen, they sat late over their wine, and with a view to promote merriment, this young man sent for one of his slaves, who was in the habit of preaching to his companions in slavery, and ordered him to preach a sermon to the company. The good man hesitated for a time, but at length began to address them. Instead of the mirth, however, which they anticipated from the ignorance and simplicity of the poor man, the piety and fervour of his discourse produced a contrary effect. The solemn truths he delivered sank deeply into the hearts of some of the company, and, through the Divine blessing, carried conviction to the heart of his master, who now seriously inquired after the way of salvation; which having learned, he began from a sense of duty to publish the grace of Christ, and became an ornament to the Christian ministry.

A ZEALOUS MINISTER.

The Rev. J. Perkins, a missionary to Persia, has recorded the following remarkable anecdote in his journal:—A physician, who had been personally acquainted with the infidel Paine, had embraced his sentiments, and was very profane and dissipated. After striving for more than a year against the convictions of the spirit of God, which were so powerful, and his stubbornness so great, like a bullock unaccustomed to the yoke, as to bring him to a bed of long confinement, and the most awful depression of mind, he became an humble, zealous, exemplary Christian. And as soon as his health was recovered, he qualified himself, by preparatory studies, to go forth to the world, and preach that Jesus, whom he for many years considered as an impostor, whose name he had habitually blasphemed, and whose religion he had counted foolishness, and a base imposition on the world.

REV. W. COOPER.

The late Rev. W. Cooper, of Boston, very early in life set his heart upon being a minister of Jesus Christ; and this object of his choice he never abandoned. At seven years old, while hearing a sermon from the Rev. Mr. Colman, with whom he afterwards was colleague, he was so attracted by the eloquence of his manner, that he went home with a determination to read like him: a circumstance which drew from that venerable man, who survived him, and preached on the occasion of his death, the following humble but affectionate remark: " I ought to thank God, if I have served, in any way, to form him for his since eminent pulpit services; and, in particular, his method of preaching Christ and Scripture. So a torch may be lighted at a farthing candle."

A NEW ENGLAND MINISTER

At a missionary meeting in New Hampshire, in 1833, a minister rose and said that he once knew a man in a very awful state, for whom the wood was drawn together, to make a cage, in which he might be kept from doing himself and others injury. "While in that state, one solitary female prayed for him; God heard her prayer, and now he is in the midst of you, a happy man, and a minister of Jesus Christ. I am," added he, "that man: and that woman was my wife, whom I wish to honour by making her a life member of the Missionary Society."

REV. DR. WEST.

Mr., afterwards Dr. Stephen West, had entered the ministry, and settled in Stockbridge, while yet a stranger to experimental religion. Like other learned men, who trust in their own righteousness, he had laboured to accommodate his theology and his preaching to his own standard of personal religion. Two pious female members of the church, who had often lamented their want of spiritual instruction and benefit from the ministry of their pastor, at length agreed to meet once a week, to pray for him. Amidst many discouragements, they continued their united supplications to the Hearer and Answerer of prayer; but, as they afterwards remarked, they were never both discouraged at the same time. On leaving the house of God, one would say, " We have had no food to-day ;"

the other would usually answer in words of encouragement,— 'God is able to do for us more than we ask; let us continue our meetings for prayer." At length their prayers were heard; there was a sudden and remarkable change in the preaching of their pastor. They met as usual at the close of worship: "What is this?" asked one. "God is the hearer of prayer," answered the other.

The means by which this change was brought about were truly interesting. Mr. West, and Mr. Hopkins, a neighbouring minister, were in the habit of frequently meeting to discuss their different views of divine truth. At those meetings Mr. Hopkins allowed Mr. West to state his views, and to exhaust his arguments before attempting a reply; and then proceeded, in the kindest and clearest manner, to show their opposition to the word of God. In one of these interviews, Mr. West, who had been walking up and down the room in great agitation, said to Mr. Hopkins, "Only reconcile Divine sovereignty with man's agency, and I will give up my sentiments to embrace yours." "And cannot *you* reconcile them, Mr. West?" "No," said he, "I cannot." "Well," said Mr. Hopkins, with great mildness and sincerity, "I have, to your conviction, proved that God is a Sovereign; and you are conscious that man is a free agent. Now, therefore, if you cannot reconcile God's sovereignty with man's agency, you *must* be damned." The solemn appeal was not in vain. The words rested on his mind day and night. He felt he was a stranger to godliness, and a blind leader of the blind. With great fearfulness he continued to preach, but became more practical, and preached the truth as he began to feel it. The first sermon he preached after this change filled the hearts of those females with holy joy. Dr. West was afterwards the author of an excellent work on the Atonement of Christ.

AN OLD CLERGYMAN.

A VENERABLE clergyman, and doctor of divinity, in New Hampshire, at the age of seventy years, lodged at the house of a pious friend, where he observed the mother teaching some short prayers and hymns to her children. "Madam," said he, "your instructions may be of far more importance than you are aware: my mother taught me a little hymn when a child, and it is of use to me to this day. I never close my eyes to rest, without first saying,

> 'Now I lay me down to sleep,
> I pray the Lord my soul to keep:
> If I should die before I wake,
> I pray the Lord my soul to take.'"

THE BEECHER FAMILY.

THE humble, weary, and anxious toils of the nursery, sometimes need glimpses of the future, to impart to them their true dignity and value. Let any mother who feels that she is of small value, and that her duties and cares are of little account, ponder over such incidents as these:

On the east of Long Island, in one of the most secluded spots in this country, more than thirty years ago, a mother, whose rare intellectual and moral endowments were known to but few, made this simple record:

"This morning I rose very early to pray for my children:

and especially that my sons may be ministers and missionaries of Jesus Christ."

A number of years after, a friend who was present, thus describes the mother's dying hour: "Owing to extreme weakness, her mind wandered and her conversation was broken; but as she entered the valley of the shadow of death, her soul lighted up and gilded its darkness. She made a feeling and most appropriate prayer, and told her husband that her views and anticipations had been such, that she could scarcely sustain them; and that if they had been increased, she should have been overwhelmed; that her Saviour had blessed her with constant peace, and that through all her sickness, she had never prayed for life. She dedicated her five sons to God as ministers and missionaries of Jesus Christ, and said that her greatest desire was, that her children might be trained up for God.

"She spoke with joy of the advancement of the kingdom of Christ, and of the glorious day now ushering in. She attempted to speak to her children, but was so exhausted, and their cries and sobs were such, that she could say but little. Her husband then made a prayer, in which he gave her back to God, and dedicated all they held in common, to him. She then fell into a sweet sleep, from which she awoke in heaven."

The prayers of this mother have been answered. All her eight children have been "trained up for God." Her five sons are all "ministers and missionaries of Jesus Christ." And the late Rev. George Beecher was the first of her offspring whom she welcomed to heaven.

REV. JOSEPH EASTBURN.

When a youth, after he had entered upon his apprenticeship to the trade at which he so long worked, this young man fell into company which would have led him into evil practices. Being removed from parental guardianship, and showing an unregenerate heart, he was disposed to follow the evil example to which he was now exposed. On one occasion he had engaged with some of his companions to spend the Sabbath in sinful amusement in the country; he had already passed the suburbs of the city, when the distant sound of a church-bell struck upon his ear. He was affected by the sound; he remembered that often, in company with his parents, he had been summoned by it to the house of God; and now what was he doing? turning his back upon the sanctuary, and violating the holy Sabbath. Entertaining such reflections for a moment, he suddenly stopped, then left his companions, and went to the house of prayer. It was the turning point of his life; this salutary remembrance of the manner in which he had been taught to regard the Sabbath, induced a change of conduct, and he subsequently became one of the most devoted servants of Jesus Christ.

This excellent minister is well known as the founder of the first Mariner's Church in Philadelphia, and as an eminent preacher to seamen. At his grave, the Rev. Dr. Green gave an account of the origin of this peculiar department of labour. When he began to preach to seamen, about 1820, he procured a sail-loft, and on the Sabbath hung out a flag. As the sailors passed by they hailed him and his friends, "Ship ahoy!" "We," says Mr. Eastburn, "answered them. They asked us where we were bound?" We told them to the port of New Jerusalem—and that they would do well to go in the fleet.

'Well,' said they, 'we will come in and hear your terms.'"
Such was the commencement of a work on which the blessing of God has so greatly rested.

REV. MR. C.

At a meeting of a Religious Tract Society, at Otsego, the Rev. Mr. C., a clergyman well known to the meeting, arose with deep emotion, and said, "My friends, I stand before this congregation as a monument of the efficacy of tracts. When a young man, careless, unbelieving, and impenitent, as I was one day passing along the road, I saw a little piece of paper half-covered with mud; it attracted my attention; I picked it up, and found it to be the tract 'POOR JOSEPH.' I seated myself on a bank beside a small stream, and read it; and oh! I shall never forget the feelings I had as I read over that simple story. The Spirit of God sent home its truths to my heart. I trembled and wept in view of my sins, and I never rested until I reposed on the blood of Christ for salvation. If I have ever done any good in the cause of Christ, and if I may be hereafter made instrumental in leading lost and perishing souls to the Redeemer, it may be all traced to that tract. It has started a train of causes that must operate through eternity."

REV. PRESIDENT EDWARDS.

Few things would tend more to encourage the Christian education of children, especially on the part of pious mothers, than a careful examination of the history of eminent Christian ministers. President Edwards was the only brother of ten sisters, and the son of eminently pious parents. He was the great-great-grandson, on his mother's side, of a minister in London in the days of Queen Elizabeth; and the family of his mother for several generations was equally singular for their devotedness to God. To his mother, especially, is the church indebted, under God, for much of the eminence to which this extraordinary man attained.

REV. DR. DWIGHT.

Still more remarkable than the case of President Edwards, was that of his grandson, President Dwight. His mother, the daughter of Edwards, possessed uncommon powers of mind; and for the extent and variety of her knowledge, she has been rarely excelled in this or any other country. Though married at an early age, and a mother at eighteen, she found time, without neglecting the ordinary cares of her family, to devote herself, with the most assiduous attention, to the instruction of this son, and a numerous family of children, as they successively claimed her regard. She began to instruct him almost as soon as he was able to speak, so that at four years of age he could read his Bible with ease and correctness. She aimed, at a very early period, to enlighten his conscience, to make him afraid of sin, and to know the way of pardon only through the righteousness of Christ. The impressions thus made were never effaced. His most valuable instructor through life was his mother.

SEVERAL YOUNG CLERGYMEN.

A few years since, some gentlemen in this country, who were associated in preparing for the Christian ministry, felt interested in ascertaining what proportion of their number had pious mothers. They were greatly surprised and delighted in finding, that out of one hundred and twenty students, more than a hundred had been blessed by a mother's prayers, and directed by a mother's counsels to the Saviour. Though some of these had broken away from all the restraints of home, and, like the prodigal, had wandered in sin and sorrow, yet they could not forget the impressions of childhood, and each was eventually brought to Jesus, and proved a mother's joy and blessing.

From the "Quarterly Register," published about the same time, we learn that of the one hundred and fourteen students whose names were then on the catalogue of the Theological Seminary at Princeton, one hundred and four, or about eleven-twelfths of the whole number, had mothers embracing Christianity; eighty-two had parents both of whom were professors. In twenty-two instances the mother professed religion, and the father did not. Not a single case where the father was a professor, and the mother was not.

A Missionary from this country says, "I recollect particularly, that once my mother came and stood by me as I sat in the door, and tenderly talked to me of God and my duty to him, and her tears dropped upon my head. That made me a missionary."

Another clergyman has stated that in his boyhood a colored nurse impressed it upon his mind, by her simple remarks, that he was to become a minister. This impression never left him, even during his most sinful years, but proved a leading instrumental cause of turning his mind to religion, and finally of constraining him to enter the ministry.

The Rev. Dr. Scudder states that a clergyman told him that when he was about five years of age he saw some pictures of the Tuscarora Indians which had been sent by a lady who had gone as a missionary from his native place. This circumstance made an impression upon his mind respecting missions which he never lost, and he considered this as one of the means which God used for his conversion.

Some years since, a gentleman was travelling from Philadelphia to Boston with his daughter. At Providence a young man, a profane sailor, entered the coach, whom the gentleman reproved for his profanity, and recommended him with much seriousness to read Doddridge's Rise and Progress of Religion; and at Boston they parted from each other with regret.

In the coach with them travelled a young man, a student at one of the colleges, of whom, however, but little notice was taken. A few years afterwards, a gentleman came into the store of our traveller at Philadelphia, whom, however, he did not know till he was informed that he was the young man who travelled with him and the sailor to Boston. The pleasing facts were now elicited, that, influenced by what the gentleman had said to the sailor, the present visitor had been induced to read " The Rise and Progress," which had been blessed to the conversion of his soul, and that he was now come to reside in Philadelphia, to study for the ministry, under the excellent Dr. Staughton. The young man thus benefited by a casual conversation in a stage-coach, became a minister in Massachusetts.

Rev. Mr. B——, of C——, related the following interesting fact at an anniversary meeting of the benevolent societies of Chittenden co., Vermont:

"Previous to entering the ministry, while on a short journey, as he stopped to water his horse, there came along a ragged, dirty boy, to whom he gave a tract. About six years after, while in the seminary, a young man called at his room and asked him if he recollected that tract—holding one in his hand. He replied in the negative. The young man then opened the tract, and inquired if he did not remember that pencil-mark? He observed that it was his own handwriting, and replied that he had a faint recollection of giving such a tract to a boy some years before. 'I am that boy,' replied the young man. 'I was very wicked and abandoned, when I received the tract, and my parents were equally bad. They never attended church or gave me any religious instruction. I read the tract again and again, and thought it was very wonderful: my wickedness seemed so great that I had no rest till I found it in the Saviour. I am now in my junior year, preparing for the ministry.'"

A drunkard having obtained possession of a good book, pledged it for liquor. Before the vendor of ardent spirits had removed it from the bar, a very dissipated young man entered the place, and being too well known to obtain credit, he was constrained to lay down three cents for a glass of rum, before he could obtain it. This troubled him, for it was the last three cents he had, and he dreaded being unable to get his usual dram in the morning. While these thoughts perplexed him, he saw the book, and judging rightly how it came there, he supposed that, could he purloin it, his difficulty would be removed, for he could in like manner pledge it at some other bar. He accomplished the theft unobserved, and, much pleased with his success, went home. That he might avoid being suspected when offering the book, he opened it to see what it was; the first words he saw were these : " There is nothing covered that shall not be revealed." In a moment this solemn truth was impressed upon his conscience; and his course of life, his deeds of darkness, his choice of wicked associates, and his future prospects, forced themselves upon his attention. He lay down, but could not sleep : and after spending a restless night, he arose to seek, not the *fire-water* to which he was accustomed, but those streams that make glad the city of God. An intolerable burden oppressed him, and in bitter anguish of spirit he went to some of the servants of Jesus Christ, and asked for their counsel and their prayers. In this state of mind he continued for a season, but at length the Lord heard his cry, and delivered him from the horrible pit, and set his feet upon a rock, and put a new song into his mouth, and established his goings. That man is now a minister of the Gospel

REV. MR. JAPHET.

Dr. Cotton Mather has related a very pleasing incident which occurred in the seventeenth century, in connection with Mr. Mayhew.

It appears that soon after he began to preach in Martha's Vineyard, the wife of Pammehannit, a leading man among the Indians, became deeply impressed with the gospel. In the confession she made before her admission into the church, she stated that long before she heard the gospel, she lost five children in succession, while very young, and that when her sixth was born, who was a son, agitated with fear lest she should lose him also, she took him in her arms, and walked into the fields. While there she mused on the insufficiency of all human help, and it was suggested to her mind that there was an Almighty God who ought to be prayed to,—that He had created all things—and that He who had given life to all was able to preserve the life of her child. With these feelings she cried to God for the life of her child, and the child lived. As soon as this poor woman heard the gospel, it was evident that her mind was fully prepared to receive it. Her son became an eminent Christian, and a laborious minister of an Indian church, consisting of some scores of regenerated souls. He was living when Dr. Mather wrote in 1696, faithfully and successfully labouring to extend the Gospel among the Indians on the main land. His name was Japhet.

REV. DR. PATTEN.

The Rev. Dr. Patten, of New York, stated, at a meeting of the American Tract Society in that city, that a pious man of colour, in the vicinity of Philadelphia, whom he knew and often conversed with, when he first began to turn his thoughts to the Christian ministry, held with him an interesting conversation. This poor Tom, for so he was called, had been converted when a slave, had learned to read, was called to the dying-bed of his master to read the Bible, was emancipated by his master's will, and, after having redeemed his wife, had removed to the suburbs of Philadelphia. Poor Tom said to Dr. P., "Massa, me hear you are going to study to be a minister!" "Yes." "Will you let poor Tom say one thing to you?" "Yes." "Well, you know the good Master says, Watch and pray. Now you may watch all the time, and if you no pray, the devil will get in. You may pray all the time, and if you no watch too, the devil will get in. But if you watch and pray all the time, the devil no get in; for it is just like the sword of God put into the hand of the angel at the entering of the garden—it turn every way. If the devil come before, it turn there; if the devil come behind, it turn there. Yes, massa, it turn every way."

REV. W. TENNENT.

The history of very few ministers has ever been found to present more remarkable events than those connected with this extraordinary man.

In early life he was a very diligent student, and made great proficiency in the languages. Being very deeply impressed with a sense of divine things, he determined to follow the example of his father, and to devote himself to the ministry. He was preparing for examination by the presbytery, when his health failed, and he became almost a skeleton. He was attended by a young but eminent physician, who was attached to him by warm friendship, but who had to grieve over the entire loss of his health and spirits. One morning, while Mr. Tennent was conversing with his brother, in Latin, on the state of his soul, he fainted, and apparently died. On the following day, the neighbours were invited to attend his funeral. In the mean time his physician, who had been in the country, returned, and was greatly affected with the news of his death. He could not be persuaded that it had taken place. He tried every means to ascertain the existence of life, but without effect. The funeral, by the determination of the physician, was delayed. On the third day the people were again invited to discharge the last duties owing to the dead; still, however, the physician was not satisfied, and implored, at length, for only one quarter of an hour more delay. At this critical moment, the body, to the great astonishment of all, opened its eyes, uttered a dreadful groan, and sunk again into apparent death. This, of course, put an end to all thoughts of burying him, and every effort was employed in hope of speedy resuscitation; in about an hour the eyes again opened, and in a few hours he was restored to life.

Still, however, for about six weeks his recovery was doubtful, and twelve months elapsed before he was in good health. After he was able to walk about the room, his sister, who had stayed from church on the Sunday afternoon, was reading in the Bible, when he asked her what book she had in her hand. She told him, and he asked, " What is the Bible ? I know not what you mean." She was deeply affected, and with tears told him that he was once well acquainted with it. On examination it was found that he was totally ignorant of every transaction of his former life. He could not read a word, nor had he any idea of what it meant. He was taught to read and write after the manner of children, and began to learn the Latin language under the tuition of his brother. One day, as he was reciting a lesson in Cornelius Nepos, he suddenly started, placed his hand on his head, as if something had hurt him, and said that he felt a sudden shock, and it seemed to him as though he had read that book before. By degrees his recollection was entirely restored.

The account he gave of the solemn transaction to which we have referred, was, in substance, that while he was conversing with his brother, he found himself in a moment in another state of existence, conducted by a superior being to an ineffable glory, an idea of which it was impossible to convey. He reflected on his happy change, and saw an innumerable company of happy beings surrounding the inexpressible glory, in acts of joyous adoration and worship. He felt unutterable joy, and requested his conductor to attend him to join the happy throng; he was informed, however, that he must return to earth. This communication greatly pained him, and in a moment he saw his brother disputing with the doctor. He added, " Such was the effect on my mind of what I had seen and heard, that if it be possible for a human being to live entirely above the world and the things of it, for some time afterwards I was that person. The ravishing sounds of the songs and hallelujahs that I heard, and the very words that were uttered, were not out of my ears when awake, for at least three years. All the kingdoms of the earth were in my sight as nothing and vanity; and so great were my ideas of heavenly glory, that nothing which did not in some measure relate to it, could command my serious attention."

Further particulars were expected to have been found among

Mr. T.'s papers after his death, as he was known to have written them; but unhappily these papers, by the calamities of war, and the sudden death of his son, were lost.

REV. S. BLYTHE.

This worthy man, who emigrated from the east to Alabama in a very early period of his history, entertained considerable doubts as to his call to the ministry; and arranged with his wife that his having preached should, for a time at least, be kept secret. Not many days after, he met with a pious old lady, who had newly arrived in the wilderness, and who deeply lamented that there was no house of God, no preaching, no preacher, and no one who felt like herself. She was anxious to find a congenial spirit with whom she could hold in rcourse. After a very little conversation, she looked anxiously and seriously in his face, and said, "My dear sir, are you not a professor of religion?" He answered, with a faltering voice, "Ah! I am a sort of one." The good old lady instantly asked, "Are you not a minister of the gospel?" He could conceal the fact no longer, but acknowledged that though he had wished to conceal it, he had been accustomed to preach. The good woman was greatly delighted, and urged him to make an appointment for preaching, which he did, and in the course of a year or two, established several churches.

AN INDIAN PREACHER.

Hiacoomes, the first Indian convert on Martha's Vineyard, was a remarkable man. He was an Indian of Great Harbor, now Edgartown. The Indian sachems and others of their principal men looked upon him as an ordinary or mean person, on account of his humble parentage, slow speech and uninteresting countenance—yet there was that within him, which afterwards appeared of greater value than the endowments of those who looked upon him with contempt. Living among the English, some of them visited him in his wigwam, and were courteously entertained by him; and he visited them in return, evidently that he might learn something that would be for his advantage. About the same time, he went also to the English meeting, where the Rev. Thomas Mayhew, who was then minister to the few English families in Edgartown, preached. Mr. Mayhew had not, as yet, made any direct efforts for the conversion of the Indians, but was revolving in his mind some plans whereby to reach them. The coming of Hiacoomes to his meeting, the disposition he manifested to hear and receive instruction, and the gravity of his demeanour, induced the preacher to try what he could do in influencing him to become a Christian He immediately sought an opportunity for conversation, and finding encouragement in his interview, he invited the Indian inquirer to come to his house every Sabbath evening, that he might speak to him of religion. The news soon spread among the Indians, and the sachems and pawwaws were much alarmed, and tried to discourage Hiacoomes from holding communication with the English and receiving their instructions, but all to no purpose, as he was strongly bent after still higher attainments in the knowledge of God. This was in 1643, and in two years afterwards, having in the meanwhile been prepared by Mr. Mayhew, he commenced teaching to the Indians the things of Christianity. He was not suffered to proceed without opposition from the pawwaws, sachems and other Indians—but he made this improvement of the injustice done him. "I had," he remarked, "one hand for injuries and another hand for God; whilst I received wrong with the one, I laid the faster hold on God with the other." These words should be written in letters of gold.

REV. CHARLES BEATTY.

Many of the most eminent ministers have been introduced to their work in a very unexpected manner. This was the case with Mr. Beatty, an excellent Presbyterian minister of the last century. He was a native of Ireland, where he obtained a pretty accurate classical education; but his circumstances being narrow, he emigrated to America, and employed several of the first years of his life on this side the Atlantic in the business of a pedlar. In the pursuit of this vocation, he halted one day at the "Log College," on the Neshaminy, then under the care of the Rev. William Tennent, the elder. The pedlar, to Mr. Tennent's surprise, addressed him in correct Latin, and appeared to be familiar with that language. After much conversation, in which Mr. Beatty manifested fervent piety, and considerable religious knowledge, as well as a good education in other respects, Mr. Tennent said to him, "You must quit your present employment. Go and sell the contents of your pack, and return immediately, and study with me. It will be a sin for you to continue a pedlar, when you may be so much more useful in another profession." He accepted Mr. Tennent's offer, returned to Neshaminy, completed his academical and theological studies, and in due time became an eminent minister. He died in Barbadoes, where he had gone to solicit benefactions for the college of New Jersey.

REV. PRESIDENT DAVIES.

A LITTLE more than a century ago, the Rev. W. Robinson had been preaching in North Carolina, having been sent there by the "New-light" presbytery of New Brunswick. He was compelled by persecution to make a precipitate retreat, which was so hasty that his many warm friends had no opportunity to contribute any thing as a compensation, or even to defray his expenses. A collection was, however, made, and sent after him by some trusty friends. But he peremptorily refused to receive a penny of it, saying he knew what his enemies would say if he should receive any part of it, and he was resolved they should have no occasion to speak ill of him or of his Master's cause. He at length consented to receive it, saying he knew a very pious and promising young man, who was in very indigent circumstances, and had been for some years prosecuting his studies for the ministry; he would, with their leave, expend it upon him, with the promise that if he should enter the ministry, he should come and preach to them. To this they consented. Samuel Davies, then studying under the care of the Rev. Samuel Blair, at Fogg's Manor, Pennsylvania, was this youth; and by his coming and labouring among them the pledge was redeemed.

One of the confidential elders of this extraordinary preacher once said to him:—"Mr. Davies, how is it, that you, who are so well-informed upon all theological subjects, and can express yourself with so much ease and readiness, should think it necessary to prepare and write your sermons with so much care, and take your notes into the pulpit, and make such constant use of *them?* Why do you not, like many other preachers, oftener preach extempore?" Mr. Davies replied, "I always thought it to be a most awful thing to go into the pulpit, and there speak nonsense in the name of God. Besides, when I have an opportunity of preparing, and neglect to do so, I am afraid to look up to God for assistance, for that would be to ask him to countenance my negligence. But when I am evidently called upon to preach, and have had no opportunity to make preparation, I am not afraid to try to preach extempore, and I can with confidence look up to God for assistance."

REV. DR. RODGERS.

THERE is something in the following anecdote equally adapted to interest the Christian and to excite a spirit of inquiry in the mind of the philosopher.

In the early life of Dr. Rodgers, he was appointed by his presbytery to visit three congregations in Virginia, in company with the Rev., afterwards President Davies. On their way a remarkable circumstance occurred. Mr. Rodgers, from his earliest years, had been unusually fearful of lightning and thunder. So great, indeed, were his agitation and suffering during thunder-storms, that the prospect of one made him unhappy. He had taken much pains to get the better of this weakness; but, to use his own language, "neither reason, philosophy, nor religion availed any thing;" and it was the more distressing, because both he and his friends thought it might seriously interfere with his ministerial usefulness. But in the course of the journey of which we are now speaking, he was entirely delivered from this infirmity, and by means the most unlikely to be imagined to produce such a happy effect.

While he and Mr. Davies were riding together in Virginia, one afternoon, they were overtaken by one of the most tremendous thunder-storms ever known in that part of the country. They were in the midst of an extensive forest, and several miles distant from any house which offered even tolerable shelter, either to them or their horses. The storm came up with great rapidity; the lightning and thunder were violent beyond all description; and the whole scene such as might be supposed to appal the stoutest heart. Their horses, terrified and trembling, refused to proceed. They were obliged to alight; and, standing by their beasts, expected every moment to be precipitated into eternity by the resistless element. Providentially, however, they escaped unhurt: and the consequence was as wonderful as the preservation was happy. From that hour Mr. Rodgers was entirely delivered from the infirmity which had hitherto given him so much distress.

A member of the Doctor's congregation in New York once complained to him that his prayers were too methodical, and that they appeared to be studied. "You are right, sir," said the doctor, "my prayers are studied. Would you have me offer to God that which costs me nothing?"

REV. DR. HARRIS.

The Rev. N. Hall, in his funeral sermon for this valued minister, relates an incident which occurred i the first year in College, interesting in itself, and which exercised a great influence on his character in the whole of his after life.

His mother, having learned, by a visit to his room, his great need of comfortable clothing, and unable herself to help him, save by her hands, had proposed to him to raise in some way the sum of money, a very small one, which would enable her to purchase for him what he needed. After many fruitless attempts to do this, he set off to meet his mother, as by previous arrangement, in Boston; having nothing in possession or prospect, but a few cents, which he had transferred from his trunk to his pocket as he left his room; and these—so strong were his benevolent sympathies—he gave to a poor crippled soldier that he met on his way, and who, faint and famishing, solicited his aid. As he went on, deeply depressed at his destitute condition, and in despair at his seeming fate, he perceived something adhering to the end of his rude staff he had cut on his way; and found it to be a gold ring, into which his staff had stuck itself as he walked, and having engraved upon it the words, "God speed thee, friend." Its pecuniary worth proved sufficient for his present exigency, and its moral value was incalculable, giving him a cheerful faith and confidence in God. The whole incident, acting upon his sensitive nature, subdued and overwhelmed him, and gave to his character a stronger religious determination. "That motto," said he in after life, "has ever been the support of my faith when it was feeble, and the strength of my heart when it was faint."

REV. DR. KING.

In the month of December, 1807, Mr. Maynard was teaching school in Plainfield, Mass. One cold, blustering morning, on entering his school-room, he observed a lad whom he had not seen before, sitting on one of the benches. He was fifteen years old; his parents lived seven miles distant; he wanted an education; and had come from home on foot that morning, to see if Mr. M. could help him to contrive how to obtain it.

Mr. M. asked him if he was acquainted with any one in that place.

"No."

"Can your parents help you towards obtaining an education?"

"No."

"Have you any friends that can give you assistance?"

"No."

"Well, how do you expect to obtain an education?"

"I don't know, but I thought I would come and see you."

Mr. M. told him to stay that day, and he would see what could be done. He discovered that the boy was possessed of good sense, but no uncommon brilliancy, and he was particularly struck with the cool and resolute manner in which he undertook to conquer difficulties which would have intimidated weaker minds. In the course of the day, Mr. M. made provision for having him boarded through the winter in the family with himself, the lad paying for his board by his services out of school. He gave himself diligently to study, in which he made good, but not rapid proficiency, improving every opportunity of reading and conversation for acquiring knowledge, and thus spent the winter.

When Mr. M. left the place in the spring, he engaged a minister, who resided about four miles from the boy's father, to hear his recitations; and the boy accordingly boarded at home and pursued his studies. It is unnecessary to pursue the narrative further. Mr. M. has never seen the lad since; but this was the early history of the Rev. Dr. Jonas King, whose exertions in the cause of oriental learning, and in alleviating the miseries of Greece, have endeared him alike to the scholar and the philanthropist, and shed a bright ray of glory on his native country.

REV. DR. KING, AND REV. HENRY LYMAN.

We propose to sketch another incident, or series of incidents, connected with Mr. King. They were communicated by an ardent friend of the missionary cause, and who has contributed largely of his abundant means for its advancement. It will be remembered that Mr. King, after his election to a professorship in one of the eastern colleges, was sent to Europe on business connected with the institution. While there, it was deemed important by the American Board of Commissioners, that he should proceed as a missionary, under their direction, to Palestine. The college, after some solicitation, was prevailed upon to consent to the arrangement, and a letter was written to Mr. King, informing him of the wishes of the Board of Commissioners. This letter reached Mr. King at Paris, and was received for him by the gentleman to whom we have alluded, who was then engaged in mercantile business in that city. This gentleman received a letter at the same time, desiring him to unite with the Board in their endeavours to procure the valuable services of Mr. King, in that most interesting and important field of labour, Palestine. When Mr. King came into the counting room, the letter was handed to him

He immediately retired with it to a small private adjoining room. He did not return for about three hours. When he came out, reaching his hand, he inquired, "What shall I do?" "Go." "Behold," says he, "I go bound in the spirit to Jerusalem, not knowing the things that shall befal me there." The gentleman immediately wrote to several friends of the missionary cause in Europe, saying, "Mr. King has consented to go to Palestine. I will give a certain sum for so many years: will you do the same?" Affirmative answers were returned in every case.

Before he left for Jerusalem, Mr. King requested his friend, on his return to America, to go and see his aged parents, and administer to them such consolation as their condition should require. This he promised; and this promise he kept, when, a few years after, he found himself at Northampton, in Massachusetts, and within a few miles of their residence. Knowing that they were still in indigent circumstances, he determined not to visit them without an open hand. It was in the winter season: a sleigh was procured and laden with provisions, and, accompanied by a young man, the son of the host from whom he had procured the sleigh, he started on his long-promised errand of mercy. On arriving at the house, he found it as he expected, small and decayed, the inmates of which might well say:

> "No beggar soils the knocker of my door:
> The child of rags by instinct shuns the poor."

When that door was opened by the aged mother, in every lineament was seen the features of Jonas King. There was no mistaking the parentage. "I have come," said the ambassador, for such he may well be termed, "from your son at Jerusalem." The venerable father rose up to receive him, and, after a few hurried questions, said, "Let us pray;" and bending down, he returned fervent thanks for his social privileges, and especially for the opportunity offered him of hearing from his long-absent and beloved son. The provisions were brought in. "These," said the ambassador, "are sent by your son; at least I present them in his name." "What!" said the aged and simple-hearted mother, "did these things come all the way from Jerusalem?" As the coffee, and tea, and sugar, were successively placed before them, the good old man said, "Of a truth God has this day abundantly blessed us: again let us return thanks;" and he bowed the knee and lifted up his voice, and gave thanks to God for his goodness to them. The table was soon spread, and the aged pair, and their son's friend and their benefactor, were gathered around it; the lad who had driven the horses was among the number. A blessing was invoked, and the meal partaken of with grateful hearts. When it was over, the day was drawing to a close, and the gentleman signified his intention of returning. Before he departed, the old family Bible was brought forward, and a chapter read. The eyes of the pious old man were dimmed with age, and he regretted their decay, especially as it prevented his reading the sacred word. Again the old man said, "Let us unite in prayer," and again he bowed himself, and invoked the choicest blessings upon his son and upon his friend. With a heart filled with love and admiration of the piety of these aged saints, and depos'ting secretly between the leaves of the old Bible a twenty-dollar bill, that friend departed, expecting in all probability never to see their faces again on earth. A few years afterwards, the same gentleman was attending a Commencement in one of the New England colleges. After the close of the exercises, a young gentleman approached him, and, addressing him by name, said, "You probably do not recollect me, but I am the person who accompanied you on your visit to the parents of Jonas King; I date my first serious religious impressions from that day." That young man was the Rev. Henry Lyman, who was afterwards missionary to India, and whose prospects of usefulness, and whose life, were terminated by the melancholy death of himself and associate, by the cannibals of the island of Borneo. The good old man has gone to his rest, and by his will, left to the friend of his son, the old family Bible.

A CLERGYMAN.

Some years ago, a clergyman, who was a widower, married the widow of a deceased minister of another denomination. She was a woman highly esteemed for her correct views of Divine truth, and for sincere and consistent piety. She had not long accompanied her new companion in his public and social worship, before she became pensive and dejected. This awakened the solicitude of her companion, who insisted on knowing the cause. At length, with trembling hesitancy, she observed, " Sir, your preaching would starve all the Christians in the world." " Starve all the Christians in the world!" said the astonished preacher ; "why, do I not speak the truth ?" "Yes," replied his wife, "and so you would were you to stand in the desk all day, and say my name is Mary. But, sir, there is something besides the letter in the truth of the gospel." The result was, a very important change in the ministerial efforts of this clergyman ; after which his partner sat and heard him with great delight.

AN INDIAN MISSIONARY.

Every Christian must review with deep interest the history of the rise and progress of religion among our Indians. The following narrative was given by a gentleman of the United States, when on a visit to England, and was published in that country in 1838:—

It was in the autumn of 1832, in the regions of the far-west, when the shadows of the forest were deepening in the twilight over the waters of the Columbian river, that a traveller, whom commerce had led to seek out the tribe of Indians dwelling upon its borders, (commonly called "the Flat-headed Indians,") appeared at the entrance of a wigwam, asking for food and water, in broken accents, but in their own language. When rested and refreshed, its owner asked his errand, which proved to be one of barter, and made him very welcome to these children of the wilderness.

The savage who received him was tall, erect, and finely formed, with an expression of intelligence about his eyes and forehead which might have bespoken the power of civilization. "You are weary," he said to the stranger, "and it was well that you reached our shelter before the voice of the great Eagle was abroad upon the mountains."

"What do you mean?" asked his guest, at the same moment looking forth at the clouded sky;—"and what is the voice of the great Eagle?"

"Hear it now," replied the savage, as the first peal of thunder rolled, and echoed round the hills. "The great Spirit is riding down the water-fall! Do you not hear him in the wind? I am afraid of him, and so surely you must be. Let us speak against his harm."

"I fear nothing," replied the hardy wanderer. "But is this spirit a good or a bad spirit?—and have you more spirits than one in your country?"

"We have a good Spirit," was the answer, "but we never speak to him—he will do us no evil: and we have a bad spirit, who is the great eagle I told you of; and we pray to him, that he may not work us harm. What spirits have you in your country?"

" I come," said the stranger, "from the Ohio; and the men in those parts have a book which teaches them a new way to heaven; or, as you would call it, to the sky. They say that they shall live again after they die, and live up there—that is, if they please their great Spirit."

" What is a book?—I should like to see it," said the Indian. "And about living after death, I want to know. How far is it to the Ohio?"

" It is three thousand miles," replied the traveller, "and all through the desert. You never will reach the Ohio;—but all I have said to you is true."

The Indian turned into his hut to sleep; but he could not sleep at all,—and he walked out again into the clear still moonlight, when the storm was hushed, to think about the book which could teach the way into the sky. There were two men in his tribe to whom he repeated, the next morning, what the traveller had said; and he asked them if they would go with him to fetch such a book from beyond the mountains. They agreed,—and after a season the traveller went on his way, and they too took their journey in an opposite direction. They lived by the chase, endured innumerable perils, and were six months on their road;—but at last arrived at their destination, and entreated to see the book of which they had heard, and to be taught that which they did not know.

Their history excited great interest—they were welcomed and instructed; but ere many months had passed, the savage who had first heard the good news from the traveller,—worn out with the fatigue and hardships of his journey—fell ill and died: not, however, before he had listened to the glad tidings of salvation by Jesus Christ; and declared that he believed the book. A still deeper feeling was occasioned by his death. A missionary offered himself to return with the two others to their homes; and did accompany them back to the Columbian River. Accounts were received from him of his safe arrival, his joyful reception by the tribe, and of his beginning to distribute among them the water of life.

SEVERAL CLERGYMEN.

Pains taken in the composition of sermons are not labour thrown away. An eminent scholar, the president of one of our universities, re-wrote the most useful of his sermons thirteen or fourteen times, and laboured, in connection with a literary friend, two whole days on two sentences. A living divine, who has been called the prince of our pulpit orators, spent a fortnight on a single discourse, which has already accomplished more good than *four thousand* sermons written by another of our pastors, at the rate of two a week. On the blank leaf of one of Dr. Griffin's manuscripts, it appeared that his discourse had been preached *ninety times!* Thus had it been touched and retouched, reviewed and rewritten, till, so far as the author's power availed, it was perfected.

A YOUNG MINISTER.

A young minister, a few years since, received a call from two different societies at once, to become their pastor. One of them was united and rich, and therefore able to give him a large salary; the other was poor, and so divided that they had driven away their minister. In this condition he applied to his father for advice. An aged coloured servant, who overheard what was said, made this reply; "Massa, go where there is the least money and the most devil." The minister took the advice, united the church, and converted many souls to Christ.

REV. MR. WILLEY.

The Rev. Mr. Willey, of New Hampshire, at a public meeting in Park Street church, Boston, gave the history of a lad in a retired part of the country, to whom a pious lady, after serious conversation, gave the "Saints' Rest." He read it, became deeply interested, and carried it to the barn where he was employed, weeping over its pages, and over his hardness of heart, and praying to be saved from the miseries of the lost. But these impressions died away; and some years after, on the Sabbath, in Boston, he wandered into the very church where the meeting was then assembled, where, under the appeals of the venerable Dr. Griffin, all his former solicitude for his undying soul was revived, and he was led immediately to apply to a clergyman of the city for the "Saints' Rest." After considerable trouble the long-sought volume was found and read, portions of it, time after time, during the week. On the Sabbath this youth was seen in this house, a weeping stranger, sometimes in one part of it and sometimes in another. It was in that gallery, referring to the west gallery, as he has since ventured to hope, he poured out his soul unto God, and that light began to dawn upon him, which has since been as the rising light of day. This youth was the eldest in a family of ten children, *all of whom, together with both parents, have since been brought to hope in the mercy of God,* and to unite with his people; and of the five sons, four are in the Christian ministry.

REV. DR. GRIFFIN.

The late Rev. Dr. E. D. Griffin was exceedingly careful in the preparation of his sermons. Dr. Sprague says that he was once at his house, and in view of preaching, went into his study to read over his sermon. He called for ink and sand, and began to strike out, and to pour on the sand. The manuscript was already black with erasures and insertions, but the work went on, the paper growing darker every moment. One of the little children coming up, and looking on the blotted and blurred manuscript, corrected and re-corrected, said, "How can you read your sermon? It is all scratched out?" He was particular in covering with ink every word erased, so that it could not be read.

The remark of the child led him to speak of his custom; and said he, " This I regard as one chief excellence of my preaching, if I have any." He continued, " I have a plain figure which I use in the study; it will not do for the public ear; but it serves to illustrate my point. If you put swingling tow upon a hetchel, you can ride to Boston on it; but if you pull out the tow," holding up his fingers to represent the process, "and let the points stick up, they will prick: so," added he, " you may cover up the truth with ornaments and words, till the conscience cannot be reached. You must *pull out the tow*—the points are the truth—pull out the tow, and let the points stick up." A better illustration, as Dr. Sprague remarks, was never given. If our sermons had less " tow," and more naked " points," they would do more execution.

SEVERAL EMINENT CLERGYMEN.

The Rev. Dr. Hill, of Virginia, some time since, made the following statement at a public meeting of a Tract Society:—

I lost my sainted mother when I was a youth, but not before the instructions which I received from her beloved lips had made a deep impression upon my mind; an impression which I carried with me into a college, (Hampden Sidney,) where there was not then one pious student. There I often reflected, when surrounded by young men who scoffed at religion, upon the instructions of my mother, and my conscience was frequently sore distressed. I had no Bible, and dreaded getting one, lest it should be found in my possession. At last I could stand it no longer, and therefore requested a particular friend, a youth whose parents lived near, and who often went home, to ask his pious and excellent mother to send me some religious books. She sent me *Alleine's Alarm*, an old black book, which looked as if it might have been handled by successive generations for one hundred years. When I got it, I locked my room and lay on my bed reading it, when a student knocked at my door; and although I gave him no answer, dreading to be found reading such a book, he continued to knock and beat the door, until I had to open it. He came in, and seeing the book lying on the bed, he seized it, and examining its title, he said,—"Why, Hill, do you read such books?" I hesitated, but God enabled me to be decided, and tell him boldly, but with much emotion, "Yes, I do." The young man replied with deep agitation, "Oh, Hill, *you* may obtain religion, but *I* never can. I came here a professor of religion; but through fear, I dissembled it, and have been carried along with the wicked, until I fear that there is no hope for me." He told me that there were two others, who he believed were somewhat serious. We agreed to take up the subject of religion in earnest, and seek it together. We invited the other two, and held a prayer-meeting in my room on the next Saturday afternoon. And Oh, what a prayer-meeting! We tried to pray, but such prayer I never heard the like of. We knew not how to pray, but tried to do it. It was the first prayer-meeting that I ever heard of. We tried to sing, but it was in a suppressed manner, for we feared the other students. But they found it out, and gathered around the door, and made such a noise, that some of the officers had to disperse them. And so serious was the disturbance, that the President, the late excellent Rev. Dr. John B. Smith, had to investigate the matter at prayers that evening, in the prayers' hall. When he demanded the reason of the riot, a ringleader in wickedness got up and stated, that it was occasioned by three or four of the boys holding *prayer*-meeting, and they were determined to have no such doings there. The good President heard the statement with deep emotion, and looking at the youths charged with the sin of praying, with tears in his eyes, he said, "Oh, is there such a state of things in this college? Then God has come near to us. My dear young friends, you *shall* be protected. You shall hold your next meeting in my parlour, and I will be one of your number." Sure enough, we had our next meeting in his parlour, and half the college was there; and there began the glorious revival of religion, which pervaded the college and spread into the country around. Many of those students became ministers of the gospel. The youth who had brought me Alleine's Alarm from his mother was my friend, the Rev. C. Still, preaching in this State. And he who interrupted me in reading the work, my venerable and worthy friend, the Rev. Dr. H———, is now president of a college in the West.

REV. E. T. TAYLOR.

A PIOUS English widow, who resided among ignorant and vicious neighbors in the suburbs of Boston, Mass., determined to do what she could for their spiritual benefit. She opened her little front room for weekly prayer-meetings, and engaged some pious Methodists to aid in conducting them.

Among others who attended was a young sailor of intelligent and prepossessing countenance. A slight acquaintance showed him to be very ignorant of even the rudiments of education; but he had evidently such superior talents that the widow became much interested in his spiritual welfare, and prayed much that God would instruct and convert him, and make him useful.

But in the midst of her anticipations, he was suddenly summoned away to sea. He had been out but a short time when the vessel was seized by a British privateer and carried into Halifax, N. S., where the crew suffered by a long and wretched imprisonment.

A year had passed away, during which the good woman had heard nothing of the young sailor. Still she remembered and prayed for him with the solicitude of a mother. About this time she also was called to Halifax on business. While there, her habitual disposition to be useful, led her with a few friends to visit the prison with Bibles and tracts. In one apartme t were the American prisoners. As she approached the grat door, a voice shouted her name, calling her mother, and a youth appeared and leaped for joy at the grate. It was the lost sailor boy! They wept and conversed like mother and son, and when she left she gave him a Bible—his future guide and comfort.

During her stay at Halifax, she constantly visited the prison, supplying the youth with tracts, religious books, and clothing, and endeavouring by her conversation to secure the religious impression made on his mind at the prayer-meetings in Boston. After many months she removed to a distant part of the province; and for years she heard nothing more of the young sailor.

We pass over a period of many years, and introduce the reader to Father Taylor, the distinguished mariners' preacher in the city of Boston. In a spacious and substantial chapel, crowded about by the worst habitations in the city, this distinguished man delivered, every Sabbath, discourses as extraordinary, perhaps, as are to be found in the Christian world. In the centre column of seats, guarded sacredly against all other intrusion, sat a dense mass of mariners—a strange medley of white, black, and olive, Protestant, Catholic, and Pagan. On the other seats in the galleries, the aisles, the altar, and on the pulpit stairs, were crowded, week after week, and year after year—the families of sailors, and the poor who had no other temple—the elite of the city—the learned professor—the student—the popular writer—the actor—groups of clergymen, and the votaries of gayety and fashion, listening with throbbing hearts and wet eyes, to a man whose only school had been the forecastle, whose only endowments were those of grace and nature, but whose shrewd sense, keen wit, glowing fancy, melting pathos, and energetic delivery would allow none to be inattentive or unaffected in his audience.

In the year 183–, an aged English local preacher moved into the city of Boston from the British provinces.

The old local preacher was mingling in a public throng one day with a friend, when they met "Father T—." A few words of introduction led to a free conversation, in which the former residence of his wife in the city was mentioned, and allusion was made to her prayer-meeting—her former name was asked by "Father T—;" he seemed seized by an impulse—inquired their residence, hastened away, and in a short time arrived in a carriage, with all his family, at the home of the aged pair. There a scene ensued which must be left to the imagination of the reader. "Father Taylor" was the sailor boy of the prayer-meeting and the prison. The old lady was the widow who had first cared for his soul. They had met once more!

REV. DR. PAYSON.

A WRITER in the Christian Mirror says:—As a preacher, Payson was eminently prayerful. It was manifest in private intercourse with his Divine Master. "Payson," said an elderly minister of Christ, respecting him, "Payson does not need to go to the throne of grace, for he is always there." About the time I was licensed, and was leaving for the field where I laboured sixteen years, he said to me—"Brother M., I would never leave my study without having first prayed." And he seemed to read the holy word with much prayer. He studied, he planned, he wrote, he pronounced his sermons in prayer. He seemed to be habitually sensible that God only could give his words success; and such was his faith in the efficacy of prayer, that he once said to the writer, "If I really knew I needed two such worlds as this for my own private accommodation, I should no more hesitate to ask for them, than I should hesitate to ask for my daily bread." And exercising this faith in the efficacy of prayer, it is not strange that he should be much in prayer for the Holy Spirit to accompany his efforts in the ministry. Here was his chief dependence for success. For though his powers of oratory were far above most in the holy office—though his imagination was most inventive and brilliant—seldom surpassed—his memory remarkably tenacious, and his reading extensive, yet his dependence for success, I repeat it, was on the promised assistance of the Holy Spirit. This was seen in his sermons. It was especially seen in his addresses at the throne of grace. The assembly to whom he administered were, by his manner in prayer, made to feel that their minister leaned upon an almighty arm, in his great work. They heard him address the Saviour in such humble confidence, as to convince them that there was his only hope.

REV. DR. STRONG.

The Rev. Mr. —— was appointed many years ago to preach the election sermon before the governor, senators and representatives of Connecticut. Unaccustomed to such an audience, he displayed no little diffidence and trepidation in prospect of appearing before so much talent and dignity. This being noticed by the company in which he was, a brother in the ministry, of a different mental character, said to him, "Why, brother ——, don't mind the governor and the great people; just think they are all cabbage heads, and then you will be at your ease." "Think no such thing," said the excellent Dr. Strong, taking his friend aside; "think that you are going to preach before the most intellectual, and honorable, and learned audience that can be assembled in the State; bear in mind that they are *immortal* men, who will stand with you in the judgment of the great day; remember that angels are present, and so is your Lord and Master; fill your thoughts with a sense of his presence, and your obligations; think of his goodness and his promises; let God fill your whole field of vision, and man will appear in his proper diminutiveness; rely upon it, the more your mind is awed by reflections like these, the more calm, and balanced, and composed will it be." The preacher took the advice thus rendered, and afterwards thanked the friend who gave it, for the happy effects which it produced.

INCIDENTS CONNECTED WITH THE PULPIT LABOURS OF THE CLERGY.

REV. DOCTOR RODGERS.

THE following is one among many instances which might be given of the striking character of the preaching of this excellent man, while he resided at St. George's, before his removal to New York.

The celebrated George Whitefield had appointed, on a certain day, to preach within a few miles of Mr. Rodgers' residence; and the people of the neighbourhood assembled to the number of from five to six thousand. Owing, however, to some circumstance, not now known, Mr. Whitefield did not arrive. The people, after waiting in vain for a considerable time, urged Mr. Rodgers, who was present, to rise and address them. For any man, with the best preparation, to take the place of Whitefield, and preach to an audience assembled to hear *him*, would have been an arduous task; but to do this on a sudden call, and with scarcely any preparation, was much more so. Mr. Rodgers, however, wisely made it one of the first principles of his ministry, never to shrink from any service to which the providence of God evidently called him. He therefore determined, without any hesitation, to comply with the request of his friends; and, after a moment's premeditation, rose and preached to the multitude in the open air. The consequences were most happy. It proved, indeed, a day of power. It was the opinion of many who heard him, that notwithstanding all the disadvantages of the occasion, the preacher scarcely ever spoke so acceptably or so well. The congregation, on dispersing, unequivocally manifested that they had not been disappointed; and very many had reason long to remember the solemnities of the day with grateful and endearing joy.

When the Doctor was a young man, in the summer of 1748, he spent some time in Maryland, where his preaching and his manners were very attractive, and where he met with considerable success.

One case, that of a Mr. Winder, a gentleman of great wealth and urbanity, may be more distinctly alluded to. He was a polite scholar, and a member of the Episcopal Church, but, nevertheless, called with much courtesy on his neighbours where Mr. Rodgers was visiting, and invited the young Presbyterian preacher to pay him a visit. Mr. Rodgers accepted, and, previously to his going, was apprized by his friends that Mr. W. was a zealous, high-toned Episcopalian, and a very determined opponent of the doctrine of Election. He was scarcely seated in his chair at Mr. W.'s house, before that gentleman introduced the controversy respecting Election, by asking his opinion of a book on the subject which lay upon the table. Our young preacher replied that he had never before seen the book, but that he was a very firm believer in the doctrine of Election, and regarded it as a very important and precious part of the Christian system. This plunged them at once into the very midst of the dispute, which was continued, with a few interruptions, during the day. At its close, Mr. W. acknowledged himself silenced but not convinced, and dismissed his guest in the evening with much respect and friendliness.

The next Sabbath Mr. Rodgers preached in the neighbourhood, and Mr. Winder was one of his hearers. The faithful and animated discourse was founded on Ephesians, ii. 8; "For by grace are ye saved, through faith; and that not of yourselves, it is the gift of God." This sermon reached the heart of Mr. W. He, in common with a number of others, was deeply affected in the course of the service, and retired from the house of worship with very different views of himself, and of the way of salvation, from those which he had entertained before. The next day he called on Mr. Rodgers, not to cavil at the doctrine of Election, nor to speculate on the mysteries of religion, but to ask, as a convinced sinner, what he must do to be saved. His heart was now softened, his difficulties in a great measure removed, and he was convinced that if he were saved at all, it must be by grace alone. He was ready to acknowledge himself an instance of the sovereignty of divine mercy, and in a short time found peace and consolation in the truths which a few days before he had opposed as unscriptural and forbidding. He united with the church, and became for many years an exemplary ruling elder, and often spoke of the revolution which his views and hopes had undergone, and of the circumstances attending it, with deep humility and fervent gratitude.

The impression which this excellent man could produce by his preaching, may be further judged of from the following facts:

At the meeting of the Synod in 1774, he was appointed to spend a number of weeks, in the summer and autumn of that year, on a missionary tour, through the northern and north-western parts of the province of New York. He devoted several months to that service, and with renewed zeal and assiduity, for the most part in places utterly destitute of the means of grace. These labours were the immediate or remote means of forming many churches, which have since proved large, flourishing, and happy.

The period at which the Doctor fulfilled this mission was that rendered memorable by the warm dispute between the settlers in the territory which is now Vermont, and the government of New York, which claimed that territory as lying within its jurisdiction. Measures of great decision, and even violence, had been taken by both parties a short time before he went into that country; so that he found the public mind, particularly in

Vermont, highly irritated and inflamed. Nothing was further from the Doctor's view than any political design; but some of the jealous and exasperated Vermonters, knowing that he came from the capital of New York, and connecting every thing with the existing disputes, suspected him of being engaged in some mission or plan unfriendly to their claims. In a particular town which he had entered by appointment, for the sole purpose of preaching, he observed, a little before the public service began, several rough and fierce-looking men approach the house in which he was about to preach, and enter into very earnest and apparently angry conversation with those who stood near the door. He was utterly ignorant at the time of their design, or of the subject of their conversation; but was afterwards informed that they were very warmly contending with his friend that he was a spy, and of course a very dangerous person, and that he ought to be immediately arrested. It was in vain that the friends of the Doctor remonstrated, on the ground of the sacredness of his office, and the solemnity of the duty in which he was about to engage, and to attend on which the people were now collected together. His angry accusers replied, that the more sacred his office, the greater his power of doing mischief; and that to allow him to escape would be treason to their cause. At length, finding that all they could say availed nothing to his exculpation, and that the most positive assurances of his being known to be a man of pious and exemplary character, only rendered these hostile and ardent spirits more determined in their original purpose, the Doctor's friends only begged them to delay the seizure of his person until after divine service should be closed, as it would be a pity to disappoint so large a congregation as had then assembled for public worship. To this proposal, after much persuasion, they reluctantly consented, and divine service began. The exercises were more than usually solemn and impressive; many of the congregation were in tears; and even those who had come into the assembly filled with so much resentment, were observed to be softened with those around them. When worship was ended, they said nothing about their plan of arresting the preacher, but quietly retired, and suffered him to pursue his journey.

Two or three days after this, while the Doctor was preaching in a more northern town in the same district of country, soon after the service had begun, he saw two men enter the assembly, marked with countenances of peculiar ferocity and rage. He afterwards learned that they had come under the same impressions and with the same views as their predecessors in violence. They had, however, resolved to wait till the service should be ended, and then to arrest the preacher. The exercises of the day, as in the former case, were the means of disarming them. When the benediction was pronounced, they withdrew, saying to each other, that they were probably mistaken in the man, and had better go home.

REV. MR. S.

The Rev. Mr. S., a distinguished Methodist preacher, who was well known in the West, was once preaching with great fervour on the freeness of the gospel, and around him was an attentive congregation, with eager eyes turned to the preacher, and drinking every word into their souls. Among the rest was an individual who had been more remarkable for opening his mouth to say amen, than for opening his purse. Though he never gave money for the support of the gospel, yet he might be said to support the pulpit, for he always *stood by it*. He had, on this occasion, taken his usual place near the preacher's stand, and was making his responses with more than usual animation. After a burst of burning eloquence from the preacher, he clasped his hands, and cried out in a kind of ecstacy, "Yes, thank God! I have been a Methodist for twenty-five years, and it hasn't cost me twenty-five cents!" "God bless your stingy soul!" was the preacher's emphatic reply.

A CLERGYMAN IN INDIANA.

On a fine summer's day, in 1840, a clergyman was called to preach in a town in Indiana, to a youthful congregation. At the close of his discourse, he addressed his young hearers in some such words as these: "Learn that the present life is a preparation for, and has a tendency to, eternity. The present is linked to the future throughout creation, in the vegetable, in the animal, and in the moral world. As is the seed, so is the fruit; as is the egg, so is the fowl; as is the boy, so is the man; as is the rational being in this world, so will he be in the next. Dives estranged from God here, is Dives estranged from God there; and Enoch walking with God here, is Enoch walking with God in a calmer and better world. I beseech you, then, live for a blessed eternity. Go to the worm that you tread upon, and learn a lesson of wisdom. The very caterpillar seeks the food that fosters it for another and similar state; and, more wisely than man, builds its own sepulchre, from whence in time, by a kind of resurrection, it comes forth a new creature, in almost an angelic form. And now, that which was hideous is beautiful; and that which crawled, flies; and that which fed on comparatively gross food, sips the dew and revels in the rich pastures—an emblem of that paradise where flows the river of life, and grows the tree of life. Could the caterpillar have been diverted from its proper element and mode of life, it had never attained the butterfly's splendid form and hue; it had perished a worthless worm. Consider her ways, and be wise. Let it not be said that you are more negligent than worms, and that your reason is less available than their instinct. As often as the butterfly flits across your path, remember that it whispers in its flight, 'LIVE FOR THE FUTURE.'"

With this the preacher closed his discourse; but, to deepen the impressions, a butterfly, directed by the Hand which guides alike the sun and an atom in its course, fluttered through the church, as if commissioned by Heaven to repeat the exhortation. There was neither speech nor language, but its voice was heard, saying to the gazing audience, "LIVE FOR THE FUTURE."

REV. J. KENNADAY.

THE following facts were narrated by the Rev. J. Kennaday, in a sermon before a Methodist Conference in the United States:

I remember, on one occasion, in the early part of my ministry, when I visited one of my appointments upon the circuit I then travelled, I was seated amid my studies, seriously reflecting upon my labours in that village, when one of the brethren, an aged and judicious man, entered my room, and after a few moments' conversation on the state of the congregation, more marked for the greatness of its numbers, and the solemnity of its general attention, than for the instances of conversion, observed, "I have thought that I would suggest to you the propriety of preaching, this evening, on the love of God. I sometimes think we hear so much of terror and of wrath, that the people become hardened." I thanked him for his advice, for I believed it was given in candour and affection. He had been gone from my room but a little while, when another entered, a brother deservedly beloved, and of no less influence. I soon perceived that the state of the congregation was the burden of his heart. In a little time he remarked, "I thought I would take the liberty of advising you to preach a sermon to-night, on the terrors of the law. It is a long time since we heard a sermon truly alarming, and the people, I fear, are presuming unjustly upon that love of which they hear so constantly. Give us something, brother, that will arouse." Could opinions be more conflicting? And yet they were men of sound piety, and of no ordinary judgment. This little incident, so early occurring, taught me, through my ministry, incessantly and intensely, so to "speak, not as pleasing men, but God."

REV. DR. GRIFFIN.

Soon after the settlement of the late Rev. E. D. Griffin at Newark, he preached a sermon on the doctrine of election. Many of his hearers were offended; and some of his principal supporters threatened to leave him. A great excitement existed; for a heavy blow had been struck. They went to Dr. Richards with their complaints. He told them to be calm—not to act rashly. If that doctrine was of God, it would stand: and he cautioned them not to be found fighting against God. Dr. G. soon after called upon him, and said, in great agitation, "I have ruined myself—I have broken up my congregation." "I hope not," said Dr. R. Dr. G. inquired what he should do. Dr. R. replied, "I will tell you. Go home, and write two sermons on the doctrine of election, with as much care and consideration as though your life depended on every sentence. Pray over them; and next Sabbath preach them, under the consciousness that the eye of the

Saviour is upon you." He sat with a fixed look, while his friend was speaking. No sooner had he ceased, than Dr. G. sprang on his feet, and said, as he left the room, "I'll do it."

The Sabbath came. Dr. Richards obtained a supply for his pulpit, and was present to hear his friend. In the interval, he had seen the disaffected persons, and others; and urged all to attend. He sat in a retired part of the house, and observed Dr. G., as he entered the church. His great soul was oppressed. His noble countenance beamed with light—his eye was full of fire. He preached like a dying man. The house was still as death. The Spirit of God was there. In the afternoon, every seat, and aisle, and corner, was crowded. All Newark was moved. Dr. G. stood up, and vindicated the law and government of God. He rose with the subject, till an awe was felt which subdued every heart. The effect was wonderful. Those very men came round him, as he descended from the pulpit, and wept. The Spirit of God subdued them. That day, "the great revival," of which every one has heard, began; and before it ceased, hundreds were converted to Jesus Christ.

A writer in the Christian Review of 1839, gives the following description of a scene he himself witnessed. Speaking of Dr. Griffin, he says:—We remember him, on one occasion, as he was about to preach before a large assembly of an evening. It was a time of deep interest in religion. He always took ample time to review his sermon, and get his heart in a proper frame, before he went into the pulpit. As he entered the sanctuary, his majestic form and snow-white head attracted every eye He seemed to be pondering awful subjects, as he ascended the sacred desk. He read the hymn in a tremulous tone. His prayer was short, simple, and earnest. As he arose behind a temporary breast-work, erected to accommodate his unusual height, he looked around the assembly with the solicitude of a parent. His text was Isa. i. 18.—" Come, now, and let us reason together, saith the Lord." His feelings, the subject, the place, the assembly, all conspired to give uncommon interest to the effort. After a few remarks, he said :—" My business, at present, is with impenitent sinners. I would single them out from the crowd, and take them aside, and say in their ear—I have a message from the Lord to deliver to you. I am sent to reason with you, in His name, about the high concerns of a future world—about your interests a thousand ages hence—about the claims which the Sovereign of the world has upon you, and the long score of uncancelled charges which He has against you. Let Christians stand by, and assist me with their prayers, while I attempt to recall from death this interesting multitude." This happy introduction seemed to divest his manner of the formality of the preacher, and his address of the regularity of a sermon. We could think of nothing but a parent speaking, in all the tenderness of his heart, to his wayward offspring. His tender spirit, and subdued tones, served to render the illusion the more complete. " My poor hearers," he continued, " you have often considered an address from the pulpit as a matter of course, and felt no personal interest in it. But it must not be so now. I have a solemn errand from the Lord to do to you, *one by one.*" Each one seemed disposed to give him his hand, and come to his side, to hear his message. He then proceeded, in an easy way, to reason and expostulate with them. There was the most breathless attention. He was short, direct, and overwhelming. We think we see him now, as he stood, at the close, referring his weeping hearers to the awful scenes of the judgment :—" My beloved friends," he said, " I expect soon to meet you at that bar, and give an account of my labours among you to-night." It is solemn to reflect, that many who heard him on that evening are in eternity. They have met him before the throne of God. As though an unwonted solemnity had come over him, he said, with deep unction: "It is in full view of that awful scene, that I am speaking thus to you. I would not have you perish; but"—gathering himself up, he said, with great deliberation—"but if you perish, I would clear my garments of your blood."

As though not satisfied, and reluctant to leave them, he came forward in the pulpit, and said, with impassioned tones: —" But you *must not* perish. The calls of mercy are still out. I have returned to my text, and found it written—'Though your sins be as scarlet, they shall be white as snow; though they be red like crimson, they shall be as wool.' These heavenly words, issuing from the eternal throne, still mingle their sounds about your ears. There is yet hope. You need not perish. The door of mercy is not yet closed. That Saviour whom you just now saw on the judgment-seat, once died on Calvary. Though you have so long trifled with his blood— though you have so long abused sermons and Sabbaths— though you have ten thousand times been found in arms against the Sovereign of the world, yet in that blood, all your stains may be washed out—all your treasons purged. Only do not now seal your damnation, by longer rejecting his mercy. Fall down now at his feet: go not from this house, till you have bathed them with your tears, and wiped them with the hairs of your head. This is an awful moment. Heaven, earth, and hell, are now opened before you. From the throne of God, which is placed in the midst, the invitation is still proceeding. Not man, but God himself, is now speaking to you. If you turn away, it will be like those who turned away when their feet touched the borders of the promised land. They could not be forgiven, but must perish in the wilderness. Take care what you do; for you are now standing near the Shechinah. Drop the weapons from your bloody hands. With those trembling arms, clasp His feet; resolving never to quit your hold:—that if he tread you down, you will sink, but that you will never leave the spot, till one look assures you that your sins are forgiven. Oh, could we see you thus! Are you *afraid* to go? Why, it is the same Being who left the realms of glory to die for you. Go, with greater confidence than you ever went to an earthly parent. Go, with all your sins upon you. It is not to *judge* that He has now come. He has come to heal the broken-hearted, and to preach deliverance to the captives. The love of Jesus looks out of his eye. His hands, bearing still the prints of the nails, are extended to receive you. Go, and give pleasure to that heart which bled on the point of the spear. Go, and find your heaven in the sweetness of that embrace. Go.—You see him there!—Oh, go!"

Some of his tones yet linger on our ear. Some of his expressions of countenance are yet present to our recollection. That picture can never fade from our mind.

REV. W. ROBINSON.

In the year 1473, the Rev. W. Robinson was sent by the "New Light" presbytery of New Brunswick to preach in North Carolina, and was engaged to pay a visit to some towns in Hanover.

On the Saturday before the Sabbath on which he had engaged to preach there, he had to ride late at night to reach a tavern, within eight or ten miles of the place. The tavern-keeper was a shrewd, boisterous, profane man; and when uttering some horrid oath, Mr. Robinson ventured to reprove him; and although it was done in a mild manner, the inn-keeper gave him a sarcastic look, and said, " Pray, sir, who are you, to take such authority upon yourself?" "I am a minister of the gospel," replied Mr. R. "Then you belie your looks very much," said the tavern-keeper. This referred to the circumstance that, owing to the small-pox, Mr. R. had a very rough face, and had lost the sight of one of his eyes. Mr. Robinson said, "If you wish certainly to know whether I am a minister or not, if you will accompany me to such a place, you may be convinced by hearing me preach." "I will," said the innkeeper, "if you will preach from a text which I shall give you." "Let me have it," said Mr. Robinson, "and if there is nothing unsuitable in it, I will." The waggish tavern-keeper, with the wish of turning him into ridicule, assigned him the text, "I am fearfully and wonderfully made," (Psalm cxxxix. 14.) Mr. Robinson promised that if he would accompany him, he would preach, among his first sermons, one from that text. He did so, and before the sermon was ended, this wicked man was made to feel that he was the monster, and that he was fearfully and wonderfully made himself. It is said that he became a very pious and useful member of the church.

A CLERGYMAN IN MAINE.

The following fact we copy from Dr. Cotton Mather's Magnolia; we are afraid that it does not present the only instance where clergymen have attributed good motives to their people without their being deserved.

There were more than a few attempts of the English, to people and improve the parts of New England, which were to the northward of New Plymouth; but the designs of those attempts being aimed no higher than the advancement of some worldly interests, a constant series of disasters had confounded them, until there was a plantation erected upon the nobler designs of Christianity; and that plantation, though perhaps it has had more adversities than any one upon earth, yet, having obtained help from God, it continues to this day. There have been very fine settlements in the north-east regions; but what has become of them? I have heard that one of our ministers, once preaching to a congregation there, urged them to consider themselves a religious people from this consideration,—that otherwise they would contradict the main end of planting this wilderness; whereupon a well-known person, then in the assembly, cried out, "Sir, you are mistaken: you think you are preaching to the people at the Bay: our main end was to catch fish."

AN INDIAN MISSIONARY.

In the year 1798, one of the missionaries to the Indians of the north-west was on his way from the Tuscarora settlement to the Senecas. Journeying in pious meditation through the forest, a majestic Indian darted from its recesses, and arrested his progress. His hair was somewhat changed with age, and his face marked with the deep furrows of time; but his eyes expressed all the fiery vivacity of youthful passion, and his step was that of a warrior in the vigour of manhood.

"White man of the ocean, whither wanderest thou?" said the Indian. "I am travelling," replied the meek disciple of peace, "towards the dwellings of thy brethren, to teach them the knowledge of the only true God, and to lead them to peace and happiness." "To peace and happiness!" exclaimed the tall chief, while his eye seemed to flash fire—"behold the blessings that follow the footsteps of the white man; wherever he comes, the nations of the woodlands fade from the eye, like the mists of morning. Once, over the wide forests of the surrounding world, our people roamed in peace and freedom, nor eve dreamed of greater happiness than to hunt the beaver, the bear, and the wild deer. From the furthest extremity of the wide deep, came the white man, armed with thunder and lightning, and weapons still more pernicious. In war he hunted us like wild beasts; in peace he destroyed us by deadly liquors, or yet more deadly frauds. But a few moons had passed away, and whole nations of invincible warriors, and of hunters that fearlessly swept the forest and the mountain, perished, vainly opposing their triumphant invaders; or quietly dwindled into slaves and drunkards, and their names withered from the earth. Retire, dangerous man; leave us all we have yet left, our savage virtues and our gods; and do not, in the vain attempt to cultivate a rude and barren soil, pluck up the few thrifty plants of native growth that have survived the fostering cares of thy people, and weathered the stormy career of their pernicious friendship." The tall chief darted into the wood, and the good missionary pursued his way with pious resolution.

He preached the only true Divinity, and placed before the eyes of the wandering savages the beauty of holiness, the sufferings of the Redeemer, and the sublime glories of the Christian heaven. He allured them with the hope of everlasting bliss, and alarmed them with denunciations of an eternity of misery and despair. The awe-struck Indians, roused by these accumulated motives, many of them adopted the precepts of the missionary so far as they could comprehend them; and in the course of eighteen months, their devotion became rational, regular, and apparently permanent.

All at once, however, the little church in which the good man was wont to pen his fold, became deserted. No votary came as usual to listen with decent reverence to the pure doctrines which they were accustomed to hear; and only a few solitary idlers were seen of a Sunday morning, lounging about, and casting a wistful, yet fearful look at their little, peaceful, and now silent mansion.

The missionary sought them out, inquired into the cause of this mysterious desertion, and told them of the bitterness of hereafter to those who, having once known, abandoned the religion of the only true God. The poor Indians shook their heads, and informed him that the Great Spirit was angry at their apostasy, and had sent a prophet from the summit of the Alleghany mountain to warn them against the admission of new doctrines; that there was to be a meeting of the old men soon, and that the prophet would then deliver to the people the message with which he was intrusted. The zealous missionary determined to be present, and to confront the impostor, who was known by the appellation of *The Prophet of the Alleghany* He accordingly obtained permission from the chiefs to appear at the council, and to reply to the charges that might be brought forward. The 12th of June, 1802, was the time for the decision of the solemn question, " whether the belief of their forefathers or that of the white men was the true religion." The usual council-house not being large enough to contain so great an assemblage of people, they met in a valley about eight miles to the westward of Seneca Lake. This valley was then embowered under lofty trees; it is surrounded on almost every side with high rugged hills, and through it meanders a small river.

It was a scene to call forth every energy of the human heart. On a smooth level, near the bank of a slow stream, under the shade of a large elm, sat the chief men of the tribes. Around the circle which they formed, was gathered a crowd of wondering savages, with eager looks, seeming to demand the true God at the hands of their wise men.

In the middle of the circle sat the aged and travel-worn missionary. A few gray hairs wandered over his brow, his hands were crossed on his bosom, and as he cast his hope-beaming eye to Heaven, he seemed to be calling with pious fervour upon the God of truth, to vindicate his own eternal word by the mouth of his servant.

For more than half an hour there was silence in the valley, save the whispering of the trees in the south wind, and the indistinct murmuring of the river. Then all at once a sound of astonishment passed through the crowd, and the prophet of the Alleghany was seen descending one of the high hills. With furious and frenzied step he entered the circle, and waving his hand in token of silence, the missionary saw with surprise the same tall chief who, four years before, had crossed him in the Tuscarora forest. The same panther skin hung over his shoulder, the same tomahawk quivered in his hand, and the same fiery and malignant spirit burned in his red eye. He addressed the awe-struck Indians, and the valley rung with his iron voice.

"Red men of the woods, hear what the Great Spirit says to his children who have forsaken him.

"Through the wide regions that were once the inheritance of my people, and where for ages they roved as free as the wild winds, resounds the axe of the white man. The paths of your forefathers are polluted by their steps, and your hunting-fields are every day wrested from you by their arts. Once, on the shores of the mighty ocean, your fathers were wont to enjoy all the luxuriant delights of the deep. Now you are exiles in swamps or on barren hills; and these wretched possessions you enjoy by the precarious tenure of the white man's will. The shrill cry of revelry or war is no more heard on the majestic shores of the Hudson, or the sweet banks of the silver Mohawk. There, where the Indian lived and died as free as the air he breathed, and chased the panther and the deer from morn till evening—even there the Christian slave cultivates the soil in undisturbed possession; and as he whistles behind his plough, turns up the sacred remains of your buried ancestors. Have ye not heard at evening, and sometimes at dead of night, those mournful and melodious sounds that steal through the deep valleys, or along the mountain sides, like the song of echo? These are the wailings of those spirits, whose bones have been turned up by the sacrilegious labours of the white man, and left to the mercy of the rains and tempest. They call upon you to avenge them—they adjure you, by every motive that can rouse the hearts of the brave, to wake from your long sleep, and, by returning to the invaders of the grave, the long arrears of vengeance, restore again the tired and wandering spirits to their blissful paradise, far beyond the blue hills.

"These are the blessings you owe to the Christians. They have driven your fathers from their ancient inheritance—they have destroyed them with the sword and poisonous liquors—they have dug up their bones, and left them to bleach in the wind—and now they aim at completing your wrongs, insuring your destruction, by cheating you into the belief of that Divinity, whose very precepts they plead in justification of all the miseries they have heaped upon your race.

"Hear me, O, deluded people, for the last time! If you persist in deserting my altars, if still you are determined to listen, with fatal credulity, to the strange, pernicious doctrines of these Christian usurpers—if you are unalterably devoted to your new Gods, and new customs—if you *will* be the friends of the white man, and the followers of his God—my wrath shall follow you; I will dart my arrows of forked lightning amongst your towns, and send the warring tempest of winter to devour you. Ye shall become bloated with intemperance; your numbers shall dwindle away, until but a few wretched slaves survive; and these shall be driven deeper and deeper into the wild, there to associate with the dastard beasts of the forest, who once fled before the mighty hunters of your tribe. The spirits of your fathers shall curse you from the shores of that happy island in the Great Lake, where they enjoy an everlasting season of hunting, and chase the wild deer with dogs swifter than the wind. Lastly, I swear by the lightning, the thunder, and the tempest, that in the space of sixty moons, of all the Senecas, not one of yourselves or your posterity shall remain on the face of the earth."

The prophet ended his message, which was delivered with the wild eloquence of real or fancied inspiration; and all at once the crowd seemed to be agitated with a savage sentiment of indignation against the good missionary. One of the fiercest broke through the circle of old men to despatch him, but was restrained by their authority.

When this sudden feeling had somewhat subsided, the mild and benevolent minister of God obtained permission to speak on behalf of Him by whom he had been sent. Never have I seen a more touching, pathetic figure, than this good man. He seemed past sixty—his figure tall, yet bending—his face mild, pale, yet highly intellectual—and over his forehead, which yet displayed its blue veins, were scattered, at solitary distances, a few gray hairs. Though his voice was clear, and his action vigorous, yet there was that in his looks which seemed to say that his pilgrimage was soon to close.

With pious fervour he described to his audience the glory, power, and beneficence of the Creator of the universe. He told them of the pure delights of the Christian heaven, and of the never-ending tortures of those who rejected the precepts of the gospel. He painted, in glowing and fervid colours, the filial piety, the patience, the sufferings of the Redeemer, and how he died on the cross for the sins of the whole human race; and, finally, he touched with energetic brevity on the unbounded mercies of the Great Being who thus gave his only-begotten Son a sacrifice for the redemption of mankind.

When he had concluded this part of the subject, he proceeded to place before his now attentive auditors the advantages of civilization, of learning, science, and a regular system of laws and morality. He contrasted the wild Indian, roaming the desert in savage independence—now revelling in the blood of enemies, and in his turn the victim of their insatiable vengeance—with the peaceful citizen, enjoying all the comforts of cultivated life in this happy land; and only bounded in his indulgences by those salutary restraints which contribute as well to his happiness as to that of society at large. He described the husbandman enjoying, in the bosom of his family, a peaceful independence, undisturbed by apprehensions of midnight surprise, plunder, and assassination; and he finished by a solemn appeal to Heaven, that his sole motive for coming among them was the love of the Creator and of his creatures.

As the missionary closed his appeal, *Red Jacket*, a Seneca chief of great authority, and the most eloquent of all his nation, rose and enforced the exhortations of the venerable preacher. He repeated his leading arguments, and with eloquence truly astonishing in one like him, pleaded the cause of religion and humanity. The ancient council then deliberated for nearly two hours; after which, the oldest man rose and solemnly pronounced the result of their conference—" That the Christian God was more wise, just, beneficent, and powerful than the Great Spirit; and that the missionary who delivered his precepts, ought to be cherished as their best benefactor—their guide to future happiness."

When this decision was pronounced by the venerable old man, and acquiesced in by the people, the rage of the Prophet of the Alleghany became terrible. He started from the ground, seized his tomahawk, and denouncing the speedy vengeance of the Great Spirit on their whole recreant race, darted from the circle with wild impetuosity, and disappeared in the shadows of the forest.

AN IMPRESSIVE PREACHER.

A MINISTER, a few years since, made the following striking statement :—

When I was travelling in the state of Massachusetts, twenty-six years ago, after preaching, one evening, a very serious-looking young man arose, and wished to address the assembly. After obtaining leave, he spoke as follows: " My friends, about one year ago, I set out in company with a young man, an intimate acquaintance, to seek the salvation of my soul. For several weeks we went on together, we laboured together, and often renewed our engagements never to give over seeking till we obtained the religion of Jesus. But all at once the young man neglected to attend public worship, appeared to turn his back on all the means of grace, and grew so shy of me that I could scarcely get an opportunity of speaking with him. His strange conduct gave me much anxiety; but still I felt resolved to seek the salvation of my soul, or perish making the publican's plea.

"After a few days, a friend informed me that my companion had received an invitation to attend a ball, and was determined to go. I went immediately to him, and, with tears in my eyes, endeavoured to persuade him to change his purpose, and to go with me, on that evening, to a prayer meeting. I pleaded with him in vain. He told me, when we parted, that I must not give him up as lost, for after he had attended that ball, he intended to make a business of seeking religion. The appointed evening came; he went to the ball, and I went to the prayer-meeting. Soon after the meeting opened, it pleased God, in answer to prayer, to turn my spiritual captivity, and make my soul rejoice in his love. Soon after the ball opened, my young friend was standing at the head of the ball-room, with the hand of a young lady in his hand, preparing to lead down the dance;

and while the musician was tuning his violin, without one moment's warning, the young man fell backwards dead on the floor. I was immediately sent for to convey his remains to his father's house. You will be better able to judge what were my emotions, when I tell you that that young man was my own brother."

REV. DR. PAYSON.

Dr. Payson, of Portland, Maine, always seized upon every uncommon occurrence, in his congregation, to turn it to religious account. So settled a habit was this with him, that whenever, during the week, any extraordinary event happened, there was frequently a considerable degree of interest felt among his people, in respect to the manner in which it would be made to tell, in the production of moral and religious impression, in their pastor's sermon on the next Sabbath.

Dr. Payson's meeting-house was situated at the corner formed by one of the principal streets in the city and another narrow street, or perhaps lane, which opened into it. Across this narrow street, opposite the meeting-house, a convenient and pleasant conference-room, or vestry, as it was sometimes called, had been erected. His people had become warmly attached to this building; a fact which all who ever attended Dr. Payson's evening meetings, will readily understand. One night, the inhabitants of the town were aroused by the cry of fire; and, on going out, they found the whole heavens in a glare, from the flames of this conference-room. It was built of wood; and the next morning nothing was left but a heap of black smoking rubbish, and the whole side of the meeting-house, opposite, was browned by the scorching heat of the flames.

The next Sabbath there was the most intense interest felt,

by all in the meeting-house, when he arose in the pulpit, and stood prepared to name his text. The whole congregation seemed to say, by the eager and inquiring expression of their countenances, "What have you to say to us about this calamity?" And he pronounced his text as if replying: "For the time is come that judgment must begin at the house of God, and if it first begin at us, what shall the end be of them who obey not the gospel of God." 1 Pet. iv. 17. Then followed one of the most eloquent and powerful appeals ever heard from his lips. He explained that one mode by which God endeavours to call sinners to him, and to arouse his people to repentance, is his providence. He tries kindness; and when that fail, he tries frowns. He enumerated a number of events which had occurred, within a few past months, each more distinct and decided than the preceding:—"And now," said he, "God has come nearer still." He then spoke for several minutes with great power and effect, in regard to the loss they had sustained, pointing to the blackened ruins, which were in full view. "Even this sanctuary," said he, "God has but just spared, and that, not without leaving upon it the marks of his frown." After further remarks to his church members, he turned to the congregation generally, and warned them of the danger of resisting God's calls. "I am no prophet," said he, "and I pretend to no extraordinary knowledge of God's will; but here is the solemn declaration of his word. Take care, then, of your houses. Take care of your stores; for if this people, in spite of God's repeated warnings, will go on obstinately in sin, they must not be surprised if he should arise in his anger and send a sweeping conflagration to desolate the town."

The impression made by the view he took of this providence, as a solemn warning from God, was universal and most powerful. The sermon was extemporaneous; and Dr. Payson, it was understood, afterwards said that he did not consider that calamities were always to be viewed as judgments, though they ought to be regarded as warnings, intended to awaken us to penitence, and to renewed fidelity in the service of God.

It would, indeed, be difficult to nicely discriminate between the judgments of God and the ordinary dispensations of Providence; but some occurrences are so clear, that we must exclaim, "This is the finger of God."

Dr. Payson being taken suddenly ill, and, as every one thought, about to die, he remarks: "What gave me most concern was, that notice had been given of my being about to preach! Whilst the doctor was preparing my medicine, feeling my pains abated, I on a sudden cried out, 'Doctor, my pains are suspended; by the help of God, I will go and preach, and then come home and die.' In my own apprehension, and in appearance to others, I was a dying man; the people heard me as such. The invisible realities of another world lay open to my view. Expecting to stretch into eternity, and to be with my Master before the morning, I spoke with peculiar energy. Such effects followed the word, that I thought it was worth dying for a thousand times." His biographer says, "He had something so peculiar in his manner, expressive of sincerity in all he delivered, that it constrained the most abandoned to regard what he said as not only true, but of the last importance to souls."

REV. E. T. TAYLOR.

THE following is an extract from the Boston Transcript of a few years since:

We happened last Sunday afternoon to be at the Bethel in North Square. The house was running over with seamen, who filled the body of the house, the stairs to the pulpit, and even the pulpit itself. We give the following extract from the sermon of the afternoon, as a fair specimen of the style in which the Rev. Mr. Taylor makes a practical application of an important truth: "I say, shipmates, now look me full in the face. What should we say of the man aboard ship, who was always talking about his compass, and never using it? What should you think of the man, who, when the storm is gathering, night at hand, moon and stars shut, on a lee shore, breakers ahead, then first begins to remember his compass, and says, 'Oh, what a nice compass I have got on board,' if before that time he has never looked at it? Where is it that you keep your compass? Do you stow it away in the hold? Do you clap it into the forepeak?" By this time Jack's face, that unerring index of the soul, showed visibly that the *reductio ad absurdum* had begun to tell. Then came, by a natural logic, as correct as that of the school, the *improvement*. "Now then, brethren, listen to me. Believe not what the scoffer and the infidel say. The Bible, the Bible is the compass of life. Keep it always at hand. Steadily, steadily fix your eye on it. Study your bearing by it. Make yourself acquainted with all its points. It will serve you in calm and in storm, in the brightness of noon-day, and amid the blackness of night; it will carry you over every sea, in every clime, and navigate you, at last, into the harbour of eternal rest."

REV. SYLVESTER LARNED.

When the gloom of the pestilence was gathering over the city of New Orleans, and multitudes leaving with a view to escape it, the late Rev. Mr. Larned entered his church one evening to perform divine service. Few were present; the lamps untrimmed and unlighted; and every thing indicated the presence of sorrow and apprehension. He assisted the sexton in his duties; and finally, in the dim light of the faintly illuminated temple, the faces of a few, who had gathered around the altar, were revealed. It was late, and as he stepped within the pulpit, he exclaimed, "Watchman, what of the night?" and, inspired by the solemn aspect of Providence, and his dread responsibilities in such an hour, spoke, as with a commission from heaven in his hand, to that fixed, silent audience; and so impressed their hearts by truths, which were the treasure and life of his own, as, amid all the changes of time and place on earth, could never be forgotten.

REV. DR. FISK.

A STRIKING instance of the power of the oratory of the late Dr. W. Fisk, is given in the funeral sermon preached for him by the Rev. Dr. Bangs:—

While preaching on a certain occasion, in the large church in Forsyth street, New York, having finished the discussion of his subject, he addressed himself directly to the heart and conscience. He described the danger of the wicked man; his exposure—his constant liability to death. He followed him to the brink of death's dark precipice, and painted him plunging over the edge into perdition's gulf. The whole scene was vividly before the eye. A preacher below him, suddenly and unconsciously, threw out his arms to catch the sinner in his fall, and carry him in faith to the Lamb of God.

After Dr. Fisk had been once showing the power of his eloquence, in the chapel of the University over which he presided, a lady of cultivated mind, decided genius, and strong feeling,—a stranger in the place,—as she came away, said to another, with a half-stifled voice, "Have you any irreligious students in your college?" and on being answered in the affirmative, added, "astonishing!"

TWO CLERGYMEN.

The villages of Gardiner, Hallowell, and Augusta, on the Kennebec river, lie near to each other. Rev. Mr. S. lived in Gardiner. He was visited by Rev. Mr. N., who preached in Hallowell and Augusta, who was allowed to look over a sketch of a sermon which Mr. S. had been writing. This, Mr. N. copied, and the next Sabbath he preached it at Augusta. It so happened that Mr. S. preached in the same church in Augusta, the Sabbath after, and delivered the same sermon, not knowing that another had used it before him. And what was a little amusing was, when he came out of church, a good lady said to him—

"Mr. S., you preached us a good sermon, but you ought to have given Mr. N. credit for it, as it was the same sermon he preached here last Sabbath!"

REV. DR. BEDELL.

One Sabbath morning, while the late Rev. Dr. Bedell, of Philadelphia, was preaching, a young man passed by, with a number of companions, as gay and thoughtless as himself. One of them proposed going into the church, saying, "Let us go and hear what this man has to say, that everybody is running after." The young man made this awful answer: "No, I would not go into such a place if Christ himself was preaching." Some weeks after, he was again passing the church; and, being alone, and having nothing to do, he thought he would go in without being observed. On opening the door, he was struck with awe at the solemn silence of the place, though it was much crowded. Every eye was fixed on the preacher, who was just about to begin his discourse. His attention was instantly caught by the text: "I discerned among the youths a young man void of understanding." Prov. vii. 7. His conscience was smitten by the power of truth. He saw that *he* was the young man described. A view of his profligate life passed before his eyes, and, for the first time, he trembled under the feeling of sin. He remained in the church till the preacher and congregation had passed out; then slowly returned to his home. He had early imbibed infidel principles; but the Holy Spirit, who had aroused him in his folly, led him to a constant attendance on the ministry of Dr. B., who had been the instrument of awakening his mind. He cast away his besetting sin, and gave himself to a life of virtue and holiness. He afterwards declared openly his faith in the Lord Jesus Christ, and his desire to devote himself to his service.

In a sermon, delivered a few years since, Dr. Bedell said, "I have now been nearly twenty years in the ministry of the gospel, and I here publicly state to you, that I do not believe I could enumerate three persons, over fifty years of age, whom I have ever heard ask the solemn and eternally momentous question, 'What shall I do to be saved?'"

REV. DR. MILLER.

The late Rev. Dr. Miller, Professor of Theology, in a sermon delivered at Baltimore, in 1820, related a fact which ought not to be forgotten by those who think lightly of the errors of Unitarianism. The preacher stated that Dr. Priestley, two or three years before his death, said to him, "I do not wonder that you Calvinists entertain and express a strongly unfavourable opinion of us Unitarians. The truth is, there neither can, nor ought to be, any compromise between us. If *you* are right, *we* are not Christians at all; and if *we* are right, *you* are gross idolaters."

REV. T. HOOKER.

The Rev. Thomas Hooker, having paid a visit to Cambridge, Massachusetts, was invited to preach on the Sabbath afternoon, and Governor Winthrop went from Boston purposely to hear him. Having read his text, he proceeded with great fluency for about a quarter of an hour, when he suddenly found himself at a loss for something to say. After several ineffectual attempts to proceed, he candidly confessed his difficulty, and, requesting the congregation to sing a psalm, withdrew for half an hour. He then returned, and preached for about two hours, with propriety and vivacity. After the sermon, he said to some of his friends, "We daily confess that we can do nothing without Christ; and what if Christ should prove this to be the fact before the whole congregation!"

A FORCIBLE PREACHER.

The Western Review, a few years since, stated the following fact :—

A clergyman was preaching in a town which was much infested with the Universalist heresy; where a preacher, holding its doctrines, was present to "withstand the truth," became greatly enraged. The sermon was no sooner closed, than he began to challenge the preacher to a defence of his doctrines. As it was rather late, the clergyman who had been preaching declined a formal debate, but proposed that each should ask the other three questions, to which a direct answer should be returned. This was agreed to. The Universalist began—put his questions, and they were promptly answered. It then came to the clergyman's turn. His first question was, "Do you pray in your family?" Thunderstruck and dismayed, the preacher of smooth things knew not what to say. At length he asked, "Why, what has that to do with the truth of my doctrine?" "Much," was the reply; "by their fruits ye shall know them." At last, he frankly confessed that he did not. Then for the second question : " When you get somewhat displeased, do you not sometimes make use of profane language?" This was carrying the war into the inner temple of his infidel abominations. There was no door of escape. Answer he must. It was of no use to deny it. He confessed he was profane. "I will go no farther," said the pious clergyman; "I am satisfied"—and turning to the congregation, added, "I presume you are also. You dare not trust your immortal welfare to a prayerless and profane guide."

Here was a practical argument. Every one saw and felt its force. A dozen lectures on the subject would not have done half so much good.

REV. DR. STAUGHTON.

The Rev. Dr. Staughton, of Philadelphia, was remarkable for the energy of his delivery, and for the originality of many of his remarks. On one occasion, he was preaching from the words, "God be merciful to me a sinner." His soul kindled, as he proceeded, with intense ardour for the salvation of his hearers. He presented, in a strain of vivid and powerful eloquence, the joy of the angelic hosts on the repentance of one sinner. Perfect silence reigned through the vast audience. There was a moment's pause, and it was obvious, from his countenance and his attitude, that his mind was preparing for some powerful and overwhelming flood of feeling. He proceeded: "Shall I retire with the desponding reflection, that, in all this congregation, there is not one soul humbled before God? Shall angels prepare their wings for flight, and the voice of contrition be unheard? It cannot be. I will cherish the hope that there is, at least, one sinner here, whose heart is melted down before the Lord, and trembling at the prospect of future retribution: that there is, even now, one whose agony is on the point of extorting from his lips the cry of the publican." Suddenly throwing up his arm, with a voice full, loud, and rapid, he exclaimed, "Hark!" The effect it is impossible to describe. His arm remained for a time elevated, during which the most awful stillness reigned, interupted only by an apparently delicate and indescribable breathing, that seemed to pass over the congregation, midway in the edifice. Then, with a grace and energy peculiar to himself, he brought down his hand upon his breast, and repeated the prayer, "God be merciful to me a sinner." The feelings of the assembly were wrought to the highest point, and some time elapsed before they were enabled to breathe freely.

On one Sabbath evening, the worthy Doctor discoursed to his congregation from the words of John the Baptist, in the third of Matthew, "He shall gather the wheat into his garner, but shall burn up the chaff with unquenchable fire," and was, of course led to describe the torments of hell. The thunder of his eloquence rolled, and its lightnings flashed in every direction. Indulging his imagination, he exclaimed, "Yonder you see a miserable group, who, while on earth, were companions in swearing and Sabbath-breaking; in another direction you behold a wretched young man who was disobedient to his parents"—at this moment turning his eye to the left hand of his vast church, he discovered a pew full of ladies laughing at some trivial incident connected with themselves, and on them he fixed his full gaze, as he closed his powerful paragraph with the words, "and here is a party that went to church to laugh." He proceeded in his sermon without any further remark on the impropriety, and it scarcely need to be added that the reproof had the desired effect.

Another beautiful illustration of the character and power of this admirable preacher's eloquence, may here be given. The following address formed the close of a sermon before a charitable association:—

What more shall I add, my brethren, to excite your liberality? Could I take you severally into the mansion of misery in our city, and show you the pallet where the child of want and distress is lying, whose former condition of life makes the idea of an alms-house afflicting, and whose distresses are cheered only by the hopes that spring will bring better days, and that Christian bosoms are not dead to sympathy;—could I place before your eyes the shivering infant, the starving grandsire the poor widow, forsaken, neglected, forgotten, or even the repenting, tattered profligate, I know you would melt : in spite of all the apologies self-love might suggest, your charity would abound.

Two boats, some time ago, were sent from Dover to relieve a vessel in distress. The fury of the tempest overset one of them, which contained three sailors, and a companion sunk. The two remaining sailors were floating on the deep; to one of them a rope was thrown; but he refused it, crying out, "*Fling it to Tom:* he is just ready to go down; I can last some time longer." They did so; Tom was drawn into the boat. The rope was then flung to the generous tar, just in time to save him from drowning. Look on the boisterous sea of this world. You have your conflicts, we acknowledge, but there are some that cannot *last* like you. *Throw* out immediately to their assistance, or it may be too late. Accomplish now, what I persuade myself you thought of yesterday, during the cold and heavy snow-storm. Come, my brethren, discharge your duty, adorn the gospel, disappoint the devil, and revere a present God.

REV. DR. HUMPHREY.

In the biography of the late Rev. Dr. Nettleton, we are furnished with a very pleasing account of a sermon preached by Dr. Humphrey, when pastor of the church at Pittsfield. It appears that in 1820, a promising state of things existed there. Dr. Nettleton was present, and it was resolved to devote the day of the declaration of Independence to religious services. To this arrangement many ungodly persons in the neighbourhood objected, and while the people were assembling and crowding the church, the rioters exploded crackers, and in other ways sought to annoy them.

The service having commenced, and having proceeded with

great solemnity, Dr. H. read as his text, John viii. 36, "If the Son, therefore, shall make you free, ye shall be free indeed." He had not proceeded far, when the word " fire" was given, and their ears were suddenly stunned, and the congregation startled, by the report of cannon. It was the attack of the adversary, and it was well kept up. But, unfortunately for him and his agents, every shot preached louder than ten thousand thunders; for while the drums beat, and the fifes played, and the soldiers marched backward and forward, animated by the noise of the cannon, and anticipating a glorious triumph over the cause of God, they were labouring hard to defeat themselves. So skilfully did the preacher allude to, and apply his discourse to the conduct of the opposition out of doors; such advantage did he take of every blast of the cannon, and every play of the drum, by some well-pointed remark, that it all went, like a two-edged sword, to the hearts of listening sinners. Nothing could possibly have subserved more the object of his discourse. A few persons trembled for the result, but Dr. Nettleton and others were more than hopeful, and they were right. That evening service crowded the place more than ever before—a most powerful impulse was given to the revival, and from that time Emmanuel spread his trophies among great and small. They who thought to crush the work of God were bitterly disappointed, and retired with shame; and one hundred and forty converts declared themselves on the Lord's side.

A FAITHFUL MINISTER.

A MINISTER, in travelling to fulfil an appointment for preaching, stopped on the way to deliver a sermon to a church that was without a pastor. In his discourse he animadverted with some severity on the disgraceful practice of intemperance, especially among professors of religion. On visiting the same place some time afterwards, he was told that he had hurt the feelings of some of the brethren; and in a second discourse he apologized to this effect:—"I understand, my brethren, that when I was last here, I was so unfortunate as to hurt the feelings of some of you by remarks upon drunkenness. Since nothing was further from my intention, I feel it my duty to make an apology, which is this:—Being a stranger here, I most solemnly declare that I did not know that there was a drunkard belonging to the church." The hint had its effect. The grumblers were drunkards, and at the next church meeting were excluded.

REV. W. TENNENT.

This eminent minister, who, in the last century, was distinguished for great usefulness, was one day passing through a town in the state of New Jersey, in which he had never preached, and stopping at a friend's house to dine, was informed that it was a day of fasting and prayer in the congregation, on account of a very remarkable and severe drought; which threatened the most dangerous consequences to the fruits of the earth. His friend had just returned from church, and the intermission was but half an hour. Mr. Tennent was requested to preach, and consented, after great hesitation, as he wished to proceed on his journey.

At church the people were surprised to see a preacher, wholly unknown to them, and entirely unexpected, ascend the pulpit. His whole appearance, in his travelling-dress, covered with dust, and exhibiting a long and meagre visage, engaged their attention, and excited their curiosity. On his rising up, instead of beginning to pray, as was the usual practice, he looked around the congregation with a piercing eye and earnest attention; and after a minute's profound silence, he addressed them, with great solemnity, in the following words: "My beloved brethren, I am told that you have come here to-day to fast and pray; a very good work indeed, provided you have come with a sincere desire to glorify God; but if your design is merely to comply with a customary practice, or with the wish of your church officers, you are guilty of the greatest folly imaginable; as you had better have stayed at home, and earned your three shillings and sixpence." (At that time this was the stated price of a day's labour.) "But if your minds are indeed impressed with the solemnity of the occasion, and you are really desirous of humbling yourselves before Almighty God, your heavenly Father, come, join with me, and let us pray.

This had an effect so uncommon and extraordinary on the congregation, that the utmost seriousness was manifested. The prayer and the sermon added greatly to the impressions already made, and tended to rouse the attention, influence the mind, command the affections, and increase the emotion which had been so happily produced. Many had reason to bless God for the unexpected visit, and to reckon the day one of the happiest of their lives.

During the great revival of religion in America, which took place under Mr. Whitefield, and others distinguished for their piety and zeal at that period, Mr. Tennent was laboriously active, and much engaged to help forward the work; in the performance of which he met with strong and powerful temptations. The following is from his own lips:—

On the evening preceding public worship, he selected a subject for the discourse intended to be delivered, and made some progress in his preparations. In the morning he resumed the same subject, with an intention to extend his thoughts further on it; but was presently assaulted with a temptation that the Bible was not of Divine authority, but the invention of man. He instantly endeavoured to repel the temptation by prayer, but his endeavours proved unavailing. The temptation continued, and fastened upon him with greater strength as the time advanced for public service. He lost all the thoughts which he had prepared on the preceding evening. He tried other subjects, but could get nothing for the people. The whole book of God, under that distressing state of mind, was a sealed book to him; and, to add to his affliction, he was "shut up in prayer;" a cloud, dark as that of Egypt, oppressed his mind.

Thus agonized in spirit, he proceeded to the house of God, where he found a large congregation assembled, and waiting to hear the word; and then he was more deeply distressed than ever; and especially for the dishonour which he feared would fall upon religion, through him, that day. He resolved, however, to attempt the service. He introduced it by singing a psalm, during which time his agitation increased to the highest degree. When the moment for prayer commenced, he arose, as one in the most painful and perilous situation, and with arms extended to heaven, began with this exclamation, "Lord, have mercy upon me." On the utterance of this petition, he was heard; the thick cloud instantly broke away, and light shone upon his soul. The result was a deep solemnity throughout the congregation; and the house, at the end of the prayer, was a place of weeping. He delivered the subject of his evening meditations, which was brought to his full remembrance, with an overflowing abundance of other weighty and solemn matter. The Lord blessed this discourse, so that it proved the happy means of the conversion of about thirty persons. This day he ever afterwards spoke of as " his harvest day."

At another time, Mr. Tennent took great pains to prepare a sermon to convince a celebrated infidel of the truth of Christianity. But, in attempting to deliver this laboured discourse, he was so confused as to be compelled to stop, and to close the service by prayer. This unexpected failure, in one who had so often astonished the unbeliever with the force of his eloquence, led the infidel to reflect that Mr. Tennent had been, at other times, aided by a divine power. This reflection proved the means of his conversion. Thus God accomplished by silence what his servant wished to effect by persuasive preaching. Mr. Tennent used afterwards to say, that his dumb sermon was one of the most profitable he ever delivered.

Those who love to become acquainted with the manners of the old men of former generations, will read with interest the description given not long since by an old man then living in Monmouth county, and furnished to the Newark Sentinel.

Mr. Tennent's manners were altogether primitive. He had three pegs behind the pulpit; and when he entered it, he took off his hat, and hung it on one of them; his wig, and hung that on the second; and often drew off his coat, and hung that on the third. His sermons were pre-eminently full " of strong meat," and were delivered with great earnestness and simplicity.

REV. BRADFORD HOMER.

We place on record the following remarks from a sermon of the late Rev. Bradford Homer, as they entirely meet the sympathy of every minister of the gospel, and apply to every congregation with which we are acquainted.

"I beseech you that you be not over-scrupulous about the height of the thermometer, or the aspect of the clouds on a Sabbath morning—that you doom not the preacher to come in from a lowering and desolate sky to the more desolate scene of an empty church. I mean not to intrude upon the delicacies of life, and I know that there are many constitutions that will not bear an exposure to the inclemency of the storm. I leave every man's conscience to be his bodily physician. But I beg of you to be consistent patients; for that admirable doctor is never more stupid than under the sound of the church-going bell; and if the fireside of home looks inviting, and the storm beats cheerlessly against the window—above all, if the heart from within does not cry out for the courts of the Lord, it is easy, too easy, to get an invalid's exemption from one unscientific guide, or to conjure up some lion, in the shape of a formidable snowdrift, or a pelting rain, or a smoky house—no one of which would excuse us to a client or a customer, but any one of them we can put off on our minister or our God. Still, politeness forbids me to enter the private circle and say to this and that person, You ought to be at church: as a gentleman, I leave you to judge for yourselves; but, as a minister, you must excuse me if I beg you to remember the man whose profession obliges him to go to church in all weathers; whose taste will not permit him to reward the faithful few with an old sermon, or a desultory talk inspired by empty pews; whose sense of justice obliges him to bring out the hard earnings of a week's toil, when one and another and another for whom that sermon was written, are not in their seats. I say I wish they would think of him from the good easy-chair, and by the blazing hearth of home, and cast on him the wing of their sympathy, if they cannot give him the light of their faces."

REV. MR. HOWE.

It is related of Rev. Mr. Howe, late of Hopkinton, Massachusetts, that during the period his people were discussing the subject of a new meeting-house, one day, while he was preaching, observing his congregation in rather a lethargic state, he stopped in the middle of his sermon, and, casting his eyes around, remarked they were talking about erecting a new meeting-house; but he did not know that it was worth while, as the timbers looked in pretty good condition, and he was sure the *sleepers* were *sound*.

REV. DR. LATHROP.

The late Rev. Dr. Lathrop, of Springfield, in a sermon intended to show how God often answers prayer in very unexpected ways, related a very striking illustration of his doctrine in the case of a negro, who had, by a contemplation of nature, while in his own country, been led to conceive of the existence of a supreme, wise, and good Being, who made and governed the world. He was accustomed to pray to him, that he might know his character, and the manner in which he could be pleased. While in this state of mind, he was, with many others, stolen, and his faith began to waver. He was brought into a pious family in New England, where he was instructed in the knowledge of Christ, and became his devoted follower. He used to admire the kindness of God, who, in this most remarkable manner, answered his prayers.

REV. DR. BEECHER.

The following anecdote of Dr. Lyman Beecher, when a young man, is related on the authority of the Philadelphia North American. While, on the one hand, it may reprove the senior brother who may be disposed to judge "according to the outward appearance," so, on the other, it may encourage the young and timid to aim after excellence.

When, in the early years of his life, Dr. Beecher was living in Litchfield, something caused him to spend a Sunday in New Haven. He was dressed in homely simplicity, and was diffident in conversation; so that it was no easy matter to judge of his quality. Dr. Strong was then settled over the Congregational Church in that city, and professional usage required that he should entertain Beecher at his house, and invite him into his pulpit. He looked distrustingly upon the plain country pastor, and lamented the terrible necessity. But there was no alternative but in the violation of courtesy. Beecher sat meekly in the pulpit, through the morning and afternoon, but was not asked to take any part in the services. In the evening, Dr. Strong intimated to him very coldly, that if he chose to do so, he could preach for him, and was shocked by his instant acquiescence. "A man who will accept an invitation tendered in such a way as this," thought Strong, "cannot preach a sermon fit for *my* congregation to listen to!" He was mistaken, however. Beecher had hardly less pride than genius, and he felt keenly the chilling coldness of the great man, as Dr. Strong was considered. The evening came on; the church was brilliantly lighted, and thronged with the beauty, fashion, and intelligence of that home of gentleness and learning. Dr. Strong had offered the opening prayer, and was sitting in stern ill-humour, while the choir were singing the hymn to precede the sermon. Mr. Beecher became restless, and his face was flushed with a sudden excitement. He turned to the Doctor, and inquired, in a low and hurried voice, if the sermon could be a few moments deferred—he had left his manuscript in his chamber. "No!" said the Doctor, with exultant but ill-natured sharpness—and grasped the Bible to select a text for himself, glad that an accident was to relieve him and his congregation from the mortifying infliction he had dreaded. He was too fast; his young brother had been stung to the heart by his manner, and recognising the words of the last line of the hymn, sprang to the desk, and ere Dr. Strong had recovered from his astonishment, announced his text for an extemporaneous discourse. "It is the will of God!" thought the vexed and humbled pastor, and prepared himself to listen with Christian resignation. For a few moments the young preacher spoke with slight hesitation, as if, while giving his introduction, he was revolving in his mind an extended argument. Soon his voice rang clear and loud, his sentences came compact and earnest, and his manner caught the glowing fervour of his thought. All was hushed but his impassioned tones; the great assembly was still as death; and leaning forward, with blended wonder and admiration, the pastor felt stealing over him from the hushed air the rebuke of his Master, for his harsh judgment and cold treatment of his young brother. In after life, he used to relate the story, and confess that he had never heard such eloquence as that of the homespun young Mr. Beecher.

AN EFFECTIVE CLERGYMAN.

A CLERGYMAN in the United States, concluding a sermon to young persons, took occasion to impress upon parents the duty of parental faith, and illustrated its power in the following manner:—

About two-and-twenty years ago, a little circle were met around the couch of an apparently dying male infant; the man of God who led their devotions, seemed to forget the sickness of the child, in his prayer for his future usefulness. He prayed for the child, as a man, a Christian, and a minister of the word. The parents took hold of the horns of the altar, and prayed with him. The child recovered, grew towards manhood, and ran far in the ways of folly and sin. One after another of that little circle ascended to heaven; but two, at least, and one of them the mother, lived to hear him proclaim the everlasting gospel. "It is," said the preacher, "no fiction; that child, that prodigal youth, that preacher, is he who now addresses you."

REV. DR. MERCER.

Few men could produce more effect in making a solemn appeal to the consciences of his hearers than Dr. Mercer. He once preached from the language of the apostle, "If any man love not our Lord Jesus Christ, let him be anathema maranatha," when one of the most distinguished men in the country was present, and was deeply impressed with the discourse. On coming away, he said, "I could feel the very curse of God running through my bones."

This excellent man had once spent a fortnight in a preaching tour, chiefly labouring in a district favoured with an extensive revival of religion. On his return he met his church at their regular meeting. He was aware that the church was in a very languid state, and his sermon was on the deceitfulness of the heart, in crying peace, peace, when there is no peace. At the close of his discourse he became deeply affected, and addressed his congregation thus:—"Dear brethren and friends, I have been a great part of the last two weeks, addressing a people that I believe are truly awakened to a sense of their lost, helpless and ruined state, and are crying out in their agony, 'What shall we do to be saved?' Amongst them, my tongue seemed to be loosed, and I could point them with great freedom to the way of salvation through a crucified Saviour. On my way hither, I have felt the deepest concern in contrasting your lifeless situation with them, until I even bedewed the pommel of my saddle with tears;" and here, lifting up his hands, he exclaimed, "O, my congregation, I fear you are too good to be saved!" and again burst into an irrepressible flood of tears. Descending from the pulpit, and recovering himself a little, he poured forth a most solemn and impassioned exhortation, during which many came forward and asked that prayer might be made in their behalf; and thus commenced one of the most interesting revivals which has ever blessed that favoured church.

———

This admirable preacher was once discoursing from Hebrews vi. 1. His main object was to impress on Christians the importance of aiming at high attainments, and going on to perfection. "Unless we aim at a high mark," said he, "we shall never attain to eminence, as we shall not be likely to rise higher than our aim. Some Christians are afraid to aim high. Alas, they have not as much courage as a chicken. As I was sitting in my piazza one pleasant evening, last summer, my attention was drawn to the fowls as they were going to their rest. One little chicken particularly attracted my notice. He fixed his eye upon a limb pretty high up a tree, and made an ineffectual aim to gain it. He then took another position, and repeated his effort to reach it, but was again unsuccessful. Still, in no wise discouraged, he kept his eye upon the limb first chosen, and tried, and tried, and tried again; but to no purpose. Six times he tried and failed, but the *seventh* time he reached it. My brethren, aim high,—press on to perfection—try to have as much courage and perseverance as that little chicken."

The Rev. President Manly, in describing Dr. Mercer, says:—

To feel his greatness it was necessary to have heard him preach *under happy circumstances.* At other times he was characterized by a solid judiciousness in all he did or said, sanctified by a simple, fervent piety. But in his happy seasons he would rouse and enchain the attention of reflecting minds beyond any minister I have ever heard. At such times, his views were vast, profound, original, striking, absorbing, in the highest degree; while his language, though simple, was so terse and pithy, so pruned, consolidated, and suited to become the vehicle of the dense mass of his thoughts, that it required no ordinary effort of a well-trained mind to take in all that he said. At a meeting of the South Carolina Baptist State Convention, held at Edgefield C. H., he preached, preparatory to communion, on Sunday, and Dr. Furman was one of his hearers. His text was, " For if the blood of bulls and of goats, and the ashes of an heifer, sprinkling the unclean, sanctifieth to the purifying of the flesh; how much more shall the blood of Christ, who, through the eternal Spirit, offered himself without spot to God, purge your consciences from dead works to serve the living God." It was one of his happy times; and after a few of his honest shrugs, and workings of his neck and shoulders, as if to push his huge frame into his armour, he got fairly under way. Dr. Furman sat next to me in the congre gation, and though much absorbed myself, I could not forbear to notice that the Doctor (whose unconscious and inordinate use of snuff, when excited and engaged, was remarkable) passed his hand to his pocket with singular celerity and frequency. At length, as the subject advanced and the interest deepened, the snuff-box returned no more to the pocket, but remained open on his knee; while the thumb and finger plied incessantly and full-freighted between it and his nose. Father Mercer was now reasoning out, by overpowering argument, the position—that the divinity of Jesus Christ is necessary to his atonement; and when he announced the conclusion, proved and clear, the venerable Dr. F. brought his hand down violently on his knee, exclaiming audibly, "*What an important thought!*"

The biographer of Dr. M. has given us another illustration of his power in the pulpit, while preaching at the Savannah River Association, in 1824. His text was, "The weakness of God is stronger than men." It was a passage admirably suited to the genius of the preacher; his mind was at the time remarkably free and unclouded, and his heart in a very tender and devout frame. He first illustrated what he supposed might be understood by the weakness of God: this he considered as referring mainly to the precious Gospel of a crucified Redeemer. He next considered in what the strength of men might be said to consist; for, said he, "the text seems to imply that men have some kind of strength with which the weakness of God is brought into conflict." He here enlarged in a manner most powerful and convincing, upon the pride, ignorance, and deep-seated corruption of the human heart. He then proceeded to show how, by weak and insignificant means, the Lord thwarted the vain and proud designs of man, and how, especially by the application of Gospel truth by the Spirit of God, the stubborn and rebellious heart was effectually and savingly subdued. His track was as clear as the noon. His simple and energetic language, his apt illustrations, and his invincible reasoning, rendered every thing visible. The audience felt that they were in the hands of a master-spirit, or rather in the hands of a glorious and Almighty Sovereign, whose power was portrayed with such pungent and heart-searching strokes; and whilst their minds were led captive by the matchless argument, their feelings were evidently much affected by the holy fervour, the tender and heavenly pathos of the venerable preacher.

A somewhat amusing incident may here be given, illustrative of the power Dr. Mercer had over his hearers. An excellent Methodist brother, who attended his preaching and was very fond of him, used frequently to express his approbation by a *hearty amen*, when any sentiment or expression pleased him, and these were very frequent. Dr. M., in private, kindly observed that he did not disapprove such expressions, if they were appropriate and well-timed; "but you sometimes manifest your assent when the denunciations of God are made against the wicked," &c. This, for a season, cooled his ardour, and he was silent, though restless. At last, when some rich doctrine of truth dropped from the preacher's lips, he exclaimed at the top of his voice, "*Amen! rough at a venture!*" The effect on the audience and on the speaker may be well conceived.

A NEW ENGLAND CLERGYMAN.

An excellent, but somewhat eccentric clergyman, whose field of labour was in the interior of New England, one Sunday, at the close of the services, gave notice to his congregation, that in the course of the week he expected to go on a mission to the heathen. The members of his church were struck with alarm and sorrow, at the sudden and unexpected loss of their beloved pastor, and one of the deacons, in great agitation, exclaimed,—"What *shall* we do?" "Oh, brother C———," said the minister, with great apparent ease, "*I don't expect to go out of town!*"

REV. T. PORTER.

Ministerial usefulness, under God, depends much on Christian activity. A few years ago, three sailors just from sea were walking up Water Street, just above Arch, in the city of Philadelphia, where they discovered the Bethel Flag of the Mariner's church, and one said to the other, "What is that—a rendezvous?" At that moment a member of the Female Bethel Flag Society passed, and hearing their conversation, invited them to go in. In the usual carelessness of impenitent seamen, they made some trifling reply; but finally went into the place. The pastor of the church, the Rev. T. Porter, preached that evening from Gen. xxxvii. 16:—"I seek my brethren." In the course of his sermon he described himself as a shipping master, and, having his papers, was desirous of shipping a crew for the good ship Zion. "Come, seamen," said he, "let me register your names;" to which one of the men alluded to, said, with a smile, "You won't ship me." However, before the meeting closed he was weeping for his sins. The impressions made on his mind were such as he had never felt before, and he left the place blessing God that he had been thus led into his house.

REV. MR. RAWSON.

MORE than one hundred years ago, there graduated at Harvard University, a clergyman named Rawson, who subsequently settled in the ministry at Yarmouth, and Cape Cod. He used to preach very pointed sermons. Having heard that some of his parishioners were in the habit of making him the subject of their mirth at a grog-shop, he one Sabbath preached a discourse from the text—"And I was the song of the drunkard." His remarks were of a very *moving* character; so much so, that many of his hearers rose and left the house in the midst of the sermon.

A short time afterwards, the preacher delivered a discourse still more pointed than the first, from the text, "And they, being convicted out of their own consciences, went out one by one." On this occasion, no one ventured to retire from the assembly; but the guilty ones resigned themselves, with as good grace as possible, to the lash of their pastor.

REV. DR. WELCH.

WE copy the following interesting narrative from the Albany Express, October, 1847. It beautifully shows the advantages of self-possession in the preacher:—

On Sunday evening last, a very large audience attended the

North Pearl Street Baptist Church, attracted in part by the fame and eloquence of the pastor, Dr. Welch, and partly, we doubt not, in consequence of the announcement made from the pulpit in the morning, that the rite of marriage would be solemnized at the close of the service.

The theme of the Rev. Doctor, was the power and goodness of God, chosen as the basis for an appeal to the Christian charities and warm sympathies of his people, in behalf of the needy widow and children of the late sexton of the church, C. S. Morton, who, though a colored man, was distinguished for his estimable Christian character, habits of industry, strict integrity, and intelligence beyond the great majority of his class and complexion. The discourse was characterized by all the high and admired qualities which have placed Dr. Welch in the front rank of pulpit orators and extemporaneous preachers, and the appeal was not made in vain. In the midst of one of his happiest illustrations, and with voice and gesture admirably suited to the sentiment, he looked out upon the audience and exclaimed—" *The Spirit and the Bride say,* Come !"

The wedding party, having been notified of the time fixed upon for the performance of the nuptial ceremony, had stationed themselves at the foot of the stairway, in readiness for the signal, which was to be communicated by the sexton. The latter, when he heard the exclamation, "The Spirit and the Bride say, Come !" and saw the gesture, verily believed the time for the marriage had arrived, and immediately beckoned the party to approach. They promptly obeyed the summons, and bride and bridegroom, bride's-maid and groom's-man, marched solemnly up the broad aisle to the pulpit! The doctor was in the midst of his discourse. The whole audience saw the awkwardness of the occurrence, many understood the true cause of the mistake, and all looked to see the confusion of the clergyman, thus placed in a painful predicament. But in this they were disappointed. Closing the sentence thus curiously interrupted, Dr. Welch calmly stepped down from the pulpit, and almost before the echo of his voice in the utterance of his discourse had died away, he was heard addressing the candidates for marriage in a manner most appropriate to the occasion, and in the beautiful style and fervid eloquence for which he is so celebrated. The ceremony over, the wedding party retired, and the preacher, as little disconcerted as if nothing unusual had occurred, re-ascended into the desk, and taking up his subject at the precise point where he had left it, (though he uses no written notes,) proceeded to finish his sermon. So admirably was the awkward incident managed, that we doubt whether the party occasioning it ever suspected any thing wrong.

AN AGED CLERGYMAN.

An aged clergyman, when preaching in New England, some few years since, raising his voice with each succeeding word, and bringing down his clenched hand with amazing force upon the Bible at the last word of the sentence, exclaimed—" A deceitful wicked man is not fit to serve either God, man, or the devil!" Then, after a pause, he added, "And I'll tell you why. He is not fit to serve God, because he's unholy; he's not fit to serve man, because he's deceitful; and he's not fit to serve the devil, because he's not content with his wages. No," said the old man, with a shrewd look, "*he's not content with his wages.* Why," added he, " my children, I once saw a rogue of a soldier, for some crime that he'd done, tied up, and flogged with forty lashes; and while he was taking his wages, he made all sorts of noises, but he never once said that he liked it. No, no, my friends, the sinner is not satisfied with the wages which the devil gives, and he never will be—' for *the wages of sin is death.*' Sinners! sinners! strike for higher wages."

REV. JOHN SUNDAY.

The Rev. Dr. Alder, in his admirable volume on the Wesleyan Missions, relates the following pleasing anecdote:

"I understand," said John Sunday, the converted Indian chief, to a congregation which he was called to address at Plymouth, in the year 1837, "that many of you are disappointed, because I have not brought my Indian dress with me. Perhaps, if I had it on, you would be afraid of me. Do you wish to know how I dressed when I was a pagan Indian? I will tell you. My face was covered with red paint. I stuck feathers in my hair. I wore a blanket and leggins. I had silver ornaments on my breast, a rifle on my shoulder, a tomahawk and scalping-knife in my belt. That was my dress then. Now, do you wish to know why I wear it no longer? You will find the cause in second Corinthians, fifth chapter and seventeenth verse: 'Therefore, if any man be in Christ, he is a new creature; old things are passed away; behold, all things are become new.' When I became a Christian, feathers and paint 'passed away.' I gave my silver ornaments to the mission cause. Scalping-knife 'done away;' tomahawk 'done away.' That my tomahawk now," said he, holding up, at the same time, a copy of the Ten Commandments, in the Ojibwa language. "Blanket 'done away.' Behold," he exclaimed, in a manner in which simplicity and dignity of character were combined, "Behold, all things are become new!"

REV. GEORGE WHITEFIELD.

The following facts relating to the distinguished George Whitefield were published a few years since in Boston :—

There was nothing in the appearance of this extraordinary man which would lead you to suppose that a Felix would tremble before him. He was something above the middle stature, well proportioned, and remarkable for a native gracefulness of manner. His complexion was very fair, his features regular, and his dark blue eyes small and lively ;—in recovering from the measles he had contracted a squint with one of them ; but this peculiarity rather rendered the expression of his countenance more remarkable, than in any degree lessened the effect of its uncommon sweetness. His voice excelled both in melody and compass ; and its fine modulations were happily accompanied by that grace of action which he possessed in an eminent degree, and which has been said to be the chief requisite in an orator. To have seen him when he first commenced, one would have thought him any thing but enthusiastic and glowing; but as he proceeded, his heart warmed with his subject, and his manner became impetuous and animated, till, forgetful of every thing around him, he seemed to kneel at the throne of Jehovah, and to beseech in agony for his fellow-beings.

After he had finished his prayer, he knelt for a long time in profound silence, and so powerful was the effect on the most heartless of his audience, that a stillness like that of the tomb pervaded the whole house.

Before he commenced his sermon, long darkening columns clouded the bright sunny sky of the morning, and swept their dull shadows over the building, in fearful augury of the storm

His text was—" Strive to enter in at the strait gate ; for

many, I say unto you, shall strive to enter in, and shall not be able."

"See that emblem of human life," said he, pointing to a shadow that was flitting across the floor. "It passed for a moment, and concealed the brightness of heaven from our view; but it is gone. And where will you be, my hearers, when your lives are passed away like that dark cloud? Oh, my dear friends, I see thousands sitting attentive, with their eyes fixed on the poor, unworthy preacher. In a few days we shall all meet at the judgment-seat of Christ. We shall form a part of that vast assembly which will gather before his throne, and every eye will behold the Judge. With a voice whose call you must abide and answer, he will inquire whether on earth ye strove to enter in at the strait gate—whether you were supremely devoted to God—whether your hearts were absorbed in him. My blood runs cold when I think how many of you will then strive to enter in and shall not be able. Oh, what plea can you make before the Judge of the whole earth? Can you say it has been your whole endeavour to mortify the flesh with its affections and lusts? That your life has been one long effort to do the will of God? No! you must answer, 'I made myself easy in the world, by flattering myself that all would end well, but I have deceived my own soul: I am lost.'

"You, O false and hollow Christians! of what avail will it be that you have done many things; that you have read much in the sacred word; that you have made long prayers; that you have attended religious duties; and appeared holy in the eyes of man? What will all this be, if, instead of loving him supremely, you have been supposing you should exalt yourselves in heaven, by acts really polluted and unholy?"

On another occasion, Mr. Whitefield was preaching in Boston, on the wonders of creation, providence, and redemption, when a violent tempest of thunder and lightning came on. In the midst of the sermon it attained to so alarming a height that the congregation sat in almost breathless awe. The preacher closed his note-book, and, stepping into one of the wings of the desk, fell on his knees, and with much feeling and fine taste repeated—

> Hark! THE ETERNAL rends the sky!
>   A mighty voice before him goes—
> A voice of music to his friends,
>   But threatening thunder to his foes.
> "Come, children, to your Father's arms;
>   Hide in the chambers of my grace,
> Till the fierce storm be overblown,
>   And my revenging fury cease."

"Let us devoutly sing, to the praise and glory of God, this hymn, Old Hundred."

The whole congregation instantly rose, and poured forth the sacred song, in which they were nobly accompanied by the organ, in a style of pious grandeur and heartfelt devotion that was probably never surpassed. By the time the hymn was finished, the storm was hushed; and the sun, bursting forth, showed through the windows, to the enraptured assembly, a magnificent and brilliant arch of peace. The preacher resumed the desk and his discourse, with this apposite quotation:

"Look upon the rainbow; praise him that made it. Very beautiful it is in the brightness thereof! It compasseth the heaven about with a glorious circle; and the hands of the Most High have bended it."

The remainder of the services were well calculated to sustain that elevated feeling which had been produced; and the benediction with which the good man dismissed the flock was universally received with steaming eyes, and hearts overflowing with tenderness and gratitude.

When Mr. Whitefield once preached before the seamen of New York, he introduced the following bold apostrophe into his sermon :—"Well, my boys, we have a clear sky, and are making fine head-way over a smooth sea, before a light breeze, and we shall soon lose sight of land. But what means this sudden lowering of the heavens, and that dark cloud arising from beneath the western horizon? Hark! Don't you hear distant thunder? Don't you see those flashes of lightning? There is a storm gathering! Every man to his duty! How the waves rise, and dash against the ship! The air is dark! The tempest rages! Our masts are gone! The ship is on her beam-ends? What next?" The unsuspecting tars, reminded of former perils on the deep, as if struck by the power of magic, arose, and with united voices exclaimed, " Take to the long-boat." It need scarcely to be added that the preacher readily caught at the reply, and beautifully applied it to the importance of fleeing to the Rock of Ages as the great Refuge.

As Whitefield was once preaching to a vast multitude on the banks of one of the noble rivers of Virginia, he spoke of the strength of depravity, and the insufficiency of the means of grace to convert the sinner without the influence of the Holy Spirit. "Sinners," said he, "think not that I expect to convert a single soul of you by any thing that I can say, without the assistance of Him that is 'mighty to save.' Go and stand by that river, as it moves on its strong and deep current to the ocean, and bid it stop, and see if it will obey you. Just as soon should I expect to stop that river by a word, as, by my preaching, to stop that current of sin that is carrying you to perdition. Father in heaven, see! they are hurried on towards hell; save them, or they perish!" The impression which this address produced upon his hearers was so strong, that they were ready to respond with trembling, "Save, Lord, or we perish."

Whitefield was once preaching to a vast crowd of people in Southern Pennsylvania, at that time ignorant and uncivilized. He was incessantly disturbed by their noise, and twice rebuked them with great severity. At length, he was so overcome by their noisy and irreverent conduct, that he stopped short, dropped his head into his hands, burst into a flood of tears, and exclaimed, "Oh! Lord God! I am ashamed that these people are provoking thy wrath, and I dare not reprove them a third time!" Such was the effect of this, that his audience were perfectly quiet till the end of his discourse.

A young man, who was a member of the college at Princeton, hearing that Whitefield was to preach in the neighbourhood, attended, anxious to satisfy himself whether the preacher really deserved all the celebrity he had acquired. The day was rainy, and the audience was small; and the preacher, accustomed to address thousands at once, did not feel his powers called forth as at other times. After hearing about one-third of the sermon, the young man said to himself, "The man is not so great a wonder after all—quite common-place and superficial—nothing but show, and not a great deal of that;" and, looking round upon the audience, he saw that they also appeared uninterested, and that old father ———, who sat directly in front of the pulpit, and who always went to sleep after hearing the text and plan of the sermon, was enjoying a nap, as usual. About this time, Whitefield stopped. His face went rapidly through many changes, till it looked more like a rising thunder-cloud than any thing else; and beginning very deliberately, he said, "If I had come to speak to you in my own name, you might rest your elbows on your knees, and your heads upon your hands, and sleep; and, once in a while, look up and say, 'What does the babbler talk of?' But I have not come to you in my own name. No; I have come to yo' in the name of the Lord God of Hosts, and"—here he brought down his hand and foot at once, so as to make the whole house ring again—"and I must and will be heard." Every one in the house started, and old father —— among the rest. "Ay, ay," continued the preacher, looking at him, "I have waked you up, have I? I meant to do it. I have not come here to preach to stocks and stones; I have come to you in the name of the Lord God of Hosts, and I must and I will have an audience." The congregation was fully aroused, and the remaining part of the sermon produced considerable effect.

———

When visiting America, Mr. Whitefield often stood on the outside steps of the court-house, in Market street, at the corner of Second, in Philadelphia, and preached to thousands who crowded the streets below. On one of these occasions, a youth pressed as near to his favourite preacher as possible; and, to testify his respect, held a lantern for his accommodation. Soon after the sermon began, he became so absorbed in the subject, that the lantern fell from his hand, and was dashed to pieces; and that part of the audience in the immediate vicinity of the speaker's station, were not a little discomposed by the occurrence.

Some years after, Mr. Whitefield, in the course of his fifth visit to America, about the year 1754, on a journey from the southward, called at St. George's, in Delaware, where Mr. (afterwards Dr.) Rodgers was then settled in the ministry, and spent some time with him. In the course of this visit, Mr. Rodgers, riding one day with his visitor in a close carriage, asked him whether he recollected the occurrence of the little boy who was so much affected with his preaching as to let the lantern fall. Mr. Whitefield answered, "Oh, yes! I remember it well; and have often thought I would give almost any thing in my power to know who that little boy was, and what had become of him." Mr. Rodgers replied, with a smile, "I am that little boy." Mr. Whitefield, with tears of joy, started from his seat, clasped him in his arms, and with strong emotions remarked, that he was the fourteenth person then in the ministry, whom he had discovered in the course of that visit to America, of whose hopeful conversion he had been the instrument.

———

Mr. Whitefield, in his diary, under date of November 9, 1740, gives the following account of the conversion of Mr. Brockden, recorder of deeds; a man eminent in his profession, but for many years a notorious deist:—" In his younger days, he told me, he had some religious impressions, but going into business, the cares of the world so choked the good seed, that he not only forgot his God in some degree, but at length began to doubt of and dispute his very being. In this state he continued many years, and had been very zealous to propagate his deistical (I could almost say atheistical) principles, among moral men; but he told me he never endeavoured to make proselytes of vicious, debauched people. When I came to Philadelphia this time twelvemonth, he told me he had not so much as a curiosity to hear me. But a brother deist, his choicest friend, pressed him to come and hear me. To satisfy his curiosity, he at length complied with the request. I preached at the court-house stairs, upon the conference which the Lord had with Nicodemus. I had not spoken much, before the Lord touched his heart. 'For,' said he, 'I saw your doctrine tended to make people good.' His family knew not that he had been to hear me. After he came home, his wife, who had been at sermon, came in also, and wished heartily that he had heard me. He said nothing. After this, another of his family came in, repeating the same wish; and, if I mistake not, after that another; till, at last, being unable to refrain any longer, with tears in his eyes, 'Why,' said he, 'I have been hearing him;' and then expressed his approbation. Ever since, he has followed on to know the Lord; and I verily believe Jesus Christ has made himself manifest to his soul. Though upwards of three-score years old, he is now, I believe, born again of God. He is as a little child, and often, as he told me, receives such communications from God, when he retires into the woods, that he thinks he could die a martyr for the truth."

Mr. Whitefield once visited Chestertown, Kent county, on the Eastern Shore of Maryland. The minister of the parish did not like Whitefield's new mode of preaching; and so, to stop him, so far as his own congregation was concerned, preached a sermon directly opposed to him, Whitefield being present, from the text, "Paul, thou art beside thyself; much learning doth make thee mad." The sermon was, of course, very pointed.

At the close of the service, Whitefield took his stand at the door of the church, and announced to the retiring congregation that he would preach that afternoon, under a fine, large oak, that stood in sight. It is not necessary to say that all who had heard the minister, and many hundreds besides, went to hear him. His text was, "I am not mad, most noble Festus, but speak forth the words of truth and soberness." Tradition says that the minister was quite outdone, and literally " used up." It was further said that Whitefield's voice was distinctly heard on the Queen Anne's side of the river; which must be a distance, from where the oak stood, of a mile and a quarter.

On one occasion, during Whitefield's residence in this country, a black trumpeter, belonging to an English regiment, resolved to interrupt him, during a discourse which he was expected to deliver in the open air. At the hour appointed for the sermon, he repaired to the field where it was to be preached, carrying his trumpet with him, on purpose to blow it with all his might, about the middle of the sermon. He took his stand in front of the minister, and at no great distance. The concourse that attended became very great; and those who were towards the extremity of the crowd pressed forward, in order to hear more distinctly, which caused such a pressure at the place where the trumpeter stood, that he found it impossible to raise up the arm which held the trumpet, at the time he intended to blow it. He attempted to extricate himself from the crowd, but found this equally impossible, so that he was kept within hearing of the gospel as securely as if he had been chained to the spot. In a short time, his attention was arrested, and he became so powerfully affected by what the preacher presented to his mind, that he was seized with an agony of despair, and was carried to a house in the neighbourhood. When the service was over, he was visited by Mr. Whitefield, who tendered some seasonable counsels; and the poor trumpeter from that time became an altered man.

The following anecdote, related by Dr. Franklin, which is equally characteristic of the preacher and himself, further illustrates the power of Mr. Whitefield's eloquence: "I happened," says the doctor, "to attend one of his sermons, in the course of which I perceived he intended to finish with a collection, and I silently resolved he should get nothing from me. I had in my pocket a handful of copper money, three or four silver dollars, and five pistoles in gold. As he proceeded, I began to soften, and concluded to give the copper. Another stroke of his oratory made me ashamed of that, and determined me to give the silver; and he finished so admirably, that I emptied my pocket wholly into the collector's dish—gold and all. At this sermon, there was also one of our club; who, being of my sentiments respecting the building in Georgia, and suspecting a collection might be intended, had, by precaution, emptied his pockets before he came from home. Towards the conclusion of the discourse, however, he felt a strong inclination to give, and applied to a neighbour, who stood near him, to lend him some money for the purpose. The request was made to, perhaps, the only man in the company who had the coldness not to be affected by the preacher. His answer was, "At any other time, friend Hodgkinson, I would lend to thee freely; but not now, for thee seems to be out of thy right senses."

The late Rev. Dr. Lathrop, of West Springfield, Massachusetts, related to Mr. Whitefield a fact which the Doctor had personally witnessed; and he related it without much feeling. The same day, Mr. Whitefield introduced the story into his sermon, and Dr. Lathrop, as he heard it, found himself drowned in tears.

REV. MR. BENNETT.

A VENERABLE clergyman, usually called Father Bennett, in an excellent sermon, preached in the city of Boston, stated that a pious minister, while speaking of the love of Christ for a lost world, alluded to his peculiar attachment to the third chapter of John. Said the minister, "It makes no difference as to what part of the Bible I begin; whether I commence at Genesis, and proceed forward to Revelation, or whether I commence at Revelation, and proceed backward to Genesis—*I can't help stopping at the 3d chapter of John.*" "But now-a-days," added Father Bennett, "a great many persons, wherever they commence in the Bible, prefer to make their stopping-place among the prophecies of Daniel, instead of stopping where the good minister did, at the third chapter of John, where their hearts would be warmed by the declaration that 'God so loved the world, that he gave his only-begotten Son, that whosoever believeth in him should not perish, but have everlasting life.'"

REV. DR. HITCHCOCK.

THE following incident was related by President Hitchcock, in a sermon preached in the College Chapel, Amherst, Massachusetts, on "The Moral Dignity of the Christian Character," and is a beautiful illustration of the subject:—

Allow me here to refer to a case that lately fell under my observation, which illustrates more forcibly than I had ever conceived, the priceless value of the Christian hope to the most unfortunate and degraded. I had descended a thousand feet beneath the earth's surface, in the coal-pits of the Mid Lothian Mines, in Virginia, and was wandering through their dark subterranean passages, when the voice of music at a little distance broke upon my ear. It ceased upon our approach, and I caught only the concluding sentiment of the hymn,

"I shall be in heaven in the morning."

On advancing with our lamps, we found the passage closed by a door, in order to give a different direction to the currents of air, for the purpose of ventilation; yet this door must be opened occasionally to let the rail-cars pass, loaded with coal. And to accomplish this, we found sitting by that door an aged blind slave, whose eyes had been entirely destroyed by a blast of gunpowder, many years before, in that mine. There he sat, on a seat cut in the coal, from sunrise to sunset, day after day; his sole business being to open and shut the door, when he heard the rail-cars approaching. We requested him to sing again the hymn whose last line we had heard. It was, indeed, lame in expression, and in the poetic measure very defective; being, in fact, one of those productions which we found the pious slaves were in the habit of singing, in part at least, impromptu. But each stanza closes with the sentiment,

"I shall be in heaven in the morning."

It was sung with a clear and pleasant voice, and I could see the shrivelled, sightless eyeballs of the old man rolling in their sockets, as if his soul felt the inspiring sentiments; and really the exhibition was one of the most affecting that I have ever witnessed. There he stood—an old man, whose earthly hopes, even at the best, must be very faint; and he was a slave—and he was blind—what could he hope for on earth? He was buried, too, a thousand feet beneath the solid rocks. In the expressive language of Jonah, "He had gone down to the bottom of the mountains; the earth, with her bars, was about him for ever." There, from month to month, he sat in total darkness. Oh, how utterly cheerless his condition! And yet that one blessed hope of a resurrection morning, was enough to infuse peace and joy into his soul. I had often listened to touching music; I had heard gigantic intellects pour forth enchanting eloquence; but never did music or eloquence exert such an overpowering influence upon my feelings, as did this scene. Never before did I feel the mighty power of Christian hope. Never before did I witness so grand an exhibition of sublimity. Oh, how comparatively insignificant did earth's mightiest warriors and statesmen, her princes and emperors, and even her philosophers, without piety, appear! How powerless would all their pomp and pageantry and wisdom be to sustain them, if called to change places with this poor slave! He had a principle within him superior to them all; and when the morning which he longs for shall come, how infinitely better than theirs will his lot appear to an admiring universe! And that morning shall ere long break in upon thy darkness, benighted old man! The light of the natural sun, and the face of this fair world will never, indeed, revisit you; and the remnant of your days must be spent in your monotonous task, by the side of the wicket-gate, deep in the caverns of the earth; but that bright and blessed hope of a resurrection morning shall not deceive you. The Saviour, in whom you trust, shall manifest himself to you, even in your deep darkness; and at the appointed hour, the chains of slavery shall drop off, and the double night which envelops you shall vanish into the light and the liberty and glory of heaven. And just in proportion to the depths of your darkness and degradation now, shall be the brightness and the joy of that everlasting day.

I would add, that on inquiry of the pious slaves engaged in these mines, I found that the blind old man had a fair reputation for piety, and that it was not till the loss of his eyes that he was led to accept of a Saviour. It may be that the destruction of his natural vision was the appointed means of opening the eye of faith within his soul.

A MINISTER IN NEW ENGLAND.

Some years since, a distinguished minister in New England thought within himself, what would be the effect at the present day of the preaching of the great divines of the seventeenth century? The more he pondered the thought, the more it interested hi mind, until at last he resolved to test the problem, by copying, and preaching to his own people, a sermon from one of their number. Mentioning to a few individuals his plan and the reasons of it, that he might not be charged with plagiarism, he made the experiment. The Sabbath came; the sermon was preached, and it told with mighty power. His large and intelligent congregation were riveted in breathless attention, and were solemn as the grave. They went from the house, a few speaking, in under-tones, of the deep impressiveness and power of the sermon, but most of them giving still higher tribute to its excellence by the thoughtful stillness in which they walked, searching their own hearts, and thinking of eternal things.

The sermon was from Richard Baxter, and its influence in that congregation, and through it, will never die; its power may go down from generation to generation, to be known in its fulness only at the judgment. By it, " he, being dead," is yet speaking, and the power of his voice may be felt for ever

---

REV. MR. S.

A devoted servant of God, on one occasion, some years ago, preached upon the Diotrephesian spirit. In his usual faithful manner, he pointed out its sad effects upon a church, until, in its application, he came so close, that some persons were surprised, knowing how delightful the harmony had always been in that church. One of them soon began to persuade himself, however, that there was a Diotrephes there, but could not satisfy himself who it was. He ventured to seek information, and turning to a good brother, an elder in the church, he said, "Mr. L——, who DOES Mr. S. mean?" "*You* and *me*," was his quick reply. That hearer has never asked since, *who his minister meant*, when he was delivering the message of his Master.

REV. DR. STILLMAN.

In the course of two weeks, the late Dr. Stillman was called to bear the loss of two children, who had attained adult age. The stroke was heavy, and the wound grievous, like the piercing of a sword to the heart; the support of religion, however, not only sustained him, but also caused him to triumph over the trial. For his first sermon after this bereavement, he took for his text, Romans viii. 18: "For I reckon that the sufferings of this present time are not worthy to be compared with the glory that shall be revealed in us." The congregation had expected to hear an account of the mournful state of his mind, but were delighted with the cheerful picture he presented of his own feelings in the prospect of that eternal glory, which faith presented to his animated vision and certain hope. On one occasion, in his study, a few who were candidates for admission into his church, had expressed their faith and hope in Christ with freedom and cheerfulness. Their views evidently affecting the pastor's heart, he looked round most affectionately upon the little group, and with a smile of delight thus made known his feelings: "What a wonderfully strange thing religion is! How happy it makes us!" His cheerful countenance indicated his entire willingness to leave all earthly society for the presence of Christ in glory. A person said, "Sir, I was recently walking in the street in happy meditation, and my mind was so delightfully elevated that heaven appeared to be but a little way off." "Ah!" replied he, "heaven is not far off when we feel right."

The Rev. Dr. Pierce, in his discourse delivered on the fiftieth anniversary of his settlement at Brookline, Mass., in alluding to Dr. Stillman, says:

"The bare allusion to this godly man recals delightful associations, of which I must ask leave to take a passing notice. When a boy, no greater boon could I ask of my father, than permission to walk five miles, on the Lord's-day morning, to hear this good man preach; and to remain, through the day, to be sure of a seat in his crowded house, for the afternoon. It has been my privilege, in my time, to hear eloquent preachers of great notoriety; but, for pulpit eloquence, I have been in the invariable habit of assigning him the very first rank. Indeed, every sermon he delivered was with an earnestness, as if he had received one more important message from his Master, and the present might be his only opportunity for delivering it."

AN EMINENT CLERGYMAN.

It is related of a clergyman, distinguished alike for his eloquence and exemplary piety, that having an appointment to preach in a certain village, he stopped on Saturday evening, at the house of one of his early acquaintances, a resident of the village. To his surprise, he found his old friend a distiller and vender of ardent spirits, and exceedingly bitter against the temperance cause. He could not refrain, all the evening, from giving vent to his feelings against all the temperance men and every temperance movement. The next day the preacher took his text from Jonah: "Dost thou well to be angry?" He showed what good was doing in the days in which we live, and especially in the temperance cause; how that cause was drying up the fountains of pauperism, and crime, and brutality; saving thousands on thousands from the drunkard's path, and restoring many a lost man to society and his family; transforming the most degraded and abject beings in the community into useful, respectable, and wealthy citizens. And as he enumerated one blessing after another, he would look down upon his friend and ask, "Dost thou well to be angry?" It was more than the poor man could bear: shame and confusion were his. He hid his face from all the congregation, and as soon as possible made the best of his way home from church; and from that day, no man became a stronger advocate of temperance reform, or made greater pecuniary sacrifices in its behalf.

REV. MR. GILLESPIE.

This energetic minister, in his "Lectures to Young Men on the Formation of Character," says, very forcibly, "*I can't do it*" never did any thing— *I'll try*" has worked wonders— and "*I will do it*" has performed prodigies

REV. MR. MOODY.

FATHER MOODY was born at Newbury, in 1675, graduated at Harvard College in 1697, was settled at York, Me., in 1700, and died, at 72 years of age, in 1747. He refused to receive from his people a stipulated salary, and lived with them half a century on their voluntary donations. The following anecdote is related of him:

Colonel Ingraham, a wealthy parishioner, had retained his large stock of corn in a time of great scarcity, in hopes of raising the price. Father Moody heard of it, and resolved upon a public attack upon the transgressor. So he arose in the pulpit one Sabbath, and named as his text, Prov. xi. 26,—' He that withholdeth corn, the people shall curse him ; but blessings shall be upon the head of him that selleth it.' Colonel Ingraham could not but know to whom the reference was made, but he held up his head, and faced his pastor with a look of stolid unconsciousness. Father Moody went on with some very applicable remarks, but Colonel Ingraham still pretended not to understand the allusion. Father Moody grew very warm, and became still more direct in his remarks upon matters and things ; but Colonel Ingraham still held up his head as high, perhaps a little higher, than ever, and would not put on the coat prepared for him. Father Moody at length lost all patience. "Colonel Ingraham!" said he, "you *know* that I mean *you;* why don't you hang down your head ?"

Mr. Moody was once on a journey, in the western part of Massachusetts, and called on a brother in the ministry, on Saturday, thinking to spend the Sabbath with him, if agreeable. The good man appeared very glad to see him, and said, "I should be very glad to have you stop and preach for me to-morrow ; but I feel almost ashamed to ask you." "Why, what is the matter?" asked Mr. Moody. "Why, our people have got into such a habit of going out before worship closes, that it seems to be an imposition upon a stranger." "If that is all, I must and will stop and preach for you," was Mr. Moody's reply. When the Sabbath-day came, and Mr. Moody had opened the service and named his text, he looked round on the assembly, and said, " My hearers, I am going to speak to two sorts of folks to-day, saints and sinners. Sinners, I am going to give you your portion first, and I would have you give good attention." When he had preached to them as long as he thought well, he paused and said, "There, sinners, I have done with you now; you may take your hats and go out of the meeting-house as soon as you please!" But all tarried and heard him through.

A young clergyman was once visiting him, and on the morning of the Sabbath, he asked him if he would not preach. "Oh, no, Father Moody," was the young gentleman's reply, " I'm travelling for my health, and wish to be entirely relieved from clerical duties. Besides, you, sir, are a distinguished father in Israel, and one whom I have long wished to have an opportunity of hearing, and I hope to-day for that gratification."

" Well," said the old man, as they wended their way to the meeting-house, " you will sit with me in the pulpit?"

It was immaterial, the young minister replied; he could sit in the pulpit or in the pew, as Father Moody preferred. So, when they entered the meeting-house, Father Moody stalked on, turned his companion up the pulpit stairs, and went himself into the parsonage pew.

The young man looked rather blank when he found himself alone, and waited a long while for his host to "come to the rescue." But there Father Moody sat before him, as straight and stiff as a statue, and, finding there was to be no reprieve for him, he opened the Bible, and went through with the exercise. Perhaps the excitement caused by this strange treatment might have enlivened his brain; at all events, he preached remarkably well. After the conclusion of the services, Father Moody arose in his pew and said to the congregation,—" My friends, we have had an excellent discourse this morning, from our young brother; but you are all indebted to me for it."

REV. MR. WILLARD.

Mr. Treat, a minister of Eastham, married a daughter of Mr. Willard, one of the pastors of the Old South Church, Boston, in the seventeenth century. The matter of his sermons, it is stated, was excellent, but it was greatly injured by the badness of his manner. After his marriage with the daughter of Mr. Willard, he was sometimes invited by the latter to preach in his pulpit. Mr. Willard possessed an agreeable delivery and harmonious voice, and as a natural consequence, he was generally admired. Mr. Treat having preached one of his best discourses to the congregation of his father-in-law, in his usual unhappy manner, excited much dissatisfaction. Several persons waited on Mr. Willard, and begged that Mr. Treat might not be invited into the pulpit again. To this request Mr. Willard made no reply; but he desired his son-in-law to lend him the discourse, which being left with him, he delivered it, without alteration, to his people, a few weeks after. The hearers were delighted, and requested a copy for the press. " See the difference," said they, " between yourself and your son-in-law. You have preached a sermon on the same text as Mr. Treat's; but while his was intolerable, yours was excellent."

REV. MR. TRUAIR.

WHEN we do a little good, who can tell us where the happy effects of it will end? In the year 1822, soon after the efforts for the benefit of seamen were commenced in New York, the Rev. Mr. Truair was on a tour, preaching and making collections for that cause. In the course of his journey he preached one evening at a school-house in a little town in Vermont, containing only a few scattered inhabitants. The next morning he met a poor woman in the neighbourhood who had heard his sermon, and felt desirous of doing something for the sailor's cause. Having no money, she brought a bag of mustard seed, which she begged him to accept, hoping it might turn to some good account. Mr. T. conveyed the mustard seed to New York, and on his stating the facts, some of the members of the board of directors purchased it for three dollars, proposing to present it to some missionaries then about to sail to Palestine, that they might sow it there. The next day, the circumstances were mentioned to a few friends, and several dollars more were added to the purchase. The following Sabbath evening it was mentioned at the Mariners' church, and twelve dollars more were added. And on the following Tuesday evening, the incident was told at a prayer-meeting, and the sum of nine dollars more was taken. The amount thus received for the poor woman's "two mites" was thirty dollars. Surely "she of her penury cast in more than they all!"

REV. DR. WADDELL.

THE following narrative, written by the late distinguished Attorney General, William Wirt, is too good either to be omitted or abridged:—

It was one Sunday, as I travelled through the county of Orange, that my eye was caught by a cluster of horses tied near a ruinous old wooden house in the forest, not far from the road-side. Having frequently seen such objects before, in travelling through these States, I had no difficulty in understanding that this was a place of religious worship.

Devotion alone should have stopped me to join in the duties of the congregation; but I must confess, that curiosity to hear the preacher of such a wilderness was not the least of my motives. On entering, I was struck with his preternatural appearance. He was a tall and very spare old man; his head, which was covered with a white linen cap, his shrivelled hands, and his voice, were all shaking under the influence of a palsy, and a few moments proved to me that he was perfectly blind. The first emotions that touched my heart were those of mingled piety and veneration. But how soon were all my feelings changed! The lips of Plato were never more worthy of a prognostic swarm of bees, than were the lips of this holy man. It was a day of the administration of the sacrament: and his subject was, of course, the passion of our Saviour. I had heard the subject handled a thousand times: I had thought it exhausted long ago. Little did I suppose that in the wild woods of America, I was to meet with a man whose eloquence would give to this topic a new and more sublime pathos than I had ever before witnessed.

As he descended from the pulpit to distribute the mystic symbols, there was a peculiar, a more than human solemnity in his air and manner, which made my blood run cold, and my whole frame shiver.

He then drew a picture of the sufferings of our Saviour; his trial before Pilate; his ascent up Calvary; his crucifixion and death. I knew the whole history; but never until then had I heard the circumstances so selected, so arranged, so coloured! It was all new: and I seemed to have heard it for the first time in my life. His enunciation was so deliberate, that his voice trembled on every syllable, and every heart in the assembly trembled in unison. His peculiar phrases had that force of description, that the original scene appeared to be at that time acting before our eyes. We saw the very faces of the Jews; the staring, frightful distortions of malice and rage. We saw the buffet: my soul kindled with a flame of indignation, and my hands were involuntarily and convulsively clenched.

But when he came to touch on the patience, the forgiving meekness of our Saviour; when he drew, to the life, his blessed eyes streaming in tears to heaven; his voice breathing to God a soft and gentle prayer of pardon on his enemies, "Father, forgive them, for they know not what they do!" the voice of the preacher, which had all along faltered, grew fainter and fainter, until his utterance being entirely obstructed by the force of his feelings, he raised his handkerchief to his eyes, and burst into a loud and irrepressible flood of grief. The effect was inconceivable. The whole house resounded with the mingled groans and shrieks of the congregation.

It was some time before the tumult had subsided so far as to permit him to proceed. Indeed, judging by the usual but fallacious standard of my own weakness, I began to be very uneasy for the situation of the preacher; for I could not conceive how he would be able to let his audience down from the height to which he had wound them, without impairing the solemnity and dignity of his subject, or perhaps shocking them by the abruptness of his fall. But—no; the descent was as beautiful and sublime as the elevation had been rapid and enthusiastic.

The first sentence with which he broke the awful silence was a quotation from Rousseau:—"Socrates died like a philosopher, but Jesus Christ like a God!"

I despair of giving you any idea of the effect produced by

this short sentence, unless you could perfectly conceive the whole manner of the man, as well as the peculiar crisis in the discourse. Never before did I completely understand what Demosthenes meant by laying such stress on delivery. You are to bring before you the venerable figure of the preacher; his blindness constantly recalling to your recollection old Homer, Ossian, and Milton, and associating with his performance the melancholy grandeur of their geniuses; you are to imagine that you hear his slow, solemn, well-accented enunciation, and his voice of affecting, trembling melody; you are to remember the pitch of passion and enthusiasm to which the congregation were raised; and then the few moments of portentous, death-like silence which reigned throughout the house; the preacher, removing his white handkerchief from his aged face, (even yet wet from the recent torrent of his tears,) and slowly stretching forth the palsied hand which holds it, begins the sentence, "Socrates died like a philosopher,"—then pausing, raising his other hand, pressing them both, clasped together, with warmth and energy to his breast, lifting his "sightless holes" to heaven, and pouring his whole soul into his tremulous voice—"but Jesus Christ—like a God!" If he had been indeed and in truth an angel of light, the effect could could scarcely have been more divine. Whatever I had been able to conceive of the sublimity of Massillon, or the force of Bourdalone, had fallen far short of the power which I felt from the delivery of this simple sentence

If this description gives you the impression that this incomparable minister had any thing of shallow, theatrical trick in his manner, it does him great injustice. I have never seen in any other orator, such a union of simplicity and majesty. He has not a gesture, an attitude, or an accent, to which he does not seem forced by the sentiment he is expressing. His mind is too serious, too earnest, too solicitous, and at the same time too dignified, to stoop to artifice. Although as far removed from ostentation as a man can be, yet it is clear, from the train, the style, and substance of his thoughts, that he is not only a very polite scholar, but a man of extensive and profound erudition. I was forcibly struck with a short, yet beautiful character which he drew of Sir Robert Boyle; he spoke of him as if " his noble mind had, even before death, divested herself of all influence from his frail tabernacle of flesh ;" and called him, in his peculiarly emphatic and impressive manner, "a pure intelligence; the link between men and angels."

PETER, THE INDIAN PREACHER.

The following anecdote equally illustrates the genius and talent of the speaker to whom it relates, and the usefulness of Mr. Kirkland, the honoured missionary under whose labours he had received his Christian instruction.

While Mr. Kirkland was a missionary to the Oneidas, being unwell, he was unable one Sabbath afternoon to preach, and told Good Peter, one of the head-men, that he must address the congregation. Peter modestly and reluctantly consented. After a few words of introduction, he began a discourse on the character of the Saviour. "What, my brethren," said he, "are the views which you form of the character of Jesus? You will answer, perhaps, that he was a man of singular benevolence. You will tell me, that he proved this to be his character by the nature of the miracles which he wrought. All these, you will say, were kind in the extreme. He created bread to feed thousands who were ready to perish. He raised to life the son of a poor woman who was a widow, and to whom his labours were necessary for her support in old age. Are these, then, your only views of the Saviour? I tell you they are lame. When Jesus came into our world, he threw his blanket around him, but the God was within!"

This anecdote was related to the late Dr. Dwight, by Mr. Kirkland himself.

REV. Z. ADAMS.

The Rev. Z. Adams was well acquainted with a neighbouring minister, a very mild, inoffensive man, and the exchange of labours for a Sabbath was proposed. Knowing Mr. Adams's peculiar bluntness of character, the minister said, "You will find some panes of glass broken in the pulpit window, and possibly you may suffer from the cold. The cushion, too, is in a bad condition; but I beg of you not to say any thing to my people on the subject; they are poor." "O no! O no!" said Mr. Adams. But before he left home he filled a bag with rags, and took it with him. When he had been in the pulpit a short time, feeling somewhat incommoded by the too free circulation of air, he deliberately took from the bag a handful or two of rags, and stuffed them into the window. Towards the close of his discourse, which was upon the duties of a people towards their clergyman, he became very animated, and purposely brought down both fists with a tremendous force upon the pulpit cushion. The feathers flew in all directions, and the cushion was pretty much used up. He instantly checked the current of his thoughts, and simply exclaiming, "Why, how these feathers fly!" proceeded. He had fulfilled his promise of not addressing the society on the subject, but had taught them a lesson not to be misunderstood. On the next Sabbath the window and the cushion were found in excellent repair.

A CLERGYMAN IN MASSACHUSETTS.

About one hundred years ago, a clergyman in Massachusetts had a respectable neighbour belonging to his parish, who was notoriously addicted to lying: not from any malicious or pecuniary motives, but from a perverse habit. The minister was every day grieved by the evil example of his neighbour This person was Captain Clark, a friend of the clergyman in all temporal matters, and a man useful in the parish. But his example was a source of much inquietude to the divine. He was determined to preach a sermon for the occasion. Accordingly he took for his text, "Lie not one to another." He expatiated on the folly, the wickedness, and evil example of lying in such a pointed manner, that nearly every person present thought that the clergyman was aiming at the Captain. The service being ended, some one said to the captain, "What do you think of the sermon?" "Excellent, excellent," he replied; "but I could not for my life keep my eyes off old mother Symington, thinking how she must feel, for he certainly meant her." This story was told by a daughter of the clergyman, who heard the sermon; to which she added, "When you hear any folly or vice exhibited from the pulpit, before you look out for a mother Symington, look within yourself, and see if Captain Clark is not there." Her advice had some effect, and may have again.

A GOOD PREACHER.

It has been well remarked that no individual is benefited by preaching, till he supposes that it means *him*. It sometimes appears so personal to wicked men, that they feel as though they were just about to be called out by name before the congregation. A minister was once preaching, and when describing certain characters, said, "If I were omniscient, I could call out by name the very persons that answer to this picture." A man called out, "Name me!" and he looked as though he were going to sink into the earth. He afterwards said that he had no idea of speaking out, but the minister described him so perfectly that he really thought he was going to call him by name. The minister did not know that there was such a man in the world.

REV. MR. S.

The Cincinnati Advertiser, some time since, gave an account of an eccentric clergyman, who, not being a very animated and interesting preacher, was often deserted by his flock, at least by parts of them, on the Sabbath. The old gentleman finally adopted some rather novel methods of keeping the delinquents up to the point of duty.

When any family was absent two or three Sabbaths in succession, Mr. S. would publicly state to the congregation that as Mr. ———'s family had been for some time absent from public worship, he presumed there was sickness or trouble in their household, and would appoint a prayer-meeting at their house on the next Tuesday afternoon.

The old gentleman on one occasion also caught the wanderers by the following piece of harmless guile:—On one Sabbath afternoon, he told his people that he should take a journey the next day, and be absent for a short time; but he would take care that some person should come from Boston, and supply his desk the next Sabbath. On the next Sabbath morning the meeting-house was filled. The whole town turned out to hear the Boston minister. They waited a while in eager expectation of his entrance, when in marched the Rev. Mr. S., and walked up the broad aisle, as he had been accustomed to do for many years gone by. On ascending his pulpit, he smiled graciously upon his large audience, and said: "I am glad, my dear hearers, that I have got you out—you're all here as you ought to be—and I hope your minds are prepared to receive instruction—I came from Boston yesterday myself."

REV. PRESIDENT EDWARDS.

This distinguished man was an eminent proof that powerful preaching consists in somewhat more than manner, and that true eloquence is truth spoken with feeling. It is believed that no preacher, who has appeared in this country, ever engrossed the attention of his audience so often, so long, and to so great a degree, except Mr. Whitefield. Yet his voice was low, his style slovenly and uncouth, and he was without gesture. During the first third part of his ministry, he read his sermons; the remaining part of his life, he preached either from short notes or extemporaneously. The propriety of his pronunciation, his earnestness, his gravity, and his singular solemnity, controlled, in the most absolute manner, the minds of those who heard him. Mr. Hooker, who succeeded him— who was distinguished for his learning, good sense, and elegance of mind and manners, as well as for his moral worth— well said to Dr. Dwight, that eloquence is so variously understood and defined, that it is difficult to determine what is intended by it; but that, if it consisted in making strong impressions of the subject of a discourse on the minds of an audience, Mr. Edwards was the most eloquent man he ever knew. Mr. Strong, afterwards Professor of Mathematics and Natural Philosophy in Yale College, in early youth heard Mr. Edwards deliver the sermons which now constitute his "History of Redemption." He says that his mind was from the beginning deeply interested in the subject; as it advanced, his feelings were more and more engaged, till, when the preacher came to a consideration of the final judgment, his mind was wrought up to such a pitch that he fully expected the awful scene to be unfolded on that day, and in that place. He waited with the deepest and most solemn solicitude, to hear the trumpet sound and the archangel call; to see the graves open, the dead arise, and the Judge descend in the glory of his Father, with all his holy angels; and was deeply disappointed when the day terminated, and left the world in its usual state of tranquillity.

The following narrative of this extraordinary man cannot but prove interesting:—

While the people in the neighbouring towns were in great distress for their souls, the inhabitants of Enfield were very secure, loose, and vain. A lecture had been appointed there; and the neighbouring people were so affected at the thoughtlessness of the inhabitants, and in such fears that God would, in his righteous judgment, pass them by, while the Divine showers were falling all around them, as to be prostrate before Him a considerable part of the evening previous, supplicating mercy for their souls. When the appointed time for the lecture came, a number of the neighbouring ministers attended, and some from a distance. When they went into the meetinghouse, the appearance of the assembly was thoughtless and vain The people hardly conducted themselves with common decency. Edwards preached. His plain, unpretending manner, both in language and delivery, and his established reputation for holiness and knowledge of the truth, forbade the suspicion that any trick of oratory would be used to mislead his hearers. He began in the clear, careful, demonstrative style of a teacher, solicitous for the result of his effort, and anxious that every step of his argument should be clearly and fully understood. His te t was Deut. xxxii. 35: "Their foot shall slide in due time." As he advanced in unfolding the meaning of the text, the most careful logic brought him and his hearers to conclusions, which the most tremendous imagery could but inadequately express. His most terrific descriptions of the doom and danger of the impenitent, only enabled them to apprehend more clearly the truths which he had compelled them to believe. They seemed to be, not the product of the imagination, but what they really were, a part of the argument. The effect was as might be expected. Trumbull informs us that "before the assembly was ended, the congregation appeared deeply impressed and bowed with an awful conviction of their sin and danger. There was such a breathing of distress and weeping, that the preacher was obliged to speak to the people and desire silence, that he might be heard. This was the beginning of the same great and prevailing concern in that place, with which the colony in general was visited.

A METHODIST CLERGYMAN.

A METHODIST preacher, at a camp-meeting held in Massachusetts, at the conclusion of his sermon, took occasion to impress upon his hearers the propriety of contributing freely of their substance for the benefit of the church; and urged them to make the "collection, which was then about to be taken up, a good one." After the collection had been made, he arose with great solemnity, and looking into the contribution boxes, which, although they contained a great number of cents, showed a lamentable dearth of silver, exclaimed, with much gravity, "I perceive that *Alexander the coppersmith hath done us much harm.*"

AN ECCENTRIC CLERGYMAN.

A SHREWD, eccentric, but withal talented preacher, of unbounded influence among his people, once administered reproof in a very effectual manner. One warm summer afternoon, his congregation, like some other congregations, got drowsy, and not a few went off into a regular doze. The orator went on, apparently undisturbed by the apathy, and finished his discourse. He paused; the silence, as is often the case after the hum-drum of a not very animated preacher, roused up the congregation: some rubbed their eyes, and all stared; for there stood the minister, sermon in hand. He waited till he saw them all fairly awake, and then very calmly said, "My good friends, this sermon cost me a good deal of labour, rather more than usual; you do not seem to have paid to it quite as much attention as it deserves. I think I will go over it again;" and he was as good as his word, from text to exhortation.

REV. PRESIDENT DAVIES.

WHEN Mr. Davies was yet under thirty years of age, he was induced to accompany the Rev. Gilbert Tennant to England, to solicit donations for the college of New Jersey, of which he afterwards became the president.

His fame, as a pulpit orator, was so great in London, that i' reached the ears of King George II., who expressed a strong desire to hear him. This was brought about; and Mr. D. preached before a splendid audience, composed of the royal family and many of the nobility. It is further said, that while Mr. D. was preaching, the king was, at different times, seen speaking to those around him, who were seen also to smile. Mr. Davies observed it, and was shocked at what he thought was irreverence in the house of God, utterly inexcusable in one, the influence of whose example was so great. After pausing, and looking sternly in that direction several times, the preacher proceeded in his discourse; but the same conduct was still observed. The American preacher then exclaimed: "When the lion roars, the beasts of the forest tremble; and when King Jesus speaks, the princes of the earth should keep silence!" The king is said to have given a significant but courteous bow to the preacher, and to have sat very composedly and reverently during the rest of the service.

The king is said to have been enraptured with the preacher's manner and eloquence, and to have been expressing his delight to those around him. He sent for the preacher, who repeated his visit, and received from the king a handsome donation for the college.

REV. BENJAMIN HARVEY.

The following anecdote, of probably the oldest clergyman of his day, is copied from the New York Baptist Register, published at Utica, in 1845. The venerable man died in 1847.

Elder Benjamin Harvey, who is to open the religious services at the meeting-house, on the fourth, is now in the one hundred and eleventh year of his age, and still retains his faculties to an astonishing degree. His health is excellent. He walks about with great ease, and to all human appearance may last several years longer. On Lord's-day of last week we had the privilege of conversing with him in regard to his employment during the winter. He informed us that since December last, he had preached every Sabbath, and several times during the week likewise.

In the afternoon, at the request of the pastor of Broad Sreet Baptist church, he made the first prayer, which he prefaced substantially with these remarks: "We are now about to pray—but we shall not change the mind of God by our prayer, if we were to pray until we drop into our graves. God will not be altered by it. He is perfectly right, and needs no alteration. If there is any alteration, it must be in us; and our prayer must be that we may be penitent and conformed to his will, and find mercy through Jesus Christ." He said he had two objects to pray to; one was the congregation, and the other the great Father in heaven—and the prayer to the congregation is, " 'We pray you in Christ's stead, be ye reconciled to God.' And now, let us unite in prayer to Him, that he would grant us poor sinners the mercy we need."

In the evening he preached a sermon of fifty-five minutes, from the passage in Revelations, "I saw an angel flying through the midst of heaven, having the everlasting gospel to preach," and was listened to with interest and astonishment. Though it was somewhat scattering, to use a common phrase, yet there was manifestly method peculiar to himself, and many thoughts truly valuable. His strength of lungs, and accuracy of Scripture quotation, were indeed wonderful; and his vigour of action, and his great animation, are not often surpassed by ministers in the meridian of life. The Bible must have been closely studied by him in former years. His animation was such frequently, in speaking of the blessedness of the Redeemer, that he would clap his hands under the exercise. He referred to the two previous sermons in his opening, that he had preached in the same pulpit, and gave the main division with astonishing accuracy; showing his memory as well as his other faculties remarkably sound, and that he is indeed the greatest wonder of the age.

A NEW ENGLAND CLERGYMAN.

An eminent minister gave, in one of his sermons, the following illustration of the Divine dealings with sinners.

A clergyman sitting in his study, saw some boys in his garden stealing melons. He quietly arose, and walking into his garden, called them; "Boys, boys." They immediately fled with the utmost precipitation, tearing through the shrubbery, and tumbling over the fences. "Boys," cried out the gentleman, "stop, do not be afraid. You may have as many melons as you want. I have more than I know what to do with."

The boys, urged by the consciousness of guilt, fled with increasing speed. They did not like to trust themselves in the gentleman's hands; neither did they exactly relish the idea of receiving favors from one whose garden they were robbing.

The clergyman continued to entreat them to stop, assuring them that they should not be hurt, and that they might have as many melons as they wished for. But the very sound of his voice added wings to their speed. They scampered on in every direction, with as determined an avoidance as though the gentleman was pursuing them with a horsewhip. He determined, however, that they should be convinced that he was sincere in his offers, and therefore pursued them. Two little fellows who could not climb over the fence were taken. He led them back, telling them they were welcome to melons whenever they wanted any, and giving to each of them a couple, allowed them to go home. He sent by them a message to the other boys, that whenever they wanted any melons, they were welcome to them if they would but come to him.

The other boys, when they heard of the favors with which the two had been laden, were loud in the expression of their indignation. They accused the clergyman of partiality, in giving to some without giving to all; and when reminded that they would not accept of his offers, but ran away from him as fast as they could, they replied, "What of that? He caught these two boys, and why should he have selected them instead of the rest of us? If he had only run a little faster, he might have caught us. It was mean in him to show such partiality."

Again they were reminded that the clergyman was ready to serve them as he did the other two he caught, and give them as many melons as they wanted, if they would only go and ask him for them.

Still the boys would not go near him, but accused the generous man of injustice and partiality in doing for two, that which he did not do for all.

So it is with the sinner. God finds all guilty, and invites them to come to him and be forgiven, and receive the richest blessings heaven can afford. They all run from him, and the louder he calls, the more furious do they rush in their endeavours to escape. By his grace he pursues, and some he overtakes. He loads them with favours, and sends them back to invite their fellow-sinners to return and receive the same. They all with one accord refuse to come, and yet never cease to abuse his mercy and insult his goodness. They say, "Why does God select some and not others? Why does he overtake others who are just as bad as we, and allow us to escape? This election of some and not others, is unjust and partial."

And when the minister of God replies, "The invitation is extended to you: whosoever will, let him come and take of the water of life freely," the sinner heeds it not, but goes on in his sins, still complaining of the injustice and partiality of God, in saving some and not saving all.

COLOURED PREACHERS.

A COLOURED preacher in Philadelphia, a few years since, showed his correct theology and his ingenuity, in telling his auditory, in language and style they could well comprehend, an important truth.—" My dear breddren, de liberal man, what gibs away his property, ain't gwine to heaben for dat, no more dan some of you wicked sinners. Charity ain't no good widout righteousness. It is like beef-steak widout gravy;—dat is to say, no good, no how."

An agent of one of our Missionary Societies, not long since, visited and addressed a coloured church in Kentucky. When the collection was about to be taken, the pastor, himself a coloured man, arose and said, " My dear brethren, when we have our meetings for prayer, you are generally present, and I am pleased to see this house filled. Whenever, at such times, any thing is said about the wants of the heathen, and the duty of praying and giving for the conversion of the world, you give me groans of approbation. Now I wish you to come forward with your money, or I shall conclude that you did not groan honestly."

An African preacher, speaking from the words, "What is a man profited if he gain the whole world and lose his own soul?" mentioned, among other things, that many lost their souls by being too charitable! Seeing the congregation astonished beyond measure at his saying it, he very emphatically repeated it, and then proceeded to explain his meaning. "Many people," said he, "attend meeting, and hear the sermon; and when it is over they proceed to divide it out among the congregation; this part was for that man, that part for that woman; and such denunciations were for such persons; these threats for you sinners—and so," continued the shrewd African, "*they give away the whole sermon, and keep none for themselves.*"

REV. DR. J. M. MASON.

Many facts are related of the power of Dr. Mason's pulpit eloquence. His mind was of the highest order, his theology Calvinistic, and his style of eloquence irresistible as a torrent. When the distinguished Robert Hall heard him deliver his celebrated discourse on *Messiah's Throne*, at a missionary meeting in London, in 1802, it is said he exclaimed, "I can never preach again!"

REV. DR. F.

An intelligent writer says :—

In one of my college years, a fellow-pupil suddenly died. On the Sabbath following, the venerated Dr. F. connected his discourse with this event, which was itself preaching very solemnly to some of us. This was a sentence: "Young man, thou art now strong and full of health; but I will tell thee, the spade which shall dig thy grave may be already forged—thy winding-sheet be lying in yonder store—and that clock (pointing to the one on the gallery) *be counting out the moments in the last Sabbath-day of thy life.*" He paused. It was the stillness of the grave, for a minute: but, oh! *the tick of "that clock!"* It entered my soul; it seemed like the sound of the keys in the doors of the eternal world. No voice, no speech, could have searched the audience as did that awful voice of our departing moments. Since that day, I have ever looked seriously upon the face, and listened solemnly to the voice, of the sanctuary clock.

REV. MR. STEVENS.

A FEW years since, the Rev. Mr. Stevens, of Boston, delivered a sermon at Newburyport, before the "Society for the Relief of Aged Females;" which he concluded, by relating a part of the history of a family in Philadelphia, with which he was intimately acquainted.

It consisted of the parents and four children. The husband was in an employment which enabled him to maintain his family comfortably, and lay by something as a provision for old age. In the midst of his joys, he was seized with consumption, nearly spent his all, and died. After his death, the mother laboured with constancy at her needle, to support her children, till almost incessant efforts brought on the same disease, and she also descended to the grave. Before this, however, the eldest boy, then about seven years of age, went from door to door, seeking employment, to keep the family from starvation. Those upon whom he thus called, were generally too busy to listen to the story of a child. He at length obtained a situation in the Globe cotton mill, in Philadelphia, receiving for his services seventy-five cents a week, and succeeded in getting a younger brother into the same establishment, who was paid fifty cents a week. This dollar and a quarter per week served for some time to sustain the sick mother and family. None interested themselves in their fate; for their neighbours were generally vicious and degraded, and as poor as themselves. For a long period, roasted potatoes were their only food, and the small pieces of wood which they collected in the streets, their only fuel.

Finally, a female, who had been bridesmaid to the mother, heard of her distress, and sought her out. Her assistance and personal services were freely given; but, alas! it was now too late—she could but smooth the pillow of death! The mother was laid in the grave, by the side of her husband, and the children were left orphans. Situations, however, were obtained for them, and at their meeting, at the end of every year, they could speak of increasing prosperity. Finally, the eldest boy was introduced into the ministry, and, added the preacher, "*is the individual who now addresses you!*"

" We have rarely," say the editors of the paper from which we transcribe this account, " witnessed a more powerful effect than the announcement of this fact produced. It was as though an electric shock had been sent through the whole audience. So entirely unprepared were the assembly for such a termination; so completely had their sympathies been given to sufferers whom they supposed were at that time many miles distant, that the declaration that one who had passed through the scene in which their feelings had been so strongly enlisted stood before them, was unexpected, and in the highest degree startling!"

REV. B. STANDFORD.

A few years since, a very interesting religious exercise was held at Bridgewater, Massachusetts, on the occasion of Deacon John Whitman's arriving at the age of one hundred years. The deacon, a rather tall, stout man, in good health, with mental faculties scarcely affected, excepting his hearing and sight failing, occupied an arm-chair in front of the pulpit. The assembly was the largest ever witnessed in that house, and intense interest was generally visible.

The Rev. B. Standford preached the sermon, from 2 Tim. iv. 6: "For I am now ready to be offered, and the time of my departure is at hand," and addressed, both to the venerable deacon and to the congregation, a variety of important remarks and counsels. He stated that Mr. Whitman was blessed with pious parents, and was from a child the subject of serious impressions. His mind was led fully to embrace the gospel of Christ, under the ministry of the distinguished George Whitefield; and that for seventy years he had adorned the religion of Jesus, during thirty of which he had sustained the office of deacon.

SEVERAL CLERGYMEN.

A clergyman, in a recent discourse, was speaking of the practice of pointing to the sins and follies of the members of the churches, as an excuse for others, when he thus illustrated the evil of such an argument: "Ah!" said he, "it is the common device of the devil, to blind the eyes of his disciples with the dust shaken from the soiled garments of Christians."

A celebrated divine, who was remarkable in the first period of his ministry, for a boisterous mode of preaching, suddenly changed his whole manner in the pulpit, and adopted a mild and dispassionate mode of delivery. One of his brethren observing it, inquired of him what had induced him to make the change. He answered, "When I was young, I thought it was the *thunder* that killed the people; but when I grew wiser, I discovered that it was the *lightning*—so I determined in future to thunder less and lighten more."

A reverend clergyman from Ohio, preaching in the city of Brooklyn, New York, observed two young ladies talking together. Stopping suddenly in his discourse, and looking seriously at them, he said, "I observe two young ladies in the congregation, earnestly engaged in conversation; and as it is not a mark of true politeness for more than one to speak at a time, in church, I will remain silent for a short time, to give them an opportunity to finish *their* discourse, when I will resume *mine*." The worthy minister, after standing in silence a moment or two, resumed his subject.

Several years ago, a town in New England was blessed with a revival of religion. One evening, a lady and her little daughter attended a meeting; and while the minister was speaking of the neglect of family duties, of reading the Scriptures, and of family prayer, the little daughter, who listened attentively, and perceived that the preacher was describing a neglect that she had noticed herself, whispered to her mother,

"Ma, is Mr. —— talking to you?" This was powerful preaching to the mother; she was immediately brought under deep convictions of sin, which resulted in her hopeful conversion to God.

REV PROFESSOR SHEPPARD.

The Rev. Professor Sheppard, of Bangor, was engaged to preach in the First Baptist Church, at the period of the occurrence of a great flood. He arrived at the church with some difficulty, and finding but few there, in the general consternation, he offered prayer, and then addressed them, in a manner which must, though short, be regarded as truly sublime :—

"God himself has the audience of the people to-day; and while He speaks, his ministers may well keep silence."

REV. DR. STANFORD.

The late Rev. Dr. Stanford, of New York, on a particular occasion preached a sermon from a passage in the Canticles: "Let my beloved come into his garden, and eat his pleasant fruits." After he had, in a very interesting manner, described a beautiful garden, and spoke of the variety and fragrance of its shrubs, flowers, trees and fruits, and then applied the subject to the state of the Christian church; as he descended from the pulpit, one of the deacons said to him, "Well, brother Stanford, you have laid out the garden in due form, and you have described the varieties and excellences of its productions; but where is your fence?" With his usual promptness he replied, "Oh! I left that for you deacons to put up; and see that you keep it in good order."

A UNIVERSALIST MINISTER.

It is not often we recommend the neglect of the pulpit; but in one instance, at least, we should unite with one of the parties in the following narrative, in thinking it desirable.

A Universalist minister was travelling to the West, and had sent on an appointment to preach in a certain place. On his arrival, he found a congregation, to whom he proclaimed the doctrine of unconditional salvation. After the sermon, he informed his hearers that he should be that way on his return, at such a time; and if they desired it, he would then preach again. No one replied till he had twice repeated his statement. At last an old *Friend*, in the back part of the congregation, rose, and said, "If thee hast told the truth this time, we do not *need* thee any more; and if thee hast told us a lie, we do not *want* thee any more."

REV. JOHN ELIOT.

This eminent man was very justly styled *The Apostle to the Indians.*

On the 28th of October, 1646, he set out from his home, in company with three friends, to the nearest Indian settlement. He had previously sent to give this tribe notice of his coming, and a very large number was collected from all quarters. If the savages expected the coming of their guest, of whose name they had often heard, to be like that of a warrior or sachem, they were greatly deceived. They saw Eliot on foot, drawing near, with his companions; his translation of the Scriptures, like a calumet of peace and love, in his hand. He was met by their chief, Waubon, who conducted him to a large wigwam. After a short rest, Eliot went into the open air, and, standing on a grassy mound, while the people formed around him in all the stillness of strong surprise and curiosity, he prayed in the English tongue, as if he could not address Heaven in a language both strange and new. And then he preached for an hour in their own tongue, and gave a clear and simple account of the religion of Christ, of his character and life, of the blessed state of those who believed in him. Of what avail would it have been to set before this listening people the terrors of the Almighty, and the doom of the guilty? This wise man knew, by long experience as a minister, that the heart loves better to be persuaded than terrified — to be melted than alarmed. The whole career of the Indian's life tended to freeze up the finer and softer feelings, and make the more dark and painful passions familiar to him. He resolved to strike a new chord; and when he saw the tears stream down their stern faces, and the haughty head sink low on the breast, as he painted the ineffable love of Christ, he said it was a "glorious and affecting spectacle to see a company of perishing, forlorn outcasts, so drinking in the word of salvation." The impressions this discourse produced, were of a very favourable nature: as far as the chief, Waubon, was concerned, they were never effaced. Afterwards, the guest passed several hours conversing with the Indians, and answering their questions. When night came, he returned to the tent with the chief, and the people entered their wigwams, or lay around, and slept on the grass. What were Eliot's feelings on this night? At last, the longing of years was accomplished; the fruit of his prayers was given him.

Such was the perseverance of this holy man in his great work, that on the day of his death in his eightieth year, the

"Apostle of the Indians" was found teaching the alphabet to an Indian child at his bedside. "Why not rest from your labours now?" said a friend. "Because," said the venerable man, "I have prayed to God to render me useful in my sphere; and now that I can no longer preach, he leaves me strength enough to teach this poor child his alphabet."

REV. JOHN GANO.

The Rev. Dr. Cone, pastor of the first Baptist church in New York, in 1845 preached a centennial sermon, in which he gave a sketch of his predecessors in office. In speaking of the Rev. John Gano, who was pastor from 1760 to 1788, he said that it might be interesting to state a reminiscence of the revolutionary war. Mr. Gano was a chaplain to the militia, and fleeing up the island before the British, the regiment to which he belonged turned to resist the pursuers, and the manœuvre bringing him in front of the line, he fought there in the place of the lieutenant-colonel, who was absent. He fought bravely, which gave courage to the men, who said, "Surely God is on our side, when our chaplain is our leader." At the close of the war he returned to the city, and found his house destroyed, and his place of worship a stable of British cavalry. He gathered what he could of his flock, and preached to them from these words in Haggai: "Who is left among you that saw this house in her first glory? Is it not now in comparison of it as nothing?"

A clergyman, some time since, imparted instruction to his congregation by relating the following facts:

Two travellers put up for the night at a tavern. Early in the morning they absconded without reckoning with their host, also stealing from him a bag of beans. A few years after they passed that road in company again; and again they asked for lodging at the same inn. The identical landlord was yet at his post; and in the evening was overheard by them, talking in one corner of the bar-room, in a suppressed voice, with one of his neighbours, about a swarm of bees. One of his dishonest guests said to the other, "Did not he say beans?" "I think he did," was the reply, and quickly they were missing.

I often think, added the clergyman, about the beans. When the church member complains that the minister means him, this anecdote about the beans will pop into my mind. On a thousand other occasions, I notice people whose consciences are not easy, saying to each other, by various modes of communication, "Did not he say beans?" though perhaps the preacher was no nearer the subject about which they were excited than the bees were to the beans.

A PRACTICAL PREACHER.

A New England clergyman enforcing on his congregation the necessity of practical godliness; and contrasting the early Christians with those of the present generation, very properly remarked, "We have too many resolutions, and too little action. 'The *Acts* of the Apostles,' is the title of one of the books of the New Testament; their *Resolutions* have not reached us."

REV. LUTHER RICE.

When Mr. Rice was travelling as an agent in the cause of foreign missions, he was once in attendance at a public meeting of the Shiloh Association, held in Culpepper county,—that part of it now forming Rappahannock county. He had been urging the claims of the heathen on the sympathies and efforts of Christians with his accustomed eloquence and effect; but among his hearers was a brother of the name of Jonathan Waters, an excellent man, but somewhat eccentric, a great stickler for sound doctrine, and perhaps not altogether uninfected with the anti-ism somewhat rife at that day in his neighbourhood. When asked what he thought of the cause, he replied he could tell better if he knew what *sort* of gospel was to be sent to the heathen. Brother Rice had not preached to them; he had only spoken to them on the subject of missions. "Well," said Mr. Rice, " suppose I preach to-night." Arrangements were accordingly made for holding the service at a private house. A goodly number was present, and among them Brother Waters, seated at some distance from the speaker. The text was announced,—John x. 27, 28,—" My sheep hear my voice, and I know them, and they follow me: and I give unto them eternal life; and they shall never perish, neither shall any man pluck them out of my hand." The preacher had proceeded a little way, when Brother W. became bent in the posture of deep thought. By and by, he raised his head, and fixed his eyes on the speaker; soon his mouth was agape; a little after, he hitched forward his chair, and gradually approached the table, until, at length, he was under the very lips of the charmer. In due time—Luther Rice seldom preached long sermons—the discourse was concluded; but no sooner was the "Amen" out, than the good brother, inflicting a "right smart" slap on the shoulders of Mr. R., exclaimed, " Well, brother Rice, YOU CAN PREACH!"

Brother Waters, from that evening to the day of his death, was known as one of the warmest friends of Christian enterprise in all his region. He continued as firm a believer as ever in the Lord doing his own work; but insisted no less strongly that it was the part of a true friend of Christ to obey his Master's commands.

Mr. Rice was eminently a practical man. He once attended a meeting in Virginia, where the people had gathered from afar, and a large number of ministers were present. Sermons on Election, Perseverance of the Saints, Justifying Faith, and the various doctrines of grace, had been preached. One of the ministers alluded to this fact, and said that there had been much strong meat given, but thought it necessary in order that young preachers and young converts should be established in the truth. It was proper to go over, at such times, the round of doctrines.

Beside him, on that occasion, sat Luther Rice. He at length arose to speak. He remarked that he could not agree with all that his predecessor had said. "Strong meat! Call the doctrines of electing love, preserving grace, justifying faith, strong meat! No, no, this is the very milk of the word, fit food for babes. It is for *me* to preach the strong meat. Give as the Lord has prospered you. *There is strong meat for you.*" His eye flashed, and the full tone of his voice, as he enunciated this, could never be forgotten. He had visited Virginia, to arouse to the work of missions. His labors were not in vain.

REV. JOHN SUMMERFIELD.

Seldom, if ever, has this or any other country produced a more zealous or eloquent preacher than this truly remarkable young man. Among many other illustrations of his power in the pulpit, we learn that in 1822, he preached in New York, in behalf of the institution for the instruction of the Deaf and Dumb, and the following were his concluding sentences; but although they are the very words of the preacher, those only who heard them in that great congregation, can conceive of the fervour with which they were uttered:—

"But I transfer these children now to you. Behold them." Here dropping his handkerchief on the platform, the objects of the charity stood up in the presence of the congregation, while he proceeded,—" They now stand before you, as you must stand before the judgment-seat of Christ. Turn away from these children of affliction, and when the Lord says, ' Inasmuch as ye did it not to the least of these, ye did it not unto me,' you too may be dumb, speechless in shame. Dare you on this occasion say:—

> The mercy I to others show,
> That mercy show to me?

Do you realize that day? You must stand stripped of every earthly treasure—naked before God! While you plead for mercy,—cast all earthly treasure from you now,—these now plead with *you*, as you will plead with God:—hear them! I do not mock you!—Silence like theirs is eloquence. The hand of God has smitten them, but the stroke which blasted, consecrated them! Heaven has cast them on you:—if you withhold, 'tis sacrilege! Will a man rob God? Are you still passing by on the other side? Still griping, with a miser's fist, the pelf of earth?—Father of Mercies! palsy not that hand! wither not that eye which can gaze on these objects, and not feel affected! On *me* be the wrong! I have failed to affect them—these children have failed. Thou canst move them;—Oh, descend as with cloven tongues of fire! and find thou an entrance into every heart.—But—I can no more!"

The sermon being concluded, the collection was taken up, which amounted to more than one thousand dollars, a gold necklace, and several rings.

Preaching once in Allen Street Church, New York, this eloquent young clergyman wished to define and illustrate Christian confidence; and he did it in this way :—"You remember Peter, when he was imprisoned, chained between two soldiers. The church was praying in tears, wondering what would become of them if their strong champion was taken from them. The enemies of God on earth, and the devils in hell, were rejoicing that they had Peter in their power. The angels in heaven, ever intent on the mysteries of Providence in redemption, were sending down to see what the Lord would do with Peter. When heaven, and earth, and hell, were thinking of Peter, what were Peter's thoughts? What was Peter doing? *Peter was asleep.*"

A YOUNG CLERGYMAN.

The following lines, descriptive of a beautiful incident, are from the pen of Mrs. A. L. Angier, and are said to describe an actual occurrence.

> The rosy light of Sabbath eve
> On hill and valley lay;
> And lingered long, as if to leave
> A blessing on the day.

The village bell had sweetly tolled
    Its chime upon the air,
To summon to their hallowed fold
    The worshippers for prayer.

The organ's deep and solemn peals
    Fell on the listening ear,
As o'er the senses gently stole
    The feeling—God is near!

The youthful preacher rose, and took
    His theme—'twas Jesus' love!
When lo! beside the sacred book
    There stood a snow-white dove!

With timid gaze and folded wing,
    It paused—then soared away;
In vain we sought to track its course,
    In vain we bade it stay.

Onward and upward still it flew,
    Till not a speck was seen,
To tell that in the vaults of blue
    Its graceful form had been.

I know not if the thought be wrong,
    But it hath *seemed* to me,
That some *mute herald* from the skies
    That gentle bird might be,

To teach us, if to innocence
    Our days on earth are given,
We too may plume our spirits' wings,
    And take our flight for heaven.

The memory of that Sabbath eve,
    That quiet sunset scene,
Did on my heart an impress leave,
    From which this truth I glean:

That nature's *simplest lessons* tend
    To show some moral plain;
For, on the page that God hath penned,
    No line is writ in vain.

DEVOTEDNESS OF CLERGYMEN TO THEIR LABOURS.

REV. JOHN BROCK.

This eminent minister, who died at Reading, Mass., in 1668, was truly remarkable for devotedness to his work, and for a spirit of fervent prayer, of which several remarkable facts are related. When he lived at the Isle of Shoals, he persuaded the people to enter into an agreement to spend one day in every month, besides the Sabbaths, in religious worship. On one of these days, the fishermen, who composed his society, desired him to put off the meeting, as the roughness of the weather had for a number of days prevented them from attending to their usual employment. He endeavoured in vain to convince them of the impropriety of their request. As most of them were determined on seizing the opportunity for making up their lost time, and were more intent on their worldly than on their spiritual concerns, he addressed them thus: "If you are resolved to neglect your duty to God, and will go away, I say to you, catch fish if you can; but as for you, who will tarry and worship the Lord Jesus Christ, I will pray unto him for you, that you may catch fish until you are weary." Of thirty-five men, only five remained with the minister. The thirty who went from the meeting, with all their skill, caught through the whole day but four fishes; while the five who attended divine service, afterwards went out and caught five hundred. From this time the fishermen readily attended all the meetings he appointed. A poor man, who had been very useful with his boat, in carrying persons who attended public worship over a river, lost his boat in a storm, and lamented his loss to his minister. Mr. Brock said to him, "Go home, honest man; I will mention the matter to the Lord; you will have your boat again to-morrow." The next day, in earnest prayer, the poor man recovered his boat, which was brought up from the bottom, by the anchor of a vessel, cast upon it without design. A number of such remarkable correspondences between the events of providence and the prayers of this holy man, caused Mr. John Allen, of Dedham, to say of him, "I scarce ever knew any man so familiar with the great God, as his dear servant Brock."

REV. PRESIDENT DAVIES.

Such was the devotedness of this excellent minister, that even in very early life, when only entering on his labours, and when he was judged to be in an irrecoverable consumption, entertaining no hope of restored health, he determined to spend the remains of an exhausted life, as he apprehended, in endeavouring to advance his Master's glory in the good of souls. Accordingly he removed from the place where he was, to another, about a hundred miles distant, then in want of a minister. Here he laboured in season and out of season; and preached in the day, and had his hectic fever by night, and sometimes to such a degree as to be delirious, and to be in need of persons to sit up with him.

It is said of this extraordinary man, that he never preached a sermon which was not instrumental in at least one conversion. Some of his sermons brought many to the foot of the cross. For the explanation of this, it need only be said that his soul was made of heavenly fires. He delighted to be in his closet.

BISHOP GRISWOLD.

Dr. Stone relates that this eminent Christian minister having once reached Newport, it became necessary to cross Narragansett Bay, in order to keep an appointment which he had made at Wickford, in the old St. Paul's or Narragansett Church. But a violent gale, which had prevented an outward-bound vessel from sailing for Cuba, was still raging, and had kept the regular ferry-packet from coming over, on that day, from Wickford to Newport. Here, indeed, was a difficulty, which would have kept most men housed. The swelling Narragansett, bowing its thousand waves before the strong blast of a still powerful wind and tempest, lay, eight miles broad, between him and his place of destination. Yet he could not give up, without an effort, his purpose of being punctual to his engagement. By the offer of an extra reward, he induced a strong boatman, in an open sea-craft, to attempt the passage. They set forth together on the dangerous essay. But by the time they were midway on the water, the boatman felt the peril to be too great for farther progress. Addressing his passenger, therefore, he said: "Bishop, I dare go no further against such a wind as this!" The announcement was full of import. Still, the bishop was undismayed. He did not, indeed, emulate the moral sublime of the ancient conqueror, in the inquiry, "Quid times? Cæsarem vehis?" "Why fearest thou? Thou carriest Cæsar." But, rising above, into the higher sublime of a calm trust in him who holdeth the waters in the hollow of his hand, he simply asked, "Why, what is the matter?" "The craft has not ballast enough," was the quick reply; if she carried more of that, she might perhaps live through the bay." "Would it help her," asked the bishop, "if I were to lie down in the boat?" "No better ballast than that could she have" said the boatman. The suggestion was no sooner made than adopted. Casting himself at full length upon his face, into the bottom of the boat, with the weight of a strong frame, much heavier than that of common men, the little vessel braced herself more strongly to the blast; and though in peril of going down, yet, after long toiling, she reached Wickford harbour, and the bishop stepped thankfully upon the firm land. Yet, so wet and encrusted had his hat and garments become, under the gray brine which had been splashed over him, that the inhabitants of the village were scarcely able to recognise in him their old and well-known visitor.

But, upon reaching the house of the rector of the parish, in season for the service which he had appointed, he found that he had not been expected, and that therefore the church had not been opened. The violence of the storm kept every one at home. The rector himself was in utter amazement at his arrival, and exclaimed, "Why, bishop, I would not have crossed the Narragansett, such a day as this, for a warranty deed of the whole Narragansett country!" Nor would the bishop, for such an inducement as that. But, under a sense of duty, he was ready to dare what no *pecuniary* consideration could have bribed him to attempt. "I had made my appointments," said he, calmly, "and was not willing that the people should be disappointed through my fault."

A MISSIONARY IN NEW YORK.

Some time in the latter part of the last century, a missionary from one of the New England societies was labouring in the nterior of the state of New York, where the settlements were very few and far between. This missionary was much devoted to his work, meek and affable, and possessed a remarkable talent for introducing the subject of religion to every individual with whom he came in contact. On a hot summer's day, while his horse was drinking from a small brook through which he rode, there came along a poorly dressed, bare-headed, bare-footed boy, about seven years old, and stood looking at the missionary from the bridge just above him.

"My son," said the missionary, "have you any parents?"

"Yes, sir; they live in that house," pointing to a cabin near by.

"Do your parents pray?"

"No, sir."

"Why do they not pray?"

"I do not know, sir."

"Do you pray?"

"No, sir."

"Why do you not pray?"

"I do not know how to pray."

"Can you read?"

"Yes, sir; my mother has taught me to read the New Testament."

"If I give you this sixpence, will you go home and read the third chapter of John, and read the third verse over three times?" The little boy said he would; and the missionary gave him the sixpence, and rode on.

Some twenty years had elapsed; and the same missionary, advanced in years, was labouring in a sparsely-peopled region, in another part of the same state. While on his way to a little village, one day, late in the afternoon, he called at a small house, and inquired the distance. "Six miles," was the reply. He then stated that himself and horse were very weary, and inquired if he could not stay all night. The woman of the house objected, on account of their poverty; but the husband said, "Sir you shall be welcome to such as we have."

The missionary dismounted and went in. The wife began to prepare his supper, while her husband proceeded to take care of the horse. As he came in, the missionary addressed him: "Do you love the Lord Jesus Christ?"

"That," said the man, "is a great question."

"True," said the missionary; "but I cannot eat till you tell me."

"Sir," said the man, "about twenty years ago, I lived in the interior of this state, and was then about seven years old. While playing in the road, one day, a gentleman in black rode into the brook, near by me, to water his horse. As I stood on the bridge above, looking at him, he began to converse with me about praying, and reading the Bible; and told me he would give me a sixpence if I would read the third chapter of John, and the third verse three times: 'And Jesus answered and said unto him, Verily, I say unto thee, except a man be born again, he cannot see the kingdom of God.' I gave him my promise, took the money, and felt wealthy indeed. I went home, and read as I had promised. That verse produced an uneasiness in my mind, which followed me for days and years; and finally I was led by its influence, as I trust, to love Jesus as my Saviour!"

"Glory to God!" said the missionary, rising from his seat; "here is one of my spiritual children; the bread cast on the waters is found after many days!"

They took their supper, and talked and sang, and prayed and rejoiced together all night long, neither of them having any disposition to sleep. The missionary found him to be poor in this world's goods, but rich in faith, and an heir of the kingdom. Early in the morning they parted, and the missionary went his way, inspired with fresh zeal for the prosecution of his holy labours.

REV. S. STODDARD.

This eminent preacher and writer was the predecessor, at Northampton, of President Edwards. He probably possessed more influence than any other clergyman in the province, during a period of thirty years. The very savages are said to have felt towards him a peculiar awe. Once, when he was riding from Northampton to Hatfield, and passing a place called Dewey's Hole, an ambush of savages lined the road. It is said that a Frenchman, directing his gun towards him, was warned by one of the Indians, who some time before had been among the English, not to fire, " because that man was the Englishman's God." A similar adventure was reported to have befallen him, while meditating, in an orchard immediately behind the church in Deerfield, a sermon which he was about to preach.

REV. SAMUEL H. STEARNS.

This young minister, who was cut off in the commencement of a highly promising course of usefulness, while yet a student at Andover, formed high and correct views of the ministry, and prepared and adopted the following resolutions, which cannot be too strongly commended as a model for others:—

I wholly renounce ambition, and self-indulgence, as motives of action.

I must be absolutely and entirely devoted to God, in heart and life; and live not unto myself, but unto him who loved me and died for me.

I must glorify God, in the improvement of my own character, and in doing good to mankind.

I will follow my own taste and genius, so far as circumstances allow; and trust in God that his providence will guide me.

I will never intrude myself on the public, or take a conspicuous part, without good and important reasons; nor will I shrink from the exposure when duty calls, but generously go forward, and endeavour to acquit myself with Christian propriety.

My intercourse with the world, so far as it extends, shall be perfectly honourable, christian, frank, kind, and magnanimous;—any good attained or done at the expense of this, costs too much.

It shall be my pleasure to exert a happy influence on all within the little circle in which I move.

I will never be disturbed or diverted from my purpose, by the remarks, conduct and opinions of those who do not know my character or understand my motives; but will ever maintain that self-possession, freedom, independence, and liberality of feeling which constitute true dignity.

Why should we be for ever undoing the work of life? Why should we wish to be just like everybody else? I will be myself, and make the best of it. God grant that I may grow better!

REV. G. WHITEFIELD.

Every thing about Whitefield commanded attention. His voice, accompanied by his look from crossed eyes, and proceeding from a man of his robust frame, must have produced wonderful effects. It is said that when once preaching in a grave-yard, two young men conducted themselves improperly, when he fixed his eyes upon them, and with a voice resembling thunder said, "Come down, you rebels!" They fell, neither of them being inclined to come into contact with such a look, or to hear such a voice again.

A CITY MINISTER.

A minister of the Gospel, in one of our Northern cities, some years ago, became deeply impressed with a desire for increased usefulness. He thought much upon the most probable means for the accomplishment of this object. The ordinary opportunities of access to his people, by pulpit ministration and customary pastoral visitings, did not satisfy his soul. He longed to lead his flock directly to Christ—to witness a greater degree of spirituality among them. At length, he resolved to visit every family, and, as far as practicable, to ascertain the spiritual condition of each of its members, by personal conversation upon religious experience. At an appointed time, he entered upon his labours of love. He called on one and another of the families of his people—had every household gathered—and with much affectionate concern, spoke to them of the necessity of living each day for God and for eternity. His own soul was comforted, and he felt that his labours were not in vain in the Lord.

A day or two after he had commenced this heavenly employment, he called at the house of one of his most pious and influential members—a man of wealth. The father was absent at his place of business; but the mother, an amiable and pious woman, was at home. On making known to the latter his desire that she should summon her family to the parlour, and acquainting her with his design to speak personally to them—to exhort, admonish, or encourage, as they might need—the mother thanked him with tears of gratitude; but said:—

"I have one request to make of you, sir."

"What is that?" said the minister.

"It is, that you will say nothing to my eldest daughter, Mary, on the subject of religion. I have prayed for that child for years. I have talked to her again and again; but her heart is set upon vanity. Fashion and the world are predominant in her affections. She has become, of late, exceedingly sensitive to reproof or admonition. Respectful in every other relation, she will not permit me to speak to her on religious subjects, without returning a violence of language entirely unbecoming a daughter. I have determined, therefore, to refrain from any direct appeal to her, until she shall give evidence of greater docility. You will please, therefore, say nothing to Mary, whatever you may say to the others. I should be very sorry to have your feelings injured, as well as my own, by the manner in which I am but too confident she would respond. May God bless your admonition to the rest."

In a few moments, the family were gathered in the presence of the minister. Mary sat among them. She had entered with a respectful courtesy, and taken her position at a window upon the street, apparently more interested in what was going on without, than attentive to the conversation within. The minister spoke first to the mother, of her responsibilities and duties; then to a son, a youth of intellect and promise; then to a younger daughter, and so on, until he had administered his kind and fatherly instruction to all—I mean all except Mary. To her he said nothing; he seemed to be unconscious of her presence.

As the tears of tenderness flowed freely from all who participated in the delightful interview, Mary sat at the window, playing idly with the tasseling of the silk curtains; her proud spirit refusing the first intimations of sympathetic feeling. The brightness of her eye was undimmed by any gathering tear; the loftiness of her carriage was not for a moment relaxed by the affecting scene before her; and when the minister said, " Let us pray !" she arose not from her seat to bow with the rest, but remained still in her position of scornful unconcern; her delicate fingers toying with the silken fringes of the drapery before her. The minister poured out his soul in a fervent prayer to the throne of grace. Oh! how earnestly committed he that family to the guardianship of Heaven; referring to them in his supplications individually, and appropriately presenting them to the mercy of the Father through the merit of the Son. But he offered no prayer for Mary. Unconcernedly and proudly, she still played with the silken toys. The prayer ceased—the good man arose. Taking each by the hand, he affectionately gave a parting admonition and invocation; and bowing coldly to Mary, who as coldly returned his civility, he left the room, and made his way to the entrance of the building.

He had scarcely passed the threshold, when the words of the Redeemer, "I am not come to call the righteous, but sinners, to repentance," flashed upon his mind. Suddenly pausing, he said to himself, "Shall I refuse exertion for any soul, to save which my Master came down from Heaven? Nay; God being my helper, I will return!"

Again he stood in the parlour. The family sat just as he had left them, musing upon the things he had spoken. Mary was, to all appearance, still cold and unmoved.

With a courage imparted by the Holy Spirit, he walked up to where she sat, and taking her hand in his, said, "It is a faithful saying, and worthy of all acceptation, that Jesus Christ came into the world to save sinners. Shall he save you?"

The rock was smitten! The waters gushed forth freely and fully! Mary, proud and scornful as she seemed to be, needed only the word of invitation to bow and weep and pray. Then was heard the bitter cry of "God, be merciful to me, a sinner!" Angels hovered over that little assembly, and ere the descending sun gave place to the gathering twilight, the shout of conversion ascended to the throne, and there was joy in heaven over the sinner that had repented.

The moral of this narrative is twofold, and is borne upon its very face. Mothers may learn from it never to despair, and ministers never to falter!

REV. SOLOMON ALLEN.

This excellent minister, who laboured in the beginning of this century, first in Hampshire county, and then in the western part of the state of New York, did not commence his ministry till he was fifty years of age. His zeal was irrepressible, and his disinterestedness exceedingly striking. He endured great hardships, making every possible sacrifice in the pursuit of his great object. And such was the happy effect, that many felt as did one avowed enemy of the gospel: "This is a thing I cannot get along with; this old gentleman, who can be as rich as he pleases, comes here and does all these things for nothing; there must be something in his religion."

REV. DR. J. M. MASON.

Being asked by a physician why he did not give to the world the result of his observations in his frequent travels in different parts of the world, Dr. M. replied, "Alas! what sort of travels can I write? I neither understand the nature of the air I breathe, nor the water I drink, nor the earth I tread upon; my life has been appropriated to *Divinity*." The frankness of this answer was characteristic of this great and nonest man, who long bore the name of the American Paul and may be considered as a rebuke of a class of the clergy not small, who know every thing but the *one* to which they have professedly devoted their lives.

REV. PRESIDENT EDWARDS.

The most eminently useful men have been those of the deepest piety. President Edwards's success may be attributed, in a very eminent degree, to this fact. He writes: "Once, as I rode out into the woods, having alighted from my horse, in a retired place, for divine contemplation and prayer, I had a view, that for me was extraordinary, of the glory of the Son of God, as Mediator between God and man. The person of the Son of God appeared ineffably excellent, with an excellency great enough to swallow up all thought and conception. This view continued, as near as I can judge, about an hour, and kept me the greater part of the time in a flood of tears, and weeping aloud. I felt an ardency of soul to be, what I know not otherwise how to express, emptied of self, to lie in the dust, and to be full of Christ alone; to love him with a holy and pure love; to trust in him; to live upon him; to serve and follow him; and to be perfectly sanctified and made pure, with a divine and heavenly purity." Such passages as these constantly occur in his moral history.

Who can wonder that such a man was eminently useful as a preacher? When he preached, it was with a heavenly unction and power that subdued a whole assembly. Many aim to be very intellectual, and avoid the manifestation of deep emotion, as if it were allied to weakness; than which nothing can be more untrue. There is in their discourses an affectation of argumentative power. Every thing is viewed by them in the mere light of reason, rather than in the soft and mellow light of fervid and holy feeling. We care not how rigid the preacher's logic; but it must be a logic warmed and vivified by a spirit of deep and earnest piety. The preacher must not be *professionally* pious. He must study the Bible with a constant reference to his own personal wants, and to the sanctification of his own heart.

REV. JOHN ELIOT.

Some of the Indian chiefs having become the open enemies of the gospel, Mr. Eliot, sometimes called the "Apostle of the American Indians," when in the wilderness, without the company of any other Englishman, was, at various times, treated in a threatening and barbarous manner by some of those men; yet his Almighty Protector inspired him with such resolution, that he said, "I am about the work of the Great God, and my God is with me; so that I fear neither you, nor all the sachems (or chiefs) in the country. I will go on, and do you touch me if you dare." They heard him, and shrunk away.

REV. DR. RODGERS.

The wisdom of Dr. John Rodgers, of New York, was in nothing more evident than in his way of opposing error, and in his dislike of persecution. When he was once strongly urged by some of the officers of his church to preach against the errors of a particular sect, and to warn his people against them by name, he firmly refused; saying, "Brethren, you must excuse me; I cannot reconcile it with my sense either of policy or duty to oppose these people from the pulpit, other wise than by preaching the truth plainly and faithfully. I believe them to be in error; but let us out-preach them, out-pray them, and out-live them, and we need not fear."

REV. DR. MANNING.

In the Rev. W. Hague's excellent "Historical Discourse," we meet with the following anecdote of Dr. Manning :—

It was the delight of Dr. Manning to aid the needy, and to throw the sunshine of Christian sympathy around the path of the afflicted. His knowledge of the world, his courtly manners, his christian meekness, combined with great energy of character, enabled him to move at ease with every class of society, and to promote the good of all. In a recent memoir which forms an elegant tribute to his memory, it is stated, that he enjoyed the confidence of the general commanding in his department, and in one instance in particular, had all the benevolent feelings of his heart gratified, even at the last moment, after earnest entreaty, by obtaining from General Sullivan an order of reprieve for three men of the army, who were sentenced to death by that inexorable tribunal, a Court Martial. The moment he obtained the order revoking the sentence, he mounted his horse at the general's door, and by pushing him to his utmost speed, arrived at the place of execution at the instant the last act had begun, which was to precipitate them into eternity. With a voice which none could disobey, he commanded the execution to stay, and delivered the general's order to the officer of the guard. The joy of the attending crowd seemed greater than that of the subjects of mercy; they were called so suddenly to life, from the last verge of death, they did not, for a moment, feel that it was a reality.

REV. D. TINSLEY.

Time was, when, under other government, persecution was rife in our land. The Rev. David Tinsley was born in Virginia, about 1749. He preached with Samuel Harris, the Virginia apostle, and Jeremiah Walker, and as the result, was imprisoned four months and sixteen days, in the winter season, in Chesterfield jail. Through the grates of his prison he proclaimed the Saviour to hundreds who came to listen. His enemies burned red pepper and tobacco in order to suffocate him, but he continued to preach.

REV. DR. COKE.

This eminent minister, who to a very great extent obeyed the Divine command, " Go ye, and preach the gospel to every creature," extended his labours to the most distant parts of the earth, and preached in the greatest variety of situations, and under the most varied circumstances. At Raleigh, the seat of government for North Carolina, he obtained the use of the House of Assembly; the members of both houses attended, and the speaker's seat served for a pulpit. At Annapolis, he occupied the theatre. "Pit, boxes, and gallery," says he, "were filled with people, according to their ranks in life; and I stood upon the stage, and preached to them, though at first, I confess, I felt a little awkward."

But preaching in the forests delighted Coke the most. "It is," said he, "one of my most delightful entertainments, to embrace every opportunity of engulfing myself, if I may so express it, in the woods: I seem then to be detached from every thing but the quiet vegetable creation, and my God.

Sometimes a most noble vista, of half a mile or a mile in length, would open between the lofty pines; sometimes the tender fawns and hinds would suddenly appear, and on seeing or hearing us, would glance through the woods, or vanish away. The deep green of the pines, the bright transparent green of the vales, and the fine white of the dogwood flowers, with other trees and shrubs, form such a complication of beauties, and is indescribable to those who have lived in countries that are almost entirely cultivated."

The manner of tracing the preacher was curious; when a new circuit in the woods was formed, at every turning of the road or path, the preacher split two or three bushes, as a direction for those that came after him, and notice was sent round to the neighbourhood at what place he was going to preach.

REV. DR. CHAPLIN.

It is related of the late Rev. Dr. Jeremiah Chaplin, as an illustration of his unwearied industry, that while he was yet a student at Brown University, a neighbouring clergyman made some inquiries into the peculiarities and merits of Dr. Hopkins' Body of Divinity, then just published, and was answered, "Ask Chaplin, he can tell you." Dr. Pattison, in his funeral oration, says that he acted to the fullest extent on the maxim, "Never to ask another to do that for him which he could do for himself."

REV. DR. RICE.

The Rev. Dr. John H. Rice was an eminently distinguished Presbyterian minister in Virginia, and for some years editor of the Evangelical and Literary Magazine. After his death, which occurred in 1831, a series of resolutions intended to govern his conduct was found, among which were the following:—" Never spare person, property or reputation, if I can do good; necessary that I should die poor. Endeavour to feel kindly to every one; never indulge anger, envy, or jealousy towards any human being. Endeavour to act so as to advance the present comfort, the intellectual improvement, and the purity and moral good of my fellow-men."

REV. DR. PAYSON.

Never has the ruling passion been more strongly exemplified in the hour of death than in the case of this excellent minister. His love for preaching was as invincible as that of the miser for gold, who dies grasping his treasure. He directed a label to be attached to his breast when dead, with the admonition, " Remember the words which I spake unto you while I was yet present with you;" that they might be read by all who came to look at his corpse, and by which he, being dead, still spoke. The same words were, at the request of his people, engraved on the plate of the coffin, and read by thousands on the day of his interment.

REV. JOHN SHEPHERD.

OF one of the eminent men bearing this name, it is recorded that he was greatly distinguished for his success in the pulpit. When on his death-bed he said to some young ministers who were present, "The secret of my success is in these three things:—

"1. The studying of my sermons very frequently costs me tears.

"2. Before I preached a sermon to others I derived good from it myself.

"3. I have always gone into the pulpit as if I were immediately after to render an account to my Master."

All who knew that devoted man would have united in expressing his secret in three words—"In the closet."

REV. DR. BYLES.

DR. MATHER BYLES, of Boston, in a period of great political excitement, was asked why he did not preach *politics*. He replied, "I have thrown up four breast-works, behind which I have entrenched myself; neither of which can be forced. In the first place, I do not understand politics; in the second place, you all do, every one of you; in the third place, you have politics all the week—pray, let one day in seven be devoted to religion; in the fourth place, I am engaged in a work of infinitely greater importance. Give me any subject to preach on, of more consequence than the truths I bring to you. and I will preach on it the next Sabbath."

REV. DR. DWIGHT.

Every year's experience, in the ministry of this country, shows the vast importance of scriptural exposition. Let ministers be encouraged to discharge this duty, from the advantages derived from it, as stated by Dr. Dwight. He says, "I took up the practice of expounding the Scriptures, when I was a minister of a parish. I never was thanked so much for any other sermons as for those. For this reason, I think it is necessary to explain the plainer truths of the Scripture, as well as the more intricate."

REV. DR. NOTT.

The following extract, from the Norwich (Conn.) Courier, February, 1848, while it shows the deserved respect due to a venerable Christian minister, will be read with interest, "for a good while to come :"—

On Monday, of last week, the people of Franklin, Conn., to the number of nearly one hundred and fifty, made their annual visit to their venerable pastor, the Rev. Dr. Nott. They have, for a number of years, celebrated his birthday in a similar manner. The doctor having reached the very advanced age of ninety-four years on Sunday, the 23d of January, his parishioners fixed upon the Monday following for their anniversary occasion.

The day being propitious, at an early hour the old time-honoured mansion was filled with happy, warm-hearted friends, of every age, from the octogenarian to the child of a year, embracing whole families as well as solitary individuals, and including not only those who were upon the stage sixty-six years ago, but the contemporaries also to the sixth generation, all commingling in happy groups, each anxious to salute and honour their devoted pastor, whose birthday had brought them together.

For all this long period he has officiated statedly, without the aid of a colleague, and has been kept from the pulpit but *eleven Sundays*, through indisposition. We think a like case can hardly be found, in which so great an amount of ministerial labour has been performed, by the same individual, for so long a period.

A POPULAR MINISTER.

An eminent and deservedly popular preacher continued, after his introduction to the pastoral office, to live in the free and generous manner to which he had been previously accustomed, and in which his pecuniary circumstances allowed him to indulge. His table contained every thing to stimulate and to gratify the appetite. He had soon to complain of headache, giddiness, and other like symptoms. After suffering in mind and body for a length of time, he was led to the philosophical examination of his own case; and the conclusion to which he came was, that he must entirely change his mode of living, or pay a heavy penalty in the loss of health, or perhaps life itself. On this conviction he acted; and he says: "I soon lost all relish for wine or porter, or any thing of the kind; and I now regard them with dislike, if not with positive loathing; and for tea or coffee, I have no longer the least appetite. I now relish plain food with a greater zest than I ever did highly seasoned dishes, when my taste was perverted by unnatural stimulants, and yet I eat as great or a greater variety than I then did. I now enjoy that perfect health, buoyancy of spirits, and corporeal and mental energy to which I was ever before a stranger; and no inducement on earth can have sufficient influence to cause me to return to my former mode of living, for I regard it almost with horror."

REV. DR. PORTER.

It was one of the excellent resolutions of the late Dr. Porter, of Andover, that he would never *identify*, nor by his example, tempt others to *identify religion with melancholy;* "for," says he, "if I were to paint a Pharisee, I should give him a *sad* countenance; but if an angel or my Saviour, a *cheerful* one. The fact that painters, who are strangers to vital godliness, so generally, in representing Christ, give him the aspect of sadness, I will endeavour to make instructive to myself."

A MISSIONARY TO THE INDIANS.

Sir William Phips, a governor of New England, in the latter part of the seventeenth century, was a man of great Christian excellence. He maintained a missionary to the Indians, and that missionary was of the right kind. When the governor first proposed the mission to him, he replied, "I shall probably endanger my life by going to preach the gospel to the Frenchified Indians; but I know that it will be in the service of the Lord Jesus Christ, and therefore I will venture to go."

REV. DR. BEECHER.

The venerable Dr. Lyman Beecher says, " we need simple and effective preaching, clear, discriminating and doctrinal. Fine polished style, painted rainbows, are of no use. Give me the close preaching which reaches the conscience, and makes the sinner say—THAT MEANS ME." *You may as well throw a whole apothecary's shop at a patient,* to cure him of his sickness, as to preach without having your sermons close and practical in their application.

The following narrative was given by the worthy Doctor, at the social fire-side, after his return from Fort Wayne—a town north of Indiana—where he was called to attend a protracted meeting, and also to assist in the ordination of one of his sons.

Well, our I landed at St. Mary's about seven o'clock, Friday afternoon, and there were over sixty-two miles of hard road between me and Fort Wayne, and I knew if I didn't make a bold push I could not get there before Sunday.

A gentleman who knew me came to the boat, as we landed, and took me to his house. Understanding I was bound for Fort Wayne, he said,

"You will remain with me to-night—for of course you can't think of going on."

" Yes, sir, I must get over fifteen or twenty miles to-night."

" Oh! impossible! the road is horrid, and it will be very dark."

" Can't help that, I must go."

"Why, but, doctor, you don't know any thing about it. I would not risk my own neck on that road."

" Very likely you wouldn't—but I think I must try it."

"Well," said my friend, " if you are so bent upon it, and will rest till ten o'clock, the moon will rise then, and I will take my horse, and go with you, and pilot you through the first fifteen miles."

Well, I thanked him, and after supper went and lay down to rest, and at ten o'clock he called me, and the moon was up and our horses ready, and we took to our saddles—and well it was that he went with me, for sure enough I never could have found the horrible way—deep in woods—half the time midleg deep in mud, amid stumps and logs, and sometimes black sloughs, and places where we had to turn off the track and make a circuit of a mile through the woods on the right, and then come back and just strike the path, and diverge off for a mile on the left. We must have made as much as eight miles additional in these crossings. At last, between two and three o'clock at night, we came out of the worst of it, on to a tolerable Western road, and as there was a little village there, I thanked my guide, and told him I would not trouble him to go farther; so he stopped to lodge in the village. As for me, I felt lively and brisk, and the moon shone clear, and I thought I would just hold on the rest of the night. About day-break I got into the town of Wiltshire, where I slept two hours, took breakfast, and then went on. At three o'clock I came within eleven miles of Fort Wayne, and really, I can tell you, I did feel tired—almost worn out. I didn't know but I had gone beyond the work. I stopped an hour for dinner, and jogged on. Soon a young man overtook me, and company and talk revived me, and seemed to revive my horse too, for he pricked up, and the first I knew we came right into Fort Wayne. It was five o'clock, and I had travelled, as I reckon, with all the windings and turnings, seventy-two miles since ten o'clock the night before. I bathed all over in cold water, and then in spirits, went to bed at nine o'clock, and slept soundly and sweetly, and rose the next morning fresh and bright, without soreness or fatigue. Preached twice that day with great delight and freedom, visited all day Monday and part of Tuesday, and preached Tuesday, Wednesday, and Thursday, besides studying and writing.

How many ministers in the *prime of life* would be willing to make equal effort, rather than encroach on the Sabbath in travelling to their place of preaching? How many young *candidates* at the East, are willing to go West and do Dr. B.'s labour, for Dr. B.'s *salary*, which is simply *trusting in God*.

A DEVOTED PASTOR.

IN a time of revival in a certain church and congregation, the pastor urged one of his brethren, an able and skilful lawyer, to converse with a scoffing infidel of their acquaintance. "You know," said he, "that Mr. R. comprehends an able argument as well as any of us; and you and I have often seen how his eye will kindle under a compact and well-drawn argument. Now, can you not go over, with him, the proofs on which the Christian system rests?"

"I have done that already," said the lawyer, "and he heard me through patiently, and then pounced upon my arguments like a tiger on his prey. Then he wound up with bitter reproaches, which made me dread to encounter him again."

One of the elders of the same church had been also to visit the infidel, and met with a like reception, and he had made similar objections to his pastor to visiting the infidel again. But on a subsequent evening he was led, by the Spirit of God, to wrestle before the throne with most agonizing prayer in that infidel's behalf. At intervals he continued all night presenting his case before God, and praying for his conversion and salvation, as a man would pray for a friend's life on the eve of his execution.

Prayer was followed by corresponding effort, and not long after, in the crowded church, Mr. R. stood up, a changed man, to relate his Christian experience!

"I am as a brand," said he, "plucked out of the burning. The change in my views and feelings is astonishing to myself; and all brought about by the grace of God and that *unanswerable argument*.

"It was a cold morning in January, and I had just begun my labor at the anvil in my shop, when I looked out and saw Elder B—— approaching. As he drew near, I saw he was agitated—his look was full of earnestness. His eyes were bedimmed with tears. He took me by the hand. His breast heaved with emotion, and with indescribable tenderness, he said, 'Mr. R——, I am greatly concerned for your salvation!' and he burst into tears. He often essayed to speak, but not a word could he utter; and finding that he could say no more, he turned, went out of the shop, mounted his horse, and rode slowly away.

"'*Greatly concerned for my salvation*,' said I audibly, and I stood and forgot to bring my hammer down! '*Greatly concerned for my salvation.*' Here is a new argument, thought I, for religion, which I never heard before, and I know not how to answer it. Had the elder reasoned with me, I could have confounded him; but here is no threadbare argument for the truth of religion. Religion must move the soul with benevolent, holy, mighty impulses, or this man would not feel as he does. 'GREATLY CONCERNED FOR MY SALVATION'—it rung through my ears like a thunder-clap in a clear sky. 'Greatly concerned ought *I* to be for my own salvation,' said I; 'what shall I do to be saved?'"

"I went into my house. My poor pious wife, whom I had so often ridiculed for her religion, exclaimed, 'Why, Mr. R——, what is the matter with you?' 'Matter enough,' said I, filled with agony—'Matter enough. Elder B. has ridden two miles this cold morning to tell me he was greatly concerned for my salvation. What shall I do?' She advised me to go and see him. No sooner said than done. I mounted my horse and pursued after him. I found him alone in that same little room where he had spent the whole night in prayer for my poor soul. 'I am come,' said I to him, 'to tell you I am greatly concerned for my own salvation.'

"'Praised be God,' said the elder. 'It is a faithful saying, and worthy of all acceptation, that Jesus Christ came into the world to save sinners, even the very chief;' and he began at that same Scripture, and preached unto me Jesus. On that same floor we knelt, and together we prayed, and we did not separate that day till God spoke peace to my soul. And here permit me to say, if you would reach the heart of such a poor sinner as I, you must get your qualification where the good elder did his, in your closet and on your knees.'" That converted infidel long outlived the elder, and was the means of the conversion of many.

DR. COTTON MATHER.

Doctor Cotton Mather, who was born at Boston, in the seventeenth century, commenced a life of the most active beneficence when very young; and at the age of sixteen, adopted as a maxim, that a power and an opportunity to do good, not only give the right of doing it, but make it a positive duty. On this maxim he determined to act; and continued to do so during the remainder of his days. Accordingly he began in his father's family, by doing all the good in his power to his brothers and sisters, and to the servants. After he had attained to man's estate, he imposed on himself a rule, "never to enter any company where it was proper for him to speak, without endeavouring to be useful in it; dropping, as opportunities might offer, some instructive hint or admonition." By way of improving every moment of his time, he avoided paying and receiving unnecessary visits; and, to prevent intrusion, he caused to be written, in large characters, over the door of his study, these admonitory words, "Be short." Not a day passed without some contrivance, on his part, "To do good;" nor without his being able to say, at the close of it, that some part of his income had been distributed for pious purposes. This is an example highly worthy of imitation.

Many men have accomplished wonders by a constant regard to method. Every business should be done in its proper place, and at the proper time. Dr. C. Mather was remarkable in his conduct, and for what he did. Besides the discharge of pastoral duties in a large church, the care of a family, an extended correspondence, an attention to the interests of numerous public societies, he wrote not less than three hundred and eighty-two distinct pieces, large and small, for the press. That all his pursuits might have their proper places, he used to propose to himself a certain question in the morning of every day, as follows:—

Lord's-day morning.—What shall I do, as the pastor of a church, for the good of the flock under my charge?

Monday.—What shall I do for my family, and for the good of it?

Tuesday.—What shall I do for my relations abroad?

Wednesday.—What shall I do for the churches of the Lord, and the more general interests of religion in the world?

Thursday.—What good may I do in the several societies to which I belong?

Friday.—What special subjects of affliction and of compassion may I take under my particular care, and what shall I do for them?

Saturday.—What more have I to do for the interests of God, in my own heart and life?

REV. MR. BAILEY.

GOOD old Mr. Bailey, one of the first divines of New England, says that his earnest desire was to get up his soul to three things:—Patience under the calamities of life; impatience under the sinful infirmities of life; and earnest longings after a better life.

REV. MR. BACKUS.

THE following anecdote is sometimes related by aged Christians in New England:—An unpleasant rupture took place between the Rev. Mr. Alden, late of Bellingham, and a Mr. Mann, a member of his church. All attempts for a reconciliation were in vain. At length, a number of ministers were called together for consultation and advice; among whom were the Rev. Messrs. Stillman, of Boston; Manning, of Providence; and Backus, of Middleborough. The conference was holden at the house of the Rev. W. Williams, in Wrentham, and they spent the afternoon, and almost all the following night, in their pious efforts; but the parties were unyielding, and there was not the least prospect of a settlement. For a long time, the Rev. Mr. Backus, author of "The Church History of New England," and other excellent works, had sat with his head bowed down, and appeared to be sleeping. A little before break of day, Mr. B. rose up, saying, "Let us look to the Throne of Grace once more;" and then knelt down and prayed. The spirit and tone of his prayer were such as to make every one feel that the heart-searching God had come down among them. The result was, the contending parties began immediately to melt; and the rising sun saw the rupture healed and closed up for ever.

I have often heard that good man pray. The efficacy of his prayers did not consist in length, nor in their gaudy dress; but it seemed that he and his God loved each other, and that he was at home before the Throne of Grace. I heard the last sermon which he ever preached. It was delivered in his own dwelling-house, from 1 Peter ii. 9. I remember well the piety, pathos, and unusual earnestness, which characterized that discourse. His religion made him willing to die.

REV. DR MERCER.

FEW ministers were ever more remarkable for punctuality in fulfilling his engagements, than Dr. Mercer. He never found a difficulty in surmounting comparatively small impediments. For instance, if he came to a creek swollen to a dangerous torrent, he could strip his horse, drive him across the stream, and with his saddle and saddle-bags on his back, search out for himself a crossing-place on some log or fallen tree. This he once did on his way to a Saturday meeting. At the next monthly meeting, some of the brethren, in making their excuses for absence at the previous Conference, observed that they started for the meeting, but, upon finding the creek impassable, they returned. His reply was very characteristic· "If you had waited a little longer, I would have shown you the way."

On another occasion, while travelling, he was compelled, by high waters, to turn aside and spend the Sabbath with a pious family. He walked the room in great disquietude of spirit; and, on being asked the cause of his uneasiness, he replied, "Ah! I feel like a fish out of water; this is the very first time, since the commencement of my ministry, that I have been absent from public worship on the Sabbath, when my health would allow my attendance.

BISHOP ASBURY.

This worthy bishop, in 1798, on a journey to Charleston, S. C., passed a creek in the parish of St. ——, on the bank of which sat a slave, fishing, and humming a tune. He was called Punch, and was notorious for his vicious character. The pious bishop rode towards him, deliberately proceeded to alight, fastened the horse to a tree, and seated himself by the side of the slave.

As the slave seemed willing, the bishop commenced a minute and close conversation with him on religion. Punch began to feel; tears ran down his sable cheeks; he appeared alarmed at his danger as a sinner, and intently listened to the counsels of the singular stranger. After a long conversation, the bishop sung the hymn,

"Plunged in a gulf of dark despair;"

prayed with him, and pursued his journey. More than twenty years elapsed before he again saw or heard of Punch.

While on another visit to Charleston, he was called upon by an aged and Christian negro, who had travelled seventy miles on foot to visit him. It was the slave he had warned and prayed over, on the bank of the creek, who had ever since been journeying on the way to heaven. When the bishop left him, on the bank of the stream, he immediately took up his fishing-tackle, and hastened home in the deepest agitation, pondering over the words of the venerable man. After some days of anguish and prayer, he found peace in believing, and became a new man. The change was too manifest not to be discovered by his fellow-servants—it was the topic of his conversation with them incessantly. In his simple way, he pointed them to the Lamb of God, which taketh away the sins of the world, and many of them became thoroughly penitent for their sins. Throngs of the neglected Africans resorted to his humble cabin, to receive his exhortations and prayers. A perverse overseer, who had charge of the plantation, perceiving the increasing interest of the slaves for their souls, and their constant attendance in the evenings, at Punch's cabin, determined to put a stop to the spreading leaven. But, on coming one night to break up a meeting, he was struck under conviction, fell down under a tree near by, and began to cry for mercy. The negroes gathered around him, and prayed with him till God in his mercy pardoned and comforted him. The overseer now became a co-worker with Punch among them: he joined the Methodist church, and in time became an exhorter, and finally a preacher! Punch had now full liberty to do good among his associates. He exhorted, prayed, and led them on, as a shepherd his flock, and extended his usefulness around the whole neighbourhood. After many years, he was removed, by the decease of his master and the distribution of the estate, to the parish of A., where he continued to labour for the souls of his fellow-bondmen with still greater success. Scores, and even hundreds, were converted through his instrumentality; and he sustained a kind of pastoral charge over them for years.

INTERCOURSE OF THE CLERGY WITH EACH OTHER.

REV. DR. RODGERS.

The Rev. Mr. Forrest, a minister of the Associate Reformed Church, in speaking of the late Dr. John Rodgers, of New York, says:—

A few years ago, I related to Dr. Rodgers an anecdote of a Scottish clergyman, who, while preaching from Hebrews xi. 32, "And what shall I more say? for the time would fail me to tell of Gideon," &c., observed, " My brethren, here are some very rough-spun saints; really, if the Spirit of God had not decided this matter, it would have been hard work to have admitted them among the number. But, my brethren, this teaches us that if we get to heaven, we shall see many folks there that we did not expect.' Dr. Rodgers observed, yes, my friend, I expect to see in heaven, among other wonders, three very great ones: some there whom I did not expect to have seen there; others not there, whom I had great expectations of seeing there; but the greatest wonder of all, will be to see myself there, the chief of sinners, pardoned and sanctified by the grace of God.

Dr. Rodgers, beautifully exemplified "the meekness and gentleness of Christ, "and so greatly added to his usefulness. A young clergyman who had paid a short visit to the city, and who had enjoyed two or three pleasant interviews with the Dr., a few years before his death, at the close of the last interview, rose and offered him his hand for the purpose of bidding him farewell. The Doctor took it, and squeezing it affectionately, with a very few simple words, expressive of pious hope, and tender benediction, dismissed him. The clergyman on retiring, inquired, whether what he had witnessed was the

Doctor's common manner of taking leave of his friends? adding that he had seldom seen anything so much like the primitive style of an apostle before. There have been better days of the church, when such things were not rare. Would to God they were less so now.

Few men ever determined more fully to live while he lived, and to persevere in the discharge of all the duties of life than Dr. Rodgers. He had long maintained a correspondence with several eminent ministers of Great Britain, when the last of them, Dr. Erskine, of Edinburgh, died. Mr. Rodgers at that time was not less than seventy-six, but he said he believed he must open a correspondence with Dr. Balfour of Glasgow, as he did not wish to be without a friend on that side of the Atlantic, with whom he could occasionaily exchange letters. Dr. Miller very wisely remarks that the premature dotage of many distinguished men has arisen from their ceasing in advanced life, to exert their faculties, under the impression that they were too old to engage in any new enterprise.

THOUGHTLESS MINISTERS.

Few things can be more important than that Christian Ministers should be careful of the manner in which they speak of each other. The influence for good or for evil, on themselves and on all who hear them is very great. A respectable pastor, some time since, was speaking of a brother in the same communion, and concluded his remarks with the exclamation, "Ah, he is a snake in the grass!" A venerable minister at the same time remarked of another, " He is as full of venom as a ser pent." Can any of our readers tell the results of this kind of remark on young people standing by? Would it not have been far better for the brother to have gone to each offender, and in "the meekness and gentleness of Christ" to have pointed out his fault, and thus to have "gained his brother?"

REV. DR. STANFORD

In one of the lectures addressed to his students, on the composition of sermons, this excellent man says:—"I cannot deny myself the pleasure of stating, that many years ago, I met with a plain, yet good old minister, who, in conversation with me, on the subject of the composition of a sermon, very pleasantly said, "I know of no better rule than the proportions observable in the structure of the human body. Let your introduction be short, like the head of the man, round, and full of expression. Make up the body of your sermon of the solids of divine truth; but be sure that Christ be the heart, and the Spirit of God like the lungs, to produce respiration. The legs to run after every class of your hearers; and a pair of arms tenderly to embrace them. This may appear to you a little fanciful, but I must confess, however singular the description, yet to my mind, it seemed worthy of being remembered."

REV. DR. HARRIS.

Nothing seems more awful than preaching what we do not ourselves fully believe; and few things can be more poignant than the reflection of having in this way preached error. A

Universalist minister once spent a Sabbath with Dr. Harris of Dunbarton. The conversation between them concluded as follows:—The doctor fastened his eye on the young man, saying, "Do you know for certainty that your doctrine is true?" "No, sir," the youth replied, "I don't pretend to a certain knowledge of the truth of it." The doctor added, "Then, sir, don't ever preach it again till you know it is true." A year or two after this conversation the young minister renounced his Universalism, and indulged a hope that he had experienced a change of heart.

A MINISTER IN NEW HAMPSHIRE.

A ministers' meeting was held, a few years since, in New Hampshire, at which was present an excellent clergyman, since removed to heaven. It was just after a time of general revival throughout the country, and his brethren generally were telling what *they* had done, how many persons had been converted under *their* preaching, &c. Our excellent friend, who was eminent for his humble piety, and who was the successor of an aged and long successful minister of Christ, sat and listened for some time to their conversation, till at length they turned to him and inquired the secret of the revival in his church. After some hesitation he arose, and, with a manner and tone which made a great impression, said, "My predecessor was a very godly man, and, in answer to his prayers, I trust about one hundred and thirty souls have been converted to God!" He then sat down. Every one *felt* the reproof, and the effect on those who had been telling what *I* had done, can be better imagined than described.

REV. GIDEON HAWLEY.

Dr. Dwight's "Travels" contain a deeply interesting account of the Rev. G. Hawley, a missionary to the Indians at Massapee, and who remained their pastor for fifty-six years, dying in 1807, in his eighty-first year.

At the time of the visit paid to him by Dr. Dwight, he had a favourite son, possessed of superior talents and learning, of distinguished piety and high reputation. He had lately come from his tutorship at Cambridge, and had just been ordained to the ministry. This lovely young man now lay in a dying state; for which, however, he was eminently prepared, looking forward to scenes suited to the elevated taste of an enlightened Christian, with the utmost serenity and confidence.

The venerable father was fully alive to the circumstances in which he was placed. He saw the setting of his fond luminous hopes in the night of the grave; and the lustre which played and trembled over this melancholy scene from the mind of his son, brilliant with hopes of immortal glory, exhibited, in their union and their alternations, a picture equally beautiful, solemn, and sublime. Into all these subjects, the father entered familiarly, and appeared equally willing to go with his son, or to stay behind. He felt deeply, but with a serene submission. He found high and sufficient consolation in the character of Him from whom the stroke came. He showed, in such a manner as to put suspicion out of countenance, the affection of a father; and Christian emotions, which a worldling or an infidel, if they could understand them, would deeply envy.

Nor was this manifestation of affection and piety, on the part of this venerable minister, without a happy effect. A young gentleman, who accompanied Dr. Dwight on this visit, who was educated in the gay world, and, as he himself declared, sufficiently addicted to its enjoyments, was entirely overcome by the scenes of this interview. After they had left the house, he burst into a flood of tears, which he had with great difficulty suppressed till that time, and was unable to utter a word till they reached the inn. In broken accents he then declared, that he had never been so deeply affected in his life; that although he had not before been accustomed to think lightly of Christianity, he had now acquired new ideas of its excellence, and that, should he ever lose them again, he should consider himself guilty as well as unhappy. Yet the whole conversation had been rather cheerful, and every thing which it involved, of a melancholy nature, had been gilded by the serenity of hope.

A MINISTER.

A CLERGYMAN relates, that he was told by another Christian minister, that he one day gave to a poor man in his congregation a tract; and, seeing him afterwards, asked him what he thought of it. "Oh, massa!" said he, "it do me soul good. I never knew before why da call 'em tracks; but when I read that little book, it track me dis way, and it track me dat way; it track me all day, and it track me all night: when I go out in de barn, it track me dare; when I go out in de woods, it track me dare; it track me ebery where I go; then I know why da call 'em tracks." This poor man became a sincere and devoted Christian.

REV. JOSEPH CRAIG.

Amongst the Baptist pioneers to Kentucky, was the eccentric Joseph Craig. His brothers, Lewis and Elijah, were distinguished Baptist preachers in Virginia, and afterwards in the wilds of Kentucky. Joe, as he was familiarly called, obtained a license to preach also; for, though eccentric, and by no means gifted as an expounder of Scripture, he could exhort feelingly, and his moral character was good. His brothers were so dissatisfied with his pulpit efforts, after twenty years' experience, that, on a church-meeting day, Lewis gravely proposed to recall his license; and gave as a reason, that he never heard of but a single instance of the preaching of Joe profiting any one, and that was an old negro woman, who, in relating her experience, mentioned his rambling exhortation as the means of her conversion. By this time, Joe was on his feet, the tears running down his cheeks, and, clapping his hands repeatedly, he exclaimed, "Bless the Lord—thank God for that! I will preach twenty years more, to be the instrument of converting another poor African." Of course Joe retained his license.

A UNIVERSALIST PREACHER.

Dr. Baird has well observed, in his excellent volume on "Religion in America," that it is a remarkable fact, established by the testimony of Universalists, on becoming converted to the Truth, that few can, however desirous, ever bring themselves to believe the doctrine of universal salvation. Most of them are like the New England farmer, who, at the close of a Universalist service, thanked the preacher for his sermon, saying that he vastly liked his doctrine, and would give him five dollars if he would only prove it to be true.

REV. DR. LIVINGSTON.

The eminent, pious, and learned theologian, Dr. Livingston, related to me, says Dr. Alexander, not many years before his decease, a pleasing anecdote, which I communicate to the public more willingly, because I do not know that he has left any record of it behind him. While a student at the University of Utrecht, a number of pious persons, from the town and among the students, were accustomed to meet for free conversation on experimental religion, and for prayer and praise, in a social capacity. On one of these occasions, when the similarity of the exercises of the pious, in all countries and ages, was the subject of conversation, it was remarked by one of the company, that there was then present a representative from each of the four quarters of the world. These were, Dr. Livingston, from America; a young man, from the Cape of Good Hope, in Africa; another student, from one of the Dutch possessions in the East Indies, and many natives of Europe, of course. It was therefore proposed, that, at the next meeting, the three young gentlemen first referred to, together with an eminently pious young nobleman of Holland, should each give a particular narrative of the rise and progress of the work of grace in his soul. The proposal was universally acceptable; and accordingly, a narrative was heard from a native of each of the four quarters of the globe; of their views and feelings, of their trials and temptations, &c. The result was highly gratifying to all present; and I think Dr. Livingston said, that it was generally admitted by those present, that they had never before witnessed so interesting a scene.

TWO CLERGYMEN.

A MINISTER was once speaking to a brother clergyman, of his gratitude for a merciful deliverance he had just experienced.

"As I was riding here to-day," said he, "my horse stumbled, and came very near throwing me from a bridge, where the fall would have killed me; but I escaped unhurt."

"I can tell you something more than that," said the other; "as I rode here to-day, my horse did not stumble at all."

We are too apt to forget common mercies.

A BAPTIST CLERGYMAN.

THE following incident, says the editor of the Christian Secretary, was related to us by a gentleman who was present; and, as we happen to be acquainted with the persons alluded to, we take the liberty to publish it. Several years since, a young man who had just entered the ministry as a Baptist preacher, took passage in the stage from this city for Albany. Among the passengers was the then pastor of the Universalist society in this city. In the course of the day, a Congregational clergyman entered the stage. The parties were all apparently strangers to each other. The conversation turned upon religious subjects, when the Universalist gave the company to understand that he was a minister of the gospel, by relating the following circumstance; without, however, stating the particular denomination to which he belonged.

"I preached, last Sabbath," said he, "from these words: 'Now, when they saw the boldness of Peter and John, and perceived that they were unlearned and ignorant men, they took knowledge of them that they had been with Jesus.' The reason of my preaching from this text," continued he, "was as follows:—My custom is, to write one sermon at least every week, and I went into my study for the purpose of writing one; but, after looking over the Bible, from Genesis to Revelation, I was unable to find a text to suit me. I then threw myself upon the bed, and, in my sleep, dreamed of reading the passage in Acts, just quoted. My mind then ran on, in a train of reflections upon the text, which, on awaking, I wrote down, as near as I could possibly recollect, and, on reading it over, I found it to be as good a sermon as I had ever written."

The preacher here paused, apparently for the purpose of seeing what effect his remarkable story had produced upon the minds of the company; when the young Baptist minister very solemnly replied, "I fear, Mr. R., it will be found, in the day of judgment, that your sermons have been nothing but *dreams*, after all." On hearing his name mentioned, Mr. R. looked somewhat confused, and manifested no disposition to discourse upon religious subjects the rest of the journey.

REV. DR. EMMONS.

It was the advice of the late Rev. Dr. Emmons, to young ministers: "Be short, in all religious exercises. Better leave the people longing than loathing. No conversions after the hour is out."

This eminent man once said to a candidate for settlement: "You have struck twelve first; fools will complain of you if you do not strike thirteen next." How many young ministers unwisely make an effort to put themselves off for more than they are worth, from a foolish desire to be popular! Such a beginning is likely to have a bad ending; for, as the same discriminating man remarked on another occasion, "Every thing that captivates will at length disgust; therefore, popularity cannot live."

A young minister having preached for the Doctor, one day, was anxious to get a word of applause for his labour of love. The grave Doctor, however, did not introduce the subject, and the young brother was obliged to bait the hook for him.

"I hope, sir, I did not weary your people by the *length* of my sermon, to-day?"

"No, sir, not at all; nor by the *depth* either."

The following sketch was furnished to the Newark Sentinel, by one who evidently understood his subject:—

It was once my good fortune to see the great Dr. Emmons, the father of Emmonite theology, and the man who boasted that he once "dandled Timothy Dwight on his knee." When I saw him, he was ninety-three, and he wore the old-fashioned cocked hat and small clothes, with huge knee-buckles. He had a broad, intellectual countenance, with long white hair falling over his shoulders. The boys followed him in the streets, to stare at him; and when he ascended the platform, in the Chatham Street Chapel, during the anniversaries, the whole body of clergy rose up to do him reverence. Very few of them had ever seen him before, as he seldom left the little town of Franklin, in Massachusetts, where he preached for more than fifty years! At the age of eighty, he gave up preaching, as he said, "before he fell into his dotage;" and, during the last fifteen years of his life, he took part in no public exercises. The late Dr. Breckenridge was in the same pulpit with him, during that visit to New York, and called on him to pray. This he declined; he even declined pronouncing the benediction. He said "he had quit work for ever here." But while he was at work, no one laboured harder. He studied twelve or fourteen hours a day, and seldom quitted his study from morning till night. Once his hired man came into his study to ask his assistance in gathering some hay, telling him that it would soon spoil. "Let it spoil," the old doctor replied; "I cannot leave *my* work to do *yours*."

At another time, an intemperate grandson of one of Dr. Emmons's friends accosted him in the presence of several bystanders, and tried to make them believe that he was familiarly acquainted with the doctor. But he was not recognised. "What!" said he, "do you not know me, doctor? I have held the stirrup for you to mount your horse, at my grandfather's, many a time." "You look as if you had never been in so good business since," replied the doctor, looking at his red face very archly. A pompous young preacher once asked him how he liked his sermon. The doctor, then ninety years old, rose from his chair, protruded his cheeks, inflated his chest, raised his eyebrows, and after a *significant puff*, sat down without saying a word. To another young man, he said, "Your sermon was too much like Seekonk Plain, long and level." He used to say of Dr. Dwight, "When I was at Yale, I used to take him up in my arms. He was a pretty boy." Dr. Emmons was a Connecticut man, and died in Massachusetts, in 1840. He was a man of most powerful intellect, and eminent, but full of the "heresies of New England divinity." Perhaps he was the clearest writer on metaphysical subjects our country has ever produced.

REV. DR. DWIGHT.

A YOUNG clergyman once called upon Dr. Dwight, and inquired respecting the best method of treating a very difficult and abstruse point in mental philosophy, upon which he was preparing a sermon. "I cannot give you any information upon the subject," the doctor replied · "I am not familiar with such topics. I leave them for young men."

REV. DR. SCUDDER.

A FOREIGN correspondent of the Congregational Journal relates the following incident of an interview between two Christian missionaries in Asia:—

The late Rev. E. Daniel, English Baptist Missionary at Colombo, was remarkable for his zeal and piety, but very plain and homely in his appearance. Dr. Scudder once fell in with him, and not imagining that he was a minister of the gospel, instantly began to talk with him about the salvation of his soul, which was taken by Mr. D. with great satisfaction and thankfulness. A gentleman hearing of it, remarked, "If Dr. S. had been one minute later, Mr. Daniel would have begun with him."

REV. THOMAS BROWN.

WHILE this gentleman was pastor of the Baptist church at Scotch Plains, New Jersey, a stranger, of respectable appearance, was announced at the parsonage door. Mr. B. went, and with his characteristic blandness, invited the stranger in; and, on learning that he was a minister of his own denomination, assured him of a welcome to the well-known hospitality of the old stone mansion. It was Saturday afternoon; and as the stranger had no engagement for the morrow, Mr. B. requested him to make himself at home for the Lord's-day. The invitation was readily and gratefully accepted; and matters being thus far settled, the pastor sat down to have a brotherly colloquy with his stranger guest. Mr. B. was remarkably communicative, where propriety allowed it, and he delighted to have his friends so too. He never wished to be "all tongue and no ear." But he found his visitor to be remarkably taciturn. He broached a number of different topics, doctrinal, ethical, statistical, domestic, and foreign. But, on each and all, the guest was provokingly uninformed and silent. He could not, or he would not, be brought out. He was all ear, and no tongue. The conclusion finally was, that he might be a very *good* brother, but he did not *know* much. That was certain; and so he was pretty much left to his own reflections. Thus, Mr. B. judged from appearances.

The arrangements for the morrow's services were now quietly settled in the pastor's own mind. It would not do for the stranger to preach in the morning, any how. The congregation was usually large and very intelligent—and strangers might be there. He might occupy the pulpit in the afternoon, for the second service, after the half-hour's intermission. All this was settled; and in due time the arrangements were kindly revealed to the stranger, who modestly consented to help his brother as best he could, if his help was desired.

The next morning came; and Mr. B. preached, no doubt, as usual, to the great satisfaction of his people. He had to preach again at a station about four miles distant, at five o'clock, which he intended to do; and the stranger was announced for the pulpit in the afternoon, after the usual intermission. There he was, accordingly; and the pastor behind him, with no little anxiety respecting the issue. The man prayed. Mr. B. was struck,—was somehow affected. Certainly, thought he, the man can *pray*, if he cannot *preach*. And he *did* preach. The most precious truths of the gospel were brought out with a rich unction, and clothed with language clear and polished, and in a manner which chained the attention and told on the hearts of the people. The pastor was astonished, confounded, mortified, delighted. He himself, he thought, could do nothing like it. The stranger was now earnestly pressed to preach the five o'clock sermon also, to which he modestly consented. "And then," said B., with his loud, hearty laugh of irrepressible delight, " he went far ahead of his first sermon! I never was more astonished in all my life."

He was taught not to "*judge according to the outward appearance.*"

REV. DR. TAYLOR

A BEAUTIFUL anecdote is told, illustrative of the Christian spirit of the Rev. Dr. Nathaniel W. Taylor. He had long been engaged in a very sharp controversy with Dr. Tyler, of East Windsor, and the late excellent Dr. Nettleton. He was one day told that Dr. Nettleton was very ill, and likely to die. He set off immediately for Dr. Tyler's house, went directly up to the room of Dr. N., without announcing his name, and as soon as he entered the sick-room, he threw his arms about the neck of his dying brother, and wept for a long time without saying a word. A most admirable exemplification of Christian feeling!

REV. LEMUEL HAYNES.

It is related in the biography of Rev. Lemuel Haynes, the coloured preacher, that some of his students having been slandered for their religious activity and zeal, went to him with their complaints, expecting his sympathy and protection. After a pause, Mr. Haynes observed, "I knew all this before." "Why, then," said one, "did you not inform us?" "Because," said he, "it was not worth communicating; and I now tell you plainly, once for all, my young friends, it is best to let the devil carry his own mail, and bear his own expenses."

There is much wisdom in this remark, and it is capable of a variety of applications. When assaults are made upon any one, in points where he is sustained by a consciousness of right, in a vast majority of cases silence is the most effective defence. For, to formally refute slander, he must first extend the publication of it; that is, must sustain the expense of carrying the devil's mail, and convey to many the information which they would not otherwise have had, that he has been subjected to imputations of wrong. And as "a lie will travel from Maine to Georgia, while truth is putting on its boots," there is little encouragement to run down a falsehood by an earnest refutation. And yet, with rare exceptions, it is not needful; a little faith and patience will serve one quite as well as laboured vindications. Habitual integrity is the best defence. Let a foul breath be breathed upon a diamond, and it will soon regain its wonted lustre.

Mr. Haynes once practised on this principle as follows:— An unprincipled man overtook him in the road, and said, "Mr. Haynes, have you heard the scandalous reports that are abroad about you?" He calmly replied, "I have heard nothing." The man proceeded, in profane and abusive language, to give the details, and allege that they were true; and that they would ruin his character. Mr. Haynes walked on in silence till he reached his own house, when he turned to the slanderer and said, "Well, Mr. ——, you see what disgrace my conduct has brought upon me, according to your own account. I want you to take warning from me, to forsake your evil course, and save your character from disgrace." They parted. But the next day, the man came with an humble acknowledgment, asking forgiveness. Thus did assaults give new lustre to his character.

> "Assailed by scandal and the tongue of strife,
> His only answer was a blameless life;
> And he that forged, and he that threw the dart,
> Had each a brother's interest in his heart."

This excellent man, happening one day to pass by the open door of a room where his daughters and some young friends were assembled, thought, from what he overheard, that they were were making too free with the character of their neighbours; and after their visitors had departed, he gave his children a lecture on the sinfulness of scandal. They answered, "But, father, what shall we talk about? We must talk of something!" "If you can do nothing else," replied he, " get a pumpkin and roll it about; that will at least be innocent diversion."

A short time afterwards, an association of ministers met at his house, and during the evening some discussions, on points of doctrine, were earnest, and their voices were so loud as to indicate the danger of losing the Christian temper; when his eldest daughter, overhearing them, procured a pumpkin, and entering the room, gave it to her father, and said, "There, father, roll it about, roll it about." Mr. Haynes was obliged to explain to his brethren; and good humour was instantly restored.

The following characteristic anecdote of this shrewd defender of the truth, is related by a correspondent of the New York Observer:—

Mr. Haynes was employed about two years, as a stated supply to the Congregational church in Manchester. In this town was a Universalist society, and, as in most other cases, its adherents were fond of discussing their sentiments with other denominations. One of these took frequent occasion to dispute with Mr. Haynes, and though he generally came off second best, he seemed determined to renew the controversy on every convenient occasion.

At the close of one of these interviews, apparently under the full conviction of his own inferiority, he said, "Mr. Haynes, you are a learned man, and I cannot argue with you; but I expect one of our ministers here before long, and I intend to bring him to see you; he will be able to defend our doctrine." Mr. Haynes replied in his usual good-natured way, "Oh, well, bring him along; I shall be pleased to talk with him."

Some weeks afterwards, the Universalist minister arrived; and the parishioner embraced the first leisure hour to take him up to the village to see Mr. Haynes. On their way, they were met by one of the brethren of their own faith, who, after learning whither they were bound, advised them to turn back; "for," said he, "*he* is an *old fox*, and you can't get to the windward of him." They, however, persisted in their purpose, and soon arrived at the parsonage.

Mr. Haynes was called from his study to receive the visitors, without knowing or receiving the least intimation who they were. As he entered the room, the parishioner, after exchanging compliments, said, "Mr. Haynes, this is Mr. X———, my minister, whom I promised to bring to see you." "How d' do, how d' do?" said Mr. Haynes, taking the minister familiarly by the hand. "Well, you are the man, then, who preaches that men may swear, and lie, and get drunk, and commit adultery, and all other abominations, and yet go to heaven, after all; ain't you?" "No, no," said the Universalist minister; "I don't preach any such thing." "Well," said Father Haynes, "*you believe so;* don't you?"

This was a blow that completely annihilated all desire for theological discussion, and well nigh took away the power of utterance from both minister and layman. After a few remarks on the state of the weather, and the pleasant situation of the village, the minister said to his attendant, "Is it not time for us to be going?" and both withdrew, apparently satisfied to dispense with all further intercourse.

REV. DR. NETTLETON.

Dr. N. had great skill in the management of difficulties which connected themselves with his engagements. He was led to visit a town where the Congregational church was nearly extinct, through the prevalence of contention. The meeting-house was in the south-east part of the town. In the centre was a large brick school-house, around which were several wealthy families, and a few professors of religion. There was a meeting-house connected with another denomination, in the north-west corner. The revival commenced in the centre. Erroneous views of religion prevailed. Soon several ministers appeared in his meetings, seeming to claim the field as their own. They made appointments for themselves. The doctor kept the minds of the people to the great subject. He publicly told the ministers that he was thankful for help, and would return their kindness, and give them as many sermons as they preached for him. This they did not expect. He made no reference to them in his preaching. There was a large public-house, directly opposite their meeting-house, occupied by an excellent family. This was opened to him, and he preached there regularly for many weeks. The consequence was, that he occupied the whole ground. More than a hundred persons were brought into the church he supplied, which has enjoyed a stated ministry ever since.

The wisdom displayed by this excellent Revivalist, in the midst of persecution, was very great. He was once labouring in a village in Connecticut, where were strong indications of the beginning of a good state of things. Christians were engaged in powerful labour, and a spirit of violent opposition manifested itself among the ungodly. The pastor of the church was called to a distant part of the parish to officiate at a wedding, and Dr. N. accompanied him. They rode together, and when they arrived at the house, the pastor left his surtout-coat hanging over the back of his chaise. Nothing particular occurred during the ceremony, but when they were preparing to return home, it was discovered that the harness was cut in several places. This, after a time, was repaired, and they arrived at the pastor's house without accident. When he took out his horse to put him into the stable, he found that the hair from the mane and tail of the animal had been shaved closely off. He brought his surtout into the study, which was then seen to have been torn from top to bottom into ribands. The good pastor was greatly excited, and declared that he would find out the perpetrators of the outrage, and prosecute them to the utmost extremity of the law. When he had time to cool, Dr. Nettleton said to him, "Brother, try on the surtout; it may not be injured so much as you suppose." He did so, and so grotesque was his appearance, that both burst into a hearty laugh. Dr. N. saw that the time was now come to make an impression upon him; and said, "Brother ——, it is evident that the Spirit of God is at work with this people, and this is a device of the adversary of souls to turn off their attention from the subject of religion. You may, I doubt not, find out the authors of this mischief, and punish them; but, in doing it, you will raise a hubbub—there will be an end of the revival, and souls will be lost for ever. Now, my advice to you is this: keep your horse in the stable; feed him yourself; do not take him out, even to water. Lay by your surtout in the bottom of your trunk, and do not mention these circumstances, even to your wife. The wrong-doers will not dare to mention their mischief; and if we are silent, it will not be known, and they will lose their labour. The parish will continue in quietness, and we shall go on in our work without molestation. We shall thus defeat the adversary of souls, and gain a blessed victory for the Redeemer." The pastor took his advice; no one ever heard of the occurrence from that time; and God blessed the church with a glorious outpouring of his Spirit. Such was the good doctor's method of dealing with persecutors.

Dr. Nettleton was most sensitively careful to sustain the influence of his brethren. He would not, when he knew there was an evident deficiency, do any thing that might tend, in the least degree, to disparage them in the estimation of their people. There was one instance in which he showed his delicacy of feeling and address in a most Christian manner. A clergyman who lived not far from the place where Dr. N. resided, bore the reputation of an indolent and inefficient pastor, and had in consequence caused considerable uneasiness amongst his people. Some of the more faithful part of the church, who deplored the low state of religion and growing laxity of morals among the youth of the congregation, went to Dr. N. and desired him to come and preach to them. To this he would by no means consent, without an express invitation from the pastor, and of that he had little hope. But there happened to be a desert spot on the borders of the town, where religious meetings were seldom held, and where the influence of the pastor did not particularly extend. When he was made acquainted with the fact, he said that he had no objection to go there and hold a few evening meetings with them. He went, and, without exciting observation, held several religious meetings. In a short time, a number of the youth were under deep conviction for sin. As soon as he perceived the joyful appearance, he requested all who were under serious impressions to meet with him the next day, informing them that he had something of an important nature, which he wished to communicate. When they had all met, he advised the young ladies to go that same evening to their pastor, and ask his counsel respecting the present state of their minds; and the young men he advised to go the evening following, for the same purpose. They all did as he had prudently directed them; and the effect was so powerfully electric, that the slothful pastor rose up at once, went to work with all his might, preached and laboured with assiduous energy, and was the favoured agent in reaping a glorious harvest of souls. As soon as the pastor got thus fairly to work, Dr. N. retired. The pastor ever remained a faithful and useful man.

AGED CLERGYMEN.

A YOUNG "divine" said to an old preacher:—"How does it happen that you write but one sermon a week? I preach three new sermons every Sabbath. I could write a sermon every day in the week, and make nothing of it."

"No doubt; precisely *nothing*," was the reply: "but that is exactly what I wish to avoid. I labour to make *something* of my sermons."

The following advice was once given from an aged minister to a young one:—

With respect to your conduct in the house of worship, I have a word or two to say to you. If you happen to make a blunder in prayer or preaching, don't stop to rectify it, but go boldly on; for, 'tis ten to one, if a single person in the whole church be listening to a word you say: but, if you stop and go back to the word, and begin to hum and haw, the hearers will immediately prick up their ears, and whisper to one another, "Ah! the minister's out, the minister's out;" and thus you'll be exposed to ridicule.

TWO CLERGYMEN.

While we must lament the existence of differences of opinion tending to destroy intercourse and fellowship among brethren, it becomes us to respect the rights of conscience, wherever they exist. There is a lesson conveyed in the following fact, although it is adapted to create a smile:—

An Episcopal clergyman resided in the immediate neighbourhood of a reverend pastor of a Baptist church. Their intercourse was kind, and they occasionally occupied each other's desk. The Baptist asked his Episcopal brother to address his people, one Lord's-day morning, to which he acceded. As they sat at dinner, after the sermon, the Baptist minister was evidently unhappy; and the Episcopalian at length elicited the fact, that this Sabbath was the time when the Baptists celebrated the Lord's Supper, and that his brother was grieving that he could not invite him to commune with them. "Oh," said his visitor, "don't let that distress you; perhaps you are not aware that, being an Episcopalian, I do not consider you ordained, and therefore could not receive the Lord's Supper at your hands." Each was amused, and each respected the conscience of his friend.

REV. DR. FURMAN.

The late Rev. Dr. Furman, of Charleston, S. C., was once present in a small company of brethren who had assembled to dine with a common friend, when the usual style by which they addressed each other was the affectionate appellation of "brother." Those present were very exact in using this mode of address. While their conversation was progressing, and they were freely "brothering" each other, there came in an aged coloured woman, well known for her piety and good character. The brethren present saluted her, one in this manner and another in that; as, "Well, old woman;" "How do, Clarinda?" and so on. When she came to Dr. F., he leaned forward, extended to her his hand, and said, "How do you do, sister Clarinda?" He probably designed this as a gentle reproof to those present, who did not seem to recognize the true equality in which all stand who belong to the family of Christ.

REV. DR. POND.

There is something so truly noble in the following handsome apology, from the pen of the Rev. Dr. Pond, that we cannot forbear to record it on our pages. Would that all of us were found to breathe the same spirit!

"I am happy in the opportunity thus afforded me, of paying what I conceive to be a merited tribute to the high missionary character of Dr. Judson. It will be recollected by many who read this article, that soon after his change of sentiments, and the publication of his sermon on the subject of baptism, I published a reply to the sermon; in the introduction to which, some things were said, impeaching the motives of Dr. J., and implicating to some extent his Christian character. In the statements there made, I had the concurrence of the then members of the American Board of Commissioners for Foreign Missions, and of most of the Congregational ministers and Christians of that day. But, in view of the course since pursued by Dr. J., his labours and sufferings, his zeal, his constancy, his well-directed and successful efforts in the best of causes, and especially after the explanations he has made of some things which, at the time of his change, were regarded by many as mysterious, I think no one *can question the purity of his motives,* or *the distinguished excellence and devotedness of his Christian character.* From the later editions of my work on Baptism, I have expunged every thing which could be interpreted as disreputable to Dr. J. I have long followed him, in what I have known of his studies and labours, with deep interest, and regard him as entitled to stand among *the foremost* of living missionaries."

REV. DRS. COOPER AND CHAUNCEY.

Dr. Cooper, who was a man of accomplished manners, and fond of society, was able, by the aid of his fine talents, to dispense with some of the severe study that others engaged in. This, however, did not escape the envy and malice of the world; and it was said, with a kind of petulant and absurd exaggeration, that he used to walk to the South End on Saturday, and, if he saw a man riding into town in a black coat, would stop and ask him to preach the next day.

Dr. Chauncey was a close student, very absent and irritable. On these traits in the character of the clergyman, a servant of Dr. Chauncey laid a scheme to obtain a particular object from his master. Scipio went into his master's study, one morning, to receive some directions, which the doctor having given, resumed his writing; but the servant still remained. The master, looking up a few minutes afterward, and supposing he had just come in, said, "Scipio, what do you want?" "I want a new coat, massa." "Well, go to Mrs. C., and tell her to give you one of my old coats;" and was again absorbed in study. The servant remained fixed. After a while, the doctor, turning his eyes that way, saw him again, as if for the first time, and said, "What do you want, Scipio?" "I want a new coat, massa." "Well, go to my wife, and ask her to give you one of my old coats;" and fell to writing once more. Scipio remained in the same posture. After a few minutes, the doctor looked toward him and repeated the former question, "Scipio, what do you want?" "I want a new coat, massa." It now flashed over the doctor's mind, that there was something of repetition in this dialogue. "Why, have I not told you before to ask Mrs. Chauncey to give you a coat? Get away." "Yes, massa; but I no want a black coat." "Not want a black coat! And why not?" "Why, massa, I 'fraid to tell you; but I don't want a black coat." "What's the reason you don't want a black coat? Tell me, directly." "Oh, massa! I don't want a black coat; but I 'fraid to tell the reason, you so passionate." "You rascal, will you tell me the reason?" "Oh, massa! I'm sure you be angry." "If I had my cane, you villain, I'd break your bones. Will you tell me what you mean?" "I 'fraid to tell you, massa; I know you be angry." The doctor's impatience was now highly irritated. Scipio perceiving, by his glance at the tongs, that he might find a substitute for the cane, and that he was sufficiently excited, said, "Well, massa, you make me tell, but I know you be angry; *I 'fraid, massa, if I wear another black coat, Dr. Cooper ask me to go preach for him!*" This unexpected termination realized the negro's calculation. His irritated master burst into a laugh. "Go, you rascal, get my hat and cane, and tell Mrs. Chauncey she may give you a coat of any colour; a red one, if you choose." Away went the negro to his mistress, and the doctor to tell the story to his friend, Dr. Cooper.

TWO MINISTERS.

The following fact, from the pen of a writer in the Newburyport Herald, contains an important truth, which our educated ministers should well understand:—

I recollect listening, when a boy, to a conversation between two Baptist clergymen; the one an uneducated, but valuable extemporaneous speaker; the other an educated man, and a writer of beautiful, clear, and logical sermons, but notorious for the hesitancy which he manifested whenever he attempted to preach " without notes." " How is it, brother L.," said the latter, " that you, without education, are able to get up, at a moment's warning, and speak so well, while I just as certainly fail as I attempt it?" "Well, brother S., I'll tell you. You're just like a rich farmer, who goes into his tool-house to get a hoe, and finds so many there that it takes him half an hour to pick out the best; and, as likely as not, after all, goes off in a hurry with a poor one; while I'm just like one of his men who hires out by the day, and comes in the morning to the corn-field, all ready for work, *with his old hoe on his shoulder.*" The thoroughly educated man very often fails as an extemporaneous speaker, from the mere excess of thought and good taste; while a man without education, and sometimes with scarcely brains enough to furnish the head of a clever parrot, "goes off" in a steady stream of words, as if he were a rain-spout in a thunder-storm. "Many a full barrel of cider," once said a witty friend of mine, "runs slower than a nearly empty one, which runs all the faster when so nearly out that it has to be propped up behind."

REV. DR. STAUGHTON.

ONE Saturday afternoon, as Dr. Staughton was preparing for the pulpit services of the following day, a stranger called at his study, and introduced himself as "the Rev. Mr. Johnson." He had no credentials, except a copy of the Minutes of an Association, in which his name was given in such a connection as to satisfy the Doctor, that in "his own country" he was "not without honor." In the course of conversation it became apparent that Mr. J. would be *willing*, if invited, to preach at least a part of the day, even in Sansom street. The Doctor did not feel very well, and was desirous to preserve his strength, as far as possible, for his evening lecture, which, as many remember, was uniformly attended by admiring crowds.

He therefore requested the "strange brother" to take the morning service, and received the prompt assurance that his wish should be gratified. Tradition has preserved no account of that "morning service," except the fact that the preacher was *heard*. His voice filled not only that spacious house, but a circle of much larger radius. As the Doctor was passing out, one of the deacons asked him what he thought of the stranger. " Oh, he is *sound*, he is *very sound*," was the significant reply.

On Monday morning, Mr. J. requested the Doctor to give him a letter of introduction to the Rev. Mr. Healy, of Baltimore. The good man was too kind to refuse altogether, and too conscientious to recommend a person of whom he knew so little. He therefore gave the applicant the following letter:

PHILADELPHIA, ———, ———.

Dear Brother Healy.—The bearer, who says his name is Johnson, and says also that he is a Baptist preacher, desires me to introduce him to your acquaintance. He cried aloud and spared not in my pulpit yesterday, and if you should find it convenient to let him preach for you, he will lift up his voice among you. Ever affectionately,

W. STAUGHTON.

Dr. Staughton cultivated a due regard to ministerial etiquette; and yet it was always so exhibited as to show that it was a spontaneous effusion of religious affection. Rather than wound the feelings, or disregard the official dignity of the plainest minister of the gospel, he would violate the fastidious taste of a whole church and congregation. Men of the most ordinary talents and acquirements, but honoured by their respective churches, he admitted to his pulpit as fully equal to himself, and worthy of all fellowship and esteem.

In a position like that of Sansom Street, there would almost necessarily be a number of supernumerary ministers. By this we mean ministers who have no pastorships. One is a teacher—another an editor—a third something else. All preaching as often as opportunity afforded, but none supported by, and therefore not devoted to the ministry. Among those at the time of which we now speak, there was one in Sansom Street church, known as Father Strawbridge. This was a very worthy old gentleman, and a very acceptable preacher; but he was never willing to occupy the Doctor's pulpit, even in the greatest emergency, for fear he might not meet the expectations of the audience, and thus, contrary to his best wishes, injure the cause he designed to promote.

Here is the way in which the Doctor managed Father Strawbridge: One Sunday, when the Doctor had to preach four sermons, he determined to apply to the old gentleman to supply his pulpit in the afternoon, when the audience was smallest, and composed chiefly of religious persons. So he went to him, and said: "Brother Strawbridge, can you do me the favour to preach this afternoon to some coloured people for me? If you can, you will very much oblige me, as my duties are very hard to-day, and I am quite indisposed." "With a great deal of pleasure, Doctor," replied the venerable old man; "you know I am always willing to render you any service in my power." "Very well," rejoined the Doctor; "I shall then rely on you; and you will find the place and the hearers in the following manner: Just pass through the vestry of Sansom Street church, ascend the flight of stairs to the right—go into the pulpit—and you will see some coloured people in the gallery on your right hand. I wish you to preach to them one of your plain, affectionate, gospel sermons, telling them of Jesus Christ and his great salvation."

The old gentleman complied with the request. It is not necessary to state that the white people who sat below all heard it, and were probably as much edified as if the sermon had been preached exclusively to themselves.

REV. DR. PAYSON.

The Rev. Dr. Payson being once asked what message he would send to the young men who were studying for the ministry, in one of the colleges, thus addressed them:—" What if God should place in your hand a diamond, and tell you to inscribe on it a sentence which should be read at the last day, and shown there as an index of your thoughts and feelings! What care, what caution, would you exercise in the selection! Now, this is what God has done: he has placed before you immortal minds, more imperishable than the diamond, on which you are about to inscribe, every day, and every hour, by your instructions, by your spirit, or by your example, something which will remain, and be exhibited for or against you, at the judgment-day."

Dr. Payson seems to have touched the right string, when, writing to a young clergyman, he says:—" Some time since, I took up a little work, purporting to be the lives of sundry characters, as related by themselves. Two of those characters agreed in saying that they were never happy until they had ceased striving to be great men. This remark struck me, as you know the most simple remarks will strike us, when heaven pleases. It occurred to me at once, that most of my sorrows and sufferings were occasioned by an unwillingness to be the nothing which I am, and by consequent struggles to be something. I saw if I would but cease struggling, and consent to be any thing, or nothing, just as God pleases, I might be happy. You will think it strange that I mention this as a new discovery. In one sense, it was not new; I have known it for years. But I now saw it in a new light. My heart saw it, and consented to it; and I am comparatively happy. My dear brother, if you can give up all desire to be great, and feel heartily willing to be nothing, you will be happy too."

REV. JOHN ELIOT.

The attachment of the Rev. John Eliot, usually called the "Apostle to the Indians," to peace and union among Christians, was exceedingly great. When he heard ministers complain that some in their congregations were too difficult for them, the substance of his advice would be, "Brother, compass them!" "Brother, learn the meaning of those three little words—bear, forbear, forgive." His love of peace, indeed, almost led him to sacrifice right itself. When a bundle of papers was laid before an assembly of ministers, which contained the particulars of a contention between parties who he thought ought at once to be agreed, he hastily threw them into the fire, and said, "Brethren, wonder not at what I have done; I did it on my knees, this morning, before I came among you."

The piety, personal and relative, of this holy man, was very distinguished, and he was always zealous in promoting the same spirit among others. When he was informed of any public news, he would say, "Brethren, let us turn all this into prayer." When he paid a visit to his friends, he used to say, "Come, let us not have a visit without prayer; let us pray down the blessing of heaven before we go." And whenever he was in the company of ministers, he said, "Brethren, the Lord Jesus takes notice of what is said and done among ministers; come, let us pray before we part." And at the end of his Indian Grammar, he records this memorable sentence: "Prayer and pains, through faith in Christ Jesus, can do any thing."

REV. DR. LATHROP.

The late Rev. Dr. Lathrop was a man of genuine piety, but was greatly opposed to the noisy zeal which seeks commendation by constantly talking about it. A young divine, who was much given to religious cant, one day said to him, "Do you suppose, sir, you have any *real religion?*" The good doctor admirably replied, "None to speak of."

This eminent man seems to have possessed considerable talent for administering reproof, as the following facts will show:—

He once engaged a young man to preach for him, who unfortunately delivered a sermon which had very little connection with his text. The day after its delivery, the author of it called on the doctor to ascertain its merits. "Well," said he, in answer to the anxious inquiry of his young friend, "your sermon was well enough; but if your text had had the small-pox, your sermon would not have caught it."

On another occasion, a neighbouring minister, not much distinguished for eloquence, had engaged to deliver a lecture for him. The hour for the service came, but not the lecturer. The doctor went through the preliminary services, and then sat down to await the arrival of his tardy brother. After an interval of a few minutes, he made his appearance, and walked to the place where the doctor was sitting. It happened to be a rainy day; and the minister of whom we are speaking, having got somewhat of a drenching, began to shake his coat, and express his sorrow for the condition he was in. "Oh," said the doctor, "never mind; go up into the pulpit; you'll be DRY enough there."

A PERSECUTING CLERGYMAN.

It has not unfrequently happened that the laity have been wiser than their clergy, and have been qualified to administer reproof to them. Here is an illustration. Soon after the late Dr. Rodgers reached Williamsburg, in Virginia, then a British colony, one of the established clergymen of Hanover appeared with him before Sir William Gooch, the lieutenant-governor, and complained that this young gentleman, before going to Williamsburg, had preached one sermon in Hanover, contrary to law, urging Sir William to proceed against him with rigour. Sir William's reply did equal honour to his religious sentiments and his official liberality :—" Mr. ——, I am surprised at you! You profess to be a minister of Jesus Christ, and yet come to complain of a man, and wish me to punish him, for preaching the gospel! For shame, sir! Go home, and mind your own duty! For such a piece of conduct, you deserve to have your gown stripped over your shoulders."

BISHOP GEORGE.

An aged traveller, worn and weary, was gently urging on his tired beast, just as the sun was dropping behind the range of hills that bounds the horizon of Springfield, Ohio. It was a sultry August evening, and he had journeyed a distance of twenty-five miles since morning, his pulse throbbing under the influence of a burning sun. At Fairfield, he had been hospitably entertained by one who had recognised the veteran soldier of the cross, and who had ministered to him for his Master's sake, of the benefits he himself had received from the hand "which feedeth the young lions when they lack;" and he travelled on, refreshed in spirit. But many a weary mile had he journeyed over since then; and now, as the evening shades darkened around, he felt the burden of age and toil heavy upon him, and he desired the pleasant retreat he had pictured to himself when that day's pilgrimage should be accomplished.

It was not long before the old man checked his tired animal at the door of the anxiously looked-for haven of rest. A middle-aged woman was at hand, to whom he mildly applied for accommodations for himself and horse.

"I don't know," said she, coldly, after scrutinizing for some time the appearance of the traveller, which was not the most promising, "that we can take you in, old man. You seem tired, however, and I'll see if the minister of the circuit, who is here to-night, will let you lodge with him."

The young circuit preacher soon made his appearance, and, swaggering up to the old man with great consequence, examined him for some moments inquisitively; then asked a few impertinent questions; and, finally, after adjusting his hair half a dozen times, feeling his smoothly-shaven chin as often consented that the stranger should share his bed for the night, and, turning upon his heel, entered the house.

The traveller, aged and weary as he was, dismounted, and led his faithful animal to the stable, where, with his own hands, he rubbed him down, watered him, and gave him food, and then entered the mansion where he had expected so much kindness. A Methodist family resided in the house, and as the circuit preacher was to be there that day, great preparations were made to entertain him; and a number of the Methodist young ladies of the neighbourhood had been invited, so that quite a party met the eyes of the stranger as he entered, not one of whom took the slightest notice of him, and he wearily sought a vacant chair in the corner, out of direct observation, but where he could observe all that was going on; and his anxious eyes showed that he was no careless observer of what was transpiring around him.

The young minister played his part with all the frivolity and foolishness of a city beau, and nothing like religion came from his lips. Now he was chattering and bandying senseless compliments with this young lady, and then engaged in trifling repartee with another, who was anxious to seem interesting in his eyes.

The stranger, after an hour, during which no refreshments had been prepared for him, asked to be shown to his room, to which he retired unnoticed, grieved and shocked at the conduct of the family and minister. Taking from his saddle-bags a well-worn Bible, he seated himself in a chair, and was soon buried in thought, holy and elevating, and had food to eat which those who passed by him in pity and scorn dreamed not of. Hour after hour passed away, and no one came to invite the old worn-down traveller to partake of the luxurious supper which was served below.

Towards eleven o'clock the minister came up stairs, and, without pause or prayer, hastily threw off his clothes, and got into the middle of a small bed, which was to be the resting-place of the old man as well as himself. After a while the aged stranger rose up, and after partially disrobing himself, knelt down, and remained many minutes in fervent prayer. The earnest breathing out of his soul soon arrested the attention of the young preacher, who began to feel some few reproofs of conscience for his own neglect of duty. The old man now rose from his knees, and after slowly undressing himself, got into bed, or rather upon the edge of the bed, for the young preacher had taken possession of the centre, and would not, voluntarily, move an inch.

In this uncomfortable position the stranger lay for some time in silence. At length the youngest of the two made a remark, to which the elder replied in a style and manner that arrested his attention. On this he removed over an inch or two, and made more room.

"How far have you come to-day, old man?"

"Thirty-five miles."

"From where?"

"From Springfield."

"Ah, indeed! You must be tired after so long a journey for one of your age."

"Yes, this poor old body is much worn down by long and constant travel, and I feel that the journey of to-day has exhausted me much."

The young minisier moved over a little.

"You do not belong to Springfield, then?"

"No; I have no abiding place."

"How?"

"I have no continuing city. My home is beyond this vale of tears."

Another move of the minister. "How far have you travelled on your present journey?"

"From Philadelphia."

"From Philadelphia! (In evident surprise.) The Methodist

General Conference was in session there a short time since had it broken up when you left?"

"It adjourned the day before I started."

"Ah, indeed!" moving still farther towards the front side of the bed, and allowing the stranger more accommodation. "Had Bishop George left when you came out?"

"Yes, he started at the same time I did; we left in company."

"Indeed!"

Here the circuit preacher relinquished a full half of the bed, and politely requested the stranger to occupy a larger space.

"How did the bishop look? He is getting old and feeble, is he not?"

"He carries his age tolerably well; but his labour is a hard one, and he begins to show signs of failing strength."

"He is expected this way in a week or two; how glad shall I be to shake hands with the old veteran of the cross! But you say you left in company with the old man; how far did you come together?"

"We travelled alone for a long distance."

"You travelled alone with the bishop?"

"Yes, we have been intimate for years."

"You intimate with Bishop George?"

"Yes, why not?"

"Bless me! Why did I not know that! But may I be so bold as to inquire your name?"

After a moment's hesitation, the stranger replied, "George."

"George! Not Bishop George?"

"They call me Bishop George," meekly replied the old man.

"Why—bless me, Bishop George!" exclaimed the now abashed preacher, springing from the bed, "*You have had no supper!* I will instantly call up the family. Why did you not tell us who you were?"

"Stop, stop, my friend," said the bishop gravely. "I want no supper here, and should not have eaten any had it been got for me. If an old man, toil-worn and weary, fainting with travelling through all the long summer day, was not considered worthy of a meal by this family, who profess to have set up the altar of God in their house, Bishop George surely is not. He is at best but a man, and has no claims beyond those of common humanity."

A night of severer mortification the young minister had never experienced. The bishop kindly admonished him, and warned him of the great necessity there was of his adorning the doctrines of Christ, by following him sincerely and humbly. Gently, but earnestly, he endeavoured to win him back from his wanderings of heart, and direct him to trust more in God, and less in his own strength.

In the morning the bishop prayed with him long and fervently before he left the chamber; and was glad to see his heart melted into contrition. Soon after the bishop descended, and was met by the heads of the family with a thousand sincere apologies. He mildly silenced them, and asked to have his horse brought out. The horse was accordingly soon in readiness, and the bishop, taking up his saddle-bags, was preparing to depart.

"But surely, bishop," urged the distressed matron, "you will not thus leave us? Wait a few minutes; breakfast is on the table."

"No, sister L——, I cannot take breakfast here; you did not consider a poor toil-worn traveller worthy of a meal; and your bishop has no claim but such as humanity urges."

And thus he departed, leaving the family and minister in confusion and sorrow. He did not act thus from resentment, for no such emotion rose in his heart; but he desired to teach them a lesson, such as they would not easily forget.

Six months from this time the Ohio Annual Conference met

at Cincinnati, and the young minister was to present himself for ordination as a deacon; and Bishop George was to be the presiding bishop.

On the first day of the assembling of Conference, our young minister's heart sunk within him, as he saw the venerable bishop take his seat. So great was his grief and agitation, that he was soon obliged to leave the room. That evening, as the bishop was seated alone in his chamber, the Rev. Mr. ——— was announced, and he requested him to be shown up.

The bishop grasped the young man by the hand with a cordiality which he did not expect, for he had made careful inquiries, and found that since they had met before, a great change had been wrought in him. He was now as humble as he was before self-sufficient and worldly-minded. As a father would have received a disobedient and repentant child, so did this good man receive his erring but contrite brother. They mingled their tears together, while the young preacher wept as a child, even upon the bosom of his spiritual father. At that session he was ordained, and became one of the most pious and useful ministers in the Ohio Conference.

TWO YOUNG MINISTERS.

Two young men entered the ministry at the same time. One of them had great success in the conversion of sinners, the other had none. Meeting one day, the one inquired of the other how this fact was to be accounted for. "Why," replied the other, "the reason is, that I *aim* at a different end in preaching from you. My object is to convert sinners, but you aim at no such thing. And then you go and lay it to sovereignty in God, that you do not produce the same effect, when you never aim at it. Here, take one of my sermons, and preach it to your people, and see what the effect will be." The other minister did so, and preached the sermon, and it produced effect. He was frightened when sinners began to weep; and when one came to him after the meeting to ask what he should do, the minister apologized to him, and said, "I did not aim toward you; I am sorry if I have hurt your feelings."

REV. DR. BELLAMY.

Holy activity in the cause of God, and caring for the souls of men, has ever been found by ministers, as well as by more private Christians, the best remedy against mental dejection. The Rev. Dr. Bellamy, of Bethlehem, Conn., whose eminence for piety and talents must long live, was often subject to great anxiety of mind, when he was filled with the impression that he was certainly going to hell. At such times, his ministerial brethren visited him, and endeavoured to relieve his mind; but all experiments having failed, one of them said to him, "Well, doctor, it may be that, after all, your convictions concerning yourself are true, and that you will certainly go to hell; but have you thought what you will do when you get there? how you will spend your time?" The doctor instantly caught up the inquiry, "What will I do when I get there? Why, I will set up prayer-meetings, and vindicate the law of God!" "But," replied his friend, "the devil will not have you there, if you engage in such employments." This had the happy effect of showing him that he had no sympathies for the employment of hell. and that his heart was united to the cause of God.

A young clergyman once visited the good old doctor, to propose the inquiry, "What shall I do to supply myself with matter for my sermons?" The doctor quaintly replied, "Fill up the cask, *fill up the cask*, FILL UP THE CASK; and then, if you tap it anywhere, you will get a good stream. But if you put in but little, it will *dribble, dribble, dribble*, and you must *tip, tip, tip*, and then you get but little, after all."

TWO CLERGYMEN.

A few years since, two New England divines were conversing together respecting the various theories concerning the origin of sin, when a lady who was present interrupted them, saying, "It seems to me that it would be far better for ministers, instead of puzzling themselves to know how sin *entered into the world*, to unite their efforts and try how much of it, with God's blessing, they can drive out." "You remind me, madam," said one of the clergymen, "of my aged deacon, who, after listening to a sermon in which I had endeavoured to explain why God suffered sin to enter the world, being asked what he thought of my theory, shook his head, and said, 'Ah, sir! all I know about it is, I am a sinner, and I WISH I WASN'T!'"

REV. GEORGE WHITEFIELD.

We transcribe the following anecdote from a recent English publication, in which it is said to have been related to a gentleman in New York, by an individual still living, who was then a boarder in Dr. Finley's family. It will be remembered by our readers how exactly Whitefield's death fulfilled his prediction :—

In the last visit but one which Mr. Whitefield paid to America, he spent a day or two at Princeton, under the roof of the Rev. Dr. Finley, then president of the college at that place. At dinner, the doctor said, " Mr. Whitefield, I hope it will be very long before you will be called home; but when that event shall arrive, I should be glad to hear the noble testimony you will bear for God." Whitefield replied, " You would be disappointed, Doctor; I shall die silent. It has pleased God to enable me to bear so many testimonies for him during my life, that he will require none from me when I die. No, no! It is your dumb Christians, that have walked in fear and darkness, and thereby been unable to bear a testimony for God during their lives, that he compels to speak out for him on their deathbeds."

A short time before the death of Mr. Whitefield, the Rev. W. Tennent paid him a visit, as he was passing through New Jersey; and one day dined with him and several other ministers, at a gentleman's house. After dinner, Mr. W. adverted to the difficulties attending the Christian ministry; lamented that all their zeal availed but little; said that he was weary with the burden of the day; and declared the great consolation, that in a short time his work would be done, when he should depart and be with Christ. He then appealed to the ministers, if it was not their great comfort that they should soon go to rest. They generally assented, except Mr. T., who sat next to Mr W., in silence, and by his countenance discovered but little pleasure in the conversation. On which Mr. W., tapping him on the knee, said, " Well, brother Tennent, you are the oldest man among us; do you not rejoice to think that your time is so near at hand, when you will be called home?" Mr. T.

bluntly answered, "I have no wish about it. Mr. W. pressed him again. Mr. T. again answered, "No, sir, it is no pleasure to me at all; and if you knew your duty, it would be none to you. I have nothing to do with death; my business is to live as long as I can, as well as I can, and to serve my Master as faithfully as I can, until he shall think proper call me home." Mr. W. still urged for an explicit answer to his question, in case the time of death were left to his own choice. Mr. T. replied, "I have no choice about it; I am God's servant, and have engaged to do his business as long as he pleases to continue me therein. But now, brother, let me ask you a question: what do you think I should say, if I were to send my man into the field to plough; and if at noon I should go to the field, and find him lounging under a tree, and complaining, 'Master, the sun is very hot, and the ploughing hard; I am weary of the work you have appointed me, and am overdone with the heat and burden of the day. Do, master, let me return home and be discharged from this hard service.' What should I say? Why, that he was a lazy fellow, and that it was his business to do the work that I had appointed him, until I should think fit to call him home."

SEVERAL CLERGYMEN.

A CORRESPONDENT of a New York paper says:—

Not many months since, I was standing in a certain store, in a city in which there were several ministers and other Christian brethren, conversing about a clergyman then just leaving the said city for another field of labour. Among other remarks, an expression was dropped, about ministers not being respected; when one of the company, a worthy deacon, spoke up with considerable apparent warmth, "Well, ministers need not expect to be respected much by the people till they respect each other a little more."

"How so?" said one.

"How so!" replied the deacon, "why, many ministers come into this store, and I often hear them talking about one another, and seldom hear them speak well. They criticise their brethren severely, and speak meanly of their talents."

A distinguished divine was not long since conversing with a Methodist clergyman of devout piety and zeal. In all their religious feelings, they perfectly harmonized, till at last the Methodist gently suggested his astonishment, that his companion should believe in the doctrine of election. "Why, my dear sir," was the reply, "if you are a Christian, did not God always intend that you should be one? There is the doctrine of election?"

What can be said upon the subject, more clear, or more convincing, by the longest dissertation that was ever penned?

REV. JOHN LELAND.

At one period of the ministry of this good man, he was considerably annoyed by a Universalist minister, who endeavoured in every possible way to draw him into controversy, but entirely without effect. At length, as the worthy pastor was riding along, finding a crowd around the shop of the village blacksmith, he turned his horse in that direction, and saw the Universalist minister addressing his neighbours, boasting of the inability of Mr. Leland to hold an argument with him. Not a few questions were proposed to Mr. L. on the subject, to which he returned mild and ready answers. At length, the preacher of error asked, in a tone of triumph, why he had neglected to answer several notes addressed to him, challenging him to a discussion on their differences. The worthy old clergyman, who had hitherto never touched the subject, now felt that he must "answer a fool according to his folly," and said, with great mildness, "Sir, when I was a lad, my father used to say to me, 'John, never kill a skunk; for, even when dead, it will be but a skunk still.'" The result was decisive; the Universalist was silent; and such was the tone thus given to public opinion, that the said preacher was soon compelled to leave the neighbourhood.

REV. DR. MERCER.

The Rev. President Manly gives the following illustration of the intense feeling of this venerable minister:—

I saw him at Eatonton, in 1824, in an aspect which I must relate, as it illustrates the simple piety and tenderness of his heart. It was on a Sunday of the meeting of the Georgia convention. Brother S—— and I were present. Brother Mercer sat in the pulpit with us. S—— got up, and, in his quaint way, surveyed the very large assembly, with several glances, and opened his address thus: "Where shall we obtain bread to feed so great a multitude? For my part, I am unprovided and penniless; but there is a lad here," turning round and putting his hand on my head as I leaned forward in the pulpit, "who has five barley-loaves and two little fishes, which, with the presence and blessing of Jesus, shall constitute a feast." This well nigh upset me. But it drove me to prayer. The Lord loosed my mind, and unlocked the fountain of tears, so that it was computed that, through a great part of the discourse, there was an average of at least five hundred persons continually bathed in tears. There was nothing in all this *Bochim* that to me was so affecting, as when I turned round and saw the sympathetic streams coursing swiftly down the furrowed cheeks of Father Mercer."

This shrewd observer, once conversing about a preacher who had a little learning and a great deal of conceit, made this remark: " He reminds me of a foolish dog I once heard of, that was in pursuit of a deer, but coming to a place where a fox had crossed the track, he left the deer and ran after the fox. He had not followed the fox far, before he arrived at a spot where a rabbit had crossed. Forthwith he leaves the fox, and pursues the rabbit; and when the hunter came up, he had left the rabbit and was barking at a mouse-hole. Brother —— sometimes sets out after something valuable, but before he stops, his folly drives him to the mouse-hole.

When this wise counsellor would at any time dissuade his brethren from projects which required pecuniary means beyond what they had in hand, he would often say, " Let us get the fodder before we buy the horse."

REV. CALEB BLOOD.

THE late Rev. Caleb Blood, of Boston, was once walking to his church, in company with the Rev. Lewis Leonard, of New York, then a very young man. On his way to worship the young minister, who felt the dignity of his friend, and who was well aware of the high respectability of the Charles Street Church, said, with much modesty, "How can I preach before *you?*" The reply of the aged minister of the cross was, "Preach before me! how can you preach before GOD?" and then went on to make to him the most soothing and comfortable remarks, which at that time inspired him with moral courage, and became eminently useful in his future life.

NTERCOURSE OF THE CLERGY WITH SOCIETY.

BISHOP CHASE.

THERE lived in Poughkeepsie a venerable lady and her talented son-in-law. The former was exceedingly anxious about the latter, because of his loose and infidel opinions on religious subjects; and yet few men were more amiable in manners, or more sprightly in conversation. "Oh, sir!" said the lady to Bishop Chase, the writer of this account, "I wish you to have a serious conversation with my son-in-law, on the subject of Christianity. Perhaps he may hearken to you, though to all of us he turns a deaf ear, whenever we speak of the Holy Scriptures."

A proposal of this kind seemed to be identified with the writer's profession. Accordingly, a day was appointed when the lady would spend a social afternoon with the writer and his family, there being no doubt that the interesting young lawyer would join the party at tea. The interview took place as was expected, and, in the full flow of talk, something was designedly introduced, touching the Christian religion. Contrary to the expectation of his relatives and friends, this interesting gentleman neither evaded nor opposed what was said, but candidly confessed he was differently impressed on that subject from what he had been. "Till a few days ago," said he, "I should have brought forward my preliminaries; and before the thresholds of Christianity were passed, I would have insisted that they should all be satisfactorily answered; but, at present, I feel differently disposed."

"And what has wrought the change?" asked the writer.

"Oh, sir!" said he, "I must tell the whole story; it relates chiefly to *General Hamilton*.

"You know," said he, "that pre-eminent character; that he is not only the greatest in the field, in the senate, and at the bar, but also the most agreeable man in social intercourse. In pursuit of his professional duties, he passes from New York to Albany, to attend the higher courts, and Poughkeepsie is his stopping-place for rest and social chat. We young lawyers delight to meet him at Hendrickson's tavern, and there breathe together the atmosphere of wit and satire. Not long since, he passed by: we gathered round him, and he greeted us with his usual cordiality. But there was something altered in his ⁋it; it was solemn, yet more affectionate. At length, to break the spell, *I* ventured, as erst, a story, the edge of which was ridicule against Christians and their creed. As I finished the anecdote, instead of the loud laugh, and responsive tale, the general gravely asked me if I knew what I had been talking of? Confusion is the best name I can give my feelings and behaviour before the great man, at such a question from his lips. Seeing my embarrassment, he said he did not design to give me pain, but by his question to call my attention to his own case.

"Not many months ago," said he, "I was, as you are, doubtful of the truths of Christianity; but some circumstances turned my thoughts to the investigation of the subject, and I now think differently. I had been in company with some friends of a similar sentiment in New York. I had indulged in remarks much to the disadvantage of Christians and in disparagement of their religion. I had gone further than ever before I had done in this way. Coming home, I stood, late at night, on the door-steps, waiting for my servant. In this moment of stillness, my thoughts returned to what had just passed at my friend's, and on what I had said there. And what if the Christian religion be true! The thought certainly was natural, and it produced in my bosom the most alarming feelings. I was conscious that I had never examined it—not even with that attention which a small retaining fee requires in civil cases. In that, I hold myself bound to make up my mind according to the aws of evidence; and shall nothing be done of this sort, in a question that involves the fate of man's immortal being? Where every thing is at stake, shall I risk all without inquiry? Wilfully blinding my own eyes, shall I laugh at that which, if true, will laugh me to scorn in the day of judgment? These questions did not allow me to sleep quietly. In the morning, I sent to my friends, the clergy, for such books as treated on the evidences of Christianity. I read them; and the result is, that I believe the religion of Christians to be the truth—that Jesus Christ is the Son of God; that he made an atonement for our sins by his death, and that he rose for our justification.

"This is the substance of General Hamilton's declaration to me at Hendrickson's, and you may judge how I feel since. As I have followed the general in many other respects, so would I imitate him here.

"Will you lend me books, that I may read as he did, before I give my opinion?"

The books were accordingly taken to his house, but he never read them. A press of business intervened. He put off his duty till a more convenient season; that season never came till it was too late. A sudden disease deprived him of reason and of life. This talented and interesting young lawyer passed from a temporal to an eternal state—and let the word of God tell the rest.

The story of General Hamilton, which this talented person was the means of communicating to the writer, ought not to be forgotten. It was, from the time the writer heard it, of the deepest interest; and when the tidings came of the general's death, it formed the basis of a sermon preached in Poughkeepsie, on the second day of July, 1804. This story is recorded here because it forms a part of the writer's reminiscences.

The Rev. Dr. Bedell relates, that while Bishop Chase was at the house of a Mr. Beck, in Philadelphia, he received a package from Dr. Ward, the Bishop of Sodor and Man, making inquiries relating to certain property in this country, of which some old person in his diocese was the heir. The letter had gone to Ohio, followed him to Washington, then to Philadelphia, and found him at Mr. Beck's. When he read it to Mr. B., the latter was in amazement, and said, "Bishop Chase, I am the *only* man in the world who can give you information. I have the deeds in my possession, and have had them forty-three years, not knowing what to do with them, or where any heirs were to be found." How wonderful that the application should have been made to Bishop Chase, and he not in Ohio, but a guest in the house of the only man who possessed any information on the subject!

A FAITHFUL MINISTER.

A MINISTER was called to conduct a conference meeting, in an extreme part of a parish where he was an entire stranger, the minister for whom he officiated being out of town. Two rough-looking men came in, as the effect of persuasion, but evidently with reluctance. In the midst of the exercises, one of them interrupted the speaker by a rude question. He was requested to be silent for a little time, when an answer should be given to him. He uttered some abusive language, and retired to another room. After a while, the minister discussed the various objections on the part of men to embrace religion, and remarked that the false religion of many professors was no more an argument for rejecting true religion, than that we should refuse genuine money because some men were wicked enough to pass counterfeits. At this remark, the other of the two men also left the room. It afterwards became known to the speaker that these men, the preceding week, had been tried for this very crime, and that, in public opinion, they were both guilty. How admirably adapted is the word of God for the conviction of sinners!

TRAVELLING CLERGYMEN.

THERE is something so interesting, so instructive, so *home-like*, in the following narrative, communicated by a plain country clergyman to one of our periodicals, that we transfer its facts and remarks to our pages:—

Once we entertained an angel. It happened in this wise My father was a country minister, and his parish lay in a lovely region of country west of the Green Mountains, on the high road from the Eastern States to the Springs. Often would ministers drive up to the door in their Yankee gigs, having previously ascertained by inquiry where the parish pastor lived, and calling to us boys at the door, would say, "Does Mr. —— live here?" On being answered in the affirmative, they would ask again, "Does he keep ministers' tavern?"— that is, does he entertain ministers *for nothing?* And being answered in the same way, they would add, "Well, take my horse and give him four quarts of oats to-night, and don't water him till he gets cool." With these laconic intimations that they felt quite at home, they would walk in to enjoy the entertainment kept for the "man," while we took care of the "beast."

Now, all this seemed sufficiently cool, not to say presuming, on the part of entire strangers; but it was the custom, and I guess no one ever went away without an invitation, and a *strong resolution*, to call again, if he ever passed that way.

But about the angel. He was not travelling to the Springs, but was an angel of the churches—a messenger sent by some one of the benevolent institutions of the day to receive the alms of God's people. Some called him a beggar; others, an agent: I have called him an angel, which title he deserved, as the sequel will show. It was in winter, and about the middle of the week, when he arrived: we had sickness in the family, and he came to stay through the week, and over the Sabbath; and would it have been strange if we had felt that his room was more desirable than his company, under such circumstances? Would it have been uncivil or unkind to have told him that it was very inconvenient for us to have him staying at our house, and we would prefer to quarter him among the people? However that may be, we preferred to keep him, and make him as comfortable as we could.

He stayed. One after another of the family was taken sick; the parents were confined to bed; the children were down; the *help* gave out and went to bed, and the travelling minister, the stranger who had turned in to tarry with us, was the only *well* person in the house. And what did he do? Did he call in some of the neighbours, and then look out for more convenient quarters? Not at all. He nursed the sick, as if nursing was his business; he went to the barn and took care of the "cattle," as if he had been brought up at the stable. He split and brought in the fuel, as if he had lived in the woods. He was at hand when he was wanted, and out of the way when he was not. He was active, clever, cheerful, as much at home as if he were among his own children, and not with strangers whom he had never seen before, and whom he might never see again.

He stayed over the Sabbath; preached for my father, who was still not able to be out; and having seen us in a good degree convalescent, he went on his way rejoicing. His name is remembered with delight by the members of that household to this day, though many years have since fled, and that family has been scattered widely; some are as far apart as earth and *heaven*.

Our folks always kept open door for the Lord's ministers, and they never had reason to regret it. Some of us have been thrown far from home and among strangers, and some of our number have sickened and died among strangers, and the Lord has always surrounded them with kind friends, whose sympathy has proved that our Father in Heaven is faithful and true, when he says, "Inasmuch as ye have done it unto the least of these, ye have done it unto me." He has provided friends for us among strangers, and we love to befriend strangers at our gate.

It was an injunction of divine wisdom that we should not be forgetful to entertain strangers, for some had thereby entertained angels unawares. And those who are most "given to hospitality," find real enjoyment in obeying this precept.

There is a vast difference among people on the subject of entertaining strangers. As a plain country minister, I have had frequent opportunities of making comparisons, and the result is this :—

When we go to Presbytery or Synod, or to a religious convention of any sort *in some places*, the good people seem to vie with each other in seeing who will most freely and handsomely entertain the strangers. Every house is open; every heart is warm; every face is pleasant; and while we stay we are treated as welcome guests; and when we go, it is with repeated and pressing invitations to come again, and never to pass through the place without favouring the family with a call.

On the other hand, I have sometimes gone to other places on such errands, and it has been with extreme difficulty that we could find lodgings, though the *ability* of Christians to entertain strangers far exceeded that of the people before described. And it is no unusual thing for ministers who have been invited by public notices to attend religious meetings in certain places, with the assurance that entertainment would be provided for them, to find on their arrival that they must seek their entertainment at a public house, and pay for it at the rate of one or two dollars a day. Now, if ministers render themselves so disagreeable by the use of tobacco, or any other vile practice, that their company is not desired, I have not one word to say. I once heard a minister apologize for his people's reluctance to accommodate guests, by saying that "angels do not chew tobacco, and therefore they were sure of *not* entertaining angels when they asked the brethren to their houses." I know such men are a great annoyance to neat housekeepers. And ministers who desire hospitality, ought to abandon those habits that render their society unpleasant.

But this *objection* is often merely an *excuse*. Hospitality is a Christian duty, and those who would, in the last great day, hear the Saviour saying unto them, "I was a stranger and ye took me in," must love to entertain Christ's friends, whether they come with the homely garb of the country, or the polished exterior of city life.

REV. DR. ARMSTRONG.

We were favoured a few evenings since, say the editors of one of our periodicals, with the presence of a valued friend, when he gave us the following story of the late lamented Dr. Armstrong. We tell it in our friend's words:—

I was, some twenty years since, travelling in Virginia by stage. We were not far from the James River, and the occupants of the stage were Dr. Armstrong, two Virginia gentlemen of the regular "young blood" breed, myself and sister. At that time the Doctor was pastor of a church in Richmond, whither the stage was bound. After some conversation, I asked him who was the owner of the lands upon James River. He said that " it was one *Wykoff*, a lawyer, who, having committed some misdemeanor in *New York*, had gone to the South to save his reputation." At this, one of the southern young men very coolly spit in his face. He turned to me, looking as much as to say, " *Isn't he crazy?*" In a moment the fellow spit again in his face, but the good man was not in the least agitated. " He who will not resent an injury should be kicked out of the stage," said the ruffian. Dr. Armstrong asked him, if he had in any way ever injured him. "Yes," said he, " you have slandered my father!" The mystery was at once solved —Wykoff, of whom he had been speaking, was his *father*. Mr. Armstrong told him he was very sorry, indeed, he had offended him, and made all the reparation in his power, but the fellow insisted that he should get out and *fight it out*. He told him *No*—he never fought—it was against his principles to fight. My sister was frightened extremely, as he had a bowie-knife with him, and we feared the consequences. At every tavern he would get out and drink, and then commence his vile language towards Dr. Armstrong. A single word of retort from him would undoubtedly have ended his life. But he was very calm and mild. At length the scoundrel's companion told him he ought to be satisfied, and when we were near Richmond he concluded to be so. Dr. Armstrong saved his life that time by being a peace-maker."

A YOUNG MINISTER IN THE WEST.

Solomon recommends us sometimes to "answer a fool according to his folly, lest he be wise in his own conceit." The principles laid down by infidels are often, when properly applied, made to appear supremely ridiculous. Let us illustrate this sentiment :—

Near the Alleghany mountains, an infidel judge was sitting with a circle of his friends, ridiculing the account of the creation of man as given in the Bible, and asserting that we came into existence by chance. "Perhaps," said he, "some of us existed a while in less perfect organizations, and at length, as nature is always tending towards perfection, we became men, and others sprang into life in other ways; and if we could find a rich country now, which had not been injured by the hand of man, I have no doubt that we should see them produced from the trees." Being fluent, self-confident, and, in most respects, superior to his audience, he made his doctrines appear very plausible, and asked this and that person of the company of their thoughts upon his statements. All answered favourable to his views, till he proposed his inquiry to a youthful stranger, who sat silent in a quiet corner. He replied, "Sir, I have no doubt at all upon the subject, for I have travelled in the richest part of Texas, where I saw the forest in its native perfection, unsullied by the hand of man, and there I have seen large hogs growing upon the trees. The nose is the end of the stem, as you see by its form; and, when ripe, I have seen them fall and proceed directly to eating the acorns that grew upon the same tree." This simple illustration of his principles, turned the laugh upon the judge, and was sufficient to counteract the evils he intended.

A COLOURED PREACHER.

Jack is a Methodist local preacher. In one of his sermons he told this story: When I was a lad, there were no religious people where I lived. But I had a young master about my age, who was going to school; and he was very fond of me. At night, he would come into the kitchen to teach me the lesson he had learned himself during the day at school. In this way I learned to read.

When I was well nigh grown up, said Jack, we took up the New Testament, and agreed to read it verse by verse. When one would make a mistake, the other was to correct him, so that we could learn to read well.

In a short time, we both felt that we were sinners before God, and we both agreed to seek the salvation of our souls. The Lord heard our prayer, and gave us both a hope in Christ. Then I began to hold meetings for prayer and exhortation among the coloured people.

My old master soon found out what was going on. He was very angry, especially because his son had become pious. He forbade my holding any more meetings, saying, that if I did, he would whip me severely for it.

From that time, I continued to preach or exhort on Sabbath nights; and on Monday morning my old master would tie me up, and cut my back to pieces with a cowhide, so that it had never time to get well. I was obliged to do my work in a great deal of pain from day to day.

Thus I lived near a year and a half.—One Monday morning my master, as usual, had made my fellow-slaves tie me to a shade tree in the yard, after stripping my back naked to receive the cowhide. It was a beautiful morning in the summer time, and the sun shone very bright. Every thing around looked very pleasant. He came up to me with cool deliberation, took his stand, and looked at me closely, but the cowhide hung still at his side. His conscience was at work, and it was a great moment in his life.

"Well, Jack," said he, "your back is covered all over with scars and sores, and I see no place to begin to whip. You obstinate wretch, how long do you intend to go on in this way?"

"Why, master, just as long as the Lord will let me live," was my reply."

"Well, what is your design in it?"

"Why, master, in the morning of the resurrection, when my poor body shall rise from the grave, I intend to show these scars to my heavenly Father, as so many witnesses of my faithfulness in his cause." He ordered them to untie me, and sent me to hoe corn in the field. Late in the evening he came along, pulling a weed here, and a weed there, till he got to me, and then told me to sit down.

"Jack," said he, "I want you to tell me the truth. You know that for a long time your back has been sore from the cowhide; you have had to work very hard, and are a poor slave. Now, tell me, are you happy or not, under such troubles as these?"

'Yes, master, I believe I am as happy a man as there is on earth."

"Well, Jack," said he, "I am not happy.—Religion, you say, teaches you to pray for those that injure you. Now, will you pray for your old master, Jack?"

"Yes, with all my heart," said I.

We kneeled down, and I prayed for him. He came again and again to me. I prayed for him in the field, till he found peace in the blood of the Lamb. After this, we lived together like brothers, in the same church. On his death-bed he gave me my liberty, and told me to go on preaching as long as I lived, and meet him at last in heaven.

I have seen, said Jack, many Christians whom I loved, but

I have never seen any I loved so well as my old master. I hope I shall meet him in heaven.

REV. MR. MOODY.

"Come, Charles, my son," said Deacon Allsworthy, "take one of these turkeys, and carry it up to Minister Moody, for Thanksgiving."

"No, father, I don't do that again, I tell you."

"What do I hear now, Charles? These five-and-twenty years I have sent the minister a turkey, and Joe has carried them, and Tom, and Jerry, and you—without ever refusing before. What's the matter now?"

"Why, father, he never thanks me for bringing it to him; besides, he took me to task a while ago, because I started out of meeting too soon."

"Well, son, you know it is the custom for the minister to go out before any of the congregation starts; this is done as a mark of respect."

"Respect or rot, he's nothing but a man, and as for creeping for him, I won't do it."

"Well, let it all pass, and carry him the turkey; and if he don't thank you for it, I will."

Charles shouldered the fowl, and in a short time was at the house of the minister, who was seated in the parlour, surrounded by a number of friends who had come to pass Thanksgiving with him. The lad entered without knocking, and bringing the turkey from his shoulders heavily upon the table, said, "Mr. Moody, there's a turkey for you; if you want it, you may have it; if you don't, I'll carry it back again."

"I shall be very glad of it," said the minister, "but I think you might learn a little manners, Charles. Can't you do an errand better?"

"How would you have me do it?" said Charles.

"Sit down in my chair," said the clergyman, "and I will show you."

Charles took the chair, while the divine took the turkey and left the room. He soon returned—took off his hat—made a very low bow, and said, "Mr. Moody, here is a turkey which my father sen s you, and wishes you to accept as a present."

Charles rose from his seat and took the fowl, and said to the minister, "It is a very fine one, and I feel very grateful to your father for it. In this and numerous and other instances he has contributed to my happiness. If you will just carry it into the kitchen, and return again, I will send for Mrs. Moody to give you half a dollar."

The good old clergyman walked out of the room—his friends laughed at the joke, and made up a purse for the lad, who ever afterwards received a reward for his services.

AN UNSUCCESSFUL MINISTER.

A WORTHY minister of the gospel was the pastor of a flourishing church. He had been a popular preacher, but gradually became less acceptable to his hearers, and his congregation very much decreased. This was solely attributed to the minister; and matters continuing to get worse and worse, some of his hearers resolved to speak with him on the subject. A deputation was accordingly appointed to wait upon him for that purpose. They did so; and when the good man had heard their complaints, he replied, "I am quite sensible of all you say, for I feel it to be true; and the reason of it is, that I have lost my prayer book." They looked quite astonished at hearing this, but he proceeded: "Once my preaching was acceptable, and many were edified by it, and numbers were added to the church, which was then in a prosperous state. But wo were then a praying people. There were many who joined together in fervent prayer that my preaching might be blest for the conversion of sinners, and for building up the saints in their most holy faith. It was this, by the blessing of God, that made us prosper. But as prayer began to be restrained, my preaching became less acceptable, the church declined, and things became as they now are. But let us have recourse to the same means, and the same effects may be expected to follow." They took the hint. Social prayer was again punctually attended to, and exertions made to induce those who were without to attend the preaching of the word. The result was, that the minister became as popular, and the church as flourishing as ever.

REV. THOMAS BROWN.

WHILE the late Rev. Thomas Brown was minister at the Scotch Plains, New Jersey, and while he was yet a young man, he went from Perth Amboy to fulfil a preaching appointment somewhere in the neighbourhood of South Amboy, on the other side of the Raritan river. He had crossed it in a small ferry-boat, worked by oars. The mouth of that river, in the channel, was sometimes very dangerous, and, for such craft, unnavigable; especially so, when the wind set down the river, or the reverse, and met the tide.

On the occasion referred to, the wind was boisterous and the waves were high. In the little boat was a number of young persons; and one, in whom the voyager felt a special interest, and who may yet remember the day. There was also another, then a child, and who, some years subsequently, related the fact. The wind blew, and the waves tossed about at pleasure the tiny vessel. The danger seemed great, and the alarm and terror of the passengers were great also. All must be lost! In the midst of the cry of distress, Mr. B. broke out, with his strong musical voice, to the good old tune of Shirland:—

> "The God that rules on high,
>   And thunders when he please;
> That rides upon the stormy sky,
>   And manages the seas;
> This awful God is ours,
>   Our Father and our love;
> He shall send down his heavenly powers,
>   To carry us above."

All were hushed, and "there was a great calm" in their feelings. And with the vigorous strokes of the oarsmen, the boat was safely brought to the welcome beach, and all gladly stepped on *terra firma*.

"What," once inquired this shrewd and venerable man, of a Scotch acquaintance with whom he sometimes reasoned—"what would satisfy you, sir, of the proper divinity of Jesus Christ?"

"Why," replied the gentleman, "if the Bible expressly declared that Jesus Christ is God—"

"Then," said my friend B., "the Bible says expressly that Jesus Christ is the *true* God, and eternal life." 1 John v. 20. No more was said.

AN AFRICAN PREACHER.

A RESPECTABLE man, who had become interested on the subject of religion, and who had begun with some earnestness to search the Scriptures, had read but a few chapters, when he became greatly perplexed with some of those passages which an inspired apostle has declared to be " hard to be understood." In this state of mind, he repaired to a coloured preacher for instruction and help, and found him, at noon, on a sultry day in summer, laboriously engaged hoeing his corn. As the man approached, the preacher, with patriarchal simplicity, leaned upon his hoe, and listened to his story. "Uncle Jack," said he, " I have discovered lately that I am a great sinner; and I commenced reading the Bible, that I may learn what I must do to be saved. But I have met with a passage here," holding up his Bible, "which I know not what to do with. It is this: ' God will have mercy upon whom he will have mercy, and whom he will he hardeneth.' What does this mean ?" A short pause intervened, and the old African replied as follows: " Master, if I have been rightly informed, it has been but a day or two since you began to read the Bible, and, if I remember rightly, that passage you have mentioned is away yonder in Romans. Long before you get to that, at the very beginning of the gospel, it is said, ' Repent, for the kingdom of heaven is at hand.' Now, have you done that? The truth is, you have read entirely too fast. You must begin again, and take things as God has been pleased to place them. When you have done all that you are told to do in Matthew, come and talk about Romans."

Having thus answered, the old preacher resumed his work, and left the man to his own reflections. Who does not admire the simplicity and good sense which characterized this reply? Could the most learned polemic more effectually have met and disposed of such a difficulty? The gentleman particularly interested in this incident, gave an account of it with his own lips; and said, "It convinced me most fully of the mistake into which I had fallen. I took the old man's advice; I soon saw its propriety and wisdom, and hope to bless God for ever for sending me to him."

REV. DR. STAUGHTON.

When the late Rev. Dr. Staughton resided at Bordentown, he was one day sitting at his door, when the infidel Thomas Paine, who also resided there, addressed him and said, "Mr. Staughton, what a pity it is that man has not some comprehensive and perfect rule for the government of his life." Mr. S. replied, "Mr. Paine, there is such a rule." "What is that?" asked Paine. Mr. Staughton repeated the passage, "Thou shalt love the Lord thy God with all thy heart, with all thy mind, with all thy soul, and with all thy strength; and thy neighbour as thyself." "Oh," said Paine, "that's in your Bible," and immediately walked away.

A PRESBYTERIAN CLERGYMAN.

Some time ago, a well-known minister of the Presbyterian church delivered a series of discourses against infidelity, in a town on the Red river, in Louisiana; many of the citizens of which were known to be skeptical. A few days afterwards, he took passage in a steamer ascending the Mississippi river, and found on board several of his neighbours, among whom was a disciple of Paine, distinguished as a ringleader of a band of infidels. He soon commenced the utterance of horrid blasphemies; and, seeing the clergyman reading at a table, he asked his companions to go with him to the other side of the table, to listen to tales which should annoy the preacher. Many, influenced by curiosity, gathered round him and heard his vulgar anecdotes, pointed against the Bible and its ministers. The preacher did not raise his eyes from the book he was reading, nor appear at all disconcerted by the presence of the rabble. At length, the infidel walked up to him, and rudely slapping him on the shoulder, said, "Old fellow, what do you think of these things?" He calmly pointed out of the door and said, "Do you see that beautiful landscape spread out in such quiet loveliness before you?" "Yes." "It has a rich variety of flowers, plants, and shrubs, that are adapted to fill the beholder with delight." "Yes." "Well, if you were to send out a dove, he would pass over that scene, and see in it all that was beautiful and lovely, and delight himself in gazing at and admiring it; but if you were to send out a buzzard over precisely the same scene, he would see in it nothing to fix his attention, unless he could find some rotten carcase that would be loathsome to all other animals. He would delight and gloat upon that with exquisite pleasure." "Do you mean to compare me to a buzzard, sir?" asked the infidel, colouring very deeply. "I made no allusion to you, sir," said the minister, very quietly. The infidel walked away in confusion, and was called "the Buzzard" during the remaining part of the passage.

A DELIGHTED MINISTER.

In a certain place, they engaged a professed infidel to instruct a reading-school. The scholars, when they came together one afternoon, were not able to read. The teacher, after several vain attempts to make them proceed as usual, sent one of his scholars to the neighbouring house of a Christian professor, to request him to come into the school. It so came to pass, that the minister of the place was also at this house, and also went with the other to the school. As an awakening had begun in the town, the minister had little doubt what was the matter. When he came in, and saw the solemn appearance, he first said to the teacher, "Sir, what is the matter with your scholars?" He replied, "I do not know." Said the minister, "Have you not been correcting them?" The master answered, "No, we have had no disturbance." "Well," said the minister, "what then *can* be the matter?" "I cannot tell," replied the master. "But you must have some opinion about it; tell me what you think it is." Not able to endure any longer the poor deist burst into tears, and said, "I believe it is the Spirit of God;" and, in a short time, the teacher and fifteen of the scholars became apparent believers.

A WISE PASTOR.

A MEMBER of a Christian church, feeling himself much aggrieved in a transaction with a Christian brother, determined upon having revenge. Conscience remonstrated; reminded him of his vows, his relation to the offender; that they were members of Christ, and that it was displeasing to God. But no—the evil rankled in his breast; revenge he would have.

How to accomplish his purpose he knew not. With these feelings, he went to his *pastor* to obtain *his* assistance. His pastor reasoned with and tried to dissuade him. Failing in this, he finally said, "I know of but one kind of revenge allowed by the Scriptures, viz.; 'If thine enemy hunger, feed him; if he thirst, give him drink: by so doing, thou shalt heap coals of fire upon his head.'" With joy beaming in his countenance, the good man, clapping his hands, exclaimed, "*I'll burn him! I'll burn him!*" Would it not be well if there were more such burning in the world? How easy would it be to melt down the hearts of thousands into love and tenderness!

A CLERGYMAN IN VIRGINIA.

A HIGHLY respectable clergyman in Virginia, some time since, gave a very interesting account of a soul-thrilling scene in which he was one of the parties concerned. He was preaching to a large and attentive audience, when his attention was arrested by seeing a man enter, having every mark and lineament of a Jew. He was well dressed, his countenance was noble, and he thought it was evident that his heart had lately been the habitation of sorrow. He took his seat, and was all attention, while an unconscious tear was often seen to wet his manly cheek. After service, the clergyman fixed his eye steadily upon him, and the stranger reciprocated the look. The minister went to him, and said, " Sir, am I correct, am I not addressing one of the children of Abraham?" "You are." "But how is it that I meet a Jew in a Christian assembly?" The substance of his narrative was as follows:—He was a very respectable man, of a superior education, who had lately come from London; and with his books, his wealth, and a lovely daughter of seventeen, had found a charming retreat on the lovely banks of the Ohio. He had buried the wife of his bosom before he left Europe, and he now knew no pleasure but the company of his endeared daughter. She was indeed worthy of a parent's love. She was surrounded by beauty as a mantle; but her cultivated mind, and her amiable disposition, threw around her a charm superior to any one or all of the decorations of her body. No pains had been spared on her education. She could read and speak with fluency several languages; and her manners charmed all who saw her. No wonder then that a doating father, whose head had now become sprinkled with gray, should place his whole affections on this only child of his love, especially as he knew no source of happiness beyond this world. Being a strict Jew, he educated her in the principles of that religion; and he thought that he had presented it with an ornament.

It was not long ago that his daughter was taken sick. The rose faded from her cheek, her eye lost its fire, and it was soon apparent that the worm of disease was rioting in the core of her vitals. The father hung over the bed of his daughter with a heart ready to burst with anguish. He often attempted to converse with her, but seldom spoke except in the language of tears. He spared no trouble or expense in obtaining medical assistance, but no human skill could extract the arrow of death now fixed in her heart. The father was walking in a small grove near his house, in great distress of mind, when he was sent for by his dying daughter. With a heavy heart he entered the door of the chamber, which he feared would soon be the entrance of death. He was now to take a last farewell of his child, and his religion gave him but a feeble hope of meeting her hereafter.

The daughter grasped the hand of her father with a death-cold hand: "My father, do you love me?" "My child, you know I love you—that you are more dear to me than the whole world besides!" "But, father, do you LOVE me?" "Why my child, will you give me pain so exquisite? Have I never given you any proofs of my love?" "But, my dearest father, DO you love me?" The father could not answer: the daughter added, " I know, my dear father, you have ever loved me—you have been the kindest of parents, and I tenderly love you. Will you grant me one request?—O, my father, it is the *dying* request of your daughter—will you grant it?" "My dearest child, ask what you will, though it take every cent of my property, it shall be granted. I *will* grant it." " My dear father, *I beg you never again to speak against Jesus of Nazareth!*" The father was dumb with astonishment. " I know," continued the dying girl, " I know but little about this Jesus, for I was never taught. But I know that he is a Saviour, for he has manifested himself to me since I have been sick, even for the salvation of my soul. I believe that he will save me, even though I have never before loved him. I feel that I am going to him—and that I shall be ever with him. And now, my dear father, do not deny me ; *I beg that you will never again speak against this Jesus of Nazareth!* I entreat you to obtain a Testament that tells of him ; and when I am no more, you may bestow on him the love which was formerly mine!"

The exertion here overcame the weakness of her feeble body. She stopped ; and her father's heart was too full even for tears. He left the room in great horror of mind : and ere he could again summon sufficient fortitude to return to her, the spirit of his beloved daughter had taken its flight, as we trust, to the Saviour whom she loved and honoured, though she had not seen him. The first thing her father did, after committing to the earth his last worldly joy, was to procure a New Testament. This he read, and, taught by the Spirit from above, he became numbered with the meek and humble followers of the Lamb.

REV. DR. NETTLETON.

A Christian minister can possess no talent more enviable than that of skill in stopping the mouths of gainsayers, and in speaking a word in season to all with whom he may meet. This talent Dr. N. possessed in a very high degree.

Being accosted by a Universalist, who wished to engage in a discussion on the doctrine of eternal punishment, he replied, "I will not enter into any dispute with you at present; but I should be pleased to have you state to me your views, that I may have them to think of." The man accordingly informed him, that in his opinion mankind received all their punishment in this life, and that all would be happy after death. Dr. Nettleton then asked him to explain certain passages of Scripture, such as the account of the judgment in the twenty-fifth of Matthew, and some others; merely suggesting difficulties for him to solve, without calling in question any of his positions. After taxing his ingenuity for some time in this way, and thus giving him opportunity to perceive the difficulty of reconciling his doctrine with the language of inspiration; he said to him, "You believe, I presume, the account given by Moses of the deluge, and of the destruction of Sodom and Gomorrah?" "Certainly," he replied. "It seems, then," said Dr. N., "that the world became exceedingly corrupt, and God determined to destroy it by a deluge of water. He revealed his purpose to Noah, and directed him to prepare an ark in which he and his family might be saved. Noah believed God, and prepared the ark. Meanwhile he was a preacher of righteousness. He warned the wicked around him of their danger, and exhorted them to prepare to meet their God. But his warnings were disregarded. They, doubtless, flattered themselves that God was too good a being thus to destroy his creatures. But notwithstanding their unbelief, the flood came, and, if your doctrine is true, swept them all up to heaven. And what became of Noah, that faithful servant of God? He was tossed to and fro on the waters, and was doomed to trials and sufferings for three hundred and fifty years longer in this evil world; whereas, if he had been wicked enough, he might have gone to heaven with the rest.

"And there were the cities of Sodom and Gomorrah, which had become so corrupt, that God determined to destroy them by a tempest of fire. He revealed his purpose to Lot, and directed him and his family to make their escape. 'And Lot went out, and spake to his sons-in-law, saying, Up, get ye out of this place, for the Lord will destroy this city. But he seemed as one that mocked to his sons-in-law.' They did not believe that any such doom was impending. They doubtless flattered themselves that God was too good a being to burn up his creatures. But no sooner had Lot made his escape, than it rained fire and brimstone from the Lord out of heaven, and they all, it seems, ascended to heaven in a chariot of fire; while pious Lot was left to wander in the mountains, and to suffer many grievous afflictions in this vale of tears; whereas, if he had been wicked enough, he might have gone to heaven with the rest." After making this statement, he requested the man to reflect on these things, and bade him an affectionate farewell.

Dr. Nettleton was once attacked by a restorationist, who quoted, in support of his doctrine, the words of the apostle Peter: "By which also he went and preached to the spirits in prison." Dr. N. observed to him that the time was specified in the next verse, when Christ preached to these spirits in prison. It was, "when once the long-suffering of God waited in the days of Noah." It was by his Spirit which dwelt in Noah, that he preached to those who are now spirits in prison.

"No," said the man, "that cannot be the meaning of the passage. The meaning is, that Christ, after his crucifixion, went down to hell, and preached to the spirits in prison." "Be it so," said Dr. N., "and what did he preach?" "I do not know," he replied, "but I suppose he preached the gospel." "Do you think," asked the doctor, "that he preached to them any thing different from what he preached on earth?" "Certainly not," replied the man. "Well," said Dr. Nettleton, "when Christ was on earth, he told sinners that, if they should be cast into prison, they should not come out thence till they had paid the uttermost farthing. If he went down to hell, to preach to the lost spirits there, he doubtless told them, 'You must remain here till you have suffered all that your sins deserve.' What influence, then, would his preaching have towards releasing them from the place of torment?"

A man once said to him, "I sincerely desire to be a Christian. I have often gone to the house of God, hoping that something which should be said might be sent home to my mind by the Spirit of God, and be blessed to my salvation." "You are willing, then, are you not," said Dr. N., "that I should converse with you, hoping that my conversation may be the means of your conversion?" "I am," he replied. "If you are willing to be a Christian," said Dr. N., "you are willing to perform the duties of religion; for this is what is implied in being a Christian. Are you willing to perform these duties?" "I do not know but I am." "You are the head of a family. One of the duties of religion is family prayer. Are you willing to pray in your family?" "I should be," he replied, "if I were a Christian. But it cannot be the duty of such a man as I am to pray. 'The prayers of the wicked are an abomination unto the Lord.'" "And is it not," said Dr. N., "an abomination unto the Lord to live without prayer? But just let me show you how you deceive yourself. You think you really desire to be converted. But you are not willing even to be convicted. Just as soon as I mention a duty which you are neglecting, you begin to excuse and justify yourself, on purpose to keep your sin out of sight. You are not willing to see that it is a heinous sin to live in the neglect of family prayer. How can you expect to be brought to repentance until you are willing to see your sinfulness? And how can you flatter yourself that you really desire to be a Christian, while you thus close your eyes against the truth?"

A young lady, who was under concern of mind, said to him, "I certainly do desire to be a Christian. I desire to be holy. I would give all the world to have an interest in Christ." He replied, "What you say will not bear examination. If you really desire religion for what it is, there is nothing to hinder you from possessing it. I can make a representation which will show you your heart, if you are willing to see it." "I am," said she. "It will look very bad," said he, "but if you are willing to see it, I will make the representation. Suppose you were a young lady of fortune; and suppose a certain young man should desire to obtain your fortune, and should for that reason, conclude to pay his addresses to you. But he does not happen to be pleased with your person. He does not love you, but hates you. And suppose he should come to you and say, 'I really wish I could love you, but I do not. I would give all the world if I could love you, but I cannot. What would you think of that young man?"

A person once said in his presence, that to inculcate upon sinners their dependence on God for a new heart, is suited to discourage effort, and to lead them to sit down in despair. He replied, "The very reverse of this is true. Suppose a number of men are locked up in a room, playing cards. Some person informs them that the roof of the building is on fire, and that they must make their escape, or they will perish in the flames. Says one of them, 'We need not be in haste, we shall have time to finish the game.' 'But,' says the person who gave the alarm, 'your door is locked.' 'No matter for that,' he replies; 'I have the key in my pocket, and can open it at any moment.' 'But I tell you that the key will not open the door.' 'Won't it?' he exclaims; and, rising from the table, flies to the door, and exerts himself to the utmost to open it. So sinners, while they believe there is no difficulty in securing their salvation at any moment, quiet their consciences and silence their fears. But when they are taught that such is the wickedness of their hearts, that they will never repent unless God interposes by his regenerating grace, they are alarmed, and begin to inquire, in deep distress, what they shall do to be saved."

A caviller once asked this excellent minister, "How came I by my wicked heart?" "That," he replied, "is a question which does not concern you so much as another, namely, how you shall get rid of it? You have a wicked heart, which renders you entirely unfit for the kingdom of God; and you must have a new heart, or you cannot be saved; and the question which now most deeply concerns you is, how you shall obtain it." "But," said the man, "I wish you to tell me how I came by my wicked heart." "I shall not," replied Dr. N., "do that at present; for if I could do it to your entire satisfaction it would not in the least help you towards obtaining a new heart. The great thing for which I am solicitous is, that you should become a new creature, and be prepared for heaven." As the man manifested no wish to hear any thing on that subject, but still pressed the question how he came by his wicked heart, Dr. N. told him that his condition resembled that of a man who is drowning, while his friends are attempting to save his life. As he rises to the surface of the water, he exclaims, "How came I here?" "That question," says one of his friends, "does not concern you now. Take hold of this rope." 'But how came I here?" he asks again. "I shall not stop to answer that question now," replies his friend. "Then I'll drown," says the infatuated man, and, spurning all proffered aid, sinks to the bottom

---

A young female, who had been for some time in a state of religious anxiety, said to him, "What do you think of the doctrine of election? Some say it is true, and some say it is not true; and I do not know what to think of it." "And what do you wish to think of it?" "I wish," said he, "to think that it is not true." "Suppose, then," said Dr. Nettleton, "that it is not true. The doctrine of repentance is true. You must repent or perish. Now, if the doctrine of election is not true, what reason have you to believe you ever shall repent?" After a moment's reflection, she replied, "If the doctrine of election is not true, I never shall repent." Her eyes were then opened upon her true condition. Every refuge failed her. She saw that she was entirely dependent on the sovereign grace of God; and there is reason to believe that she was soon brought out of darkness into God's marvellous light.

A certain individual said to him, "I cannot get along with the doctrine of election." "Then," said he, "get along without it; you are at liberty to get to heaven the easiest way you can. Whether the doctrine of election is true or not, it is true that you must repent, and believe, and love God. Now, what we tell you is, that such is the wickedness of your heart, that you never will do these things unless God has determined to renew your heart. If you do not believe that your heart is so wicked, make it manifest by complying with the terms of salvation. Why do you stand cavilling with the doctrine of election? Suppose you should prove it false; what have you gained? You must repent and believe in Christ, after all. Why do you not immediately comply with these terms of the gospel? When you have done this, without the aid of Divine grace, it will be soon enough to oppose the doctrine of election. Until you shall have done this, we shall still believe that the doctrine of election lies at the foundation of all hope in yonr case."

A woman, who was known to be a great opposer of the doctrine of election, said to him, one day, "You talked to mo yesterday, as if you thought I could repent." "And can you not?" said he." "No, I cannot, unless God shall change my heart." "Do you really believe," said he, "that you cannot repent unless God has determined to change your heart?" "I do, said she. "Why, madam," said he, "you hold to the doctrine of election in a stricter sense than I do. I should prefer to say, not that *you cannot*, but that you *never will* repent, unless God has determined to change your heart."

To a young woman, who had long been thoughtful, but not deeply impressed, and who seemed to continue from week to week in the same state of mind, he said, one day, " There are some who never will become true believers. Christ said unto the Jews, ' Ye believe not, because ye are not of my sheep.' Perhaps this is your case; and I tell you now, that if you are not one of Christ's sheep, you will never believe on him; and I hope it will ring in your ears." And it did ring in her ears. From that moment she found no peace till, as she hoped, her peace was made with God.

To a man who manifested great opposition to the doctrine of election, he once said, "If I should go to heaven, I feel as if I should wish to say, in the language of the apostle, ' who hath saved us, and called us with an holy calling; not according to our works, but according to his own purpose and grace, which was given to us in Jesus Christ before the world began.' Now, if we should meet in heaven, and I should make use of this language, would you quarrel with me there?"

" Do you believe," said an Arminian to him, one day, " that God influences the will?" " I do," he replied. " How do you prove it?" " I prove it by this passage of Scripture: ' For it is God that worketh in you both to will and to do.' " " But that does not mean," said the Arminian, " that God influences the will. And *now*, how do you prove it?" "I prove it," said Dr. N., by this passage : ' For it is God that worketh in you both to will and to do.'" " But that, I say, does not mean that God influences the will." "And what does it mean?" said Dr. N. " It means," said the Arminian " that God gives us a gracious power to will and to do." "Then it does not mean," said Dr. N., "that *God works in us both to will and to do.*"

He once fell in company with two men who were disputing on the doctrine of the saints' perseverance. As he came into their presence, one of them said, "I believe this doctrine has been the means of filling hell with Christians." "Sir," said Dr. N., "do you believe that God knows all things?" "Certainly I do," said he. "How, then, do you interpret this text, 'I never knew you?'" said Dr. N. After reflecting a momoment, he replied, "The meaning must be, I never knew you as Christians." "Is that the meaning?" said Dr. N. "Yes, it must be," he replied; "for certainly God knows all things." "Well," said Dr. N., "I presume you are right. Now, this is what our Saviour will say to those who, at the last day, shall say to him, Lord, Lord, have we not eaten and drunken in thy presence? &c. Now, when Saul, and Judas, and Hymeneus, and Philetus, and Demas, and all whom you suppose have fallen from grace, shall say to Christ, Lord, Lord—he will say to them, 'I never knew you'—I NEVER *knew you as Christians.* Where, then, are the Christians that are going to hell?"

A person who objected to some of the doctrinal views of Dr. Nettleton, said to him, "Doctor, you believe in the doctrine of the saints' perseverance?" "It is my opinion," replied he, "that that doctrine is taught in the Bible." "I should like, then," said this friend, "to hear you explain Ezek. xviii. 24. 'When the righteous turneth away from his righteousness and committeth iniquity, and doeth according to all the abominations that the wicked man doeth, shall he live? All the righteousness that he hath done shall not be mentioned; in his trespass that he hath trespassed, and in his sin that he hath sinned, in them shall he die!'"

Dr. N. replied, "You have imposed upon me a hard task. That is a difficult text to explain; and what renders it the more difficult is, that the commentators are not agreed as to its meaning. Some have supposed, that by a righteous man in this passage, is meant a self-righteous man." "I do not believe that," said the individual. "Neither do I," replied the Doctor, "for, in that case, it would seem to teach that if a self-righteous man should persevere in his self-righteousness, he would be saved. Some have supposed that by a righteous man is meant one who is apparently righteous." "I do not believe that," said his friend. "Neither do I," said Dr. N., "for in that case the text would seem to teach, that if a hypocrite should persevere in his hypocrisy, he would be saved. You suppose, do you not, that by a righteous man in this passage, is meant a true saint?" "Certainly I do." "And you suppose that by a righteous man's turning away from his righteousness, is meant falling away, as David did, and as Peter did?" "Certainly." "And you believe that David and Peter are now in hell?" "No, by no means. David and Peter repented and were restored to the favor of God." "But," said Dr. N., "when the righteous turneth from his righteousness—in his trespass that he hath trespassed, and in his sin that he hath sinned, *in them shall he die—in them shall he die.* Now, if David and Peter did turn from their righteousness in the sense of this passage, how can we possibly believe that they were saved?" The gentleman now found the labouring oar in his own hands; and after attempting for some time unsuccessfully to explain the difficulty in which he found his own doctrine involved, Dr. N. said to him, "If there is any difficulty in explaining this text of Scripture, I do not see but you are quite as much troubled with it as I am."

Dr. Nettleton was once labouring in an interesting revival, when a gentleman of considerable influence, a member of the church, but whose principles and conduct were a reproach to religion, told him that he opposed all religious meetings except those held on the Sabbath. At the same time, he made no objections to balls and parties of pleasure, but encouraged his children to attend them. Two of his daughters, one evening, without his knowledge, went to hear Dr. Nettleton preach. Finding that they had gone, he went to the place, and interrupted the meeting by ordering his daughters immediately to return home. Then, addressing the preacher, he said, "Mr. Nettleton, will you call and see me to-morrow morning at nine o'clock?" "I will, sir," he replied. Accordingly, at the time proposed he was at the house. "Mr. Nettleton," said the gentleman, "I do not approve of night meetings." "Neither do I approve of balls," said Dr. Nettleton: "I think that their influence upon young people is bad." "I do not approve of such meetings as yours," said the gentleman. "Oh!" replied Dr. N., "it is to *religious* meetings that you object, when people meet together to worship God. If I understand you, you feel no opposition to meetings of young people for amusement, if they are held in the night, and continue all night. Did you ever take your children from the ball-room?" "The command," said he, "is, Six days shalt thou labour." "Did you ever quote that command," asked Dr. N., "to prove that it is wrong to attend balls and parties of pleasure?" Then, assuming a solemn and affectionate mode of address, he said to him, "My dear sir, you are a member of the church, but you must not wonder if you are regarded by your acquaintance as in heart the enemy of religion, unless you pursue a more consistent course of conduct. While you encourage balls, and oppose meetings for religious worship, you will find it difficult to make anybody believe that you have any regard for the religion you profess." The gentleman wept, and a decided change took place in his future deportment.

In his visits from house to house, Dr. Nettleton was peculiarly careful to leave a deep impression; he therefore conversed but little on general topics, and soon left the house. He knew not only what to say, but when to be silent. Many have been thrown into distress by his apparent neglect. He had a significant way of addressing individuals. While preaching in Malta, where his efforts were signally blessed, he found a young lady, the daughter of a deacon, who was very stubborn; she was masculine in appearance, and apparently in the way of the conversion of many young persons; he dreaded her influence. He had a serious, direct conversation with her, apparently without any good effect. When about to leave her, he approached her with a resolute step and look, and said, calling her by name—"Do not think of shutting your eyes to-night without prayer; before you retire to rest, go down on your knees and call upon God; remember, I tell you to do it." This he said with great emphasis. He left her abruptly. She was more offended than ever, and said many hard things against him. When she went to her room at the close of the evening, as he predicted, the struggle commenced. She thought of his words; she was alone; her proud heart resisted, and she exclaimed aloud, "What right or authority has he to dictate to me my duty?" It rung in her ears, "I tell you to do it." "You tell me! old Nettleton, I will not do it." "Perhaps he spoke by the Spirit; what will become of me if I refuse?" The struggle was long; she trembled in every nerve. She finally fell upon her knees and cried for mercy. She became an humble Christian, and was instrumental in turning many to righteousness. How many such instances, where he displayed wonderful tact! Truly the Lord was with him. He was therefore a host. He had but one object, that was—to do good. He knew the importance of keeping the mind intent upon the great subject; he therefore requested his friends who laboured with him to avoid all levity, and, as much as possible, worldly conversation. He watched every cause which might divert the attention.

The following facts we copy from "The Christian Index."

We have heard an anecdote of Dr. Nettleton, a Presbyterian revivalist, which is apropos here. A parcel of gay young persons got up a ball in a neighbourhood in which Dr. N. had been preaching with great success, and for the amusement of themselves and others, inserted the reverend gentleman's name at the head of the list of managers. The company assembled at the time appointed. About the hour for commencing the dance, Dr. N. made his appearance, and observed to the company that he perceived, from the tickets that had been issued, that he had been appointed a manager, and therefore, he proposed to open the services with prayer. He then offered up a very affecting prayer for the thoughtless group; which was blessed of God, to the conviction of a number of those present, several of whom afterwards professed conversion, united with the church, and were never afterwards found within the walls of a ball-room. This anecdote we believe to be true. The circumstances were narrated to us in Virginia, while Dr. N. was labouring in the county in which we then resided.

A young man just completing his professional studies, was induced to accompany some female friends to the pastor's study. He there gave a promise that before he retired that night, he would, on his knees, offer prayer for himself. Possessing strict integrity, when he went to his room, he thought of his promise; he was embarrassed—he walked the room, in a cold winter's night, till late, before his proud heart would yield; and when he fell on his knees, such was the struggle in his mind, he said, " He would not, if he could be President of the United States, that any should know he was on his knees in prayer." There he was awakened, and after more than a week's struggle, he was made willing in the day of God's power. He became, not only distinguished as a physician, but as a Christian and an officer—in the church.

A writer in the American Messenger says:—

More than twenty years ago, I had the pleasure of spending some time in two places in the state of New York, in which powerful revivals of religion were in progress, by the blessing of God, upon the labours of the Rev. Dr. Nettleton.

In the course of the first revival, in the town of ——, a gentleman of my acquaintance became deeply anxious for his soul. He wept, he mourned, he sighed, and no doubt prayed for days and days together. But he was proud and obstinate; he would not submit to God.

One day, his amiable wife, whose anxieties about her husband were almost beyond control, came into his room, and, finding him still lingering in his wretched condition, and solemnly fearing that he would grieve away the Holy Spirit, and turn back to the world, she fell upon her knees, in his presence, and fervently prayed for him. The husband's state of mind, after that prayer, may be conjectured, but not easily described. He literally *writhed* in mental anguish.

Dr. Nettleton was the wisest man that I ever saw, in tracing out the operations of the human mind, when under the influences of the Divine Spirit. He seemed to possess almost intuitive knowledge of this subject. When he saw a sinner long lingering under conviction, he judged that there was a special cause, and he was pretty sure to detect that cause.

One day, after my friend Lambert (for so I will call him) had been struggling with and stifling his convictions for some time, Dr. Nettleton called to see him once more. He talked with him, pointed him to the Saviour, and perhaps prayed with him. But there Lambert lingered still—a miserable, disconsolate, lost sinner. No light, no hope. What could be the matter? Dr. Nettleton smelt ardent spirits. That was enough. He immediately intimated to Lambert that he was drinking with a view to drive away his convictions; and, I believe, the latter did not deny the charge. Dr. Nettleton solemnly warned the wretched man, and left him. What was the result? The Spirit of God left my friend, and the unclean spirit, who had gone out, returned to his old habitation, accompanied by seven other spirits, more wicked than himself; and the last state of that man was worse than the first.

Perhaps ten months pass away, when a blast and a mildew rest upon all that pertains to this miserable man. Nothing prospers in his hands. His business, though formerly flourishing, is in ruins; and he is compelled to leave the beautiful house in which he lived. This is not the worst; he is given up of God; he is undone, to all appearance, for time and eternity. His lovely wife and his interesting children are disconsolate and broken-hearted.

Go with me now through yonder street of the town, at night, and what do we see? There lies poor, wretched, ruined Lambert, a drunkard in the ditch! Oh, God! what is man, when left of thy Spirit? Let a veil, for the present, cover the sequel.

Reader, if the Spirit of God strive with you, as you value salvation, grieve him not away.

A BAPTIST MINISTER.

The doctrine of the perseverance of the saints is often abused. Common sense, however, will sometimes sweep away the sophisms of Antinomianism, and I leave it without any disguise for its ugly absurdity. A recent instance of this occurred in the city of Philadelphia. A man, who had been a professor of religion, was in a very backslidden state, to say the least of it. He was approached by a minister, who endeavoured to awaken him to a sense of danger, and arouse him to efforts such as his case demanded.

"I cannot believe," the man replied, "that I never have known the grace of God. It is impossible that I can have been deceived in my former feelings; and I am very well assured that the work which God has begun, he will carry on till the day of the Lord Jesus."

Here he rested, and seemed perfectly contented to abide in his backslidden condition, supporting himself by his misquotation of Scripture.

The minister listened to him patiently, until he had finished, and then replied,

"Yes, I know very well, that where God commences a work of grace in the heart, he will carry it on. This is what makes me fear for you. In your case, the work has stopped. I cannot believe, then, that God ever began it. You must certainly be deceived."

The man was silent, and appeared moved. At length, he frankly confessed that this was a death-blow to the false hope on which he had been depending.

A POOR MINISTER.

I heard a story, the other day, says a writer in one of our periodicals, which seems too good to be lost. A church in the country had just engaged a good minister, who had not attended long, when, after preaching on a Sunday, the deacon gave him a pull, and said,

"I want to speak with you."

After going aside, the deacon said,

"Brother, I saw something about you, to-day, that hurt my feelings."

"What was it, my dear brother?" said the minister, in surprise; "*do tell me.*"

"It was about your arm, while you were preaching, I saw it."

The poor minister became still more alarmed, and anxious to know in what way he had hurt the dear old father's feelings.

The deacon pointed to his elbow. "There it is yet," said he

The minister began to brush his sleeve.

"Stop," said the deacon; "you can't mend it now; there is a hole in your coat, right on the elbow. I am hurt to see our minister have to wear such a coat. Now, I want you to go to —— and choose a coat pattern, and I'll pay for it."

The minister thanked him kindly, and was entirely relieved of his fright.

A COURTEOUS CLERGYMAN.

Some years ago, a young man, a bricklayer by trade, removed from New Hampshire to work in the city of Lowell. He cherished at heart a strong prejudice against professed Christians, considering them as proud and supercilious, and ever ready to say to him, "Stand by thyself; we are holier than thou!" His feeling of repugnance was so deep-seated, and had such a controlling influence over his intellectual nature, as to generate skeptical thoughts, and lead him to question the truth of the Bible. One day, as he was going to his work, he saw a gentleman approaching, who had been pointed out to him as the Rev. Mr. ——, and represented as one of the most affable and courteous of his profession. "Now," said he, "I will put this matter to the test. Here I am in my work-day clothes. If this man notices me, I will think there is, after all, something good in religion."

They met. The clergyman raised his hat, bowed, smiled, and looked as if he would say, "I should be happy to become acquainted with you." The young bricklayer passed on to his labour, but could not forget his promise. The next Sabbath, he went to hear that "gentlemanly minister," and an acquaintance of the most agreeable and salutary kind ensued. His skeptical notions melted away before kind treatment, like snow in an April shower; and he soon became an honest inquirer after truth and mercy. Now, he is the beloved pastor of a flourishing church.

How clearly does this fact prove that a kind and courteous attention to young men, is a very cheap and effective mode of usefulness. No men ought practically to study the apostolic injunction, "Be courteous," more than the ministers of Christ.

REV. JOSEPH EASTBURN.

MANY of our readers entertain an affectionate remembrance of the late Joseph Eastburn, the preacher to the mariners, and for many years esteemed for his patriarchal piety and unwea ried zeal. In his doctrinal views, Mr. Eastburn was Calvinistic; and, among other points, he believed fully in the sovereignty of God in election. An Arminian acquaintance, who highly esteemed Mr. Eastburn, frequently expressed his regret that he should believe in so *horrible* a doctrine, and took occasion oftentimes to endeavour to argue him out of his belief. Mr. Eastburn, who was unobtrusive in his manners, and disinclined to controversy, endeavoured to appease him, but without effect. At a religious conference meeting, at which they were both present, the subject was again in some way introduced; when Mr. Eastburn arose, and, in his peculiarly striking manner, addressed this gentleman before the persons assembled, in the following manner:—" Brother ———, have you not told me that, in your earlier life, you were an avowed and malignant infidel, and that you were the leader of an infidel club, and that you and your companions treated every sacred subject with impious ridicule? And have you not told me that, out of that profane company, you were the only one who was brought, by the grace of God, to a sense of your sins, and to embrace the Saviour?"

"Yes, yes," said the gentleman, with emphasis—" glory be to God!"

"Then," said Mr. Eastburn, quietly, "I have often been disposed to tell you, *that that was election*." There was no reply.

Thus it is. The opponents of this doctrine hesitate not to say that it would be unjust and cruel in God to determine from eternity who should be saved, and who should be left in their sins; but they make no such charge on the Almighty, when, in fact, by his sovereign grace, he calls one into his kingdom, and leaves others to perish. The determination is mysterious, but the execution of that determination is all right. This gentleman was ready to ascribe glory to God for selecting him as a trophy of grace from the midst of his ungodly compa nions, but, according to his profession, he would have been struck with horror at the thought that God should have loved and have chosen him from eternity.

REV. JOHN WESLEY.

THE first time I had the pleasure of being in the company of the Rev. John Wesley, says a correspondent of the New York Evangelist, was in the year 1783. I asked him what must be done to keep Methodism alive when he was dead? To which he immediately answered, "The Methodists must take heed to their doctrine, their experience, their practice, and their discipline. If they attend to their doctrines *only*, they will make the people *Antinomians;* if to the experimental part of religion *only*, they will make them *enthusiasts;* if to the practical part *only*, they will make them *pharisees;* and if they do not attend to their discipline, they will be like persons who bestow much pains in cultivating their garden, and put no fence round it, to save it from the wild boar of the forest."

Mr. Wesley, in the course of his voyage to America, hearing an unusual noise in the cabin of General Oglethorpe, the governor of Georgia, with whom he sailed, stepped in to inquire the cause of it. The general addressed him: " Mr. W., you must excuse me; I have met with a provocation too great for a man to bear. You know the only wine I drink is Cyprus wine; I therefore provided myself with several dozens of it, and this villain Grimaldi" (his foreign servant, who was present, and almost dead with fear) " has drunk up the whole of it. But I will be revenged on him. I have ordered him to be tied hand and foot, and to be carried to the man-of-war which sails with us. The rascal should have taken care how he used me so, for I never forgive." "Then I hope, sir," said Mr. W., looking calmly at him, " you never sin." The general was quite confounded at the reproof; and, putting his hands into his pocket, took out a bunch of keys, which he threw at Grimaldi. "There, villain," said he, "take my keys, and behave better for the future."

REV. DR. SPRING.

Dr. Spring, of New York, related, some time ago, that during the period of a revival of religion in that city, a young lady, the object of high hope, the centre of wide influence, capable of noble things, yet careering on the giddy steep of fashion and of folly, created in him no small solicitude, as he would have to give an account for her soul, every avenue to which seemed most sedulously guarded. He delayed the visit of counsel and exhortation; and delayed till, rebuked by conscience, he could do so no longer. As soon as he called, and was ushered into the saloon, the first and only person whom he saw was this young lady, bathed in tears, who immediately exclaimed, "My dear pastor, I rejoice to see you. I was fearful I was the only one who had escaped your friendly notice." What a rebuke to fear! What an encouragement to hope and to action!

REV. MR. CLAP.

The late Rev. Mr. Clap, of Rhode Island, was asked by a member of his church, whether he thought it right to engage in dancing? His reply was, "I should think that those who are out of Christ should have no heart to dance, and those who are in Christ will have enough else to do."

REV. DR. WADDELL.

Those who have read Mr. Wirt's fine work, the "British Spy," will remember the graphic and touching description of the preaching of the blind Presbyterian preacher, as already narrated in this volume. It is no fancy sketch; the scene actually occurred as it is described. A descendant of his has lately published a letter which was originally addressed to Mr. Wirt, but not printed by him. It will be read with great interest.

To the Author of the British Spy:

The distinguished notice you have taken of the Rev. James Waddell, of Virginia, in the character of the "Blind Preacher," has induced me to give you some account of an event unnoticed by you, and which forms an era in his life. I refer to the restoration of his sight. I do this with less reserve, since it is generally understood that the "British Spy" had been long a warm friend of the subject of this notice; and that nis removal from the vicinity of the "Blind Preacher," in whose hospitable mansion he had received many and warm greetings, had left him uninformed of the event to which I have alluded, and of the circumstances which I propose to detail. You have described him as blind, and, while occupying the rude enclosure of a forest pulpit, addressing an unseen multitude in strains of eloquence which might captivate cities and win the admiration of grave senates. The incidents to which I refer were more private; in his own house, and in the midst of his family. For eight years he had been blind—a stranger equally to the cheerful light of day and the cheering faces of kindred and friends. It will readily be supposed, that in this lapse of time great changes had taken place. The infant had left the knee to rove amidst the fields; the youth had started into manhood, and, bidding adieu to the haunts of his childhood, had gone forth to act for himself upon the theatre of life; with the hope, indeed, of again and again looking upon his venerable father, but without hope of that father's ever looking upon him. A calm and patient resignation had settled over the mind of this man of God, as a summer's cloud settles over the horizon of evening. Peaceful, hopeful, and reclining upon the bosom of heaven, every painful solicitude about himself had fled away. This personal peace and Christian submission were calculated, however, to concentrate his reflections and solicitudes upon the destinies of his family, here and hereafter. His eye could not now see for them; but he had a heart to invoke the watchfulness of an eye that neither slumbers nor sleeps; that neither grows dim with age nor infirmity. His palsied hand could guide them no longer, but patriarchal counsel was freely given, and enforced by the tremendous realities of a future existence. The thread to be followed through the labyrinth of life, it was taught, had its fastenings in eternity; time and all sublunary things should be viewed in the light of eternity. But, although the mental vision was acute and wisely circumspect, the dark curtain still hung over the organs of sight, and seemed to rise no more.

And what if it should be otherwise; that hope of sight

should take the place of resignation to blindness; and, more than this, that hope should be turned into fruition; that, after the darkness of eight years, he should be presented with a broad daylight view of every thing around him! And this, I assure you, was almost a fact; for, after an operation for cataract, which, in the progress of years, had rendered light sensible, and then objects faintly visible, a strong and well constructed convex lens, procured by the kindness of a distant friend, enabled him to see with considerable distinctness. At this juncture, I happened to be at his residence—called by himself, long before, " Hopewell," and now fulfilling, in happy reality, the import of a soft and cheerful name. The scene, without dispute, was the most moving that I ever witnessed. The father could again see his children, who riveted his attention and absorbed his soul. Among these, emotions of intense interest and varied suggestions were visible in the eye, the countenance, and the hurried movements. The bursts of laughter—the running to and fro—the clapping of hands—the sending for absent friends—and then the silent tear bedewing the cheek in touching interlude—the eager gazes of old servants, and the unmeaning wonder of young ones—in short, the happy confusion from the agitation of joy—all taken together, was a scene better adapted to the pencil than the pen, and which a master's hand might have been proud to sketch. How I regretted that the mantle of some Raphael or Michael Angelo had not fallen upon me; then had my fame and my feelings each been identified with the scene, and others should have been permitted to view upon the canvas what I must fail to describe upon paper.

The paroxysm produced by the arrival of the glasses having passed away, and a partial experiment having satisfied all of their adaptation to the diseased eye, behold the patriarch seated in his large arm-chair, with his children around him, scanning with affectionate curiosity the bashful group. There was a visible shyness among the lesser members of the family community, while undergoing this fatherly scrutiny, not unlike that produced by a long absence. The fondness of a father in contemplating those most dear to him, was never more rationally exemplified, or exquisitely enjoyed, than on this occasion.

And now, the venerable man, arising from his seat and grasping a long staff which lay convenient to him, had proceeded but a short distance, when the staff itself seemed powerfully, but momentarily, to engage his attention: it had been the companion of his darkest days, the pioneer of his domestic travels, and the supporter of a weak and tottering frame.

He next proceeded to the front door, to take a view of the mountains; the beautiful south-west range stretching out in lovely prospect, at the distance of about three miles. All followed, myself among the rest; and the mountain scene, though viewed a thousand times before, was now gazed upon with deeper interest, and presented a greater variety of beauties than ever. Indeed, this mountain scenery ever after continued to delight my unsatisfied vision: whether my attention had not before this been carefully drawn to its beauties, or that the suggestive faculty, linking the prospect with the sympathetic pleasures previously enjoyed, had thrown around me a pleasing delusion, I am unable to decide. Delusion apart, however, this sunny base of the south-west mountains is a delightful region, distinguished not only by the natural advantages of a fertile soil, salubrious climate, and beautiful scenery, but by a race noted for the social virtues and for a higher order of intellect.

But to return to the individual whom I had left exercising a new-born vision upon the external world. The book-case interviews I had looked for with solicitude, and presently had the pleasure of witnessing. Watts, and Doddridge, and Locke, and Reid, with a host of worthies, had been the companions of his best days: there had been a long night of separation. The meeting and communion was that of kindred souls, and complimentary alike to his piety, scholarship, and taste. The sight of his own handwriting, upon the blank leaves of his books, was in itself a small circumstance, but seemed to affect him not a little, associated no doubt with varied circumstances of past days.

I left the house, full of reflections. I had been always awed by the solemn sanctity and personal dignity of the "Blind Preacher." The yearning solicitude which I had just witnessed, of such a father over his children, seen now for the first time after the dreary blindness of years, had melted my feelings. My imagination took flight, and, passing rapidly through time, was conducted by the incidents of this day to the resurrection morning; when the saint of God, throwing off the trammels of the tomb, with quickened vision and more than mortal solicitude, looks around for the children of his pilgrimage.

REV. MR. SPENCER.

The Rev. Mr. Spencer, of New York, has furnished the following statement:—

A poor minister once called upon me, saying that his horse and carriage were under a mortgage, which was soon to be foreclosed, and he had no money to pay it. During the night on which he stayed at my house, I was much disturbed in thinking over his case. I felt that I must help him, though my circumstances, at first view, seemed to forbid even the idea. On parting with the good man, in the morning, I presented him with five dollars, which was all the money I had. He hesitated when he saw the amount, and said that so large a donation might embarrass me. "No," said I; "it is, indeed, all I have, but you should have more if I had it. I consider that I am lending to the Lord, and have no doubt that it will soon be returned again." The same day, making a call upon one of my parishioners, who paid regularly towards my support, three dollars were unexpectedly put into my hand. And not long after, as I was dining with another family of my congregation, who likewise helped to make up my salary, we were conversing on the reflex benefits of beneficence; and I remarked, that all I had ever lent to the Lord, had been paid back in some unexpected way, with the exception of two dollars. The lady of the house immediately arose and stepped towards the mantel-piece, while the husband smilingly observed that his wife, a short time ago, had laid up two dollars in the clock for me, and that they were now happy to have this opportunity of completing my recent loan to the Lord.

REV. BELA JACOBS.

The late Rev. B. Jacobs, of Cambridgeport, Mass., could, when necessary, administer reproof very forcibly, though the gentleness of his character was always seen in the manner in which it was done. Some young ladies at his house were one day talking about one of their female friends. As he entered the room, he heard the epithets "odd," "singular," &c., applied. He asked, and was told the name of the young lady in question, and then said, very gravely, "Yes, she is an odd young lady; she is a *very* odd young lady; I consider her extremely singular." He then added, very impressively, "She was never heard to speak ill of an absent friend." The rebuke was not forgotten by those who heard it.

This excellent minister rarely punished his children; his own evidently sincere grief at any wrong committed, was usually sufficient to deter from what was so sure to grieve one so tenderly loved. On one occasion, however, one of his children had committed a serious act of disobedience. They were all called into his study; and when he had, with tears, expressed his sorrow at his child's misconduct, he knelt, and, putting his arm around the offending one, he implored the Father of all to forgive a child who had broken His commands by refusing to obey her mother. That child never forgot that prayer; nor would the most stubborn heart have refused to repent of a sin, punished, not in anger, but in such sorrowful affection. Penitence was expressed before leaving him, and his kiss seemed to seal her forgiveness on earth and in heaven.

REV. MR. ESTABROOK.

Mr. Estabrook, formerly a clergyman of Athol, was well known for his pleasant turn of mind, no less than for fervent, unaffected piety, and genuine benevolence. He died at a very advanced age. Towards the close of his life, a proposition was made in parish—or, as it then was, in town meeting, to increase his salary, to an amount corresponding with the increased expenses of living and the growing wealth of the society. The motion was in a fair way of passing, when, to the surprise of every one, the old gentleman rose and begged his friends not to vote a larger sum for him. He asked it as a favour of the parish. Some one inquired if it was not the fact, as had been stated, that the present salary was insufficient for his support. Mr. Estabrook admitted this, but begged that they would not vote him a larger sum. His friends pressed around him to inquire the reason, which he declared peculiar, and of rather a private nature. On being pressed, however, he stated his inducement to the course he had taken. He declared that he was opposed to voting any more money, because it was difficult to get what had formerly been voted! The hint was taken—the increase was voted, and, what was better, promptly paid.

AN ANXIOUS PASTOR.

During the closing service, one Sabbath, says a pastor, my eyes rested on a lovely youth. I approached him, and exhorted him to repentance and faith in the Lord Jesus Christ. He replied, "I am not ready now, but in two weeks I am resolved to seek the salvation of my soul." A few days after, his minister was summoned to visit him upon a bed of sickness. He said to the minister, "I was invited to the Saviour at the meeting of the Sabbath. I replied that I was not ready then, and now I am not ready to die." On a subsequent visit the dying youth exclaimed, "I was not ready to seek God at the meeting, I was not ready to die when the message came, and now I am not ready to lie down in hell! My two weeks have not yet elapsed, when I hoped to have made my peace with God, and sickness, death, and hell have overtaken me, and I am for ever lost."

A CLERGYMAN.

A GENTLEMAN who had formerly been very skeptical, was one day met by a clergyman who had frequently been accustomed to converse with him, but who had not seen him for some time. The clergyman asked him, "Well, my dear sir, what do you think now of the doctrine of the resurrection?" The former skeptic replied, "Oh, sir, two words from the apostle Paul conquered me, 'Thou fool.' Do you see this Bible, taking up a copy of the Scriptures, fastened with a clasp, "and will you read the words upon the clasp which shuts it?"

The clergyman read what was deeply engraven, "Thou fool." "There," said his friend, "are the words that conquered me; it was no argument, no reasoning, no satisfying my objections; but God convinced me that I was a fool; and henceforward I was determined I would have my Bible clasped with those words, and would never again come to the consideration of its sacred mysteries but through their medium. I will always remember that I am a fool, and that God only is wise."

The words, "Thou fool!" were used, both by the apostle and by this convert to his doctrine, to express the unspeakable folly of man, in setting up his own pretended wisdom in opposition to the pure and perfect wisdom of God.

REV. DR. JUDSON.

THIS veteran missionary of the cross of Christ, on his recent visit to Boston, when asked, by "an old disciple," "Do you think the prospect bright for the speedy conversion of the heathen?" nobly replied, "As bright as the promises of God!"

A GOOD PASTOR.

It is evident that some persons do not understand the sentiment which is sometimes advocated, that the more the Christian advances in holiness, the more he will see of his own sinfulness. The following conversation occurred more than fifteen years since, between a pastor and a lamb of his flock. The young inquirer said to his experienced teacher, "I do not fully understand what you preached to-day. You observed, that the more a child of God increases in holiness, the greater his own sinfulness appears in his view. Is the man really growing *worse* while advancing in holiness?" The watchful pastor, "apt to teach," smiled, and thus replied: "I will illustrate the idea. Suppose a dark room, which for a long time has not been cleansed. You enter it, and view it by moonlight; you say that it is filthy. More light is introduced, and more, and *more*. During this process of introducing more light, a cleansing process is going forward. But, though much filth has been removed since you began to examine the room, yet it now appears tenfold more filthy than when you first surveyed it by mere moonlight." The youth saw and felt the force of the illustration; and while writing this, he distinctly recollects the appearance of the affectionate pastor as he gave it.

A MINISTER IN NEW YORK.

Some few years since a person called on a minister in New York, requesting him to go without delay to a certain house, to visit a person who was sick. The minister went, and, on entering the room where he expected to find the sick person, he found it occupied by a company of gamblers, who arose from their seats, and, in a very peremptory manner, demanded why he came there? At the same time, two or three of them went to the door and bolted it, while the others surrounded the minister, demanding the reason of his presence. He first offered each one a tract, which was received; then took out his Bible, and began to read; and, not knowing what would follow, fell on his knees and raised his voice in prayer to Him who delivered Daniel from the mouth of the lions. While thus pouring out his heart to God, the door was thrown open, and one after another of the company went out, till he was left alone, "and Jesus standing in the midst," by his Spirit, to sustain and protect him.

BISHOP GRISWOLD.

DURING the residence of this excellent clergyman in Bristol, a minister, with more zeal than discretion, became impressed with the conviction that the bishop was a mere formalist in religion, and that it was his duty to go and warn him of his danger, and exhort him to *"flee from the wrath to come."* Accordingly, he called upon the bishop, very solemnly made known his errand, and forthwith entered on his harangue. The bishop listened in silence till his self-constituted instructor had closed a severely denunciatory exhortation, and then in substance replied as follows: " My dear friend, I do not wonder that they who witness the inconsistency of my daily walk, and see how poorly I adorn the doctrine of God my Saviour, should think that I have no religion. I often fear for myself that such is the case, and feel very grateful to you for giving me this warning." The reply was made with such an evidently unaffected humility, and such a depth of feeling and sincerity, that if an audible voice from heaven had attested the genuineness of his Christian character, it could not more effectually have silenced his kindly intending, but misjudging censor, or more completely have disabused him of his false impression. He immediately acknowledged his error, begged the bishop's pardon, and ever afterwards looked upon him as one of the distinguished lights of the Christian world.

A NEW ENGLAND CLERGYMAN.

A FARMER of good substance, possessing much influence in his neighbourhood, not far from Boston, had not for a long time been seen at church. His minister was deeply grieved, and called to remonstrate with the farmer, both on his own account and on account of the pernicious influence of his example. The farmer heard him with attention, and seemed penitent. "I hope, friend," said the good pastor, as he was leaving him, "I hope I shall see you at church next Sabbath?" The farmer looked down to the ground in an attitude of deep thought; then suddenly raising his head, with a cheerful look, as if conscience had conquered, replied quickly, "Well, I'll go; but," pausing a moment, he added, "yes, I'll go—or I'll *send a hand.*" Alas! how many, in different ways, evade the duty of *personal religion!*

REV. DR MERCER.

The late Dr. Mercer seems to have had a very happy talent of so conversing with disconsolate Christians as to lead them to rich sources of consolation. On one occasion, a good man rode twenty-five miles to converse with him. He had been for more than twenty years a member of a Christian church, but was exercised with great darkness and sorrow of mind. After he had told his sad tale of woe to Dr. M., he wound up all by saying, "I would not for a thousand worlds say that I am a Christian." "Would you," asked Dr. M., "for as many worlds say that you are not a Christian?" "No, I would not." "Do you believe that the devil suggests to one deceived, that he is deceived, and that he strives to convince him of it?" "Certainly not." "Do you not believe that he often worries the Christian by such suggestions, persuading him that he is deceived, and, in proof of it, calls to his mind his daily departure from the paths of rectitude and purity?" "No doubt of it." By this short category, and by narrating some of his own trials, the brother was greatly relieved, and went home with a light heart.

Another brother, who had not been long in the church, while reading the Scriptures regularly through, was greatly shocked at many of the heinous sins of the saints of old, particularly some of the actions of Lot and of David. He inquired within himself, how could holy men commit such deeds, and could the vilest sinners do worse? He became almost convinced that religion was a farce, and the Scriptures an imposition. Under these circumstances, he obtained an interview with Dr. Mercer, and told him his difficulties. "Why," said he doctor, "if the Scriptures had recorded none but virtuous and holy actions of the ancient saints, they would not have met *my* case; but they give an honest and impartial history, their bad and their good acts, and from their weakness I gather strength." The brother went away consoled, and was no more troubled in that way.

It is said of this valued minister, that he presided at his church conference meetings with great gravity and dignity, seldom allowing any irregularity to pass unreproved. The clerk of one of his churches was calling over the names of the male members, preparatory to the adjournment of the conference. It was a cold day and a cold church. The members answered to their names in such a lifeless tone of voice, that they could scarcely be heard; and, in some instances, the languid answer would not come until the name had been two or three times repeated. The clerk, however, patiently persevered in his task, attentively listening for answers till he had finished the list. The worthy pastor, whose head all the while had been hanging very low, arose from his seat with much concern on his countenance, and gravely said, "Well, brethren, if your religion is as weak as your voices, it is weak indeed: let us pray." The reproof was deeply felt, and during the prayer, which was the concluding service, many indications of deep feeling were manifested. Its good effects were seen for a long time afterwards.

A CLERGYMAN IN PHILADELPHIA.

I once heard a little incident, said to have occurred to a venerable clergyman of Philadelphia city, now no more, but who, if named, would be instantly recognised as familiar to many.

It occurred some thirty years since, at which time our reverend friend was called upon to officiate at the nuptials of the only child and daughter of a wealthy retired merchant, then residing a few miles in the country.

The time which had been appointed for the wedding, proved to be a chilly, rainy day, toward the latter end of the month of September. The rain having commenced falling on the night previous, continued throughout the day. The roads were in a miserable condition; the rain fallen upon them, still heavy with dust, rendered them almost impassable in mud. This was any thing but a pleasant prospect for the doctor; but weddings must not be delayed, nor do clergymen generally in the least desire it; they entertain a peculiar partiality for them; they find pleasure in uniting " two fond hearts," and profit in it. So, barring the weather, the doctor had no cause to complain, and, rain or shine, he was bound to go. Accordingly, a horse and chaise were procured, and the doctor, fully equipped for the journey, was soon on his way to the scene of bridal festivity. At the country mansion, all was in readiness for his coming; and when he reached there, some time after nightfall, he found the bride and her lover already waiting for him. It was not necessary to lose any time, and the doctor was not long in entering upon his appropriate duties. The necessary preliminaries being speedily arranged, within a spacious hall, richly ornamented, and in the presence of a gay and numerous company, the doctor pronounced the nuptial ceremony.

The scene was unusually affecting, even to the doctor himself. The bride, as we have said, was an only child, and, aside from her education and accomplishments, upon which every care and attention had been bestowed, she possessed qualities of the heart which endeared her to all. She was amiable and affectionate; and these traits, combined with sincere and early piety, had won the reverend old gentleman's highest friendship and esteem. To one thus interested in the happiness of a bride, the joy attendant upon her nuptials is never unmingled with tender emotions; and tears of parental sympathy trickled down the pious countenance of the old gentleman, as, at the conclusion of the ceremony, he invoked the smiles of Heaven for the future happiness of the newly wedded. Nor was he alone in these feelings: a solemn stillness for a while pervaded the whole company, yet, like a transient cloud in the morning, it was soon dispelled, leaving all bright and cheerful as before.

Shortly after the ceremony was over, the doctor prepared himself for home. So, taking an affectionate leave of the bride and her happy partner, he ordered his vehicle. Not a word had yet been hinted to him concerning a marriage fee: as for himself, he was too much absorbed in reflection to have given a thought upon the matter. The "fee," however, such as it was, had not been forgotten; but Mr. E., the bride's father, after accompanying and assisting him into his chaise, placed in his hands a little package, containing, as he said, a "present" for himself, and a "little notion" for his wife. The doctor, presuming, of course, that it was his fee, and no doubt a rich one, which was thus modestly tendered, accompanied with some small token for his wife, thanked Mr. E. accordingly; and the courtesies of the night being exchanged, the doctor lost no time in regaining his home.

Imagine, now, the old gentleman, after two hours' hard ride, through mud and rain, well drenched and bespattered, sitting by his fireside, opening, with the eager assistance of his wife, the above described package. Imagine, also, if possible, the surprise and disappointment of both, as, contrary to the lowest expectations of either, in lieu of a fifty dollar note, and a rich laced cap, the package was delivered of a plain neckcloth and an unpretending pair of gloves.

Now, fortunately for our friend the doctor, of all things he knew best how to brook disappointment; it is characteristic of the profession in general. Hence his share of the disappointment was soon smothered, and he contented himself with the reflection that his services had been well repaid already, in having been rendered to one whom he felt most happy in serving.

Not so with his wife; like the most of her sex, ay, and of her kind, disappointments were not in the least agreeable to her. Besides, on this occasion, as she was personally interested, hers was by no means small. The marriage of Miss E. had long been in contemplation; and as long had the doctor's wife been anticipating a rich fee for her husband, which, according to a good-natured agreement existing between them, in relation to the above marriage, they were to divide equally; and no marvel is it that she had magnified her share into "something very handsome."

For some time she was speechless with vexation and disappointment. She knew not how to vent her feelings; she felt hurt as well as vexed and disappointed.

"Certainly, I am greatly at a loss to account for this," at length she exclaimed, recovering herself; "surely, I would never have expected such conduct from Mr. E."

"Tut! tut! my dear," returned the doctor; "I am sure it's not worth while grieving about it."

"Indeed, I think it is," rejoined his wife, somewhat vexed, and tossing, at the same time, the gloves from her; "I'm sure your ride through mud and rain was itself well worth ten times as much."

"Well, well," said the doctor, "I'm very well satisfied, and I see no reason why you should be otherwise." So saying, he was in the act of spreading out the neckcloth, to examine its dimensions, when lo! a hundred dollar note dropped upon the floor.

If, by the touch of a magic wand, the doctor had converted the cambric into a silken sash, the surprise of his wife could not have exceeded what she now felt. She knew not what first to say. No time, however, was lost in re-obtaining the gloves; and if her surprise was great before, it was in no degree diminished, when a ten dollar note was discovered snugly stuffed away in each thumb and finger.

"My patience! did you ever!" shouted the old lady, in ecstacy.

"Ha! ha!" laughed the doctor.

But let us drop the curtain upon the happy doctor and his wife.

REV. MR. F.

WHILE the Rev. Mr. F. was pastor of a Presbyterian church in the state of New York, he enjoyed the happiness of witnessing several very delightful revivals among his people. One old man, however, withstood all, and, by the perversion of truth, seemed to seal the doom of his eternal misery. He had used to say, that as he could not convert himself, it was not his fault if he perished. During the last revival Mr. F. enjoyed, he called at the house of this old man, to converse and to pray with his family, and was going away without speaking to the old man himself. Perceiving, however, that he had something to say, Mr. F. listened to him, and found it was pretty much the same tale as usual. Mr. F. at length turned to him, and, with somewhat of a severe tone, said, "Jesus Christ demands to be received by you, and proposes himself as your Mediator with the eternal God; but you continue to reject him, and so you must perish for ever. Good bye." The old man's heart was broken—he wept over his sins—sought for mercy, and found it through Christ Jesus. In old age, he became the humble, child-like follower of the Son of God.

A FAITHFUL MINISTER.

PROFESSORS of religion have never yet felt, as they should do, that their property is the Lord's, given to them to sustain his cause. Hence they talk about giving *their property* for the support of the gospel; as though the cause of the Lord Jesus were to be supported as an act of alms-giving. A merchant, in the state of New York, was in the habit of paying a large part of his pastor's salary. One of the members of the church was relating the fact to a minister from a distance, and speaking of the *sacrifice* which this merchant was making. At this moment, the merchant came in. "Brother," said the minister, "you are a merchant; suppose you employ a clerk to sell goods, and a schoolmaster to teach your children, and you order your clerk to pay your schoolmaster out of the store, such an amount for his services in teaching. Now, suppose your clerk gave out that *he* had to pay this schoolmaster his salary, and should speak of the sacrifices that *he* was making to do it; what would you say to this?" "Why," said the merchant, "I should say it was ridiculous." "Well," said the minister, "God employs you to sell goods as his clerk, and your minister he employs to teach his children, and requires you to pay the salary out of the income of that store. Now, do you call this *your* sacrifice, and say that you are making a great sacrifice to pay this minister's salary? No; you are just as much bound to sell goods for God, as he is to preach for Him."

A MINISTER IN BOSTON

A MINISTER in Boston paid a visit to a lady of his acquaintance, who was newly married, and who was attired in the modern fashion, with bare arms. After the usual compliments, he familiarly said,

"I hope you have got a good husband, madam?"

"Yes, sir," replied she, "and a good man, too."

"I don't know what to say about his goodness," added the minister, rather bluntly, "for my Bible teaches me that a good man should clothe his wife, but he allows you to go half naked."

TWO CLERGYMEN.

Two very gayly dressed ladies, being in company with a clergyman, on his being informed that they were professed Christians, were kindly, but very solemnly reproved by him for their extravagance in dress. He reminded them that God had commanded that "women adorn themselves in modest apparel, with shamefacedness and sobriety; not with broidered hair, or gold, or pearls, or costly array, but (which becometh women professing godliness) with good works; whose adorning, let it not be that outward adorning of plaiting the hair, and the wearing of gold, or of *putting on of apparel*; but let it be the hidden man of the heart, in that which is not corruptible, even the ornament of a *meek and quiet* spirit, which in the sight of God is of great price." They were somewhat offended, and, with the hope of quieting their consciences, went to another clergyman, and asked him if *he* thought there was any harm in their wearing feathers in their hats, with artificial flowers, &c. He gravely replied, "There is no harm in *feathers* and *flowers*. If you have in your hearts the *ridiculous vanity* to wish to be thought *pretty*, you may as well hang out the *sign*, and let every one know what is your ruling passion."

REV. JOHN GANO.

This gentleman warmly espoused the cause of his country in the contest with Great Britain, and at the commencement of the war joined the standard of freedom in the capacity of chaplain. His preaching, in which he was inferior only to Whitefield, greatly contributed to impart a determined spirit to the soldiers; nor was his private intercourse less adapted to usefulness. When a lieutenant, after uttering some profane expressions, accosted him, saying, "Good morning, Dr. Good Man;" he replied, "You pray early this morning." The man thus reproved answered, "I beg your pardon." "Oh!" retorted Mr. G., "I cannot pardon you; carry your case to God." Of such a man we do not wonder to read the testimony, "The careless and irreverent stood arrested and awed before him, and the most insensible were made to feel."

REV. T. P. BENEDICT.

A MAN having heard the late Rev. Thomas P. Benedict preach a sermon, the object of which was to show that salvation is entirely of grace, said to him, "If what you have preached is true, what is it my duty to do?"

"It is your duty to believe it."

"What else is it my duty to do?"

"It is your duty to love it. You ought surely to love the truth."

"What else is it my duty to do?"

"I fear I have told you now more than you will ever do. If you will do these things, you will find no difficulty in regard to any other part of your duty. It will be very plain."

AN UNKNOWN PREACHER.

THE spontaneous preference which all persons, free from prejudice, are ready to yield, other things being equal, to a preacher who has had the advantages of education, may be illustrated by the following incident:—

In the vicinity of one of our literary institutions, where several young Baptist ministers were pursuing their studies, a church, whose members were violently prejudiced against college-learned ministers, had passed a vote that they would admit no one from the neighbouring institution into their pulpit. Shortly after this they sent to a minister then residing near the institution, whom they did not know, but with whose preaching they supposed from information they should be pleased. The minister agreed to attend and preach for them, on the day named in their request. Circumstances, however, prevented his going in person; he therefore engaged a young ministering brother, who had nearly completed his studies at the institution of which he was a member, to go in his stead. This young brother was unknown to any of the church. He came to the place at the hour appointed; and, with a fluent and ready utterance, with a warm heart and fervent spirit, and with a well-furnished mind, he delivered his Master's message. The members of the church, who supposed all this while that the preacher was the individual for whom they had sent, and who had never been in a literary institution, were delighted. Their hearts were opened. They pressed him to visit them again, to which he consented. In the mean time, they ascertained who their preacher was, that he was a member of the neighbouring institution. But they had committed themselves; he had gained their hearts, and the approbation of their judgment. It was the end of their prejudice against learning in a minister. After this they were ready to admit and act on the principle, that learning cannot MAKE a minister, but that it can greatly increase his power of being useful.

REV. SAMUEL HARRIS.

THIS excellent minister, who laboured in the last century, was called the Apostle of Virginia. In his power over the affections of his hearers, he was thought to be equal to Whitefield. The Virginians say that he seemed to pour forth streams of lightning from his eyes. The following anecdotes may illustrate his character. Meeting a pardoned criminal, who showed him his pardon received at the gallows, he asked, "Have you shown it to Jesus Christ?" The reply was, "No, Mr. Harris, I want you to do it for me." Accordingly, the good man dismounted and kneeled, and with the pardon in one hand, and the other on the offender's head, rendered thanks and prayed for pardon from God. He once requested a debtor to pay him in wheat, as he had a good crop; but the man replied that he did not intend to pay until he was sued. Unwilling to leave preaching to attend a vexatious suit, he wrote a receipt in full and presented it to the man, saying he had sued him in the court of heaven; and that he should leave the affair with the Great Head of the Church, with whom he might settle another day. The man soon loaded his wagon and sent him the wheat.

REV. DR. LAIDLIE.

SHORTLY after the arrival of the Rev. Dr. Laidlie, one of the early emigrants from Europe to New York, he was thus accosted by some excellent old Dutch people, at the close of a prayer-meeting: "Ah, Domine!" (the title which the Dutch, in their affection, give to their pastors,) "we offered up many an earnest prayer in *Dutch* for your coming among us; and truly the Lord has heard us in *English*, and sent you to us!"

AN AGED MINISTER.

A VENERABLE minister at H— preached a sermon on the subject of eternal punishment. On the next day, it was agreed among some thoughtless young men, that one of them should go to him, and endeavour to draw him into a dispute, with the design of making a jest of him and of his doctrine. The wag accordingly went, was introduced into the minister's study, and commenced the conversation by saying, "I believe there is a small dispute between you and me, sir, and I thought I would call this morning and try to settle it." "Ha!" said the clergyman, "what is it?" "Why," replied the wag, "you say that the wicked will go into everlasting punishment, and I do not think that they will." "Oh, if that is all," answered the minister, "there is no dispute between you and me. If you turn to Matt. xxv. 46, you will find that the dispute is between you and the Lord Jesus Christ, and I advise you to go immediately and settle it with him."

REV. DR. STANFORD.

It is every way important that Christian ministers should secure the love of young persons. The late Rev. Dr. Stanford, of New York, always did this in a very eminent degree. Though the peculiar gravity and dignity of his appearance was such as to preclude rather than to invite juvenile familiarity, yet scarcely any other man was so universally a favourite among children as "Father Stanford." One little boy, the son of a clergyman, was asked whom he liked best as a preacher. "Oh," said he, "I like old Father Stanford best, because he is a very good man, and he speaks out, so that I can understand him."

In their intercourse with their friends, the ministers of Christ often gain instruction as well as give it. So it occurred to Dr. S. After having once preached to the inmates of the state prison of New York, he was passing through the middle hall, to visit the sick prisoners in the hospital, when Mr. Hauman, a foreigner by birth, and one of the keepers, stood at the back-door with the key in his hand, and pleasantly offered him a pinch of snuff. After the usual salutation, the following dialogue ensued:—

"Sir, wot use you come here to visit dis vicked people?"

"My heavenly Master has made it my duty to visit the sick, and especially those who are in prison."

"Den, let me ask you, vot use it be for de rain to come down upon de ocean?—de sea be full enough of vater vidout it."

"I am somewhat surprised at the intention of your question."

"Sir, I vill tell you; dere be von ship go along 'pon de sea, vich be vant of vater, and de sailors dey be ready to die ob dirst; dey no drink de vater out de ocean. By and bye dey see cloud, and de rain begin to come down; den de sailors spread deir sails on de deck; dey catch de rain vater; dey do drink, and den go on lifely. So you come to dese poor wretches—you spread de sail—de rains ob Got's blessing come down, and den dey drink and be glad. So, sir, I vill now open de door, an you may spread your sail." Dr. S. says in his diary, "Thanking Mr. H. for his remarks, I passed through to the hospital, with a design to spread my sails of instruction and prayer, in the pleasing hope that some mercy-drops from above might descend to refresh the souls of the poor prisoners. I have often indulged pleasing reflections on this little incident, as conveying to me valuable instruction. For, as the mariner can only spread the sail, it is the Lord alone that can raise the wind, or give the gentle rain; so I can only spread the gospel sail of instruction, and wait for drops of mercy from heaven."

This eminent clergyman, in the discharge of his official duties, had once closed his sermon to the prisoners, in New York, when one of them, familiarly called "Ned Craig," formerly a lawyer, was, at his own particular request, permitted to propound a doctrinal question to the preacher. Among the individuals present, were several prisoners who formerly ranked high in the learned professions, and one who had occupied the chair of professor of languages in a university.

"Pray," asked Ned, "how can you reconcile the general invitations of the gospel with the doctrine of a particular election?"

Dr. Stanford, turning to those present, replied, "These gentlemen know, that it is not customary to teach children abstruse doctrines in any science, until they have first learned their grammar. I am no polemic, but preach to you the plain gospel; but you must learn the A. B. C. of divinity before I shall attempt to explain the subject of your inquiry."

This pungent reply to an impertinent question, propounded not with a view to improvement, but for the purpose of embarrassing the preacher, afforded great satisfaction to the other prisoners.

How awful are the scenes which the Christian minister is sometimes called to witness; at once reminding him of the dreadful consequences of sin, and rousing all his energies to action! Dr. Stanford was once travelling through New Jersey in the stage. When they stopped at Plainfield, the driver informed the company that, a short distance further on the road, an intoxicated man had, on the preceding night, murdered his two sons, his wife, and himself. As the stage had to pass by the door, the passengers insisted on stopping at the house, and requested Dr. S. to accompany them. It was one of those neat little cottages which now and then attract the admiring gaze of the traveller, and seemed, from the silence that prevailed, to be an abode of blessedness and of peace. But, alas! it was the silence of death that reigned within its blood-stained walls. On entering the front room on the lower floor, they found a table plentifully spread on the preceding evening for the family repast. Here was every thing to secure contentment and domestic comfort; but the demon of intemperance had entered the enclosure. As they ascended to the room immediately above, they beheld one of those awful spectacles, from which, with instinctive horror, the heart unsteeled by crime involuntarily recoils. In the cradle lay a lovely little boy, about eight years old, murdered in a shocking manner; and on the floor, at a short distance from him, and covered with wounds and blood, lay his brother, about ten years of age. The unhappy mother of these victims of a father's rage, was found in the back parlour, to which, it is probable, she had fled for safety, but was there stabbed to the heart, by the hand of him who had vowed at the altar to love and protect her. Near the gory bosom of the martyred woman was seen the ghastly corpse of the sanguinary monster. After perpetrating the diabolical crime of murdering his unoffending family, it was supposed that he loaded his rifle, and receiving the muzzle into his mouth, deliberately discharged its contents, by which one half of his head was entirely blown away, and the barrel of the gun severed from the stock. The apartments were literally a human slaughter-house, where death reigned in undisturbed dominion. This tragic scene closed the lips of the beholders in silence, and astonishment seemed to have paralyzed them. No one was able to give utterance to the deep and oppressive feelings of the heart, and the company retired, increasingly convinced that great indeed is the depravity of man.

The biographer of Dr. Stanford records his interviews with many dying persons. The following is very instructive:—

This morning I was requested to visit a man, supposed to

be near death. After tenderly inquiring about the state of his mind, he replied, "It is very easy—I know that there is one God—I believe that there is a future state—I believe God, when I die, will take my poor soul—I believe all these." I asked, "Do you know that you are a sinner, and that you need mercy?" "Oh, we are all sinners." I answered him, that God could not save him at the expense of divine justice; that we both stood in need of a Saviour; that God had in mercy given his dear Son, whose blood cleanseth from all sin; and that there was none other name given under heaven, whereby we may be saved, but the name of the Lord Jesus; who is, therefore, the only Saviour. To my great astonishment, this man replied, "I don't know any thing about him." "Then," I replied, "it is high time that you should know him. It is, indeed, our encouragement that this Jesus is able and willing to save to the uttermost all who come unto God by him; and it becomes you, under your circumstances, to pray to him for mercy." I was equally surprised at his answer: "I never prayed in my life." I thought it my duty solemnly to warn him of his danger. After which, I prayed.

At four o'clock, I ordered the coachman to put me down at the hospital-gate, and I went into the sick man's room; but, what was my astonishment, as I looked around, to find both the man and the bed removed. "Nurse, what have you done with the patient?" "He is in the dead-house; he died at twelve o'clock." "How did he die?" Instead of giving me a direct reply, she told me, that soon after I left him, in the morning, two of his friends came to visit him, who informed her that he was a deist, and had lived a very irregular life. "But, nurse," I said, "you do not answer my question; how did he die?" She replied, "Sir, when he knew he was going, he cried loudly enough to Jesus Christ to save him: he died a coward, and, with his last breath, renounced his former infidelity." "Men may live fools, but fools they cannot die."

A VILLAGE CLERGYMAN.

An active and skilful young minister, while engaged under circumstances of the most promising kind in the village of J——, was told of a miller who, with more than usual profaneness, had repelled every attempt to approach him on the subject of religion, and had discouraged the hopes and efforts of the few serious persons in his vicinity. Among other practices of sinful daring, he uniformly kept his windmill, the most striking object in the hamlet, going on the Sabbath. In a little time, the minister determined to make an effort for the benefit of the hopeless man. He undertook the office of going for his flour, the next time, himself. "A fine mill," said he, as the miller adjusted his sack to receive the flour; "a fine mill, indeed; one of the most complete I have ever seen." This was nothing more than just—the miller had heard it a thousand times before; and would firmly have thought it, though he had never heard it once: but his skill and judgment were still gratified by this new testimony, and his feelings conciliated, even towards the minister. "But, oh!" continued his customer, after a little pause, "there is one defect in it!" "What is that?" carelessly asked the miller. "A very serious defect, too." "Eh!" replied the miller, turning up his face. "A defect that is likely to counterbalance all its advantages." "Well, what is it?" said the miller, standing straight up, and looking the minister in the face. He went on: "A defect which is likely to ruin the mill." "What is it?" rejoined the miller. "And will one day no doubt destroy the owner." "And can't you say it out?" exclaimed the impatient miller. "It goes on the Sabbath!" pronounced the minister, in a firm, solemn, and monitory tone. The astonished man stood blank and thunderstruck; and remained meek and submissive under a remonstrance and exhortation of a quarter of an hour's length, in which the danger of his state and practices, and the call to repentance towards God, and faith in our Lord Jesus Christ, were fully proposed to him.

A TRAVELLING MINISTER.

A minister who was urged by his people to go out on a begging excursion, to solicit money to liquidate a debt on their meeting-house, put up on Saturday night with the deacon of a church to which he was to present the subject on the ensuing Sabbath. He seemed to be quite wealthy; and, as he treated his guest with great cordiality and kindness, the preacher cherished glowing expectations of a very generous contribution from his purse. On the Sabbath, after setting forth the claims of his object in as forcible and eloquent a manner as possible, the plates were passed around for money. As the deacon sat near the pulpit, the preacher could not resist the temptation of rising up a little and peeping over the pulpit, to witness the expression of the good man's liberality. As the plate approached the deacon, he leisurely put his hand into his pocket. The preacher's heart palpitated with anxiety. But, alas! the deacon just dropped from his thumb and fingers two red cents upon the plate, and allowed it to pass! The preacher suddenly sank back into his seat, and hope and faith died within him. The collection was small, and the preacher, mortified and indignant, went straight back to his people, told them the story of the two cents, and assured them they must raise the funds needed themselves, or send some one else forth to beg, rather than him. The people caught his spirit—they determined to solicit no further—increased their subscriptions, and paid their debts themselves.

REV. MR. GRAFTON

Father Grafton, as he was called, was for nearly half a century a Baptist pastor at Newton, in the vicinity of Boston. He was highly esteemed, and often invited to the corporate and other public dinners of that city. On one of these occasions, he was greatly annoyed by the profane swearing of a young man who sat opposite to him; whom he sometimes reproved, but without effect. At length, the old gentleman determined to settle the affair, and rising, with a sharp voice, he called out, "Mr. President!" That gentleman immediately commanded silence, and called on the company to hear " the Rev. Mr. Grafton." "Mr. President," said he, "I beg leave to move that there be no swearing done here"—looking at the young man, and attracting the general attention towards him—"except by my friend, the Rev. Dr. Homer," a well-known, estimable clergyman then present. The resolution was carried by acclamation, and the good old minister enjoyed himself for the remaining part of the afternoon.

REV. CALVIN COLTON.

When this gentleman was in England, a few years ago, he published an interesting little book, under the title of "The American Cottager." In it he gave an account of a female cottager on a missionary station, in one of the Western States, who had recently been received as a member of a Christian church, but who had not yet had the privilege of obeying the Saviour's command: "This do in remembrance of me." She was suddenly laid on a sick-bed, which indeed proved the bed of death. She sent for Mr. C., and expressed a most ardent desire that he should administer to her the holy ordinance of the Supper. Her ardor on the subject was so great, that he began to fear she was attaching to it too much importance, and was regarding obedience to it as a passport to heaven, and delicately expressed his fear on the subject. Her reply, however, was more than satisfactory. "No, sir, I do not think that the reception of the Lord's Supper is essential to the salvation of my soul; but I do feel that if I die without it, I can never be happy, because I shall never forget that there was a command of my Saviour, who loved me, that I never obeyed."

On the voyage of Mr. Colton to England, a few years since, he had, one Sabbath, complied with the request of the captain and passengers in preaching to them; and, towards evening, was hanging over the stern of the ship, engaged in meditation, when the current of his thoughts was interrupted by the appearance of a young man, one of the cabin passengers, before him. He begged pardon for the intrusion, and observed that he owed an apology, on his own behalf, for he was unjustly suffering in the estimation of the preacher.

"Pray, sir," said the preacher, "explain yourself." He went on, regardless of this request; adding, much to the surprise of the minister, "I bought those books at an auction-room; they were struck off to me in one parcel, the night before I left New York. I was ignorant of what they were.

"What books?" interrupted the minister.

"I intend to destroy them," continued the young man; "and I should suffer injustice if I allowed you to suppose that I had not been better educated, or that I can relish such vile trash."

It turned out, after the parties in this colloquy had come to a better understanding, that the said books were of an infidel and otherwise vile character. Soon after the commencement of the voyage, the young man had politely offered the minister the use of any of his books that might interest him. Of this privilege he had availed himself, but had not happened to have seen any of the bad ones. It had also happened that, in his sermon of that day, the preacher had taken occasion to make some remarks on the absurdity of infidelity, and the vicious state of the moral affections that could relish it. The young man felt mortified and ashamed, supposing himself to be directly aimed at in the preacher's remarks, and took this opportunity to vindicate himself. The interview proved that "conscience needs no accuser."

REV. DR. BEECHER.

When the venerable Dr. Lyman Beecher was a young man, he was once returning to his native town in Connecticut, and fell into conversation by the roadside with an old neighbour, an Episcopalian, who had been mowing. "Mr. Beecher," said the farmer, "I should like to ask you a question. Our clergy say that you are not ordained, and have no right to preach. I should be glad to know what you think about it." "Suppose," replied Dr. Beecher, "you had in the neighbourhood a blacksmith, who said he could prove that he belonged to a regular line of blacksmiths which had come down all the way from St. Peter, but he made scythes that would not cut; and you had another blacksmith, who said he could not see what descent from Peter had to do with making scythes that would cut. Where would you go to get your scythes?" "Why, to the man who made scythes to cut, certainly," replied the farmer. "Well," said Dr. Beecher, "*that minister which cuts, is the minister which Christ has authorized to preach.*" In a more recent conversation on the same subject, Dr. Beecher gave his opinion by relating this story.

In my early ministry, says Dr. Beecher, I was called to attend a neighbour at East Hampton, Long Island. He was skeptical and intemperate. "Pray for me!" he exclaimed, "pray for me!—pray for me!" "You must pray for yourself," I replied. "Pray—I cannot pray! I am going straight to perdition!" He lived three days, almost without food, and then died—so far as we know—*without any disease.* It was the power of conscience.

REV. DR. C.

A YOUNG gentleman fresh from college, who had more knowledge of books than of men, was wending his way to the residence of the Rev. Dr. C.—The Doctor was extensively known and respected for his energy of character, his learning, piety, and moral worth. But, like the great apostle, he did not disdain to "labour with his own hands."

With a letter of introduction to the aged divine, whom he had known only by reputation, our genteel young friend was seeking the privilege of an acquaintance with him.

"Old daddy," said he to an aged labourer in the field by the way-side, whose flapped hat and coarse-looking over-coat —it was a lowering day—and dark complexion and features, contrasted strongly with his own broadcloth and kid gloves and fair person:—"Old daddy, tell me where the Rev. Dr. C—— lives." "In the house you see yonder" the old man modestly replied.

Without condescending to thank him for the information, the young man rode on, and soon found himself seated in the parlour of Dr. C.'s hospitable residence, at the invitation of the lady of the house, awaiting the expected arrival of the Doctor.

In due time the host appeared, having returned from the field, laid aside his wet garments, and adjusted his person. But, to the surprise and confusion of the young guest, whom should he meet in the Reverend Dr., but the same old daddy he had so unceremoniously accosted on his way!

"It was very respectful in you," said the venerable divine, with an arch look, and in a pleasant tone—for the aged man was not wanting in wit and humor—"it was very respectful in you to call me old daddy; I always love to see young men show respect to old age."

The confusion and mortification of the young man were indescribable. He could have sunk through the floor, and buried himself in the darkness of the cellar beneath him. With a countenance crimsoned with blushes, he began to stammer out an apology for his incivility.

"No apology," said the doctor, very pleasantly, "no apology,—I always love to see respect shown to old age." But the kindness and assiduity of the family could not relieve the unpleasantness of his situation; a sense of the mortifying blunder which he had committed, marred all his anticipated pleasure from the interview, and he was glad to take his leave as soon as he could do it with decency.

REV. MR. COLEY

Several years ago, a man, decently clothed, of good appearance and address, with some degree of intelligence, called on the Rev. Mr. Coley, of Albany, whose benevolent feelings readily sympathized with the distressed, exhibiting testimonials of being a good Christian, and professing, in rather an Irish accent, to be a Scotch Baptist, but possessing no formal letter from a Baptist church. Mr. C. told him that to receive him as a good Baptist brother, a letter was indispensable. Still, he protested solemnly, loudly, and with tears, that he was a Baptist.

In about two months afterwards, he returned, with a letter, but an exceedingly doubtful one, and professing that all he wanted was, to raise money enough to get back to Halifax. Mr. C. having been often imposed upon, and suspicions running high on this occasion, invited him to dinner, determining to try, by a very proper test, whether he was really a Baptist or not. Sitting around the dinner-table, he asked him to pray for God's blessing upon the food of which they were about to partake.

"O, yes, sir, yes, sir."—A few minutes' silence.

"Pray out loud, brother," said Mr. C.—A mutter.—"I can have no such sacrifice as that at my table," said Mr. C.; "pray out loud, brother."

"O," said the man, "I can't pray before a minister."

Mr. C. then excused him. Dinner being over, Mr. Coley observed, if he were a good Baptist brother, he loved prayer; as for himself, like Daniel, he had prayers three times a day, and now he wanted the privilege of hearing him pray. The family being called in, they knelt down.—Silence.—"I want you to pray, brother," said Mr. C.—A mutter.—"I want you to pray out loud, brother," said Mr. C. "O," said the man, who by this time was wrought up to a dreadful state of perturbation, "I could not pray before a minister." "If you are a Baptist brother," said Mr. C., "you *can* pray." Upon this, the man muttered over some parts of the Lord's prayer "Now," said the minister, "I have all the evidence I need that you are an impostor. You are not a Baptist, sir." "I have called on ministers all over the United States," said the man, "and you are the sharpest man I ever met with."—With this, he made towards the door, which Mr. C. locked, and, in the tones of a second Stentor, said, "*You shall not go, sir.* James, fetch a police officer." By this time the man trembled like an aspen leaf, and cried, "Don't send for a police officer." "Confess, then, who and what you are," said Mr. C. He then confessed that he was not a Baptist, and lived by getting money in such a manner, and added that his honour was the sharpest man he ever met with. After some conversation and much entreaty, Mr. Coley allowed him to go, satisfied that he had found out a tolerably sure method of detecting impostors.

Were every minister to adopt some such expedient, such characters would become exceedingly scarce, and their acts of benevolence centre on needy and deserving objects. When ministers help such persons, they are a party to an extensive robbery among the most benevolent members of the church, though unconscious of it.

A CLERGYMAN IN NEW YORK.

A clergyman of New York related from the pulpit the following facts:—A clergyman in a neighbouring town, some time since, as he was riding, passed some young females, near a school-house, and dropped from his carriage two tracts, which he had previously marked. Some time after, he was conversing with a young woman with reference to her spiritual state, and found her rejoicing in the hope of pardoned sin. He inquired the history of her religious feelings, and she traced them to a tract dropped by a traveller, which was manifestly one of the two above referred to. He was afterwards called to visit another young woman on a sick-bed, whose mind was calm and composed in view of death, which the event proved was near at hand. She traced her first serious impressions to the circumstance of two tracts being dropped by a traveller; one of which, she said, was taken up by her cousin, and the other by herself; "and now," said she, "we are both hoping in Christ." She had retained the tract as a precious treasure, and putting her hand under her pillow, showed it to the clergyman, who immediately recognised the marks he had written on it.

REV. E. BYNE.

The late Rev. Edmund Byne, though somewhat eccentric in his manners, was an eminently faithful and fearless servant of the Lord Jesus. When a young man, soon after he had joined the church, he was invited, with his wife, by some of his old companions in sin, to attend a dancing-party, which he agreed to do on the express condition that he should entirely direct the whole proceedings of the evening. When the company had collected, a young lady stepped forward and invited the preacher to dance. He so far accepted her invitation as to walk out on the floor with her, when the violin struck up a lively air. Mr. Byne claimed his right to give direction to the exercises of the evening, and immediately sang a hymn, in which he was joined by several of the party, and then knelt down and offered up a fervent prayer. By the time he had completed his second hymn many were in tears. The dance was converted into a prayer-meeting, and no other frolic was ever attempted in that house.

REV. MR. BAKER.

Rev. Mr. Baker, a Free-will Baptist evangelist, was visiting from house to house, in a certain neighbourhood, in New England; and met on his walk three young men with axes on their shoulders. He stopped and conversed with them. Two appeared somewhat serious: the third, a gay, frank young man, replied, "You see, sir, that splendid white house on that farm yonder?" "Yes." "Well, sir, that estate has been willed to me by my uncle; and we are now going to do chopping in the woodland that belongs to it. There are some incumbrances on the estate which I must settle, before the farm can be fully mine; and as soon as I have cleared it of these incumbrances, I mean to become a Christian." "Ah! young man," said the minister, "beware; you may never see that day; while you are gaining the world, you may lose your soul." "I'll run the risk," said he, and they parted. The three young men went into the woods; and this daring procrastinator, and another, engaged in felling a tree. A dry, heavy limb, hung loosely in the top; and as the tree was jarred by the successive strokes of the axe, it quitted its hold, and as it fell crashing through the branches to the earth, it struck the head of the young heir, in its way, and stretched him on the ground, a lifeless corpse. Thus were his hopes cut off; and, hazarding the delay of months, he lost his soul in an hour. His fellow-labourer was converted; for conviction struck his mind when he saw the young heir quivering in death! "I felt then such a horror at the danger of delaying religion, when I thought of what he had just said, and saw his end, that I determined to neglect my soul no longer." His example was followed by others; and a great revival ensued

REV. DR. TODD.

The following account of a Sabbath in the solitudes was given by the Rev. Dr. Todd, at one of the benevolent celebrations at Boston:—

In the northern part of the state of New York, between the St. Lawrence and Lake Champlain, and between the Mohawk and the Hudson, there is a wilderness one hundred and fifty miles long and one hundred miles wide. I had no conception that there was such a wilderness this side of the Mississippi. This wilderness is filled with lofty mountains, little inferior to the White Mountains of New Hampshire. On the tops of these mountains, clouds gather and pour down their rains and scatter their snows, so that large reservoirs are needed to hold the superabundant waters. The hand of God has hollowed out a number of beautiful lakes, in the bosom of these mountains, for this purpose—and here arise the rivers which flow in various directions to the sea.

In the course of the last summer, in company with a learned friend, I entered that wilderness, and penetrated to the centre, where is a beautiful lake of twenty or thirty miles in length, and several miles wide, interspersed with little islands. Here we found seven families that lived alone. They had a little foot-path through the wilderness, so that when they wanted to step into a store to buy any necessaries, they could do so by following this foot-path only forty-three miles; or if a man wanted bread for his family, he had only to take his grain on his back and go the same distance and get it ground, and then bring it back in the same way. These people were keen at hunting and fishing, but children at every thing else. But death had entered even there, and taken a beautiful girl of seventeen, who had just died, with no one to administer the consolations of religion, or to perform religious services at her funeral.

It was Saturday night. The sun was an hour high. When it was known that we were ministers of the Gospel, two young ladies jumped into a little boat and rowed four or five miles, to tell the neighbours. The next morning was still. There was no hunting or fishing. The 'coons screamed unmolested after their prey. It was the first Sabbath that was ever kept there, and I was to preach. We met in a little hut covered with bark. All were there. We could not sing, for no one knew how to raise a tune. In the afternoon, to accommodate a mother that had a young child, the meeting was appointed seven miles up the lake. We found them all there. One of our boats was rowed by the father, and the other by the two sisters. One old hunter came down from forty miles farther up; and he was able to raise a tune—a half-hunter's and half-psalm tune.

What a meeting was that! There were only thirty-three souls; but they came round me, and said, if I would come and live among them, they would give me fish enough to eat, and stop hunting on the Sabbath. When we separated, as we got out a little way from them, there was a pause—they raised the tune and began to sing the hymn,

"People of the living God," &c.

Was I weak because I wept? These are the sheep which have strayed from our fold—the poor ones of the family, whom we are to send after

---

A CLERGYMAN IN TENNESSEE.

A CONVENTION being held in Tennessee, a clergyman, with a friend, made their home at the house of Dr. D., an eminent physician, who, it was said, was greatly addicted to profanity in ordinary conversation. No evidence of this fact presented itself for the several days of their visit.

At length, on the evening before their departure, the clergyman determined to draw a bow at a venture, and contrived incidentally to refer to profane swearing. He then said, "Doctor, we leave you to-morrow; and be assured we are very grateful to Mrs. D. and yourself; but, may I add, my dear sir, that we have been disappointed here?"

"Disappointed!"

"Yes, sir, but most agreeably."

"In what, Mr. C.?"

"Will you pardon me, if I say we were misinformed, and may I name it?"

"Certainly, sir, say what you wish."

"Well, my dear sir, we were told that Dr. D. was not guarded in his language; but, surely, you are misrepresented."

"Sir," interrupted he, "I do honour you for candor; yet, sir, I regret to say, you have not been misinformed. I do, and perhaps habitually, use profane language; but, sir, can you think I would swear before religious people, and one of them a clergyman?"

Tears stood in the eyes of the clergyman as he took him by the hand, and said, "My dear sir, you amaze me! Can it be that Dr. D., so courteous and intelligent a man, has greater reverence for us than for *the infinite God?*"

"Gentlemen," replied the doctor, with a tremulous voice, "I never did before see the utter folly of profane swearing. I will abandon it for ever."

REV. W. TENNENT.

The eminent minister of this name was settled as a pastor, several years before he married. Totally ignorant of the way in which he ought to manage his temporal concerns, he was frequently embarrassed. In this emergency, a friend from New York told him the only remedy against the recurrence of the evil, was to get a wife. "I do not know how to go about it," was the answer. "Then I will undertake the business," said his friend; "I have a sister-in-law, a pious and prudent widow." The next evening found Mr. Tennent in New York, and the following day he was introduced to Mrs. N——. Pleased with her appearance, he abruptly told her that he supposed she knew his errand; that neither his time nor inclination would allow him to use much ceremony; and that, if she pleased, he would return from his charge on the following Monday, and be married. With some little hesitation, the lady consented; and she proved a most excellent wife.

Mr. Tennent and the Rev. S. Blair were sent, by the synod to which they belonged, on a mission to Virginia. They stopped, one evening, at a tavern for the night, where they found a number of persons, with whom they supped, in a common room. After supper, cards were introduced; when one of the gentlemen politely asked them if they would not take a cut with them; not knowing that they were clergymen. Mr. Tennent pleasantly answered, "With all my heart, gentlemen, if you can convince us that we can serve our Master's cause, or contribute any thing towards the success of our mission." This drew some smart reply from the gentleman; when Mr. T., with solemnity, added, "We are ministers of the Lord

Jesus Christ; we profess ourselves his servants; we are sent on his business, which is to persuade mankind to repent of their sins, to turn from them, and to accept of that happiness and salvation which are offered in the gospel." This very unexpected reply, delivered in a tender, though solemn manner, and with great apparent sincerity, so engaged the attention of the gentlemen, that the cards were laid aside, and an opportunity was offered for explaining, in a social conversation during the rest of the evening, some of the leading doctrines of the gospel, to the entire satisfaction and apparent edification of the hearers.

When Mr. Tennent was once travelling in Virginia, he lodged one night at the house of a planter, who informed him that one of his slaves, a man of more than seventy years of age, and who could neither read nor write, was eminent for his piety and knowledge of the Scriptures. Having some curiosity to learn what evidence such a man could have of their divine origin, he went out in the morning, alone, and without making himself known as a clergyman, entered into conversation with him on the subject. After starting some of the common objections of infidels against the authenticity of the Scriptures, in a way adapted to confound an ignorant man, he said to him, " When you cannot even *read* the Bible, nor examine the evidence for or against its truth, how can you *know* that it is the word of God?" After reflecting a moment, the African replied, " You ask me, sir, how I *know* that the Bible is the word of God? *I know it by its effect upon my own heart.*"

AN AGED CLERGYMAN.

The following fact may show Christian ministers the importance of the greatest possible simplicity in the language they use:—

A young clergyman, who had delivered a discourse in the place of an aged brother minister, requested the opinion of the latter respecting it.

"Oh," said he, plainly, "many of the words you used were beyond the comprehension of your hearers. Thus, for instance, the word 'inference,' perhaps not half of my parishioners understand its meaning." "Inference, inference!" exclaimed the other, "why, every one must understand that." "I think you will find it not so. There's my clerk, now; he prides himself upon his learning, and in truth is very intelligent: we will try him. Zechariah, come hither, Zechariah; my brother here wishes you to draw an inference; can you do it?" "Why, I'm pretty strong, but Johanadab the coachman is stronger than I; I'll ask him." Zechariah went out a few moments, to look after the coachman, and returned. "Johanadab says he has never tried to draw an inference, sir; but he reckons his horses can draw any thing that the traces will hold!"

REV. DR. HARRIS.

The late Rev. Dr. Harris, of Dunbarton, walking out one day, in one of the large villages of a neighbouring state, met one of the champions of Universalism. It was General P——, the leader and main supporter of the large Universalist society which had for many years existed in that place. He was a high-minded man, quite wealthy, and very influential; having a good deal of general information, and considerable skill in argument, which last he did not hesitate to use whenever opportunities were presented. He and Dr. H. were personally strangers; but, knowing something of each other by reputation, they readily introduced themselves to each other. The general very soon lifted up his standard, and began his war of words; not doubting that, though he might fail to convince his opponent, he should at least show him that he was no ordinary combatant, but knew well on what ground he stood, and how to wield the sword of sectarian warfare to good advantage. The doctor heard him through; then calmly turned to him and said, "General P——, it is of no use for us to contend. We shall not convince each other by arguments ever so protracted. But there is one thing, in relation to this matter, which deserves consideration. It is this: I can treat your religion just as I please; I can turn from it, as an utter abomination. I can *despise* it; I can *spit* on it, and trample it under my feet; and yet, after all, I SHALL BE SAVED; *shan't I, General P——?*" The general, of course, was obliged to assent, or give up the doctrine. There was no room for evasion. "But," added the doctor, while the general was writhing at the contempt thus thrown upon his gods, "it will not do for you to treat my religion so. If you do, YOU ARE A LOST MAN!" This was enough—nothing more was said.

Dr. Harris was settled in Dunbarton, in August, 1789, over a church gathered one month previously, consisting of twelve members, all males. His ministry with that church continued more than forty years, during which time the place was visited with repeated and extensive revivals, by which the church was greatly enlarged and strengthened.

A short time before his death he penned the following retrospect of his method of preaching, and of his feelings in view of it. We copy it from the Congregational Journal:

"In my late sickness, though very distressing for eight or ten weeks, yet I had no choice between life and death: this I chose to leave with God to decide; and I could rejoice and did rejoice, that infinite wisdom and goodness would do all for the best; and my greatest desire is, that I may spend my future remaining days to the glory of God, and in doing good to man.

"And now, standing on the borders of eternity, I find that I have arrived at old age, and gray hairs, and many infirmities, much sooner than I had expected. Truly, few and evil have the days of my life been. Though I am sensible that God has seen much heart-wickedness and coming short of duty in me, yet I am not aware that since I professed religion, men have accused me of any immoralities, or charged me with delinquencies in ministerial or Christian duties; yet I do not by any means extend charity so far towards myself; I know that I have a great account to settle with God, which nothing can cancel but the blood of Christ.

"There is no part of my life and conduct upon which I can look back with greater approbation and peace of mind, than my manner of preaching the word, and the pains I have taken to support the discipline of Christ's church, though it has cost me much labour and toil, and I have passed through evil report as well as good report in defending the truth. For a long time I had to bear the reproach of bringing in new and strange doctrines; of being a hard, severe, and unfeeling preacher, whose doctrines and manner of preaching were calculated to divide the people, to set the father against the son and the son against the father, to break up the church and throw society into disorder. And why? Because I preached that God is unchangeably the same for ever; that he is a holy sovereign, and works all things according to his own most holy, just, and good will, and that it is man's duty to submit to that will in all things—instead of doing which, man has resisted that will, and violated God's law, and thus become the enemy of his Maker. For this God pronounced his curse upon him, binding him over to everlasting punishment; under this curse, all the human race must have suffered the vengeance of eternal fire, had not God in his own sovereign grace provided a way of escape. He so loved the world that he gave his own Son to die that sinners might live; still, none can be saved, but those who repent and forsake their sins; who believe in Christ, and become holy. Faith, repentance, a new heart and true love, are all the sovereign gifts of God; he hath mercy on whom he will have mercy, and whom he will he hardeneth. I preached all the doctrines of strict Calvinism; and truly this was new doctrine and strange preaching in these parts at that day; for when I began to preach in this town, the whole region was given over to Arminianism, both ministers and churches embracing that system, with but few exceptions; of course, in whatever direction I went, I met with opposition. The new minister brought new and strange things to their ears, which they were not willing to endure. But I found it necessary, and believed it to be my indispensable duty, to dwell much on the doctrines of grace, wherever I went; and it was often thrown out against me, that I always preached on doctrines, and the hardest doctrines too; such as would raise the opposition of the human heart, and turn the feelings of unreconciled men against the preacher. I very well knew then, as ministers do now, that I was not taking the way to be popular; but I believed it to be the right way to do good, to gain the approbation of God and save the souls of men. I believed it the only way to make men acquainted with the true character of God, with the nature and requirements of God's holy law, the condition of man before and after the fall, and the way in which sinners can be saved through the atonement of Christ.

"I am now entirely satisfied that the course I pursued was correct; the course which God will approve; the course which promoted sound doctrine in this and neighbouring churches, and led to the conversion of many souls; finally, it has fixed the churches in this region firmly on the doctrines of Christ and his apostles. Instead of regretting that I have preached these doctrines so much, I am glad, and rejoice with exceeding joy. There is no part of my life in respect to which I can look forward to the Judgment with greater composure, than that which was spent in preaching plainly and pungently, to the best of my ability, the great and glorious doctrines of sovereign grace, as understood by the fathers of New England. And I think if the ministers of the present day would preach more like the ministers of a hundred years ago, they would be much more likely to do good, and save the souls of men. The historical, biographical, geographical, astronomical, rhetorical, and egotistical preaching, which we frequently hear in these latter days, will do but little to feed the hungry souls of the saints, and much less to convict the hard hearts of poor, dying sinners; *and therefore I leave my dying testimony against such an unprofitable and unscriptural mode of preaching.*"

REV. MR. HYDE.

The memoir of the Rev. Mr. Hyde, of Lee, Mass., who died in December, 1833, presents him in a very lovely view as the head of a family. One of his sons writes:—

He never came to the family altar as if to perform an unmeaning and irksome ceremony; but it ever seemed to him a delightful spot—a spot where he loved to linger. And I believe we were all happy in the hour of family devotion. They are delightful spots in the retrospect; and nothing, *nothing* makes such a chasm at home; nothing makes the paternal mansion appear so gloomy, as not to hear the well-known accents of our much-lamented father ascending in affectionate supplication at the hours of morning and evening devotion, and invoking a blessing upon the bounties of Providence at the social repast. And he was not content with supplicating the best of Heaven's blessings upon his children at family prayers only. Often has he taken me with him in solitude, particularly when I was about to leave home, and there, upon our bended knees, has he committed me to the special care and keeping of our heavenly Father. What he has done for me in this respect, I presume he has done for the others.

SEVERAL CLERGYMEN.

An old Connecticut pastor, whose peculiarities of preaching were proverbial, and who was blest with a temper of great value, was one day told by a parishioner that he did not like his sermons. "Well," said the old man, "I don't wonder at it; I don't like 'em myself."

A deacon went to his minister, and professing to speak the sentiments of the congregation, began to complain of his style of preaching. "I do not say these things for myself," said the deacon; "I am not at all dissatisfied; but the people are very uneasy, and I am afraid we shall have trouble." "How is it," inquired the pastor, "that *you* hear all these complaints? No other member of the church seems to be so familiar with them as you are?" "Oh," said the deacon, "they all know that I am on terms of intimacy with you, and they make me the tunnel into which they pour every thing which they wish you to hear." "Yes," replied the pastor, "and it is because you *are* a tunnel that they use you as such."

———

A lady of suspected chastity, and who was tinctured with infidel principles, conversing with a minister of the Gospel, objected to the Scriptures on account of their obscurity and the great difficulty of understanding them. The minister wisely and smartly replied, "*Why, madam, what can be easier to understand than the seventh commandment,* 'Thou shalt not commit adultery?'"

———

An elder of a church in the state of New York, a few years ago, owned a distillery, and manufactured ardent spirits. The elder was an active Christian, and seemed quite awake to the benevolent efforts of the day. His pastor was grieved that so worthy a man should be engaged in a business which brought temporal and eternal ruin upon his fellow-men, and resolved to give him faithful warning. While visiting the elder, at his house, the elder looked toward the grave-yard, and said, "I love to look there; it seems to be the way to heaven." "Yes," said the pastor, "and that," pointing to the distillery, "is the way to hell." It was a word in season; and, in a few weeks, the distillery was levelled to the ground.

———

The North American Review gives us the following dialogue between a clergyman and a female parishioner:--

Parishioner.—It amazes me that ministers don't write better sermons. I'm sick of their dull, prosy affairs.

Minister.—But it is no easy matter, my good woman, to write good sermons.

Parishioner.—Yes, but then you are so long about it. I could write one myself, in half the time, if I only had the text

Minister.—Oh, if a text is what you want, I will furnish that. Take this one, from Solomon: "It is better to dwell in a corner of the house-top, than in a wide house with a brawling woman."

Parishioner.—Do you mean me, sir?

Minister.—Oh, my good woman, you will never make a good sermonizer; you are too soon in your *application*.

"It is true I have but little to give," said Dr. Finley to an agent; "but I consider it a privilege and an honour, so far as the Lord allows, to have something, if it be but a single nail, in every edifice that is going up for Christ."

A lady, in genteel but very moderate circumstances, when presenting the clergyman of ———— with a small sum for a charitable object, said, "You may put it down as the *Widow's Mite, sir.*" "Not so, my friend," replied the worthy pastor. "I beg you may," the lady earnestly added; "it is but a trifle." "I am aware of that, madam, but it is not *all your living*." How very few have in truth presented the "widow's mite," although many apply the passage to themselves.

A minister, not favourable to the doctrine of the eternal election of the people of Christ, intending once to puzzle an aged woman, who was regarded as "a mother in Israel," said to her, "Do you really believe that God chose you to salvation *before* you were born?" Her answer was remarkable for its promptness. "Oh, most certainly; for I know He never could have seen any thing in me for which to choose me *since* I was born."

A skeptic, meeting a clergyman of one of our large cities, with a view, probably, of showing his wit, asked, "If we are to live after death, why have we not some certain knowledge of it?" The clergyman, feeling it important sometimes to answer a fool according to his folly, asked in return, "Why didn't you get some knowledge of this world before you came into it?"

"If we go to war, father," said a bright-eyed boy to his clerical parent, "from what part of the Bible shall you get a text for a new sermon?" The good minister, being taken by surprise at the question, thought a moment, and then, smoothing the locks of the child with a sort of paternal pride, answered that he believed it would be from *Lamentations*.

Some years since, as the venerable Father Patterson of Philadelphia, of excellent memory, was riding in a public conveyance, through one of the most fertile counties of Pennsylvania, his attention was attracted by the many large farms in that part of the country. He admired the beauty of the landscape, the richness of the soil, the luxuriance of vegetation, the extensive meadows and ample fields waving with the yellow harvest, and ripening for the sickle. As he looked abroad, over the highly cultivated fields, on the right hand and on the left, he said to a friend, " Indeed, indeed, the Lord has many fine farms in this region; but I fear He receives very little rent from them all." We fear this passing remark is applicable to farms in many other parts of this as well as other countries.

———

That was a noble answer which was given by a clergyman to one of his acquaintances, when urged to drink wine at a wedding.

"What! Mr. M.," said one of the guests, "don't you drink wine at a wedding?"

"No, sir," was the reply; "I will take a glass of water."

"But, sir," said the officious guest, "you recollect the advice of Paul to Timothy, to take a little wine for his infirmity."

"I have no infirmity," was the reverend gentleman's reply.

———

As the Rev. Mr. Field, formerly of Westminster, Vermont, went to give his vote at an election, a man of opposite politics expressed his surprise at seeing him there; and, to confirm his objection, quoted the remark of the Saviour, that his "kingdom was not of this world." "Has no man a right to vote," rejoined the witty clergyman, "unless he belongs to the kingdom of Satan?"

———

A minister writes:—In obtaining subscriptions for a benevolent purpose, I called upon a gentleman, in one of our largest cities, who generously contributed to the object. Before leaving, I said to him, "How much, think you, will such an individual subscribe?" "I don't know," said he, "but could you hear that man pray, you would think that he would give you all he is worth." So I called upon him; but, to my surprise, he would not contribute. As I was about to take my leave, I said to him, "As I came to your house, I asked an individual what you would probably give? 'I don't know,' said he, 'but could you hear that man pray, you would think he would give you all he is worth.'" The man's head dropped, tears gushed from his eyes, he took out his pocket-book, and gave me seventy-five dollars.

Bishop Elliot, of Georgia, has published a sermon, in which he says:—

It will be a happy day for the church when her clergy and laity shall plant themselves firmly upon the four principles of this sermon: That wealth can be lawfully and innocently gotten only by labour. That, in the choice of rulers, virtue and wisdom are to be preferred to party. That education is not the mere acquisition of knowledge, but includes moral and religious training. That the religion of Christ is not the fruit of excitement, but of scriptural instruction, united with prayer and watchfulness. Such principles would, in these days, make her members what Scripture says all Christians ought to be, a "peculiar people!"

The Rev. John Elliot was once asked by a pious woman, who was vexed with a wicked husband, and bad company frequently infesting her house on his account, what she should do? "Take," said he, "the Holy Bible into your hand, when bad company comes in, and that will soon drive them out of the house."

A clergyman, in New York, not long since, remarked from the pulpit, while preaching on faith, that Faith was "God's Magnetic Telegraph." One of his hearers, who was perhaps more inquisitive than *thoughtful*, was desirous of knowing " where the office is ?" To which the admirable answer was given, "*In every lowly heart of prayer.*"

An aged clergyman, in Baltimore, states, " that during the time he was chaplain to the Maryland Penitentiary, he took great pains to ascertain from the convicts, what was the commencement of their downward career; and that the testimony of about ninety-nine out of a hundred was, that their career of wickedness commenced with *Sabbath-breaking*."

A clergyman in New England, eminent for talents, was one day accosted by a parishioner, who highly commended some of his performances, of which he himself had a very low opinion. After patiently hearing him a few minutes, the clergyman replied, " My friend, all that you say gives me no better opinion of myself than I had before, but it gives me a much worse opinion of you."

A venerable minister, who has preached some sixty-five years in the same place, being asked what was the secret of long life, replied, " Rise early, live temperately, work hard, and keep cheerful!"

An English publication gives an anecdote of a clergyman of this country worth transcribing. He was desirous of communicating the idea of faith to a little boy, and taking a chair, he placed it at a distance from him, and setting the boy upon it, told him to fall forward, and he would catch him. The boy had readily mounted the chair, but declined to fall forward as requested. He wished to obey, but was afraid the clergyman would fail to catch him. He, however, put one hand on the mantelpiece, thinking to save himself if not caught; but the minister told him that would not do—he must trust to him alone; adding that he would surely catch him, provided he would fall forward. The boy summoned all his courage, placed confidence in what had been said to him, he fell, and was immediately caught. The clergyman then told him that was faith, and that he wished him to go with the same confidence to Jesus Christ. Any child may comprehend this illustration; but alas, the disposition is too often manifested to lay hold of some " mantelpiece,"—something in which self is interested, rather than go direct to the arms of the Saviour!

A Christian pastor, in America, was in the frequent habit, during the tours he made in his extensive parish, of stopping for a night at a village inn, and of continuing his journey the next day. On one occasion he found the principal apartment converted into a ball-room. The host apologized for his not being able to accommodate him as comfortably as usual; but the pastor, without being disconcerted, asked to have his supper served to him in a corner of the room. When it was ready, he begged the assembly to grant him a few moments' silence, that he might, according to his practice, make an audible prayer before partaking of the meal. He accordingly commenced praying, but before he had finished, the dancers had disappeared.

A Universalist clergyman was once robbed on the road by a man who had formerly lived with him as a servant. After his arrest, the preacher asked the man how he could be so base as to rob his old employer. The robber's answer speaks volumes against the soul-destroying heresy:—"You yourself tempted me to commit this offence against the law; for I have often heard you say, both in public and private, that *all* men will enjoy everlasting bliss after death, and that there *is no such thing as eternal punishment in the next world.* You thus removed my *greatest* fear: why should I dread the *less?*"

A NEW ENGLAND MINISTER.

A WORTHY minister of the gospel, in one of the New England States, was in the habit of inviting any of his lay brethren, who might feel impelled by a sense of solemn duty, to exhort, or pray, or to perform any other religious acts which might to them seem proper, at the close of the preaching. It accordingly became a common practice, for some one or other of the members of the church to engage in exhortation or prayer, at the conclusion of the service. Among those who seemed anxious to take a part on such occasions, was a rough, uncouth sort of a lad, who would seldom permit an opportunity to pass, without ministering some word of admonition to the people. At ordinary times the forwardness of the lad produced no particular inconvenience. He was, therefore, generally permitted to go through his regular harangues. On one occasion, when the minister rose to preach, he saw in the meeting several very genteel-looking strangers, who had come in to hear his sermon, and appeared to be prepared to give very earnest heed. He thought at the moment that it would be a fine opportunity for him to make a powerful impression upon the hearts of these strangers; and prepared his mind for one of his best efforts. Still he was apprehensive that if the boy got a chance to exhort at the end of the service, he might frustrate all the benefit of his sermon; and he was therefore exceedingly anxious to close, and dismiss before the young man had time for his speech. But this could not be done; for the boy was watching his opportunity, and as soon as the preacher had finished, he commenced, and continued his speech for some time, to the no small mortification of the minister. After some time, this same preacher was travelling at a distance from home, when he met a very interesting stranger, who appeared instantly to recognise him, and approached and cordially saluted him, after which the following conversation took place:

Stranger.—Did I not have the pleasure of hearing you preach at ———, on a certain day, when there were several strangers of us present?

Minister.—I was preaching there at that time.

Stranger.—I shall have reason to remember that day, not only in time, but in eternity; for it pleased the Lord there to fasten an arrow in my heart, which left me uneasy and wretched, until I found peace in Christ.

Minister.—I desire to be very thankful to God, that he was pleased to make my public ministry on that occasion, the means of doing good to you, and I shall ever desire to be humble before him, for such honour put upon me.

Stranger.—My friend, it is true that the Lord has made me, as I trust, one of his jewels; but I shall not sparkle in your crown, in that day, but in the crown of that boy, who exhorted when you had done. The Lord made use of that boy to convert my soul.

REV. DR. GRIFFIN.

Dr. E. D. Griffin was often extremely felicitous in his allusions to Scripture, especially on public occasions. In his Memoir, we have an affecting account of the dangerous illness of his eldest daughter, and of his trials connected with it. Some years afterwards, when by marvellous grace that daughter had been brought into the kingdom of heaven, and had become the mother of children, she came forward, with her husband, according to the practice of the Christian denomination to which they belonged, to "offer them to the Lord;" Dr. G. stood for a moment before he uttered a word, and then, with deep emotion, said, in a way that affected every person present to tears, "I had not thought to see thy face; and lo, God hath showed me also thy seed!"

A PENITENT MINISTER.

A Christian minister, writing from Boston to England in 1795, remarks that the religion of the gospel is the grand restorative of the disturbed soul. In illustration of the remark, he states that he was once told a story by one of his hearers in reference to another, which he improperly believed, and made some strong remarks on the conduct of the offender. These were soon carried to him, losing nothing of their asperity on the road, and in his turn the offender was offended; both were very angry, the one stayed from church, and the minister was rather pleased than otherwise that he did so.

After a short time the rupture was public, and each had a party to commend and another to censure him. The conscience of the minister convicted him of wrong-doing, but it was very long before he could persuade himself to do what was right. At length he went to his brother, whom he found quite indisposed to receive him. At last the minister said, "You are justified, sir, in your conduct on this occasion; I deserve it all, yea, and more than this; and I can bear all with more ease than I can the reproaches of my own heart. I am come, sir, to acknowledge my error; I have done wrong in taking up a report of you, or saying any thing about you but to yourself; I beseech you to forgive me." He was going on—but his friend rose, his face being suffused with tears, and would have spoken, but could not. He extended his hand, and it was received with as warm a heart as ever beat in a friend's bosom. Their hearts never cooled towards each other, till they were made cold by death, and doubtless their friendship shall extend throughout eternity.

A UNITARIAN MINISTER.

An old *friend*, or Quaker, a few years since, happening one Lord's-day morning to meet a Universalist minister in front of a meeting-house in Providence, R. I., fell into conversation with him upon his favourite doctrine of universal salvation. The minister endeavoured to support his system with considerable warmth; but the Quaker professed to doubt its correctness, which served to increase the zeal of his opponent. At length, finding it in vain to reason, he remarked, "Well, friend, I think thee must be very happy when walking round the market, and seeing men women, and children of every description, to think that they are all safely bound to heaven." The Universalist could only reply, "I don't know—I think we shall do very well, if we can make out faith enough for ourselves."

A METHODIST CLERGYMAN.

Not many years ago, the Rev. Mr. ———, a native of Baltimore, was stationed by the Conference at Augusta, Georgia, where, by his exalted piety, zealous devotion to the Christian cause, and uniform cheerfulness and kindness of disposition, he made many friends, who will long continue to remember him with sentiments of veneration and esteem. His eloquence, and especially his logical mode of reasoning, never failed to interest and impress the minds of his hearers; but the old gentleman was of that old-fashioned school of preachers who entertain a higher reverence for the sanctuary in which they worship, than for the feelings of any who dared to profane it by indecorous conduct, and quaint and harsh as it seemed to the thoughtless offenders, he permitted none to interrupt the services, or deport themselves unbecomingly in his church, with impunity.

It was his custom from time to time, whenever a travelling preacher chanced to be present to fill his place, to extend the sphere of his usefulness, by preaching in the neighbourhood wherever he could obtain a congregation. On one of these occasions he had gone to fulfil an afternoon appointment in Hamburg, on the opposite side of the river from Augusta, where, at that time, there was no regular preaching. He had ascended the pulpit, and was earnestly addressing a very respectful and attentive audience, when a man entered and seated himself in a conspicuous part of the room. After looking listlessly about him for a few minutes, vainly endeavouring to adjust himself in a comfortable position, he extended his person at full length upon the bench. The preacher paused in the midst of his discourse, and fixed his eyes upon the reclining auditor.

"My friend," said he, in the blandest tone, "get up. Sit up in your seat as you should. You would not deport yourself thus in the house of a neighbor for whom you had any respect."

The eyes of all were directed upon the delinquent, who read, in every countenance, an approval of the minister's rebuke.

He rose from his position—sat erect with a crimsoned face for a few minutes, and then left the house.

The minister went on with his discourse. When the services were over, he received the thanks and congratulations of his Christian friends, who pressed around him at the door, and promising to meet them again on the following Sunday, took his leave. He had not proceeded far from the house before he was overtaken by the man whom he had rebuked for his improper conduct.

"Stop, Mr. ——," said he, "I want to have a talk with you."

The preacher turned smiling to hear what he had to say.

"You have insulted me, sir," said the man, with extreme agitation; "and I did promise to whip you on sight; but as you have given out that you will preach here next Sunday, and in consideration that you are an old man, I have concluded to give you a chance to apologize."

"For what?" inquired Mr. ——.

"Why, for insulting me in the manner you did before everybody."

"My dear sir, I can do no such thing. I cannot apologize for doing what I conceived my duty."

"But you must, sir; and I now give you notice, that if you don't apologize for insulting me to the congregation next Sunday—if you don't make the apology as public as the insult was—preacher as you are, I'll give you a thrashing."

"Tut, tut,—you would not do any thing so rash. You——"

"I will!—so help me——"

"Stop, my friend—make no rash promises," said the

preacher; "I did not desire to insult you, or to wound your feelings unnecessarily; but you must not expect me to apologize for doing my duty as a faithful steward of the house of God."

"Well, you come here next Sunday and preach without making an apology, and you know what to depend upon," replied the man as he turned away.

The following Sunday, true to his appointment, the preacher was there. The insulted auditor was there also, and kept his eyes steadfastly fixed on the preacher during the whole of his discourse. But not the slightest allusion was made to the occurrence of the previous Sunday.

After the congregation were dismissed, the man followed Mr. ———, as before.

"Well, sir," said he, "you did not make the apology which I required of you?"

"No, my friend; I told you that I could not. I feel that I have done no wrong. If I were to make a public apology to appease your feelings, I would acknowledge that I had done wrong, which would be falsifying myself. I would do any proper thing to serve you, but, as I said before, I can make no such apology."

"Well, sir, you need not think to put me off in this way. I will permit no man to insult me; and I now tell you, once more, that if you don't apologize for the insult to me last Sunday, the next time you preach in Hamburg, I will whip you, as sure as I live."

"I hope you may live to form better resolutions, my friend," said the smiling clergyman; "but you require of me what I cannot do, even to avoid a whipping."

They parted; Mr. ——— with a polite bow, and the man with fierce threats and violent gestures.

On the following Sunday, the preacher was punctual to his appointment. As on the former occasion, the belligerent individual was in his place, an attentive listener to the sermon. The meeting was an extremely interesting one, and did not break up until later than usual.

This time the man did not accost him, nor did the worthy clergyman see him again for several days. But, about a week after the last meeting, as he was going down Broad street, he saw the man who had so solemnly promised him a whipping, approaching him on the same side of the street. He easily guessed the object of his visit to Augusta, and determined to meet his fate as gracefully as possible. The man approached within a foot or two of the minister, and, with apparent timidity, drew a letter from his pocket, placed it in the clergyman's hands, and passed on, without uttering a single word.

The first thought the worthy minister had was, that possibly the unhappy man had sent him a challenge; but, on opening the letter, what was his surprise to read,

Hamburg, S. C., April 10, 1832.

"Respected Sir :—Enclosed you will find fifty dollars, a part of which I have collected from your Hamburg friends. It is tendered to you in acknowledgment of your praiseworthy efforts in the cause of religion. Hoping that you will continue to visit us, whenever your pastoral engagements will permit, I remain,   Gratefully yours,

         ——— ———."

Such was the happy result of faithful preaching. The good minister pleasantly remarked, that he would have no objection, every now and then, to receive such a flogging; and continued to visit Hamburg whenever opportunities presented.

A NEW ENGLAND CLERGYMAN.

As a minister was walking upon one of our eastern wharves, he heard a man in a fishing boat just pulled up, swearing very profanely, and resolved on reproving him. For this purpose he stepped up to the boat, and began to enquire concerning the manner of taking fish. The fisherman answered this enquiry by saying, that for one kind of fish he baited his hook with such a material, and for such other kind of fish, baited his hook with such an article. The clergyman asked, "Do you not take any without bait?" "No," said the fisherman, "I never did but one; one fool bit the naked hook." "Well," said the clergyman," the devil is a great fisherman, and to take the ambitious he baits with the honor of the world, and to take the avaricious he baits with silver and gold, and for the pleasure-seekers he baits with sensual gratifications, but the profane swearer is like your foolish fish, he bites at the naked hook.

REV. DR. WITHERSPOON.

The Rev. Dr. Witherspoon, formerly president of Princeton College, was once on board a packet ship, where, among other passengers, was a professed atheist. This unhappy man was very fond of troubling every one with his peculiar belief, and of broaching the subject as often as he could get any one to listen to him. He did not believe in a God and a future state, not he! By-and-bye there came on a terrible storm, and the prospect was that all would be drowned. There was much consternation on board, but no one was so greatly frightened as the professed atheist. In this extremity, he sought out the clergyman, and found him in the cabin, calm and collected, in the midst of danger, and thus addressed him: "Oh, Dr. Witherspoon! Dr. Witherspoon! we're all going; we have but a short time to stay. Oh, how the vessel rocks; we're all going; don't you think we are, doctor?" The doctor turned to him with a solemn look, and replied in broad Scotch, "Nae doubt, nae doubt, man; we're a' ganging; but you and I dinna gang the same way."

A GOOD PREACHER.

How beautiful is simplicity! Who can read the following illustrations of faith without emotion?

A beloved minister of the gospel was one day speaking of that active living faith, which should at all times cheer the heart of the sincere follower of Jesus; and related a beautiful illustration that had just occurred in his own family.

He had gone into a cellar, which, in winter, was quite dark, and entered by a trap-door. A little daughter, only three years old, was trying to find him, and came to the trap-door; but, on looking down, all was *dark, dark*—and she called, "Are you down cellar, papa?"

"Yes; would you like to come, Mary?"

"It is dark; I *can't* come, papa."

"Well, my daughter, I am right below you; and I can see you, though you cannot see me, and if you will drop yourself, I will catch you."

"Oh! I should fall; I can't see you, papa."

"I know it," he answered; "but I am really here, and you shall not fall or hurt yourself. If you will jump, I will catch you safely."

Little Mary strained her eyes to the utmost, but she could catch no glimpse of her father. She hesitated, then advanced a little farther, then, summoning all her resolution, she threw herself forward, and was received safely in her father's arms.

A few days after, she again discovered the cellar door open; and, supposing her father to be there, she called, "Shall I come again, papa?"

"Yes, my dear, in a minute," he replied; and had just time to reach his arms towards her, when, in her childish glee, she fell shouting into his arms, and, clasping his neck, said, "I *knew*, dear papa, I should not fall."

REV. DR. BALDWIN.

The Rev. Dr. Baldwin, when living in New Hampshire, was under an engagement to preach at some distance from home; but, having set out too late to reach the place of his appointment on the same day, he found himself at night on a rough and dreary road, which lay, for the most part, through the woods. Being very much fatigued with his ride on horseback he resolved to tarry, for the night, at the first house he might find. He came to a sort of cabin, at the door of which he knocked. A woman presented herself, of whom he begged the favour of a night's entertainment for himself and his horse. She eyed him suspiciously, for the doctor, (when in his old hat and threadbare clothes, was not particularly prepossessing in his appearance,) but finally told him that he might stay. The doctor put up his horse in the old, rickety barn, and then returned to the house. Here, upon a pine-wood table, he found a bowl of milk, a loaf of bread, and a small quantity of butter—the materials for his supper. The good woman, after giving him an invitation to be seated and partake, added, as she looked earnestly in his face, "There, such as the house affords, I give you—*if you are a good man, it is good enough; and if you are not a good man, it is altogether too good.*"

REV. MR BUSHNEL.

Mr. Bushnel, of Utica, New York, a Wesleyan Methodist preacher, having business at a neighbouring town, was obliged, in consequence, to see the landlord of the village inn; so he stopped at his house. When he entered the bar-room, he saw about twenty men, most of whom were intoxicated—several of them quite drunk. After a little time, one of them said something to Mr. Bushnel, who replied in a courteous manner, and spoke of the subject of temperance. Immediately the attention of the assembly was arrested, and the cause was denounced as the work of priests and politicians.

Mr. Bushnel, finding it impossible to stem the current of abuse by an appeal to their reason, proposed to sing a temperance song; to which they all agreed, and he accordingly commenced the "Staunch Teetotaller." On glancing around the room, after he had concluded, he observed the tear trickling down the cheek of almost every man. The sentiment of the song, and the melodious, touching manner in which it was sung, had awakened their purest sensibilities—had carried their thoughts back to their families and firesides, surrounded, as they once were, with plenty, happiness, and affection; and then the contrast of a drunkard's home—its dark wretchedness and misery, were wisely presented to their minds; and those hardened men could not resist the appeal, but acknowledged its truth by tears! The song was unanimously called for again, and their wishes were gratified by its repetition. Soon after, the landlord came in; and Mr. B. was requested to repeat it for his especial benefit. It produced the same effect upon him; and, after he had concluded, he grasped him by the hand, and exclaimed, " I will never sell another glass of liquor as long as I live!" He acted immediately on his resolution, cut down his sign-post, and closed his bar; the others promising to go to the temperance meeting that evening, and sign the pledge. And they all did so, except one.

REV. MR. WALKER.

A DIFFICULTY having arisen in the Presbyterian church of Rome, New York, between the pastor and the people, a council was called. Mr. W. made out charges of slander against five or six of his brethren, and procured his witnesses. They also made out charges against Mr. W. for his improper expressions concerning them. But the council, soon after its organization, decided, for certain reasons, that it was improper for them to act as a council in the case, and so dissolved. Thus the way to adjust the difficulties of the church seemed hedged up. Rev. Mr. L., of Auburn, now rose and delivered a solemn address to the church; and his address was followed by a moving scene. One of the brethren who was complained of by Mr. W. had been to Sherburne, to engage Rev. Mr. Truair, of that place, as an advocate. In that town God was pouring out his Spirit; and Mr. D. returned convicted of his errors. At this interesting moment he came forward, took his pastor by the hand, and made the most humble and melting confession of his faults. Mr. W. as frankly forgave him, and cordially embraced him as a friend and brother. No sooner had he done this than Mr. D. kneeled down and poured out his soul in an appropriate, humble, penitential prayer. Before he concluded, two-thirds of the audience were bathed in tears. He was followed by addresses and prayers from some of the council; and then another was ready to confess his faults, and then another, to the last of the accused; each one taking Mr. Walker by the hand, and receiving forgiveness. He in turn asked their forgiveness wherein he had expressed himself improperly towards them. Pardon was also asked of the church, and cheerfully granted. This opened the door for Mr. W.'s friends, who, one after another, confessed whatever they had said, in an unchristian manner, against the opposite party. Thus two whole days, with the exception of time occupied in hearing two sermons, was spent in mutual confession and forgiveness. Before the council separated, they took the papers which contained the charges on both sides, held them up to the view of the audience, declared they were about to make a burnt-sacrifice of them, and committed them to the flames. On the evening of the second day, a conference meeting was held, in which several were so deeply impressed as to ask for prayers. From that time a revival of religion commenced. The above facts occurred in Rome in 1819–20.

A CLERGYMAN IN VIRGINIA.

A CLERGYMAN in Virginia, speaking very highly in commendation of Legh Richmond's excellent tract "The Negro Servant," describes a very interesting scene in connection with it. He says that he was riding one day, and saw a group of coloured persons sitting under a tree, and eating their homely dinner. He asked them if they would like to hear an account of one of their own colour who became religious. They consented; and says he, "I leaned against the tree, which spread out its branches far beyond us, and I began to read. The was soon breathless attention. It was sultry noon-tide, and the leaves of the tree made no rustling. Sighs and groans were audible, though evidently suppressed; and tears coursing one after another down their sable cheeks, showed that the story of poor William had reached their hearts."

REV. JOHN COTTON.

The Rev. John Cotton, of Boston, was distinguished for his forbearance and meekness, which greatly contributed to his happiness and usefulness. When he was once told that his preaching was very dark and comfortless, he replied, "Let me have your prayers, brother, that it may be otherwise." Having once observed to a person, who boasted of his knowledge of the book of Revelation, that he wanted light in those mysteries, the man went home, and sent him a pound of candles; which insolence only excited a smile. "Mr. Cotton," says Dr. Mather, "would not set the beacon of his great soul on fire at the landing of such a little cock-boat." A drunken fellow, to make merriment for his companions, approached him in the street, and whispered in his ear, "Thou art an old fool." Mr. Cotton replied, "I confess I am so; the Lord make both me and thee wiser than we are, even wise unto salvation."

REV. DR. COKE.

The following anecdote was related by Dr. Coke himself, to his brother in-law.

In attempting to cross a river in the United States, Dr. Coke missed the ford, and got into deep water, and was carried, with his horse, down the stream. Feeling himself in danger, he caught hold of a bough, and with some difficulty got upon dry land, but his horse was lost. After drying his clothes in the sun, he commenced to finish his journey on foot; and at length met a man who directed him to the nearest village, telling him to inquire for a Mrs. ———, from whom, he had no doubt, he would receive very kind treatment. Dr. C. found the good lady's house, and received all the kindness and attention she could show him. The next morning he proceeded on his journey. After a lapse of five years, the Doctor happened to be in America again. As he was on his way to one of the provincial conferences, in company with about thirty other persons, a young man requested to be allowed the favour of conversing with him; to which he assented with Christian politeness. The young man asked him if he recollected being in such a part of the States about five years before, to which he replied in the affirmative. "And do you recollect, sir, in attempting to cross the river, being nearly drowned?" "I remember it quite well." "And do you recollect going to the house of a widow lady in such a village?" "I remember it well," said the doctor, "and never shall I forget the kindness she showed me." "And do you remember, when you departed, leaving a tract at that lady's house?" "I do not recollect that," said he, 'but it is very possible that I might do so." "Yes, sir," said the young man, "you did leave there a tract, which that lady read, and the Lord blessed the reading of it to the conversion of her soul; it was also the means of the conversion of several of her children and neighbours; and there is now in that village a flourishing Christian society." The tears shed by Dr. Coke showed something of the feelings of his heart. The young man resumed, "I have not, sir, quite told you all. I am one of that lady's children, and owe my conversion to God, to the gracious influence with which he accompanied the reading of that tract to my mind; and I am, Dr. Coke, on my way to conference, to be proposed as a preacher."

REV. MR. CROSS.

This gentleman is one of the colporteurs of the American Tract Society, and the following interesting anecdote of the success of his labours was related by the Rev. S. T. Wells.

While visiting from house to house, with an elder of Rev. Mr. J.'s church, they came to the hut of a coal-digger. "We will not go into that house," said the elder, "the man is so wicked, it would be of no use." Mr. Cross maintained that such were the very men he was sent to. They entered the hut, which indicated great poverty both within and without, and found sitting on a broken bench in the corner, a large athletic man, nearly naked. He had remained unwashed so long that the coal-dust lay like scales all over his body. The face of his wife was black and swollen with bruises which he had given her, and his own countenance was very fierce. "We have come," said Mr. Cross, "to sell you some good religious books, and to have some conversation with you on the subject of religion." "I have no money, sir," he said, "and don't want any of your books." "If you have no money," said Mr. Cross, "you shall have the books and welcome. You have a soul, and you must die; you are not prepared to die now, are you, friend?" His eye, which had been fixed with a savage glare upon him till this question, lowered a little, and began to soften, and he replied that he was not ready to die. Before Mr. Cross left him, he wept like a child, and told him that he was the first man who had ever come there to talk with him about his soul.

REV. DR. COTTON MATHER.

The following anecdote is full of instruction, both as illustrative of Dr. Mather's ingenuity in the communication of divine truth, and as suggesting a valuable hint to ministers of the present day.

In the year 1696, Bommaseen, a chief of the American Indians, was a prisoner in Boston, with some others of his countrymen. He desired a conference with one of the Boston ministers; Dr. Mather waited upon him, and was told that he wished to be instructed in the Christian religion, for he was afraid that the French had imposed upon them in what they had taught them respecting Christianity. The doctor inquired of him what appeared to them most suspicious in the instructions of the French, and Bommaseen said that they had told him that the Lord Jesus Christ was of the French nation; that his mother, the Virgin Mary, was a French lady; that Englishmen murdered him; and that as he rose from the dead, and had ascended to heaven, all who would recommend themselves to his favour must avenge his quarrel on the English, as far as they could. The doctor, knowing that the best medium of communicating religious knowledge to the Indians was to deal much in similitudes, began to think of some suitable imagery, and as a cup of drink stood upon the table, he employed that as his medium of instruction.

He told them that the Lord Jesus had given to men a good religion, which might be compared to the good drink in the cup on the table. That if we take this good religion, like the good drink, into our hearts, it will do us good, and preserve us from death. That the Bible, God's book, is the cup wherein that good drink of religion is offered unto us. That the French, having the cup of good drink in their hands, had put *poison* into it, and then made the Indians drink, and that this made them mad, leading them to kill the English, though they knew it would end in their own destruction. That it was plain the English had put no poison into the drink, for they set the cup wide open, and invited all men, even the Indians, into whose language Mr. Elliot had translated the Bible, to come and see before they tasted; but that they might fairly infer the French had put poison into the good drink, because they kept the cup closely shut, (not having given them the Bible,) and kept their hands to the eyes of the Indians when they put it to their mouths.

The poor Indians, having expressed their satisfaction with what he had said, entreated him farther to explain about the cup of good drink and the poison. He then, in the most simple manner, placed before them the chief points of Christianity; and showed them how the Catholics had poisoned and corrupted most of its truths, and that it was important for them to distinguish between truth and error. He then said—" To obtain the pardon of your sins, you must confess them to God, and pray that he would pardon them for the sake of Jesus Christ, who died for poor sinners; and if you place your eye on Jesus Christ only, when you beg the pardon of your sins, God will forgive them. You need confess your sins to none but God, except in cases where men have known your sins, or have been hurt by them; but even then, none but God can pardon them." He then showed them how the French had corrupted the truth, by enjoining them to confess their sins to a priest, to carry skins to him, and to do penance at his bidding.

The poor creatures were much delighted with this discourse of the doctor, fell at his feet, kissed his hands, and showed every mark of affection. Bommaseen, lifting his eyes and hands to heaven, said, " Sir, I thank you for these things; I resolve to spit up all the French poison; you shall be my father, I will be your son; I beseech you continue to instruct me in that religion, which may bring me to the salvation of my soul."

Dr. Franklin once received a very useful lesson from the excellent Doctor, which he thus relates in a letter to his son:—

The last time I saw your father, was in 1724. On taking my leave, he showed me a shorter way out of the house, by a narrow passage, which was crossed by a beam over head. We were still talking as I withdrew, he accompanying me behind, and I turning towards him, when he said hastily, "Stoop, stoop!" I did not understand him till I felt my head hit against the beam. He was a man who never missed an opportunity of giving instruction; and upon this he said to me, "You are young, and have the world before you; learn to stoop as you go through it, and you will avoid many hard thumps." This advice, thus beat into my head, has frequently been of use to me; and I often think of it, when I see pride mortified, and misfortune brought upon people by their carrying their heads too high.

Dr. Mather was remarkable for the sweetness of his temper. He took some interest in the political concerns of his country, and, on this account, as well as because he faithfully reproved iniquity, he had many enemies. Many abusive letters were sent him, all of which he tied up in a packet, and wrote upon the cover, "Libels;—Father, forgive them."

I happened once, says Dr. Mather, to be present in the room where a dying man could not leave the world until he lamented to a minister whom he had sent for, the unjust calumnies and injuries which he had often cast upon him. The minister asked the poor penitent what was the occasion of this abusive conduct; whether he had been imposed upon by any false report. The man made this answer: "No, sir, it was merely this; I thought you were a good man, and that you did much good in the world, and therefore I hated you. Is it possible, is it possible," he added, " for such a wretch to find pardon?"

What a contrast did the character of the doctor himself present to all this! It was his laudable ambition to say, that "He did not know of any person in the world who had done him any ill office but he had done him a good one for it."

AN AGED CLERGYMAN

An aged clergyman, in the State of New York, not long since gave a very interesting narrative of scenes in which he was personally concerned.

Two young men from Birmingham, in England, emigrated to the United States in 1793. On the vessel arriving in sight of her destined port, a storm suddenly arose, the ship was wrecked, and the two brothers, always affectionately attached to each other, died locked in each other's arms. Their bodies being washed ashore, they were decently buried, and our reverend friend preached a funeral sermon from the counsel of Solomon, " Boast not thyself of to-morrow, for thou knowest not what a day may bring forth." It was ascertained from their papers from whence they came, and how their friends could be addressed: the minister wrote to their widowed mother, now most affectingly bereaved of her sons, and deeply sympathized with her under her accumulated sorrows. A correspondence ensued, and our friend ultimately received a piece of plate with a suitable inscription on it, recording his kindness This he carefully placed in his study.

Many years afterwards, a gentleman from England, overtaken in a violent storm, sought for shelter at the house of the minister, where he was invited to stay for the night. As, on the next morning, he was looking over the worthy pastor's study, his eye caught the plate, the inscription on which he read with deep interest, for these young men were his cousins. The character of the subsequent intercourse between the minister and his new friend need not be described.

REV. MR. BENNETT.

The following is an extract from an anniversary sermon, delivered by the Rev. Mr. Bennett, of Woburn, Mass. The introductory remarks are so judicious in their character, and are so very naturally connected with the anecdote which follows, that no apology will be needed for their appearance:—

I am sorry to say it, the first open complaint is made against the pastor, in three cases out of four, by a deacon of the church. Deacons, the world over, are like Jeremiah's figs—that is, very sweet or very sour. They either aid their pastor, and, like Aaron and Hur, stay up his hands, or decidedly the reverse. It is a sober fact, and it ought to make the ears of such deacons tingle, that at least three out of four of all the ministers in New England, who have been driven away from their people, have been driven away by deacons; by men who, in one respect, have with a vengeance " magnified their office." I might point you to numerous examples all over the land. But I forbear. I thank God, however, that I have never been plagued by such deacons. I have never had the slightest difficulty with any of my deacons, except in a single instance, and that lasted but five minutes. It was with good deacon Wyman, at the commencement of the Temperance Reformation in 1826. Some one had told him that I said at a church meeting that I would never drink another drop of ardent spirit, (unless ordered by a physician,) or give it to a workman or a visitor, while I lived. The deacon called upon me the next day, and asked me if I said so. I told him I *did*, and should *stick to it*, at all hazards. "Well," said he, "then you will not be a minister of this parish three months." "Very well," said I, "I have taken my stand, and if I knew I should be drawn in quarters within three months, if I did not recant, I would not do it." Said the deacon, " You are a crazy man, and I will not talk with you ;" and arose to go out of my house, when I thus accosted him: "Deacon Wyman, the next time you enter your closet, will you ask God to teach you by his Spirit, who is right on this subject, you or I?" "I tell you," said he, "I will not talk with you," and marched out of doors. The next morning, long before sunrise, some one knocked—I went to the door, and behold, there stood deacon Wyman. He instantly grasped my hand, and, with tears rolling down his cheeks, exclaimed, "My dear pastor, I went home from your house yesterday, and in accordance with your advice, retired to my closet, and asked God to teach me by his Spirit, who was right in regard to the use of ardent spirits, you or I. In five minutes a flood of light broke in upon my mind, and I was fully convinced that you were right, and I was wrong. And now," said he, "go ahead with your temperance reformation—to the day of my death I will do all in my power to sustain you." He was as good as his word. He did sustain me as long as he lived."

REV. DR. L.

It has been well said that weighty solemn sentences, dropped into the ear of the sinner in private, are often far more useful than even the most elopuent sermons. Some years since,

Mr. B., a worldly man, who dealt in lottery tickets, was one of the committee of supply for a rich evangelical congregation, and the Rev. Dr. L. was invited to supply the pulpit for a Sabbath or two. On their way from the meeting-house to the residence of Mr. B., Dr. L., who had discovered that several persons had been opposed to his being invited to preach, remarked, "If I had known that so many had been opposed to me, I do not know that I should have preached; but I have one consolation—I preached the *truth* to them." "Yes," replied Mr. B., somewhat hesitatingly. The faithful minister then looked him full in the face, and said to him, with great solemnity and emphasis, "*Why do you not believe it then?*" The inquiry seemed to strike him dumb; he retired to reflect, to weep over his misspent life, to repent and pray. The solemn inquiry, of which conscience told him the justice, was like "a nail fastened in a sure place." He was soon brought to "the feet of Jesus, clothed, and in his right mind," and became one of the most active and useful Christians in the city of his residence.

A WISE CLERGYMAN.

"An Atheist!" exclaimed a devout clergyman, when Mr. B. was introduced to him to advocate the cause of infidelity; ' it is impossible."

"Yes, sir," said Mr. B., "I am an Atheist; and I should be glad of an argument, as I hold it impossible for any man to prove that there is a God; and, sir,"——

"But hold," said the minister; "I must first be satisfied that you are an Atheist."

"Well, sir," said Mr. B., "do I not tell you that I am so?"

"But, my Bible." said the minister, "declares that every

human heart, which of course includes yours, is not only desperately wicked, but deceitful above all things; and the Holy Ghost, therefore, asks, Who can know it? Peradventure, you may be deceived in this matter."

"But, sir," said Mr. B., "*do I not know* what I believe?—am I not a rational creature?"

"Well," said the minister, "let us try the point. I will propose a test to which you can submit without difficulty or trouble; if you will pledge yourself to pursue the course which I shall direct, I will then proceed to the argument which you seem so much to desire."

"I do not wish." said Mr. B., "to pledge myself thus blindly to do any thing. What would you have me to do?"

"It shall be," said the minister, "such a thing as shall be perfectly consistent with your professed belief, and reasonable, and easy. If (yourself being the judge) it shall not be so, *according to your own scheme*, you shall be under no obligation to perform it."

"Very well," said Mr. B. promptly, "I will. What do you propose, sir?"

"This night," said the minister, "when deep sleep shall fall upon man, and thick darkness shall cover the world, you shall, taking solemn thought, and after deep meditation, walk deliberately and alone to yonder hill, and in the thick darkness of the forest which covers its summit, you shall stand and raise your eyes and your clenched hands to the firmament above you, and then shall declare:—'There is no God who created me—There is no God who preserves me—There is no God whom I fear.' Will you do this?"

The Atheist was confounded with the proposition.

"Oh," said the minister, you are no Atheist; I was sure you were mistaken. We agree on this point. There is no ground for an argument."

REV. MR. HULL.

Father Hull was a preacher of the old school, connected with the South Carolina conference. Passing along the highway one evening, in a strange and wicked part of the country, weary and faint, he called at a respectable-looking house to ask for a lodging. After a while, as he sat by the fireside, a number of well-dressed ladies and gentlemen entered his room, and very shortly they began to dance to the music of a violin. It was a ball, at which the stranger looked silently on. At length a partner was wanted, and the old gentleman was invited to take the floor. "Certainly, madam," he replied, walking out on the floor as he spoke; "but I have long made it a rule never to commence any business till I have asked the direction of the Lord, and his blessing upon it. Will you all join in the prayer with me?" He instantly fell on his knees, and began to pray. Some kneeled, others stood still, all were petrified with astonishment. In prayer he was intensely earnest and powerful, and the heavens and the earth seemed drawn together. Some groaned, others shrieked aloud, and many fell prostrate like dead men on the floor. The dance was turned into a religious meeting, from which many dated their conversion to God, and was the commencement of an extensive revival

---

REV. JOHN SUMMERFIELD.

On a journey in the stage from Brunswick to Trenton, this worthy young clergyman, with two others, occupied the middle seat. His pale, youthful countenance, with his general appearance, led an elderly respectable gentleman, who occupied the front seat, to suppose him to have been a student from Princeton college. Under this impression, he requested him, —rather *peremptorily*, however,—to change seats. Though struck with surprise, rather perhaps at the *manner* in which the request was made, than at the request itself, after a momentary hesitation—during which his pale cheek was tinged with a momentary flush—he changed seats without uttering a word. Of all in the stage, not one, on the ground of health, (which was the reason assigned *afterwards* for making the request,) required accommodation so much as Mr. S. As it was, the change of seat affected him considerably. It is pleasant to add, however, that the gentleman having arrived in Trenton, and discovered his mistake, took the earliest opportunity to apologize to him, and by the greatest kindness endeavoured to remove any unpleasant feeling which he might inadvertently have occasioned. The meek spirit of his Master, with which Mr. S. was imbued, led him at once to forget the occurrence, and to cherish the most sincere gratitude for all the after kindness of this gentleman, with whom an interesting correspondence was kept up.

It has been well remarked that that clergyman cannot have the feelings of a pastor, who does not cherish special love for the young of his flock. The following is one of many instances of attention to the lambs of the Christian fold in the life of this highly popular minister:—

A boy, about eleven years of age, after one of his sermons to children, remained till the congregation had nearly dispersed, when he attracted Mr. Summerfield's notice; who, stepping forward, said, "My little boy, do you want any thing with me?"—The little fellow appeared overcome with his feelings, and could only say, "Mr. Summerfield." "Well, my love, what do you want with Mr. Summerfield?" The boy, being now encouraged, said that he wished Mr. Summerfield would call at his mother's house: on inquiring where his mother lived, the name of the street and the number of the house were given. "What is your name?"—"John Brown," replied the boy. "Well, John Brown, to-morrow at eleven o'clock, I shall pay you a visit." Accordingly, at the time appointed, Mr. Summerfield waited upon him; he found John busily employed sweeping and fixing the fire, and preparing for his visitor. "Well, John, here I am, according to my appointment."—John requested him to take a seat, until he had found his mother. She was a pious woman, and said that her son had heard him preach, whenever he had addressed the children, and that his mind in consequence had been much impressed. Mr. S. knelt down and prayed with them; and before he went away, encouraged John, and gave him some good advice; entered his name on the list of those for whom he felt a peculiar interest, and told him that he should keep his eyes upon him; requesting him to come and speak to him whenever he had an opportunity, that he might ascertain what progress his little friend John Brown was making. Carping criticism, or cold philosophy may despise these little traits of character, but ministerial wisdom will admire them.

REV. DR. J. M. MASON.

Every one, says the late Rev. Dr. J. M. Mason, of New York, has remarked the mixed and often ill-assorted company, which meet in a public packet or stage-coach. The conversation, with all its variety, is commonly insipid, frequently disgusting, and sometimes insufferable. There are exceptions. An opportunity now and then occurs of spending an hour in a manner not unworthy of rational beings; and the incidents of a stage-coach may produce or promote salutary impressions.

A few years ago, one of the stages which ply between the two principal cities of the United States of America, was filled with a group which could never have been drawn together by mutual choice. In the company was a young man of social temper, affable manners, and considerable information. His accent was barely sufficient to show that the English was not his native tongue; and a very slight peculiarity in the pronunciation of the *th*, showed him to be a Hollander. He had early entered into military life, had borne both a Dutch and a French commission, had seen real service, had travelled, was master of the English language, and evinced, by his deportment, that he was no stranger to the society of gentlemen. He had, however, a fault, too common among military men, and too absurd to find an advocate among men of sense—he swore very profanely and frequently.

While the horses were changing, a gentleman who sat on the same seat with him took him by the arm, and requested the favour of his company in a short walk. When they were so far retired as not to be overheard, the former observed, "Although I have not the honour of your acquaintance, I perceive, sir, that your habits and feelings are those of a gentleman, and that nothing can be more repugnant to your wishes than giving unnecessary pain to any of your company." He started, and replied, "Most certainly, sir! I hope I have committed no offence of that sort?"

"You will pardon me," replied the other, "for pointing out an instance in which you have not altogether avoided it."

"Sir," said he, "I shall be much your debtor for so friendly an act; for, upon my honour, I cannot conjecture in what I have transgressed."

"If you, sir," continued the former, "had a very dear friend, to whom you were under unspeakable obligations, should you not be deeply wounded by any disrespect to him, or even by hearing his name introduced, and used with a frequency of repetition and a levity of air, incompatible with the regard due to his character?"

"Undoubtedly, and I should not permit it; but I know not that I am chargeable with such indecorum to any of your friends."

"Sir, my God is my best friend, to whom I am under infinite obligations. I think you must recollect that you have very frequently, since we commenced our journey, taken his name in vain. This has given to me, and others of the company, severe pain."

"Sir," answered he, with very ingenuous emphasis, "I have done wrong; I confess the impropriety. I am ashamed of a practice which I am aware has no excuse; but I have imperceptibly fallen into it, and I really swear without being conscious that I do so. I will endeavour to abstain from it in future; and, as you are next to me on the seat, I shall thank you to touch my elbow as often as I trespass." This was agreed upon; the horn sounded, and the travellers resumed their places.

For the space of four or five miles, the officer's elbow was jogged every few seconds. He always coloured, but bowed, and received the hint without the least symptom of displeasure; and, in a few miles more, so mastered his propensity to swearing, that not an oath was heard from his lips for the rest of his journey, which was the greater part of it.

After this, he was more grave; and, having ruminated some time, after surveying first one and then another of the company, turned to his admonisher, and addressed him thus:

"You are a clergyman, I presume, sir?"

"I am considered as such."

He paused; and then, with a smile, indicated his disbelief

in Divine revelation in a way which called for further conversation on this subject.

He avowed himself an infidel, and an animated conversation followed. At length he exclaimed, "I own I am beaten, completely beaten; I have nothing more to say."

A silence of some minutes succeeded; when the young military traveller said to his theological friend, "I have studied all religions, and have not been able to satisfy myself."

"No, sir," answered he; "there is one religion which you have not yet studied."

"Pray, sir," cried the officer, roused and eager, "what is that?"

"The religion," replied the other, "of salvation through the redemption of the Son of God; the religion which will sweeten your pleasures, and soften your sorrows; which will give peace to your conscience, and joy to your heart; which will bear you up under the pressure of evils here, and shed the light of immortality on the gloom of the grave. This religion, I believe, sir, you have yet to study."

The officer put his hands upon his face; then, languidly clasping them, allowed them to fall down, forced a smile, and said, with a sigh, "We must all follow what we think best." His behaviour afterwards was perfectly decorous, but nothing further is known of him.

To a young infidel, who was scoffing at Christianity, on account of the misconduct of some of its professors, Dr. Mason once said, "Did you ever know an uproar to be made because an infidel went astray from the paths of morality?" The infidel admitted that he had not. "Then, don't you see," asked Dr. M., "that by expecting the professors of Christianity to be holy, you admit it to be a holy religion, and thus pay it the highest compliment in your power?" The young man was silent.

The Doctor was once requested to visit a lady in dying circumstances, who, together with her husband, openly avowed infidel principles, though they attended on his ministry. On approaching her bedside, he asked her if she felt herself a sinner, and perceived the need of a Saviour. She frankly told him, she did not; and that she wholly disbelieved the doctrine of a Mediator. "Then," said the doctor, "I have no consolation for you; not one word of comfort. There is not a single passage in the Bible that warrants me to speak peace to any one who rejects the Mediator provided for lost sinners. You must abide the consequences of your infidelity." Saying that, he was on the point of leaving the room, when some one said, "Well, but, Doctor, if you cannot speak consolation to her, you can pray for her." To this he assented, and kneeling down by the bedside, prayed for her as a guilty sinner, just sinking into hell; and then, arising from his knees, he left the house. A day or two after, he received a letter from the lady herself, earnestly desiring that he would come and see her without delay. He immediately obeyed the summons; but what was his amazement, when, on entering the room, she held out her hand to him, and said, with a benignant smile, "It is all true; all that you said on Sunday is true. I have seen myself the wretched sinner which you described me to be in prayer. I have seen Christ that all-sufficient Saviour you said he was; and God has mercifully snatched me from the abyss of infidelity in which I was sunk, and placed me on the Rock of ages. There I am secure; there I shall remain. I know in whom I have believed!" All this was like a dream to him; but she proceeded, and displayed as accurate a knowledge of the way of salvation revealed in the gospel, and as firm a reliance on it, as if she had been a disciple of Christ for many years. Yet there was nothing like boasting or presumption—all was humility, resignation, and confidence. She charged her husband to educate their daughter in the fear of God; and, above all, to keep from her those novels and books of infidel sentimentality, by which she had nearly been brought to ruin. On the evening of the same day, she expired, in fulness of joy and peace in believing.

The account which the Doctor received from her attendants was, that his prayer at his first visit was fastened on her mind,—that soon after he left her, she became alarmed respecting the state of her soul,—that at one period, though her voice had previously been so feeble that she could scarcely be heard, yet her cries were distinctly audible from the second floor to the cellar of the house, and that at length she found peace in believing in Christ as he is exhibited in the gospel.

Dr. Mason was accustomed to visit some small congregations in the country, and was returning from one of these excursions, when he stopped at a house for some refreshment. Some bread and milk were handed to him, which he ate with an iron spoon. On his return, he smilingly mentioned the circumstance among his friends; and his remark about the iron spoon soon reached the ears of his kind hostess. She replied, with grief, that she was sorry Dr. Mason had made himself merry at her expense: for if she had possessed a silver spoon, he should certainly have used it: as it was, she furnished him with the best she had. This being related to him, he mounted his horse, and rode more than fifty miles, to apologize for his thoughtless speech, and to ask the old lady's pardon.

REV. MR. WORCESTER.

The Rev. Mr. Worcester, of Salem, at a Convention, said, that as he was once putting on his over-coat to go out on a visit to his parishioners, he heard a loud and unusual knock at the door. He opened it, and there stood a miserable-looking man in a state of intoxication. He was kindly invited to come in, and he did so. "You don't know me," said the stranger, "but I know you. My mother is a member of your church, and I used to go to your father's meeting." A long conversation ensued, in which the minister caught the substance of his story. He had known him when they were boys, but not since. The unfortunate being had become an infidel, and a degraded drunkard, and actually debated on his way, whether to eat opium and die, or go and see the minister, and let him know his case. Finally he determined on the latter course. He had then been drinking, but after serious, solemn conversation, he determined to drink no more. A day or two after, Mr. Worcester called to see him, and found him in the depths of despair on account of his sins. "I had never seen," said Mr. Worcester, "such misery; but I pointed him to 'the Lamb of God, which taketh away the sins of the world.' At length he found peace and forgiveness at the cross of Christ, and finally, with his wife, united with my church; and, as I see the individual in this house, I will only say he has since sustained an honourable and consistent profession."

Mr. Worcester sat down, when an individual, of a gentlemanly bearing, rose and said, "I am the individual to whom the pastor has referred; and it is all true." He spoke for some time, with much force, and related the trials he had gone through by imbibing infidel principles, and following the paths of intemperance; and his remarks were laid up in many a heart, who felt then, as they never felt before, the stupendous change that may be produced by total abstinence, and the influence of the faithful ministers of true religion.

REV. J. ARMSTRONG.

SEVERAL years ago, the Rev. James Armstrong preached at Harmony, near the Wabash; when a physician of that place, a professed deist or infidel, called on his associates to accompany him while he "attacked the Methodists," as he said. At first, he asked Mr. Armstrong if he followed preaching to save souls. He answered in the affirmative. He then inquired, "Did you ever see a soul?" "No." "Did you ever hear a soul?" "No." "Did you ever taste a soul?" "No." "Did you ever smell a soul?" "No." "Did you ever feel a soul?" "Yes, thank God," said Mr. Armstrong. "Well," said the Doctor, "there are four of the five senses against one, that there is a soul." Mr. Armstrong then asked the gentleman if he was a doctor of medicine, and he was also answered in the affirmative. He then asked the doctor, "Did you ever see a pain?" "No." "Did you ever hear a pain?" "No." Did you ever taste a pain?" "No." "Did you ever smell a pain?" "No." "Did you ever feel a pain?" "Yes." Mr. Armstrong then said, "There are also four senses against one, to prove that there is no such thing as a pain; and yet, sir, you know that there is a pain, and I know there is a soul." The doctor appeared confounded, and walked off.

A CLERGYMAN AT NEW ORLEANS.

A Presbyterian minister, American by birth, but of Scottish parentage, happening to be in New Orleans some time ago, was asked to visit an old Scottish soldier who had wandered to that city, sickened, and was conveyed to the hospital. On his entrance, and on announcing his errand, the Scotchman told him, in a surly tone, that he desired none of his visits,—that he knew how to die without the aid of a priest. In vain he informed him that he was no priest, but a Presbyterian minister, come to read to him a portion of the word of God, and to speak to him of eternity. The Scotchman doggedly refused to hold any conversation with him, and he was obliged to take his leave. Next day, however, he called again, thinking that the reflection of the man on his own rudeness would prepare the way for a better reception. But his tone and manner were equally rude and repulsive; and at length he turned himself in bed, with his face to the wall, as if determined to hear nothing and relent nothing. The minister bethought himself, as a last resource, of the hymn well known in Scotland, the composition of David Dickson, minister of Irvine, beginning, "*O mother dear, Jerusalem, when shall I come to thee,*" which his Scottish mother had taught him to sing to the tune of "Dundee." He began to sing his mother's hymn. The soldier listened for a few moments in silence, but gradually turned himself round, with a relaxed countenance, and the tear in his eye, to inquire, "Wha learned you that?" "My mother," replied the minister; "And so did mine," rejoined the now softened soldier, whose heart was opened by the recollections of infancy and of country, and now gave a willing ear to the man that had found the Scottish key to his heart.

REV. MR. CASE.

This valued minister relates a very interesting and striking conversion, which may show us the possibility of a work of Divine mercy in the heart of a sinner, after he has ceased to hold communication with the outward world, though assuredly it can furnish no rational ground for indolence and presumption :—

A Mrs. D., whom he baptized in Charleston, Maine, in 1811, when but a young lady, was one of a party who rode out on a sleigh, drawn by two horses, on the river from Hampden to Bangor; the ice gave way, and she, with her companions, was plunged beneath the watery element. Happily, however, the lives of the whole party were saved. During this immersion, her soul, by the instantaneous and powerful work of the Holy Spirit, was converted to God. The rapid progress of thought and feeling in this short moment, as she distinctly recollected, was, as she was falling, a most vivid and impressive thought of death filled her mind. This was instantly succeeded by an overwhelming consciousness of her sins, her guilt, and her just condemnation, and this was combined with a view of the character and law of God, shining in incomprehensible brightness, reflecting his love and justice; and then, in a moment, every energy of her soul seemed concentrated in one unyielding desire for mercy. At this instant, those who escaped from the water drew her upon the unbroken ice, when her soul was filled with love to God and Christ, and her tongue unloosed to praise his name. She said that she hardly thought of her temporal salvation, but with unutterable astonishment and gratitude she beheld that glorious grace which gave her heavenly delight. This was no delusion. Her subsequent life of piety gave evidence of its reality.

REV. DR. LATHROP.

I was once requested, says Dr. Lathrop, to preach against prevailing fashions. A remote inhabitant of the parish, apparently in a serious frame, called upon me one day, and pressed the necessity of bearing my testimony against this dangerous evil. I observed to him, that as my people were generally farmers, in middling circumstances, I did not think they took a lead in fashions. If they followed them, it was at an humble distance, and rather to avoid singularity than to encourage extravagance; that as long as people were in the habit of wearing clothes, they must have some fashion or other; and a fashion that answered the ends of dress, and exceeded not the ability of the wearer, I considered as innocent, and not deserving reproof. To this he agreed; but said, what grieved him was, to see people *set their hearts* so much on fashions. I conceded that as modes of dress were trifles compared with eternal concerns, to set our hearts upon them must be a great sin. But I advised him to consider, that to set our hearts *against* such trifles, was the same sin as to set our hearts *upon* them; and as his fashion was different from those of his neighbours, just in proportion as he set his heart *against theirs*, he set his heart *upon his own*. He was therefore doubly guilty of the very sin he imputed to others.

REV. T. HOOKER.

The Rev. Dr. Dwight, in his excellent travels, describes this eminent colonist of New England, as one of their wisest and most influential men. He was universally respected for his excellent qualities. He was remarkable, among other things for his mildness. A story, illustrating this trait in his character, is still preserved.

It is said that he was once suddenly awakened, in the night time, by an unusual noise in the cellar of his house. He suspected that some person had crept in without leave, and immediately arose, dressed himself, and went silently to the foot of the cellar stairs. There he saw a man, with a candle in his hand, taking pork out of a barrel. Mr. Hooker stood still and looked on till he had taken the last piece. He then stepped towards him, and accosted him in perfectly good humour:—"Neighbour, you act unfairly; you ought to leave a proper share for me." Thunderstruck at being detected, and especially by a man of Mr. Hooker's character, the culprit fell at his feet, condemned himself for his crime, and implored his pardon. Mr. Hooker cheerfully forgave him, and concealed his crime, but seriously admonished him, and then made him carry half the pork to his own house.

REV. MR. C.

During the progress of a protracted meeting, held in Johnstown, Ohio, by the Rev. Mr. C., of the Methodist Episcopal Church, it happened that most of the persons who desired the prayers of the church, were females. This led some objectors to say that weak-minded persons were generally the first to seek religion. This came to the knowledge of the worthy clergyman; and the next evening, he took occasion, at the meeting, to notice the objection.

"Well, friends," said he, "we have had a very profitable meeting to-night; but I wish to notice a fact which I have heard to-day. Some persons have said that this is not the work of the Lord, because nearly all who profess to seek him are females. They, moreover, challenge us to tell them why there is so large a proportion of the weaker sex thus engaged. Now, sirs, I will not answer you directly; but see here:—Two years ago, I had occasion to preach to the prisoners in the Ohio Penitentiary. Now, how did it happen that there were more than four hundred males, and but about half a dozen of the weaker sex? When you answer this, I will be prepared to speak to your question."

A PASTOR.

Dr. Goodrich has beautifully said that it was the reflection that there was bread enough and to spare in his father's house, which compelled the prodigal to exclaim, "I will arise, and go unto my father." Some years ago, two young ladies, under deep conviction of sin, went, after an evening meeting, to the house of a pastor for further instruction. As he conversed with them much at large, and was urging them, by motives drawn from the love of Christ, instantly to accept the offered salvation, one of them was observed to rest her head upon her hand, as if in deep abstraction, till her face at last sunk upon the table, in solemn and overpowering emotion. After a few moments of entire silence, she looked up with a countenance of serene joy, dropped upon one knee before her companion, and said, with the simplicity of a child, "Julia, *do* love Christ. He is so beautiful! Do come with me, and love him!" This led Julia to the reflection, "She has entered in, while I remain out. One shall be taken, and another left." This, under God, was the means of bringing her also to Christ, before she laid her head that night upon her pillow.

REV. DR. LIVINGSTON.

The late Rev. Dr. Livingston, of this country, and Louis Bonaparte, ex-king of Holland, happened once to be fellow-passengers, with many others, on board of one of the North River steamboats. As the doctor was walking the deck in the morning, and gazing at the refulgence of the rising sun, which appeared to him unusually attractive, he passed near the distinguished stranger, and, stopping for a moment, accosted him thus: "How glorious, sir, is that object!" pointing gracefully with his hand towards the sun. The ex-king assenting, Dr. Livingston immediately added, "And how much more glorious, sir, must be its Maker, the Sun of Righteousness!" A gentleman who overheard this short incidental conversation, being acquainted with both personages, now introduced them to each other, and a few more remarks were interchanged. Shortly after, the doctor again turned to the ex-king, and with that air of polished complaisance for which he was so remarkable, invited him first, and then the rest of the company, to attend morning prayer. It is scarcely necessary to add, that the invitation was promptly complied with.

REV. DR. JOHN H. RICE.

A late eminent judge, of Virginia, once remarked, that the most cutting reproof he had ever received for profaneness, was without words. He happened to be crossing a ferry with the late Dr. John H. Rice. On account of shallows, the boat could not be brought to land, and they were carried to the shore by the coloured ferrymen. One of these was so careless as to suffer the judge's clothes to become wetted, and he expressed his anger by an imprecation. Dr. Rice, without saying a word, turned to him his large, speaking eye, with sorrowful expression. "I never so felt a reproof," said the judge, "in my life; and instantly asked his pardon. 'Ask pardon of God,' said Dr. Rice. I shall never forget it." At this time, the judge was entirely ignorant who his reprover was.

A fine instance of the disinterestedness of this excellent clergyman, has been recorded by his biographer. A Mrs. Randolph, a lady of his congregation, and who died in his house, some time before her death made her will, and felt exceedingly desirous to leave him a handsome legacy, as a token of Christian regard for him. Apprehending, however, that such an act might possibly expose him to some unworthy imputations of mercenary views, and prizing his honour above every other consideration, she resolved to suppress her inclination, and leave him nothing. Still, she could not feel satisfied to do so, without having the reason of her conclusion communicated to him. This was accordingly done; and she was much gratified to find that her conduct was entirely approved by him. After all, however, when her will came to be opened, it was found that she had so far altered her mind as to have left him one thousand dollars. But on hearing of the fact, Dr. Rice at once resolved not to touch a cent of it. He instantly gave it all to public Christian charities, which he knew she had favoured while living.

REV. DR. PAYSON.

Dr. Payson was very eminently devoted to his work as a minister of Christ, and never at a loss, in the pulpit or out of it, for plans to accomplish the great object to which he had devoted his life. The following rencontre with a lawyer of Portland, who ranked among the first in the place for wealth and fluency of speech, will show the doctor's insight into character, and also that his conquests were not confined to " weak women and children."

A lady, who was the common friend of Mrs. Payson and the lawyer's wife, was sojourning in the family of the latter. After the females of the respective families had interchanged several "calls," Mrs. —— was desirous of receiving a foraml visit from Mrs. Payson; but to effect this, Doctor P. must also be invited; and how to prevail on her husband to tender an invitation was the great difficulty. He had been accustomed to associate experimental religion with meanness, and of course felt or affected great contempt for the divine, as if it were impossible for a man of his religion to be also a man of talents. He knew, by report, something of Dr. Payson's practice on these occasions, and dreading to have his house a place for what appeared to him gloomy conversation, resisted his wife's proposal as long as he could do so and retain the character of a gentleman. When he gave his consent, it was with the positive determination that Dr. Payson should not converse on religion, nor ask a blessing over his food, nor offer a prayer in his house. He collected his forces, and made his preparations in conformity with this purpose. When the appointed day arrived, he received his guests very pleasantly, and entered at once into animated conversation; determined, by obtruding his own favourite topics, to forestal the divine. It was not long before the latter discovered his object, and summoned together his powers to defeat it. He plied them with that skill and address for which he was remarkable; still, for some time, victory was inclined to neither side or to both alternately. The lawyer, not long before, had returned from Washington city, where he spent several weeks on business at the supreme court of the United States. Dr. Payson made some inquiries respecting sundry personages there, and among others, the chaplain of the house of representatives. The counsellor had heard him in the devotional services of that assembly. "How did you like him?" "Not at all; he appeared to have more regard to those around him than he had to his Maker." Dr. Payson was very happy to hear him recognise the distinction between praying to God, and praying to be heard of men; and dropped a series of observations on prayer, passing into a strain of remark, which, without taking the form, had all the effect on the lawyer's conscience, of a personal application. From a topic so unwelcome, he strove to divert the conversation; and every few minutes would start something as wide from it as the east is from the west. But as often as he wandered, his guest would dexterously, and without violence, bring him back; and as often as he was brought back, he would wander again. At length the trying moment, which was to turn the scale, arrived. The time for the evening repast had come; the servant had entered the parlour with the provisions; the master of the feast became unusually eloquent, resolved to engross the conversation, to hear no question or reply, to allow no interval for "grace," and to give no indication, by the eye, the hand, or the lips, that he expected or wished for such a service. Just as the distribution was on the point of commencing, Dr. P. interposed the question, "What writer has said, 'The devil invented the fashion of carrying round tea, to prevent a blessing being asked?'" Our host felt himself "cornered;" but, making a virtue of necessity, replied, "I don't know what writer it is; but if you please, we will foil the devil this time. Will you ask a blessing, sir?" A blessing, of course, was asked; and he brooked, as well as he could, this first certain defeat, still resolved not to sustain another by the offering of thanks on closing the repast. But in this, too, he was disappointed. By some well-timed sentiment of his reverend guest, he was brought into such a dilemma, that he could not, without absolute rudeness, decline asking him to return thanks. And thus he contended every inch of his ground, till the visit terminated. But, at every stage, the minister proved too much for the lawyer. He sustained his character as a minister of religion, and gained his point in every thing; and that, too, with so admirable a tact, in a way so natural and unrestrained, and with such respectful deference to his host, that the latter could not be displeased, except with himself. Dr. Payson not only acknowledged God on the reception of food, but before separating from the family, read the Scriptures and prayed; and that, too, at the request of the master. though this request was made, as in every other instance, in violation of a determined purpose. The chagrin of this disappointment, however, eventually became the occasion of his greatest joy. His mind was never afterwards entirely at ease, till he found peace in believing. Often did he revert, with devout thankfulness to God, to the visit which had occasioned his mortification; and ever after regarded, with more than common veneration and respect, the servant of God whom he had despised; and was glad to receive his ministrations, in exchange for those on which he had formerly attended.

Once, in the progress of a revival of religion among his people in Portland, Dr. Payson, after having repeatedly invited meetings at his house, one day gave an invitation to all those young persons who did not intend to seek religion. Any one who did not know the Doctor, would be surprised to hear that thirty or forty came. He had a very pleasant social interview with them, saying nothing about religion, until, just as they were about to leave, he closed a very few plain and simple remarks, in the following manner :—

"Suppose you should see coming down from heaven, a very fine thread, so fine as to be almost invisible, and it should come and attach itself to you. You knew, we will suppose, that it came from God. Should you dare to put out your hand and brush it away?"

He dwelt a few minutes on this idea, until every one had a clear and fixed conception of it, and of the hardihood which any one would manifest who should openly break even such a tie. "Now," continued he, "just such a slender delicate thread has come from God to you this afternoon. You do not feel, you say, any interest in religion; but by coming here this afternoon, God has fastened one little thread upon you all: it is very weak and frail, and you can, in a moment, brush it away. But you certainly will not do so. Welcome it, and it will enlarge and strengthen itself, until it becomes a golden chain to bind you for ever to God."

A few years before his death, he visited, at their most crowded season, the Springs of Saratoga. He sojourned at the principal hotel, where he was surrounded by the very *elite* of the United States. From day to day he mingled in general intercourse, and took his full share in conversations on philosophical, literary, and general topics, to the delight of every one. At length he proposed that, on a coming day, which he named, the hour after dinner should be devoted to *religious* conversation. Some of his most intimate friends were fearful lest the mighty talent by which he was surrounded, which, alas, was lamentably stained with infidelity, should prove more than equal to his pious zeal, or that he might be left alone to regret that he had made the proposal. At length the hour arrived, and after the cloth was removed, he found himself surrounded by a very large assembly. He sat for some time in deep and solemn silence, and then made some remarks, simply to elicit observations and inquiries in return. A leading statesman, among others, rose, determined to try the Doctor's strength to the ut-utmost, and boldly, and with great energy, attacked Christianity in some of its strongest holds. Interest was excited to its highest intensity, as the worthy minister rose to reply. With candour, clearness, and power he re-stated the strongest arguments which his opponents had brought forward, and with simplicity and eloquence which absolutely electrified his audience, he demolished every objection they had urged, and triumphantly won the unbounded admiration of all who heard him, every one of whom declared they had never before listened to such strains of wisdom of benevolence, and of piety.

A gentleman, who conversed with Dr. Payson in Boston, when he visited that city toward the latter part of his life, was led by his preaching and conversation to a considerable degree of serious concern for his soul. His wife was still in a great measure indifferent to the subject. One day, meeting her in company, he said to her, "Madam, I think your husband is looking upwards; making some effort to rise above the world, towards God and heaven. You must not let him try alone. Whenever I see the husband struggling alone in such efforts, it makes me think of a drone endeavouring to fly upwards, while it has one broken wing. It leaps, and flutters, and perhaps raises itself up a little way, and then it becomes wearied, and drops back again to the ground. If both wings co-operate, then it mounts easily."

One day he went to visit a mother, who was disconsolate from the loss of a child. He said to her:—" Suppose, now, some one was making a beautiful crown for you to wear; and you knew it was for you, and that you were to receive it and wear it as soon as it should be done. Now, if the maker of it were to come, and, in order to make the crown more beautiful and splendid, were to take away some of your jewels, to put into it,—should you be sorrowful and unhappy, because they were taken away for a little while, when you knew they were gone to make up your crown?"

The mother said, that no one could conceive of the relief, the soothing, quieting influence which this comparison had on her mind.

Dr. Payson was once going to one of the towns in Maine, for the purpose of attending a ministers' meeting, accompanied by a friend; when they had occasion to call at a house, on the journey, where Dr. Payson was unknown. The family had just sat down to tea; and the lady of the house, in the spirit of genuine hospitality, invited the strangers to partake of the social repast. Dr. Payson at first declined; but, being strenuously urged, he consented. As he took his seat, he inquired if a blessing had been asked; and, being answered in the negative, requested the privilege, which was readily granted, of invoking the benediction of Heaven. This was done with so much fervour, solemnity, and simplicity, that it had the happiest effect. The old lady treated the company with the utmost attention; and, as Dr. Payson was about to leave, he said to her, "Madam, you have treated me with much hospitality and kindness, for which I thank you sincerely; but, allow me to ask, how do you treat my Master? That is of infinitely greater consequence than how you treat me." He continued, in a strain of appropriate exhortation; and, having done his duty in the circumstances, proceeded on his journey. This visit was sanctified to the conversion of the lady and her household. The revival continued in the neighbourhood; and, in a short time, a church was built, and the regular ordinances of religion established.

On another occasion, he went to see a sick person, who was very much troubled because she could not keep her mind all the time fixed upon Christ, on account of the distracting influences of her sufferings, and the various objects and occurrences of the sick-room, which constantly called off her attention. She was afraid that she did not love her Saviour as she found it so difficult to fix her mind upon him. Dr Payson said, "Suppose you were to see a sick little child, lying in its mother's lap, with its faculties impaired by its sufferings, so that it was generally in a troubled sleep; but now and then, it just opens its eyes a little, and gets a glimpse of its mother's face, so as to be recalled to the recollection that it is in its mother's arms; and suppose that always, at such a time, it should smile faintly with evident pleasure to find where it was; should you doubt whether that child loved its mother or not?" The poor sufferer's doubt and despondency were gone in a moment.

A MINISTER IN NEW YORK.

A minister, in the city of New York, was, a few years since, called in to visit a dying young lady, about twenty years of age, who was heiress to a large estate, whose parents were doatingly fond of her, and whose education was of the highest and most fashionable character. The minister talked of death, judgment, and eternity; but the young lady had never before heard such language addressed to her, and she trembled. In the dying hour, she called for some of her fine clothes; and, when they were brought, she looked at her mother, and said, "These have ruined me. You never told me I must die. You taught me that my errand into this world was to be gay and dressy, and to enjoy the vanities of life. What could you mean? You knew I must die and go to judgment. You never told me to read the Bible, or to go to church, unless to make a display of some new finery. Mother, you have ruined me." She died in a few moments after.

A CLERGYMAN AT ST. LOUIS.

A worthy minister from England brought over a habit, common, we believe, even in the religious families of that country, of playing at drafts, sometimes even for a small stake. He was once brought very strongly to feel its impropriety. Some ladies, who were members of his church, had acquired somewhat of a love for dancing, which their pastor found out and reproved. A cousin of one of these ladies determined to have somewhat of harmless revenge on the clergyman. By some management, the pastor was drawn to the chess-board, and a few segars were staked on the game.

They played; and, in the end, the clergyman lost, but insisted on his friend playing again. His eyes were fully opened, when the gentleman replied "that his principles forbade him to play at games of hazard;" and he wisely resolved henceforth to "avoid the appearance of evil."

REV. DR. HENRY.

The excellent Dr. T. C. Henry records the following interesting dialogue:—

"You believe yourself guilty of the unpardonable sin?"

"I am sure of it."

"In what did the crime consist?"

"I opposed the work of God."

"So did Saul."

"I denied Jesus Christ."

"So did a disciple, afterwards honoured by his Master."

"I doubted the power of Jesus Christ, after strong evidence in its favour."

"So did Thomas."

"What! are you attempting to prove by such examples that I am a Christian?"

"Not at all. I am only inquiring into the nature of your guilt; and, thus far, I can see no reason for despair."

"I have hated God," rejoined the self-condemned, "and openly avowed my enmity in sight of his divine operations."

"Thus far your case is lamentable, indeed; but not hopeless, still. Our hearts are naturally at enmity with God; and I do not see why the open avowal of this, drawn out by the sight of the law into visible form, must necessarily and always constitute the guilt of which you accuse yourself."

"I feel that I am cut off from salvation."

"It is very difficult to reason against your feelings; but they are no proof on the present subject. Let me inquire whether you desire the pardon of your sins?"

"Assuredly, if it were possible."

"Do you regret the conduct of which you accuse yourself?"

"Certainly."

"Do you sincerely desire repentance?"

"I would give the world, if it were mine, to be able to do so."

"Then it is not possible that you have been guilty to an unpardonable extent; for these are characteristics of a state of mind faithless, but far from being desperate; and they come within the design of the gospel invitations."

There was something simple and touching in this mode of ministering to a mind diseased; and it produced an effect which probably no other process could have accomplished. Mr. L. did not long survive this interview. But his living and dying hours were those of a favoured Christian.

REV. MR. TREFIT.

I was called upon, says the Rev. Mr. Trefit, some years ago, to visit an individual, a part of whose face had been eaten away by a most loathsome cancer. Fixing my eyes on this man, in his agony, I said, "Supposing that Almighty God were to give you your choice: which would you prefer, your cancer, your pain, and your sufferings, with a certainty of death before you, but of immortality hereafter; or health, prosperity, long life in the world, and the risk of losing your immortal soul?" "Ah, sir!" said the man, "give me the cancer, the pain, the Bible, the hope of heaven; and others may take the world, long life, and prosperity!"

A SHREWD MINISTER.

A MINISTER had travelled far to preach to a congregation. After the sermon, he waited very patiently, expecting some of the brethren to invite him home to dinner. In this, he was disappointed. One and another departed, until the house was almost empty. Summoning resolution, however, he walked up to an elderly-looking gentleman, and gravely said,

"Will you go home with me to dinner, to-day, brother?" "Where do you live?" "About twenty miles from this, sir." "No," said the man, colouring, " but *you* must go with *me*." "Thank you; I will, cheerfully."

After that time, the minister was no more troubled about his dinner.

A TRAVELLING CLERGYMAN.

AN excellent clergyman, "whose praise is in all the churches," was once spending the night at a large inn. "It is my custom," said he to the mistress of the inn, "wherever I am, to have family worship. I am now going to have it with my wife; and I shall be glad if you and as many of your servants as can come in, will join us." "I shall be very happy," was the reply, " and all the servants shall come in." Accordingly, she gave her directions to this effect; and all the servants, waiters, chambermaids, hostlers, and postilions attended. The worthy clergyman, before he prayed, expounded a portion of Scripture; and, at the close of his exposition, with much affectionate earnestness and solemnity, exhorted his hearers to pray for the Holy Spirit. About a year after, he was travelling the same road. As he drew near the inn, he was accosted by a post-boy. "Sir, do you remember me?" "No, my friend, I cannot say that I do." "Well, sir, I recollect you. You were here some time ago, and had us all into your room, in the house, and explained a chapter in the Bible, and prayed for us. And when you were explaining the chapter, you told us, if we had not been accustomed to pray, to begin at once, and pray, 'Lord, give me thy Holy Spirit. Lord, convert my soul.' I thought much of those words, and was determined to follow your advice. But then I was at a loss for a place in which I could be alone, to pray for the Lord to give me his Spirit. At last I thought of the stable; and I used to take the key and lock myself in, and kneel down and pray that the Lord would convert my soul. And I bless God, I have reason to believe that he has heard and answered my prayers; that he has given me his Spirit, and converted my soul." This should encourage ministers to "sow beside all waters," and also shows the truth of the old saying, that "where there is a will, there is a way."

SUCCESS AND ENCOURAGEMENT OF THE CLERGY.

REV. PRESIDENT EDWARDS.

When President Edwards had preached one of his first sermons, after the remarkable outpouring of the Holy Spirit on his labours, he observed two families, when the congregation had withdrawn, remaining, as if by joint consent. Upon approaching them, he found they had, till that day, been in a state of variance; but, owing to the influence they were now under, they could not depart from the house of God till they were reconciled.

REV. MR. S.

Mr. S., a faithful and devoted minister in Georgia, some time since was in company with Mr. H., who was passing to one of his regular appointments for preaching. The residence of Mr. W., an unconverted and careless sinner, lay in the way; and, at the suggestion of Mr. S., it was agreed that they should stop, and try to pray with the ungodly old man. A few months after, the church to which they were going, was visited by a season of refreshing from the presence of the Lord; and Mr. W. was among the first who united with it. He stated that, on a certain day in the Spring, he was in his field, and that his mind was suddenly arrested by serious thoughts. He retired to the woods to pray; after which he went home, in a dreadful state of mind, to his dinner. His pious wife accosted him with, "Mr. S. has been here this morning." "Ah, indeed! and what does he say?" "Why," said the wife, "he prayed most devoutly for you." "At what hour," asked Mr. W., "was he here?" She told him; and it was found that, in that same hour, the Holy Spirit began to work upon his heart. He was joyfully received into the church, and walked worthy of the vocation with which he was called.

REV. DR. RODGERS.

When the late Rev. Dr. Rodgers, afterwards of New York, resided in New Castle county, on the Delaware, he offended a part of his congregation, by voting, at a disputed election, for a sheriff; in consequence of which, he never voted at a general election afterwards. In this act of self-denial, he showed a practical knowledge of the scale of duties; for how feeble is the obligation, in a minister of the gospel, to promote the supposed prosperity of his country by a solitary vote, compared with his obligation to preserve a commanding and undivided influence over his whole congregation, in order more effectually to direct their attention to subjects of an imperishable nature.

A UNIVERSALIST MINISTER.

The following fact is one among many, which show how even erroneous ministers may extend the truth, when they do not mean it:—

There lived in England, many years since, a man who professed to believe in the final salvation of all men. To sustain this doctrine, whenever he came to a passage which seemed favourable to his creed, he *turned down a leaf.* In this way, he converted his Bible into a kind of Universalist Text-Book, for the indoctrination of his family. He had a son, who imbibed the sentiments of his sire. At the death of the father, the son inherited the Bible referred to; and, in accordance with paternal example, he used to read where the leaves were turned down, and comfort himself in the belief that the way of sin is not death.

After a few years, the young man removed to the western part of this country. He went to hear a Universalist minister preach. The sermon being rather a lame performance, the man, so far from being confirmed by it, was rather shaken in his confidence. He thought, however, that he could make a stronger argument himself. He went home, and sat down to the task. But the Bible, with the leaves turned down, was away in England; and he had forgotten where to look for the detached portions upon which he had rested his faith, and thus was forced to read his Bible in its legitimate connections and dependencies. So he read on, chapter after chapter, looking all the while for his favourite doctrine. But he did not find it. Nay, he was soon convinced, that in order to salvation, he must be born again. He sought, and soon found peace in believing. For a few years, he lived the life of a consistent Christian; and, when called to die, he left the world in the full enjoyment of those consolations which it is the province of evangelical faith alone to give.

REV. JOHN BAILEY.

The usefulness of this eminent minister, who died in New England in 1697, did indeed begin in early life. His father, then in England, was a very licentious man. John was a little boy, but very pious, and used to pray with his mother and the whole family. This coming to the knowledge of his father, his mind became deeply impressed. The fact led him to the cross of Christ for pardon; and he would afterwards sometimes retire, with his beloved child, to confess his past sins, and to present thanksgivings for the grace he enjoyed.

AN AGED MINISTER.

An aged clergyman, who died a few years ago, not unfrequently heard of the usefulness of some of his sermons twenty or thirty years after they had been delivered. He once rode thirty miles, on a stormy Saturday, and had but very few hearers on the following day. He frequently thought afterwards, how foolish he had been to take such a journey to preach to a few persons, when he might have staid at home and addressed many more. Nearly twenty years afterwards, he fell into the company of a very pious gentleman, who, after a long conversation, asked him if he remembered to have preached at ———, at such a time? The aged pastor replied, "Yes; and I have often thought how foolish I was to leave my own congregation, and ride thirty miles, in a storm, to preach to a dozen people." The gentleman rejoined, "But your sermons that day were the means of my conversion." Never afterwards did the good clergyman think any journey too long, or any audience too small, to accomplish his object.

SEVERAL PASTORS.

When a certain pastor, whose ministry had been very highly blessed in the conversion of sinners, was asked the secret of his great usefulness, he replied, "We have a praying church." This is an eminently powerful auxiliary to success.

A fact is recorded of another minister, who enjoyed revivals in his church for fourteen successive winters. Many did not know how to account for this, till one of his members once rose at a prayer-meeting and made a confession. "Brethren," said he, "I have been long in the habit of praying, every Saturday night, till after midnight, for the descent of the Holy Ghost among us. And now, brethren," and he began to weep, "I confess that I have neglected it for two or three weeks." The secret was out; that minister had a praying church.

A worthy minister in ill health became greatly depressed in his mind, and began to think that he could preach no more. A member of his church became deeply interested in his situation, and was led to pray, with great fervour, for the descent of the Holy Spirit on his ministry. One Sabbath morning, this member's mind was greatly exercised; and he began to pray as soon as it was light, and prayed again and again for a blessing *that day*. In some way, the minister was directed within hearing of his prayer, the light broke in upon his mind, he went into the pulpit and preached with unwonted power, and a revival of religion commenced in his church that very day.

A minister was preaching in one of our large cities, and after retiring into the vestry, a respectable woman came in, and offering her hand to the man of God, said, "Sir, I am thankful to see your face once more; this is indeed a joyful day to me."

"I have not the pleasure of knowing you, ma'am," answered the minister, shaking hands with the stranger.

"Oh no, sir, you do not know me, but I have reason to remember you; and four words I once heard you read, I shall remember for ever."

"Indeed, what were they?"

"Fifteen years ago, sir, you were preaching in this city, and I was then in a dreadful state of mind, living far from God and happiness, and at length became so miserable, I resolved to jump into the river just below, and there end, as I foolishly imagined, my life and my sorrow together. I passed this place of worship in my way, just as you, sir, gave out your text, which was in the sixteenth chapter of the Acts, and a part of the twenty-eighth verse, "Do thyself no harm." My attention was arrested, and I hope my heart changed by the Spirit of God that evening; and I have now for many years been happy, sitting at the feet of Jesus, and I hope trying to learn of him. He is to me all and in all."

The minister was deeply affected, and kneeling down, gave thanks to God for restoring this wandering sheep to the fold of Jesus. And now they live together in the land afar off, where they behold the King in his glory, and rejoice evermore, singing the new song of Moses and the Lamb.

AMERICAN MISSIONARIES.

Five young men embarked from this country, seven years ago, on their own responsibility, as missionaries to the coloured population of Jamaica. The second day after their arrival, they heard in the streets of Kingston an inquiry for missionaries. They found that a deputation of four coloured men had come from the interior to seek an instructor who would go and reside among them. When first emancipated, they had agreed among themselves that they must have a missionary, and had, for his accommodation, erected a chapel where they habitually assembled to pray that Heaven would send them a teacher. Becoming weary of waiting for an answer, they said, "How do we know but our prayers have been answered? Let us go to Kingston and see."

One of the five young men who had just arrived from America, returned with these simple-hearted Africans, and found a field waiting for the reaper.

These missionaries, says the Recorder, have established five churches, which contain more than three hundred members, and have seven schools, numbering five hundred pupils, besides a high school to prepare teachers for other schools. They hope ultimately to prepare teachers and preachers for Africa also. No sooner do the coloured people become interested in religion themselves, than they begin to think and pray for their "father-land."

THE PURITAN MINISTERS.

It is a delightful testimony which Prince bears in his "Christian History," in reference to the usefulness of the first minisers from the old country in New England. Such was the piety of their people, that one of their ministers, in preaching before a very large assembly, affirmed that he had lived among his people seven years, and during the whole time had not heard a profane oath, nor seen a drunken man.

REV. DR. L. BEECHER.

The doctor once engaged to preach, by way of exchange, for a country minister, and the Sabbath proved to be excessively cold, stormy, and uncomfortable. It was mid-winter, and the snow was piled in heaps all along the roads, so as to make the passage very difficult. Still the doctor urged his horse through the drifts, till he reached the church, put his horse into a shed, and went in. As yet, there was no person in the house, and after looking about, he took his seat in the pulpit. Soon the door opened, and a single individual walked up the aisle, looked about, and took a seat.

The hour came for commencing service, but there were no more hearers. Whether to preach to such an audience or not, was only a momentary question with Lyman Beecher. He felt that he had a duty to perform, and that he had no right to refuse to do it, because one man only could reap benefit; and accordingly he went through all the services, praying, singing, preaching, and the benediction, with his *one* hearer. And when all was over, he hastened down from the desk to speak to his "congregation," but he had departed.

So rare a circumstance was, of course, occasionally referred to, but twenty years after a very delightful discovery came to light in connection with this service. The good doctor was travelling somewhere in Ohio, and alighting from the stage in a pleasant village, a gentleman stepped up to him and fami liarly called him by his name. "I do not remember you," said Dr. B. "I suppose not," said the stranger, but we spent two hours together in a house, alone, once, in a storm." "I do not recall it, sir," added the old minister; "pray where was it?" "Do you remember preaching twenty years ago, in such a place, to a single person?" "Yes, yes," said the doctor, grasping his hand, "I do, indeed; and if you are the man, I have been wishing to see you ever since." 'I am the man, sir; and that sermon saved my soul, made a minister of me, and yonder is my church! The converts of that sermon, sir, are all over Ohio!'

So striking a result made no little impression on the doctor's mind. He learned that the man was at the time a lawyer, who was in the town on business, and tired of a sunday morning at a country hotel, went in despite of the storm to church, and heard that sermon. The doctor added, "I think that was about as satisfactory an audience as I ever had."

REV. DR. HOPKINS.

SELDOM has the pulpit been honoured with a great man who composed and uttered his discourses in so clumsy and awkward a style as Dr. Samuel Hopkins. It was the burden of his daily complaint that he had so little success in the ministry, and he is now often mentioned as a pious divine who added but little to the stock of public virtue. But let us glance at the effects produced by this "unsuccessful" labourer. Whatever may have been the extent of his indebtedness to the manuscripts of President Edwards, which were left in his possession, he has certainly done much towards moulding the theological character of New England. By his system of divinity, his four religious biographies, and his ten additional publications, he has given an impulse to many who have been esteemed more useful than himself. Dr. Jonathan Edwards ascribed his own speculative convictions of the truth to the reasoning of Hopkins. A pastor of one of the largest churches in Massachusetts, who was extensively admired for his rich and varied eloquence, who was honoured as an instrument of many religious revivals, in one of which more than a hundred persons were gathered into the fold of his church, who was withal somewhat eminent as a theological instructor and controversialist, and who has now several descendants in the ministry, was converted to the truth by the blessing of Heaven upon the labours of Hopkins. And there was another divine, who owed his renovation to the same instrumentality;—a divine whose acquaintance was sought and prized by the most eminent theologians in our own land, and by some in England;—a polished gentleman, who was said by his parishioner, Judge Sedgwick, to be "sure of silencing with his urbanity of manner those who were not convinced by his logic." For more than fifty-nine years he retained the pastoral care of a people among whom Edwards had written his treatise on the will, in whose cultivated village lived six judges of our courts, and from whose intellectual circle there have come forth one president of Cambridge University, one president, as well as the original founder of Williams College. He wrote and preached more than three thousand sermons, published nineteen books, some of standard value. His reputation as a theological teacher is illustrated by the fact, that on the list of his divinity students, are found the names of President Kirkland, Dr. Hyde, Dr. Catlin, and Dr. Samuel Spring. During his pastoral life he was active in six different revivals of religion among his people, and he admitted to his church three hundred and eighty-four persons from the world, and one hundred and twenty from other churches. He died with the title of "patriarch of his neighbourhood," and the seeds which he scattered are still bearing fruit. In the extended usefulness, then, of these two divines, both of whom were so largely indebted to Dr. Hopkins, we see a portion of the results of his labours. In the churches where their influence will long remain, in the churches of which he himself was the pastor, he has been and still is enlarging the intellect and purifying, through grace, the affections of men. He saw, at the last, a hundred of his own parishioners subscribe with their own hands to be the Lord's, and he started more than a hundred circles, which will widen and expand upon the lake, wave following wave, silently pursuing in all future time, but never overtaking each other, and never permitting the sheet of waters to become stagnant.

REV. J. PATTERSON.

The New York Christian Magazine, for 1810, tells us that the Rev. Joseph Patterson, of Washington county, in that State, with a view to promote Christian zeal among his people, fixed up a box in his church, with the inscription, "O give me a Bible!" At the end of three months the box was opened, and was found to contain thirty-two dollars and fifty cents, which sum was forwarded to the Bible Society, in Philadelphia.

REV. MR. M.

The following incident may serve to show what can be done by a single individual, when animated with ardent love to Christ and solicitude for the souls of men; and the part borne in this narrative by a poor simpleton, proves how God can make use of the weakest and most despised instrument in bringing about His purposes of mercy. When the Rev. Mr. M. was a student at Princeton, N. J. in 1841, he was equally distinguished for his glowing and unwearied zeal as he is at present. There were but few Baptists, the denomination to which he belonged, in that region, but his zeal for the cause of the Lord won for him the hearts of all Christians of whatever name. It was his delight to go out and preach the gospel wherever he could collect hearers. One evening during vacation, when he had been thus preaching, a poor half-witted man came up to him and asked him if he would not visit the part where he lived, and preach for the neighbours there. Mr. M., always ready to accept such an invitation by whoever given, assented. The intervening day was spent by the simpleton in going from house to house, telling the neighbours, in allusion to the extreme youth of the preacher, that " a boy was coming to preach for them," adding, "and he will convert you all." Considerable interest and curiosity were excited, and when evening came the place of meeting was crowded. A front seat was occupied by a number of young ladies, who were talking and laughing together; some of them afterwards owned that they never felt more light and trifling than they did when they came together that evening. The young preacher arrived, and as he passed, he heard the derisive whisper run through this front seat—" This, then, is he who is to convert us all." He took his place and gave out a hymn. The earnestness of his tones seemed at once to arrest the attention of the assembly; and when he began to preach, he had not proceeded far before many of his hearers were in tears. The young ladies, to whom we have before alluded, were deeply affected, and the blessed results of that meeting will be felt throughout eternity. The careless were arrested in their thoughtless course, and though the words of the simpleton were not fulfilled to *all*, yet they were to many, who can look back to that season as the time when they were turned "from darkness to light, and from the power of Satan unto God." One of these young ladies afterwards became the wife of the preacher. She was one of fifty who gave hopeful evidence of conversion, and were added to the church as the result of the revival thus commenced.

A CLERGYMAN IN NEW YORK.

A SHORT time since, a minister of New York city, with a view to encourage others in attempts to do good, related the following fact.

Some three or four years ago, we were building our house Our money was all gone. We had done to the utmost of our ability, and had resolved to stop when our funds were expended. One day I was standing with rather a sad heart looking at the workmen. I knew we had just enough money left to pay the bricklayers for that day's work, and that, at night, unless God should appear for us in some unexpected providential way, they must all be discharged, for we knew not where to get the next dollar. What to do, I did not know, but silently sent up my prayer to God, that he would appear for our help. While standing there, a gentleman stopped to look at the building, and presently addressed me. "Can you tell me," said he, "who is erecting this building, and where I can see any of the managers or trustees?" "Yes, sir, I am the pastor—what did you wish?" "Why I am one of a Committee to obtain a suitable room for a public primary school in this neighbourhood; and, if you can let us have the basement of this house, we will be at the expense of finishing that room, and, if it will be any help, we will furnish you with *a thousand dollars* or so, as the advance rent for three or four years." The engagement was soon concluded, and our house was before long completed with the money that God thus providentially sent us.

A NEW ENGLAND MINISTER.

A MINISTER in New England not very long since related the following fact:—

One of the ministers in Essex county made an appointment on the Sabbath for a meeting of the friends of foreign missions, on a designated evening of the same week. He was punctual to his own appointment, but found only a single individual present to participate in the duties of the evening. They determined, however, that the object should not be defeated, and discussed the question, "What ought to be done by that church and people towards the conversion of the world?" and came to the resolve, *unanimously*, that a hundred dollars *could* be raised, *ought* to be raised, and *should* be raised for the object forthwith. The meeting was then adjourned; and, before the expiration of the week, they had secured more than ninety dollars. This was a greater amount than they had ever raised in a single year before. Who will not persevere in doing good, in spite of all the difficulties which may encompass his path?

REV. MR. PRINCE.

THE Rev. Dr. Wisner remarks that the destruction of the French armament under the duke D'Anville, in the year 1746, should be remembered with gratitude and admiration by every inhabitant of America. This fleet, consisting of forty ships of war, was destined for the destruction of New England. It sailed from Chebucto, in Nova Scotia, for this purpose. In the mean time, the pious people, apprized of their danger, had appointed a season of fasting and prayer, to be observed in all their churches. While Mr. Prince was officiating in Old South church, Boston, on this fast-day, and praying most fervently that the dreaded calamity might be averted, a sudden gust of wind arose, (the day had till then been perfectly calm,) so violent as to cause a loud clattering of the windows. The reverend pastor paused in his prayer; and looking round upon the congregation with a countenance of hope, he again commenced, and with great devotional ardor, supplicated the Almighty to cause that wind to frustrate the object of their enemies. A tempest ensued, in which the greater part of the French fleet was wrecked. The duke D'Anville, the principal general, and the second in command, both committed suicide. Many died with disease, and thousands were consigned to a watery grave. The small number who remained alive returned to France, without health and without spirits, and the enterprise was abandoned, and never again resumed.

With reference to this and other similar instances, the late President Dwight remarks, in a discourse on answers to prayer: "I am bound, as an inhabitant of New England, to declare, that, were there no other instances to be found in any other country, the blessings communicated to this would furnish ample satisfaction concerning this subject, to every sober, much more to every pious man."

BISHOP M'ILVAINE.

Bishop M'Ilvaine says:—I was called from my study, to see a man who had come on business. I found in the parlour a well-dressed person, of respectable appearance, good manners, and sensible conversation—a stranger. After a little while he looked at me earnestly, and said, "I think, sir, I have seen your face before." "Probably," said I, supposing he had seen me in the pulpit. "Did you not once preach in the receiving ship at the navy-yard, on the prodigal son, sir?" "Yes." "Did you not afterwards go to a sailor, sitting on his chest, and take his hand, and say, 'Friend, do you love to read your Bible?'" "Yes." "I, sir, was that sailor; but then I knew nothing about the Bible, or about God; I was a poor, ignorant, degraded sinner." His history was, in substance, as follows: He had been twenty-five years a sailor, and nearly all that time in the service of the British navy, indulging in all the extremes of a sailor's vices. Drunkenness, debauchery, and profaneness, made up his character. The fear of death, or hell, or God, had not entered his mind. Such was he, a sink of depravity, when a preacher one day assembled a little congregation of sailors in the ship to which he was attached, and spoke on the text, "Behold, now is the accepted time; behold, now is the day of salvation." He listened, merely because the preacher was once a sailor. Soon it appeared to him that the preacher saw and knew him, though he was sitting where he supposed himself concealed. Every word seemed to be meant for a description of him. To avoid being seen and marked, he several times changed his place, carefully getting behind the others. But, wherever he went, the preacher seemed to follow him, and to describe his course of life, as if he knew it all. At length the discourse was ended; and the poor sailor, assured that he had been the single object of the speaker's labours, went up and seized his hand, and said, "Sir, I am the very man: that is just the life I have led. I am a poor miserable man; but I feel a desire to be good, and will thank you for some of your advice on the subject." The preacher bade him pray. He answered, "I have never prayed in my life; but that I might be damned, as when I was swearing; and I don't know how to pray." He was instructed. It was a day or two after this, while his mind was anxious but unenlightened, that Providence led me to him, while sitting on his chest. He said I showed him a verse of the Bible as one that would guide him. I asked if he remembered which it was. "Yes, it was, 'Him that cometh unto me I will in no wise cast out.'" Soon after this, his mind was comforted with a hope of salvation through Jesus Christ. His vices were all abandoned. He became from that time a new creature in all his dispositions and habits; took special care to be scrupulously attentive to every duty of his station; gained the confidence of his officers, and, having left the service, continued an exemplary member of society and of the church of Christ. He was so entirely renewed, that no one could imagine, from his appearance or manners, that he had been for twenty-five years a drunken, abandoned sailor.

A MINISTER AMONG THE CHEROKEES.

Some years ago, three ministers went to preach to the Cherokee Indians. One preached very deliberately and coolly; and the chiefs held a council to know whether the Great Spirit spoke to them through that man; and they declared he did not, because he was not so much engaged as their head men were in their national concerns. Another spoke to them in a most vehement manner; and they again determined in council that the Great Spirit did not speak to them through that man, because he was mad. The third preached to them in an earnest and fervent manner; and they agreed that the Great Spirit might speak to them through him, because he was both earnest and affectionate. The last was ever after kindly received.

A PREACHER FROM ENGLAND.

About the year 1773, a great revival of religion took place in the southern part of our country, by means of some preachers from England. Many, both whites and blacks, were brought to an acquaintance with God, by faith in Christ. Two of these, a white man and an African, meeting together, began to speak of the goodness of God to their souls. Among other things, they were led to inquire how long each had known the salvation of God, and how long it was, after they were convinced of their sin and danger, before each got a satisfactory evidence of their pardoning mercy. The white man said, "I was three months in deep distress of soul before God spoke peace to my guilty conscience!" "But it was only a fortnight," said the black man, "from the time I first heard of Jesus, and felt that I was a sinner, till I received the knowledge of salvation by the remission of sins." "But what was the reason," asked the white man, "that you found salvation sooner than I did?" "This is the reason," replied the other, "You white men have much clothing upon you, and when Christ calls, you cannot run to him; but we poor negroes have only this," pointing to the mat or cloth which was tied round his neck, "and when we hear the call, we throw it off instantly, and run to him."

REV. G. WHITEFIELD.

Who can tell the results of a single sermon, or trace the consequences of one conversion? When Mr. Whitefield was preaching in New England, a lady became the subject of Divine grace, and of course devoted to prayer. But in her Christian exercises she was alone; she could induce no one to pray with her but her little daughter, about ten years of age. She took this dear child into her closet from day to day as a witness of her cries and tears. After a time, it pleased God to touch the heart of the child, and to give her the knowledge of salvation by the remission of sin. In a transport of holy joy, she then exclaimed to her mother, "O mother, if all the world knew this! I wish I could tell every body! Pray, mother, let me run to some of the neighbours, and tell them, that they may be happy, and love my Saviour too!" "Ah, my dear child," said the mother, "that would be useless, for I suppose that were you to tell your experience, there is not one within many miles but what would laugh at you, and say it was all delusion." "O mother," replied the dear girl, "I think they would believe me. I must go over to the shoemaker, and tell him, he will believe me." She ran over, and found him at work in his shop. She began by telling him that he must die, and that he was a sinner, and that she was a sinner, but that her blessed Saviour had heard her mother's prayers, and had forgiven all her sins; and that now she was so happy, that she did not know how to tell it! The shoemaker was struck with surprise; his tears flowed down like rain; he threw aside his work, and by prayer and suplication sought for mercy. The neighbourhood became excited, and within a few months there were more than fifty brought to the knowledge of Jesus, rejoicing in his power and grace.

A MISTAKEN MINISTER.

The following anecdote bears strong testimony in favour of labouring and praying for the immediate conversion of young children in our Sabbath-schools. A minister in Massachusetts, who felt a lively interest in the Sabbath-school, used to pray that the seed there sown might spring up in due time and bear fruit. He not only prayed in this manner himself, but by his example, taught the teachers thus to pray. They never once thought of praying for the immediate conversion of the scholars. At length this minister heard that some two or three of the scholars who had been in the school for some time were beginning to indulge the hope that they had passed from death unto life. He called to see them, and on inquiring, found that their feelings began to change at just about the age that he and the teachers had supposed would be the due time, when the seed might begin to spring and grow and bear fruit. This led him to believe that if he had only fixed upon an earlier time, and laboured accordingly, they might have given their hearts to the Saviour long before. He was convinced of his error. He met the teachers and said to them, we have been wrong entirely wrong. We ought to have prayed for their immediate conversion then exhorted them to direct all their efforts to this point, and not to rest satisfied so long as one child in the school was unreconciled to God. They began to pray, and God soon poured out his spirit upon the school, and convinced minister and teachers that it is right to pray for the immediate conversion, of little children. Let all who have any thing to do with the religious instruction of little children, take heed lest their garments be stained with the blood of their souls.

REV. DAVID BRAINERD.

There are some interesting facts connected with the labours of this extraordinary young man among the Indians, which ought never to be forgotten. It is well known that in June 1745, he first began to labour among a small body of these people in New Jersey. For the first six weeks they manifested such entire indifference and stupid unconcern, that he was about to leave them in despair, when he was somewhat encouraged by the conversion of his interpreter. The interest with which this man now entered into the subject, and the warmth and unction with which he translated Mr. Brainerd's discourses, struck the Indians with surprise, and arrested their attention. On the 8th of August, he preached to about sixty-five of them, among whom he discovered much anxious concern. In private intercourse with them afterwards, the power of God seemed to descend upon them like a mighty rushing wind. Almost all persons, of all ages, were bowed down with concern together, and were scarcely able to withstand the shock. Old men and women, who had been drunken wretches for many years, and some children, appeared in distress for their souls. One who had been a murderer, a *pow-wow*, or conjuror, and a notorious drunkard, was brought to cry for mercy with many tears. A young Indian woman, who never before knew that she had a soul, had come to see what was the matter; she called on Mr. Brainerd on her way, and when he told her that he was about to preach to the Indians, she laughed, and seemed to mock. He had not proceeded far in his sermon before she felt effectually that she had a soul, and before it was ended, was so distressed with concern for its salvation, that she seemed like one pierced through with a dart. Such scenes were frequently repeated during the following eight weeks. Mr. Brainerd says: " This surprising concern was never excited by any harangues of terror, but always appeared most remarkable when I insisted on the compassion of a dying Saviour, the plentiful provisions of the Gospel, and the free offer of divine grace to needy sinners. The effects have been very remarkable. I doubt not but many of these people have gained more *doctrinal* knowledge of divine truth since I visited them in June last, than could have been instilled into their minds by the most diligent use of proper and instructive means for whole years together without such a divine influence. They seem generally divorced from their drunkenness, which is the sin that easily besets them. A principle of honesty and justice appears among them, and they seem concerned to discharge their old debts, which they have neglected, and, perhaps, scarcely thought of for years. Love seems to reign among them, especially those who have given evidence of having passed through a saving change. Their consolations do not incline them to lightness, but, on the contrary, are attended with solemnity, and often with tears and apparent brokenness of heart." After some months' probation, he baptized forty-seven out of less than one hundred, who composed the settlement.

REV. PRESIDENT DAVIES.

The influence of the Pulpit in stimulating the heroes of the Revolutionary war was unquestionably great. The eloquent Samuel Davies, in an address to one of the Militia companies, pronounced a celebrated encomium on Washington, in a single sentence, which animated his hearers, and proved prophetic as to its subject. After praising the zeal and courage which had been shown by the Virginia troops, the preacher added:—" As a remarkable instance of this, I may point out to the public that heroic youth, Colonel Washington, whom I cannot but hope Providence has hitherto preserved in so signal a manner for some important service to his country." This was but the echo of the general voice.

The fruits of this devoted minister of Christ were not ephemeral—they did not end in excitement. *He* went to his rest long since. But the fruits of his ministry still remain, in the consistent piety of those who were reared under the influence of parents brought into the church by his labours. A gentleman in Tennessee says:—"The fruits of the great revival in Hanover under the preaching of Samuel Davies, are now spreading and growing in the valley of the Mississippi. There are many of the children and children's children of those persons who professed religion in Hanover, under the ministry of that eminent man of God, now scattered in this great valley; and I know of no instance where they go, but an altar is reared for the worship of God in their families and neighbourhoods."

REV. GILBERT TENNENT.

DR. FRANKLIN gives an interesting account of this excellent man. It is well known that he was the friend and companion of Mr. Whitefield, and that he became the minister of the people whom that eminent minister collected together in Philadelphia.

Dr. F. says:—The Rev. Gilbert Tennent came to me with a request that I would assist him in obtaining a subscription for erecting a new meeting-house. It was to be for the use of a congregation he had gathered among the Presbyterians, who were originally the disciples of Mr. Whitefield. Unwilling to make myself disagreeable to my fellow-citizens, by too frequently soliciting their contributions, I absolutely refused. He then desired I would furnish him with a list of the names of persons I knew by experience to be generous and public-spirited. I thought it would be unbecoming in me, after their kind compliance with my solicitations, to mark them out to be worried by other beggars, and therefore refused to give such a list. He then desired I would at least give my advice. "That I will readily do," said I; "and, in the first place, I advise you to apply to all those who you know will give something; next, to those who you are uncertain whether they will give any thing or not, and show them the list of those who have given; and, lastly, do not neglect those who you are sure will give nothing, for in some of them you may be mistaken." He laughed, and thanked me, and said he would take my advice. He did so, for he asked of *everybody;* and he obtained a much larger sum than he expected, with which he erected the capacious and elegant meeting-house that stands in Arch street.

REV. DR. B.

Some years since, a merchant at Boston sent a variety of useful articles as a present to the Rev. Dr. B., his pastor, accompanied with a note, desiring his acceptance of it as a comment on Gal. vi. 6: "Let him that is taught in the word, communicate to him that teacheth in all good things." The good doctor, who was then confined by sickness, returned his compliments to Mr. W., thanked him for his excellent *Family Expositor,* and requested him to give him a practical exposition of Matt. xxv. 36: "I was sick, and ye visited me."

REV. DR. BACKUS.

The Rev. Dr. Backus, of Somers, was more than once invited to accept the professorship of Divinity, both in the college of Dartmouth and in Yale. The reasons of his refusal he did not communicate, but the principal one is not improbably found in the following anecdote:—A gentleman, who was a representative from Somers, in the legislature, sitting at New Haven, while Dr. Backus was deliberating on this subject, was urged by one of his friends to use his influence in persuading the people of Somers to unite with their minister in calling an ecclesiastical council, which should decide on the propriety or impropriety of his acceptance. He replied, "You solicit me in vain. If Dr. Backus resolves to leave us, we cannot help it; but we will never consent to call a council for the purpose of determining on our own destruction. If he leaves us, we are undone; and no people can be reasonably expected, or desired, voluntarily to take measures to accomplish their own ruin."

A HOME MISSIONARY.

It was a fine day in ———, when a steamboat left St. Louis for Cincinnati. More than two hundred passengers enjoyed the beauty of the scene and scenery, and the excitement of the passage. Among them were all classes and conditions, professions and characters. There was seen the missionary, who had spent many years in preaching the gospel among the heathen of Eastern Asia. There was a Home Missionary, too, who had spent his tour of labour in the Great Valley, in proclaiming to destitute thousands the gospel of the grace of God, and who was now returning to his home in one of the

Middle States. There was the reckless and profane, the Sabbath-breaker and the infidel; there, too, was the civilian of firm and decisive Christian character, as well as many a nominal Christian. The Sabbath was at hand, as the boat approached a city on the noble river Ohio. Those who loved the Sabbath, and made it a rule of life to honour God, in the observance of that day "made for man," had settled their arrangements to leave the boat at this city, and, after the Sabbath, to pursue their journey. A goodly number thus honoured the God of the sacred day. The Foreign Missionary led the way; the Home Missionary hesitated, doubted, and finally said that he had only the money to carry him home in the shortest time, and that he could not stop on expense over the Sabbath, and be able to pay his way homewards. "What shall I do, and what ought I to do?" was his inquiry, made with deep interest in view of his condition. The reply of the civilian was, "Obey the commands of God, and then trust Him; hundreds know you are a missionary and a minister of the gospel, and will feel the influence of your pernicious example. The cause of Christ will bleed, that a missionary should travel on the Sabbath—that a clergyman should violate the Sabbath. 'Trust in God;' no other course is safe or cheap." He was convinced, moved, resolved, and went on shore with the others, and passed the Sabbath, not without some apprehensions that he might be troubled by the expense. On Monday, another boat took them on their way. The Home Missionary came with a cheerful countenance; even the lines of solicitude on his face had disappeared. His expenses had been paid by some unknown friend; and he felt constrained to declare with gratitude, "I will obey, and hereafter trust the Lord."

A MINISTER IN NEW YORK.

How often is the pulpit introduced into a neighbourhood by very unexpected means! The Rev. Mr. Cook, of New York, not long since related the following pleasing fact:—

In 1807, a gentleman, journeying in the interior of New York, then regarded as the *far* West, took with him some copies of Doddridge's " Rise and Progress of Religion in the Soul," for distribution. As he stopped at a cabin tavern, he noticed that the woman who waited on him at table, was busily engaged in reading. He inquired what book she had, and learned that it was the " Rise and Progress," which a neighbour had lent to her, and from which she was copying passages which had peculiarly interested her mind. He gave her a copy of the book, which she received with great delight. In 1839, he was again passing that way; and, on inquiring for this woman by name, he was pointed to an elegant house as her residence. He called on her, and asked her if she remembered him. She did not. " But do you not remember the man who gave you Doddridge's Rise and Progress, thirty years ago?" " Oh, yes!" said she; " are you the same man? Why, that book was the means of converting my soul; and it was lent around, and others read it, and we had meetings to read it together. It was read at huskings and bees, and on the Sabbath day, and a revival followed; and by and by, we sent for a minister, and formed a church. The church at Wyoming is the fruit of that seed."

REV. MR. MASSEY.

There are many ways of assisting ministers in the discharge of their important duties, which seldom occur to common minds, but eminently conduce to the advancement of religion. One of these may be told in connection with General Washington, whose usefulness extended to every object within the sphere of his influence. In the affairs of Truro parish, to which Mount Vernon belonged, he took a lively concern, and exercised a salutary control. He was a vestryman of that parish. On one occasion, he gained a triumph of some moment, which Mr. Massey, the clergyman, who lived to an advanced age, used to mention as an instance of his address. The old church was falling to ruin, and it was resolved that another should be built. Several meetings were held, and a warm discussion arose respecting its location; the old one being remote from the centre, and inconveniently situated for many of the parishioners. A meeting for settling the question was finally held. Mr. George Mason, who led the party for adhering to the ancient site, made an eloquent harangue, in which he appealed, with great effect, to the sensibilities of the people, conjuring them not to desert the spot consecrated by the bones of their ancestors and the most hallowed associations. Mr. Massey said that every person present seemed moved by this discourse, and, for the moment, he thought there would not be a dissenting voice. Washington then rose, and drew from his pocket a roll of paper, containing an exact survey of Truro parish, on which was marked the site of the old church, the proposed site of the new one, and the place where each parishioner resided. He spread this map before the audience, explained it in a few words, and then added, that it was for them to determine whether they would be carried away by an impulse of feeling, or act upon the obvious principles of reason and justice. The argument, thus confirmed by ocular demonstration, was conclusive, and the church was erected on the new site.

A DISCOURAGED YOUNG MINISTER.

A YOUNG minister was settled in a large and popular congregation, under very flattering circumstances. The church and people had settled him in the belief that he was a young man of more than ordinary talents, and with the expectation of his becoming a distinguished man. After a year or two, when the novelty of the thing had worn off, the current seemed to change, and the feeling prevailed that Mr. B. was not, nor likely to be, quite what they had expected. He did not grow as they had thought he would; he did not perform the amount of labour which was needed to build up the church, and interest the congregation. Things dragged heavily. The young man felt the influence of the chill atmosphere which thus surrounded him. His spirits sunk, his health failed, and it was soon whispered around in the society and in the neighbouring towns, that Mr. B. would probably have to leave—he was not the man for the place. He was not the man of talents they had anticipated.

While things were in this state, at a meeting of the church, when the pastor was absent, (perhaps one called to see what should be done,) Mr. O——, an intelligent and influential member, arose and said:

"Brethren, I think we have been in the fault respecting our minister. I think that he is a young man of superior talents, and will one day be a distinguished man. But we have not sustained him and encouraged him as we should. We have been standing and looking on, expecting him to raise both himself and us to eminence. Now, let us adopt a different course. Let us encourage our minister with our prayers, our sympathies, and our efforts. Let us speak of him with esteem and confidence to others, and say that we think him a man of talent, and one who bids fair to be a distinguished man."

The thing was agreed upon. The leading men set the example. Very soon every one was speaking in favour of Mr. B. His people visited him, sympathized with him; and people out of the society began to remark, how Mr. B. was rising in the estimation of his people.

The young man felt the change. The cold, damp chill with which he was surrounded, and which was benumbing the energies of his soul, was changed by the influence of such kindly beams, and a warm atmosphere came over him. His spirits rose; his health returned; his energies awoke, and he showed to all that he had within him the elements of a man. Several revivals attended his labours. In the affections of the church and the people, he firmly established himself. His name became honourably enrolled among authors, and he was one whom his own church and other churches delight to honour.

REV. DR. STANFORD.

Ministers of the gospel, though it does not become them to talk of it, are often very poor, and kindness should be shown to them, both in act and in manner. The following may suggest an important and useful hint:—The late Rev. Dr. Stanford was once walking in Wall street, in New York, when he met a gentleman, who, judging from the threadbare appearance of his garments, that a new suit of clothes would not be unacceptable, invited him to step into a merchant tailor's shop, opposite. After they had entered, Mr. W. remarked to the tailor that they had called for the purpose of requesting him to decide a point upon which there was some doubt, namely, who was the largest man, Dr. Stanford or himself. They were accordingly measured, and nothing more was said on the subject. The following week, a new suit of clothes were brought to Dr. S., accompanied with an anonymous note, requesting his acceptance of them. When relating this circumstance to his biographer, Dr. S. remarked, with his usual pleasantry, "Well, what could I do but pocket the affront?"

A NEW ENGLAND MINISTER.

At the first settlement of one of the New England towns, the inhabitants, with their characteristic piety, erected a house of worship, and procured the services of an eminent minister. Without a fixed salary, he was partially dependent upon gratuity for support.

For the more effectual supply of his wants, as well as to testify their attachment and respect, the members of his flock appointed a day for general contribution. On that day, they came to the residence of their minister, some in carriages and some on foot, bringing with them their various gifts, all zealous to testify their love, and some, perhaps, anxious to exhibit their superior wealth. Be this as it may, they formed a happy group; cordial salutations were interchanged, love attuned every heart, and joy sparkled in every eye.

Among the last to arrive, were two neighbours who resided in a remote part of the parish; and whom want and privation, incident to a new settlement, had left nothing to give. Anxious to be the bearers of some token of their attachment and gratitude, they had, alas! nothing but honest hearts and kind wishes.

After much perplexity, they went into the woods, dug up each a small elm-tree, and came with their humble offerings.

Silently and unobserved, they planted them in front of their pastor's dwelling. Not venturing to mingle among the wealthier givers, their work accomplished, they returned to their homes

Two hundred years have rolled over the events of that day. The shepherd and his flock are sleeping side by side. They that gave, and he that received, have passed away; givers and their gifts forgotten. Nay, they are not all forgotten. Near by, and designating the site of the parsonage, stands an aged *elm*. Until within a few years, there were two of them. Interlocking their giant branches, they had long battled with the tempests, and drank together of the morning dews; for their shadows reached back through two centuries. Others have been planted beside them; and long and densely shaded streets, like arched passages, have given character, beauty, and a name to the *City of Elms*.

Of these two trees, thus planted, one has fallen a victim to time; the other yet stands, in hale old age, rich in its memories and associations—not the least of which is, that it was the *poor man's gift*.

A SOUTHERN CLERGYMAN.

Two coloured men, in the South, had just been hearing a sermon, and were conversing together about it. One of them remarked that he could understand but little of it, but the other said that he understood all but one word. "What is dat?" asked his companion. "De word *perseverance*," was the answer. To which the other rejoined, "Oh! me tell you what dat is; it mean, *take right hold; hold fast; hang on, ana no let go.*"

REV. JOSEPH SMITH.

Our story will carry the reader back a little more than fifty years; when all north of the Ohio river was an almost unbroken wilderness—the mysterious red man's home. On the other side, a bold and hardy band from beyond the mountains had built their log cabins, and were trying to subdue the wilderness.

To them every hour was full of peril. The Indians would often cross the river, steal their children and horses, and kill and scalp any victim who came in their way. They worked in the field with weapons at their side; and, on the Sabbath, met in the grove of the rude log church to hear the word of God, with their rifles in their hands.

To preach to these settlers, Mr. Joseph Smith, a Presbyterian minister, had left his parental home east of the mountains. He, it was said, was the second minister who had crossed the Monongahela river. He settled in Washington county, Pennsylvania, and became the pastor of the Cross Creek and Upper Buffalo congregations, dividing his time between them. He found them a willing and united people, but still unable to pay him a salary which would support his family. He, in common with all the early ministers, must cultivate a farm. He purchased one on credit, proposing to pay for it with the salary pledged to him by his people.

Years passed away; the pastor was unpaid; little or no money was in circulation; wheat was abundant, but there was no market; it could not be sold for more than twelve-and-a-half cents, in cash. Even their salt had to be brought across the mountains on pack-horses, and was worth eight dollars per bushel: twenty-one bushels of wheat were often given for one of salt.

The time came when the last payment must be made, and

Mr. Smith was told he must pay or leave his farm. Three years' salary was now due from his people.

For the want of this, his land, his improvements upon it, and his hopes of remaining among a beloved people, must be abandoned. The people were called together, and the case laid before them. They were greatly moved. Counsel from on high was sought. Plan after plan was proposed and abandoned. The people were unable to pay the tithe of their debts, and no money could be borrowed.

In despair they adjourned, to meet again the following week. In the mean time it was ascertained that a Mr. Moore, who owned the only mill in the country, would grind for them wheat on moderate terms. At the next meeting, it was resolved to carry their wheat to Mr. Moore's mill. Some gave fifty bushels, some more. This was carried from fifteen to twenty-six miles, on horses, to the mill.

In a month, word came that the flour was ready to go to market. Again the people were called together. After an earnest prayer, the question was asked, Who will run the flour to New Orleans? This was a startling question. The work was perilous in the extreme. Months must pass before the adventurer could hope to return, even though his journey should be fortunate. Nearly all the way was a wilderness; and gloomy tales had been told of the treacherous Indians. More than one boat's crew had gone on that journey, and came back no more.

Who, then, would endure the toil and brave the danger? None volunteered. The young shrunk back, and the middle-aged had their excuses. Their last scheme seemed likely to fail. At length a hoary-headed man, an elder in the church, sixty-four years of age, arose, and, to the astonishment of the assembly, said, "Here am I; send me." The deepest feeling at once pervaded the whole assembly. To see their venerated elder thus devote himself for their good, melted them all to tears. They gathered around old Father Smiley, to learn that his resolution was indeed taken; that, rather than lose their pastor, he would brave danger, toil, and even death. After some delay and trouble, two young men were induced, by hope of a large reward, to go as his assistants.

A day was appointed for starting. The young and old, from far and near, from love to Father Smiley, and the deep interest in the object of his mission, gathered together, and, with their pastor at their head, came down from the church, fifteen miles away to the bank of the river, to bid the old man farewell. Then a prayer was offered by their pastor. A parting hymn was sung. "There," said the old Scotchman, "untie the cable, and let us see what the Lord will do for us." This was done, and the boat floated slowly away.

More than nine months passed, and no word came back from Father Smiley. Many a prayer had been breathed for him; but what had been his fate, was unknown. Another Sabbath came. The people came together for worship; and there, on his rude bench, before the preacher, composed and devout, sat Father Smiley. After the services, the people were requested to meet early in the week, to hear the report. All came again.

After thanks had been rendered to God for his safe return, Father Smiley arose and told his story:—That the Lord had prospered his mission; that he had sold his flour for twenty-seven dollars per barrel, and then got safely back. He then drew a large purse, and poured upon the table a larger pile of gold than most of the spectators had ever seen before. The young men were paid each a hundred dollars. Father Smiley was asked his charges. He meekly replied that he thought he ought to have the same as one of the young men, though he had not done quite as much work. It was immediately proposed to pay him three hundred dollars. This he refused to receive, till the pastor was paid. Upon counting the money, there was found enough to pay what was due Mr. S., to advance his salary for the year to come, to reward Father Smiley with three hundred dollars, and then to leave a large dividend for each contribution. Thus their debts were paid, their pastor relieved; and, while life lasted, he broke to them the bread of life. The bones of both pastor and elder have long reposed in the same church-yard; but a grateful posterity still tell this pleasing story of the past.

A MISSIONARY AMONG THE INDIANS.

Few anecdotes are more interesting, as connected with the ministry, than some of those relating to the Indians. In 1803, these persons at Stockbridge delivered a speech to a missionary who laboured among them, which shows their affection to him, while it also illustrates not a few passages of the sacred volume. The following is an extract:—

Father! when I look at you, I see the tears are falling down your cheeks, on account of the many dismal objects you have seen. Now, according to the ancient custom of my forefathers, I stretch forth my hand and wipe the tears from your eyes, that you may see clearly. And, likewise, I see that your ears are stopped with the dust that flies about. I now clear your ears, that you may hear distinctly. I also loosen your tongue, that you may speak freely. Having done this, I see that your legs and feet are muddy, by reason of the wet path by which you travel. I likewise wash your legs and feet. While I do this, I feel some briars stick in your feet. I pluck them out, and take the healing oil, which our forefathers used to keep for that purpose, and oil them, that they may feel comfortable, while you sit by the side of our fire-place.

MORAVIAN MISSIONARIES.

A LARGE body of Indians had been converted by the Moravian missionaries, and settled in the West, where their simplicity and harmlessness seemed a renewal of the better days of Christianity. During the Revolutionary war, these settlements, named Dichtenau and Guadenhutten, being located in the seat of the former Indian contests, were exposed to outrage from both parties. Being, however, under the tuition and influence of the whites, and having adopted their religion and the virtuous portion of their habits, they naturally apprehended that the hostile Indians, sweeping down upon the American frontier, would take advantage of their helplessness, and destroy them as allies of the whites. Subsequent events enable us to compare the red and white man, and determine which is the savage. A party of two hundred Hurons fiercely approached the Moravian Indian town. The Christian Indians conducted themselves, in this trying extremity, with meekness and firmness. They sent a deputation with refreshments to their approaching foes, and told them that, by the word of God, they were taught to be at peace with all men, and entreated for themselves and their white teachers, peace and protection. And what replied the savage, fresh from the wilds, and panting for blood? Did he mock to scorn the meek and Christian appeal? Did he answer with the war-whoop, and lead on his men to the easy slaughter of his foes? What else could be expected from an Indian? Yet such was *not* the response of the red warrior. He said he was on a war party, and his heart had been evil, and his aim had been blood; but the words of his brethren had opened his eyes. He would do them no harm. "Obey your teachers," said he, "worship your God, and be not afraid. No creature shall harm you."

A DISCOURAGED PASTOR.

I once heard of a minister who stated that he preached a number of years in a certain place, without any visible benefit to any one. Finally, he concluded it was not right for him to preach, and in consequence thought he would give it up. But, while musing on the subject, he fell asleep and dreamed. "I dreamed," said he, "that I was to work for a certain man for so much, and my business was sitting upon a very large rock, with a very small hammer, pounding upon the middle of it, in order to split it open. I worked a long time, to no effect; and at length I became discouraged, and began to complain, when my employer came. Said he, 'Why do you complain? Have you not fared well while in my employ?'

"'Oh! yes.'

"'Have you not had enough to eat?'

"'Yes.'

"'Have you been neglected in any way?'

"'No, sir.'

"'Then,' said he, 'keep to work, cease your complaints, and I will take care of the result.'

"He then left me.

"I then thought that I applied my little hammer with more energy, and soon the rock burst open with such force that it awoke me. Then," says he, "I ceased to complain; I seized my little hammer with new vigor; I hammered upon that great rock, Sin, with renewed energy, nothing doubting, and soon the rock burst. The Spirit of the Lord rushed in, and the result was a reward of a glorious ingathering of souls."

REV. SYLVESTER LARNED.

The communication of reproof, however painful it may be is one of the most important and most useful duties of the Christian ministry. A Spanish gentleman once called on the late Rev. Sylvester Larned, of New Orleans, one of the most eloquent pulpit orators of his day, to say that he wished to join his church, and to receive the sacrament of the Lord's Supper; "for," said he, with an oath, "you are the most eloquent man I have ever heard!" Mr. Larned spent an hour with him in explaining what was required in order to becoming a member of his church: in other words, what it is to be a true Christian; and the Spaniard went away with a heavy heart, to reflect on a subject which had never been presented to his mind in the same light before.

A CLERGYMAN.

A clergyman, who was not very remarkable for his zeal in the cause of his Divine Master, while travelling in New York state, stopped for a night in a place where there was an extensive revival of religion. After resting for a short time at the inn, his curiosity to view the place led him to stroll through the streets. He had not proceeded far on his evening ramble, before his ear was arrested by the voice of prayer. He paused and listened; and, finding that the voice issued from a retired and humble dwelling by the roadside, stranger as he was, he resolved to enter. On entering, he found himself unexpectedly surrounded by a band of disciples, assembled for special prayer. He cast his eye about, upon the little group, in a vain endeavour to find some one whom he could recognise as an acquaintance; but all were strangers in person, through brethren in Christ. Collecting his wandering thoughts, he bowed himself in the humble attitude of prayer, and, to his infinite surprise, he soon discovered that himself, by name, and the people of his charge, were the subjects of ardent and importunate supplication. The person who was leading their devotions, was an entire stranger to him; and yet he seemed to wrestle in spirit with God, that he might be aroused to greater faithfulness and zeal in his ministerial duties and private devotions, and that God would prepare him to become an agent in reviving his work in the church and congregation over whom he was placed as a spiritual watchman. After the meeting had closed, being deeply impressed with the guilt of his past negligence, and with the responsibility of the ministerial office, he silently withdrew and returned to his lodgings. Not long after this event, he returned to his people, and resumed, with renewed vigour, the duties of his office. Within a short time, a revival commenced in his congregation, and three hundred were early numbered as the hopeful subjects of redeeming mercy.

INDEX

OF

PERSONS AND PLACES.

	Page		Page
A., Rev. Mr.	22	Bailey, Rev. Mr.	217, 433
Adams, Rev. Z.	160	Baird, Rev. Dr.	229
African	448	Baker, Rev. Mr.	356
Albany, N. Y.	131, 231, 353	Bangor, Me.	177
Alden, Rev. Mr.	217	Bangs, Rev. Dr.	108
Alder, Rev. Dr.	134	Baldwin, Rev. Dr.	385
Alexander, Rev. Dr.	230	Balfour, Rev. Dr.	224
Alleghany mountains	282	Baltimore, Md.	111, 379
————, prophet of the	98	Barbadoes	60
Allen, Rev. J.	190	Baxter, Rev. R.	148
——, Rev. S.	200	Beatty, Rev. C.	59
Allison, Rev. Dr. F.	18	Beck, Mr.	276
Allsworthy, Deacon	285	Bedell, Rev. Dr.	109, 110, 276
Amherst, college at	145	Beecher, family of	44
Andover, college at	195, 210	————, Rev. Dr.	123, 211, 350, 438
Angier, Mrs. A. L.	185	————, Rev. G.	45
Annapolis	204	Bellamy, Rev. Dr.	263
Arminian, and Dr. Nettleton	393	Bellingham, Mass.	217
Armstrong, Rev. Dr.	290	Benedict, Rev. T. P.	338
————, Rev. J.	409	Bennett, Rev. Mr.	145, 396
Asbury, Bishop	219	Bethlehem, Conn.	263
Atheist	398	Birmingham, Eng.	395
Athol	323	Bishop, a pious	40
Auburn, N. Y.	387	Blair, Rev. S.	60, 360
Augusta, Ga.	379	Blood, Rev. Caleb	269
————, Me.	109	Blythe, Rev. S.	57
		Bohemia, Del.	19
		Bommaseen, Indian chief	392
		Bonaparte, Louis	415
B., Elder	213	Bordentown, N. J.	290
——, Mr.	398	Borneo	68
——, Rev. Dr.	454	Boston, Mass.	21, 41, 50, 63, 72, 73, 76, 101, 111, 135, 137, 145, 154, 162, 173, 207, 215, 217, 269, 325, 328, 336, 357, 377, 389, 392, 421, 454
——, Rev. Mr.	51, 459		
Backus, Rev. Dr.	455		
————, Rev. Mr	217		

472 INDEX OF PERSONS AND PLACES.

	PAGE
Boyle, Sir R.	159
Brainerd, Rev. D.	451
Breckenridge, Rev. Dr.	234
Bricklayer	312
Bridgewater, Mass.	175
Bristol, R. I.	327
Brock, Rev. J.	189
Brockden, Mr.	141
Brooklyn, N. Y.	176
Brown, John	402
———, Rev. T.	235, 287
Brunswick, N. J.	400
Buffalo, Upper	463
Bumstead, Mr.	22
Burr, President	20
Bushnell, Rev. Mr.	386
Byles, Rev. Dr. M.	207
Byne, Rev. E.	355
C———, Mr.	51, 13
———, Rev. Dr.	351
———, Rev. Mr.	47, 413
Cadet	25
Cambridge, Mass.	111, 131, 152, 227, 440
Cambridgeport, Mass.	322
Cape Cod	131
Case, Rev. Mr.	411
Caviller, and Dr. Nettleton	300
Catlin, Rev. Dr.	440
Champlain, Lake	357
Chaplain, U. S. Military	25
Chaplin, Rev. Dr. J.	205
Charleston, Me.	411
———, S. C.	219, 246
Chase, Bishop	273
Chauncy, Rev. Dr.	248
Chebucto, N. S.	445
Cherokees, minister among	447
Chesterfield, Va.	204
Chestertown, Md.	142
Child	449
Chittenden, Vt.	51
Cincinnati	162, 261, 455
Clap, Rev. Mr.	317
Clarinda, the African	216
Clark, Captain	161
Clergyman	23, 50, 68, 205, 228, 325, 354, 370, 371, 374, 469
——— ——— at St. Louis	424
——— ———, a Baptist	231
——— ———, a courteous	312
——— ——— in Indiana	88
——— ——— in Maine	95
——— ——— in Massachusetts	161

	PAGE
Clergyman in New York	373, 443
———, a New England	35, 130, 169, 181, 328, 373, 375, 383
——— at New Orleans	410
——— in Philadelphia	381
——— in Tennessee	358
——— in Virginia	293, 388
———, a Methodist	165, 267, 370
———, an eccentric	166
———, an effective	124
———, an eminent	150
———, an Episcopal	245
———, an old	44, 133, 362, 395
———, a persecuting	256
———, a Presbyterian	290
———, a southern	462
———, a travelling	427
———, a Universalist	375
———, a village	346
———, a wise	398
———, a young	34, 153, 185, 223, 245, 264
Clergymen, aged	244
———, several	71, 74, 175, 266
———, several young	49, 367
———, travelling	277
———, two	25, 109, 231, 245, 264, 336
Clerk, a church	330
Coke, Rev. Dr.	204, 389
Coley, Rev. Mr.	352
Coleman, Rev. Mr.	41
Cotton, Rev. C.	348
Columbian river	69
Cone, Rev. Dr.	180
Connecticut	234, 242, 350, 367
Cook, Rev. C. S.	457
Cooper, Rev. Dr.	248
———, Rev. W.	41
Cotton, Rev. John	389
Craig, Mr.	342
———, Rev. Messrs.	229
Cross, Rev. Mr.	391
Cross Creek	463
Cuba	191
Culpepper, county of	181
D., Dr.	358
—, Mrs.	411
Daniel, Rev. E.	235
D'Anville, Duke	444
Dartmouth college	455

INDEX OF PERSONS AND PLACES.

	PAGE
Davies, Rev. President	60—62, 166, 190, 452
Deacon	312, 367
Deerfield, N. E.	195
Delaware	8, 19
Dickson, Rev. D.	410
Divine, a celebrated	176, 267
———, a New England	23
Drunkard	51
Dunbarton	226, 362
Dwight, Rev. Dr.	48, 160, 163, 208, 227, 233, 235, 412, 445
———————, mother of	48
Eastburn, Rev. J.	46, 313
Eastham	154
East Hampton, L. I.	351
East Indies	230
East Windsor	237
Eatonton	268
Edgartown	58
Edgefield C. H.	127
Edwards, Rev. President	48, 163, 195, 201, 431, 439
Elder	368
Elizabeth, Queen	48
Eliot, Rev. J.	178, 202, 254, 372
Elliot, Bishop	372
Ely, Rev. Dr.	37
Emmons, Rev. Dr.	232
Enfield	164
England	377, 424, 432, 458
Erskine, Rev. Dr.	224
Estabrook, Rev. Mr.	323
Europe	65
F., Rev. Dr.	172
—, Rev. Mr.	334
Fairfield	257
Family, a Methodist	258
Field, Rev. Mr.	371
Finley, Rev. Dr.	261, 369
Fisk Rev. Dr.	108, 109
Fogg's Manor, Penna.	60
Forrest, Rev. Mr.	223
Fort Wayne	211
Franklin, Dr.	144, 394, 453

	PAGE
Franklin, Mass.	233
Friend	178
Furman, Rev. Dr.	127, 246
Gano, Rev. J.	180, 337
Gardiner	109
Gentleman	326, 460
———————, and Dr. Nettleton	306
———————, a young	351
George, Bishop	257
———— II., King	167
Georgia	238, 315, 372, 379, 431
Gillespie, Rev. Mr.	151
Gooch, Sir W.	256
Good Hope, cape of	230
Goodrich, Rev. Dr.	414
Grafton, Rev. Mr	318
Great Harbour	58
Great Valley	455
Green mountains	277
Green, Rev. Dr.	46
Gregory, Dr. O.	36
Griffin, Rev. Dr.	71—73, 90, 91, 377
Grimaldi, an African	315
Griswold, Bishop	191, 327
H., Rev. Mr.	431
Hague, Rev. W.	203
Hall, Rev. N.	63
—, Rev. R.	172
Halifax, N. S.	76
Hallowell, Me.	109
Hamburg, Ga.	379
Hamilton, General	273
Hampden Sidney, college at	74
Hampshire, county of	200
Hanover, N. C.	94, 453
Harmony	409
Harris, Rev. Dr.	63, 225, 362
———, Rev. S.	204, 339
Harvey, Rev. B.	167
Hatfield, N. E.	195
Hauman, Mr.	341
Hawley, Rev. G.	227
Haynes, Rev. L.	238
Healy, Rev. Mr.	251
Henry, Rev. Dr. T. C.	425

INDEX OF PERSONS AND PLACES.

	Page		Page
Hiacoomes	58	L., Mr.	149
Hill, Rev. Dr.	74	——, Rev. Dr.	397
Hitchcock, Rev. President	145	——, Rev. Mr.	249
Hodgkinson, Mr.	144	Lady	369, 449
Holland	230	——, a dying	406, 424
Homer, Rev. B.	120	——, a gay	35, 368
——, Rev. Dr.	348	——, a young	299, 301, 307
Hooker, Rev. T.	111, 163, 412	Laidlie, Rev. Dr.	340
Hopkins, Rev. Dr.	205, 439	Lambert, Mr.	310
——, Rev. Mr.	43	Larned, Rev. S.	107, 469
Hopkinton, Mass.	122	Lathrop, Rev. Dr.	122, 144, 255, 412
Howe, Rev. Mr.	122	Lawrence, river St.	357
Hull, Rev. Mr.	400	Lawyer, a young	273
Humphrey, Rev. Dr.	115	Leland, Rev. John	267
Hyde, Rev. Mr.	366	Leonard, Rev. L.	269
——, Rev. Dr.	440	Litchfield	123
		Livingston, Rev. Dr.	230, 415
		London	17, 36, 166
		Long Island	44
		Louisiana	290
		Lowell, Mass.	312
Indiana	88, 211	Lyman, Rev. H.	65
Indian woman	451		
Indians, a missionary to the	210, 466		
——, Flat-headed	69		
Infidel, a young	405		
Ingraham, Colonel	152		
Ireland	18, 59	M., Rev. Mr.	78, 371, 441
		M'Cartee, Rev. Dr.	36
		M'Ilvaine, Bishop	25, 446
		Maine	238, 422
		Malta	307
		Man, a white	448
J., Rev. Mr.	391	Manchester	240
Jack, a colored preacher	283	Manly, Rev. President	127, 268
Jacobs, Rev. B.	322	Mann, Mr.	217
James, Rev. J. W.	33	Manning, Rev. Dr	203, 217
James river	250	Martha's Vineyard	53
Japhet, Rev. Mr.	53	Maryland	84
Jerusalem	66	Mason, Rev. Dr. J. M.	172, 200, 402
Jew	293	——, Mr. G.	458
Johnson, Rev. Mr.	250	Massachusetts	22, 103, 152, 161, 165, 234, 450
Judson, Rev. Dr.	247, 325		
		Massey, Rev. Mr.	458
		Mather, Rev. Dr. C.	53, 95, 215, 389, 392
		Mayhew, Rev. T.	53, 58
		Maynard, Mr.	64
Kennaday, Rev. J.	89	Mercer, Rev. Dr.	125, 218, 268, 399
Kennebeck river	109	Methodist brother	129
Kentucky	171, 229	Methodist preacher	87, 386
King, Rev. Dr.	64, 65	Middleborough, Mass.	217
Kirkland, Rev. Mr.	159	Middleton, Del.	19
——, President	440	Mid Lothian, Virginia	145
Knox, Rev. Hugh	18	Miller, a Sabbath-breaking	346

INDEX OF PERSONS AND PLACES. 475

Miller, Rev. Dr	111, 224
Minister	228, 370, 371, 435, 436, 447
———, a Baptist	311
———, a circuit	257
———, a city	197
———, a country	277
———, a delighted	282
———, a faithful	116, 276, 335
———, in New Hampshire	226
———, in Boston	336
———, in New York	326, 424, 457
———, a mistaken	450
———, an able	27
———, an aged	340, 373, 434
———, a New England	42, 148, 375, 444, 460
———, an unsuccessful	286
———, a penitent	377
———, a poor	312
———, a popular	209
———, a shrewd	427
———, a travelling	347
———, a Universalist	158, 225, 240, 267, 375, 378, 432
———, a young	71, 233, 282, 459
———, a zealous	40
Ministers, Puritan	437
———, several young	30
———, six young	28
———, thoughtless	224
———, two	249, 262
Missionaries, American	437
Missionary	50, 192
———, a home	455
———, an Indian	69, 96, 466
———, a Moravian	467
Mississippi river	290, 453
Monmouth, N. J.	120
Monongahela river	463
Moody, Rev. Mr.	152, 285
Moore, Mr.	464
Morton, Rev. C. S.	132
N , Mrs.	360
—, Rev. Mr.	109
Narragansett bay	191
Negro, an old	29
Neshaminy	59
Nettleton, Rev. Dr.	115, 237, 241, 296

Newark, N. J.	20, 90, 120, 233
New Haven	455
New Brunswick	17, 60, 94, 400
Newbury	152
Newburyport	173, 249
Newcastle, Del.	432
New England	95, 122, 133, 148, 176, 210, 217, 356, 433, 438, 444, 445
New Hampshire	42, 44, 72, 226, 312, 357, 385
New Jersey	17, 60, 117, 166, 265, 287, 343, 451
New London, Penn.	18
New Orleans	107, 410, 464, 469
New Plymouth	95
Newport, R. I.	191
Newton, Mass.	348
New York	39, 54, 62, 83, 85, 108, 138, 155, 177, 184, 185, 192, 200, 202, 233, 240, 264, 269, 274, 315, 316, 321, 326, 334, 335, 341, 342, 349, 4, 357, 360, 368, 373, 386, 387, 395, 402, 424, 457, 460, 469
Nightingale, Rev. S.	37
North Carolina	60, 94, 204
Northampton, Mass.	38, 66, 195
Norwich, Conn.	208
Nott, Rev. Dr.	206
O., Mr.	459
Oglethorpe, Governor	315
Ohio	70, 176, 276, 414, 456, 463
Otsego	47
P., General	362
Paine, Thomas	40, 290, 291
Palestine	65
Pammechannit	53
Paris	65
Party, a gay, and Dr. Nettleton	308
Pastor, a Baptist	245
———, a Christian	374, 414
———, a devoted	213
———, a discouraged	466
———, a good	26

INDEX OF PERSONS AND PLACES.

	PAGE		PAGE
Pastor, an anxious	324	R., Mr.	213, 232
——, a wise	292	Raleigh, N. C.	204
Pastors, several	435	Randolph, Mrs.	416
Patten, Rev. Dr.	54	Rappahannock, county of	182
Patterson, Rev. J.	370, 441	Raritan river	287
Pattison, Rev. Dr.	205	Ravencross, Rev. Mr.	22
Payson, Rev. Dr.	78, 104, 206, 253, 417	Rawson, Rev. Mr.	131
Pennsylvania	18, 24, 139	Reading, Mass.	189
Perkins, Rev. J.	40	Restorationist	297
Persia	40	Rhode Island	317
Perth Amboy	257	Rice, Rev. Dr. J. H.	206, 415
Peter, the Indian preacher	159	——, Rev. Luther	182
Philadelphia	23, 37, 38, 46, 50, 54, 109, 113, 123, 130, 140, 141, 171, 250, 259, 276, 311, 331, 441, 453	Richards, Rev. Dr.	90
		Richmond, Rev. L.	388
		————, Va.	281
Phips, Governor	210	Robinson, Rev. W.	17, 60, 94
Physician	409	Rodgers, Rev. Dr.	18, 61, 83, 84, 141, 202, 223, 256, 432
Pierce, Rev. Dr.	150		
Pittsfield	115	Rome, N. Y.	387
Plainfield, Mass.	64	Rousseau	157
————, N. J.	343		
Plato	156		
Plymouth	134		
Polk, Rev. Mr.	36		
Pond, Rev. Dr.	247	S., Rev. Mr.	87, 109, 148, 162, 249, 268, 431
Porter, Rev. Dr.	210		
——, Rev. T.	130	Sailor, a profane	50, 446
Portland, Me.	104, 419	Salem	408
Poughkeepsie, N. Y.	273	Saratoga, springs at	420
Preacher	269	Savannah river	129
————, a forcible	112	Scipio, an African	248
————, from England	448	Scotch Plains, N. J.	235, 287
————, a good	161, 384	Scudder, Rev. Dr.	50, 235
————, an impressive	103	Sedgwick, Judge	410
————, an unknown	335	Seneca Lake	98
————, a practical	181	Shepherd, Rev. John	207
————, a Universalist	229, 231	Sheppard, Rev. Professor	177
Preachers, coloured	171, 283, 289	Sherburne	387
Priestley, Rev. Dr.	111	Shoals, Isle of	189
Prince, Rev. Mr.	444	Skeptic	370
Princeton, college at	49, 111, 139, 265, 383, 442	Slave, a blind	146
		Smiley, Elder	464
Providence, R. I.	50, 205, 378	Smith, Rev. Dr. J. B.	75
Punch, a Christian negro	219	————, Rev. Joseph	463

INDEX OF PERSONS AND PLACES. 477

	Page		Page
Socrates	157	Treat, Rev. Mr.	154
Soldier, a Scottish	410	Trefit, Rev. Mr.	426
Somers	455	Trenton, N. J.	400
South Amboy	287	Truair, Rev. Mr.	155, 387
South Carolina	127, 400	Truro, parish of	458
Spencer, Rev. Mr.	321	Tuscarora Indians	50, 96
Sprague, Rev. Dr.	73	Tyler, Rev. Dr.	237
Spring, Rev. Dr.	316, 440		
Springfield, Mass.	122, 124		
———, Ohio	257		
Standford, Rev. B.	175		
Stanford, Rev. Dr.	177, 225, 341, 460	United States, Military Academy of	25
Staughton, Rev. Dr.	113, 114, 250, 290	Universalist	112, 296
Stearns, Rev. S. H.	195	Utica	167, 386
Stevens, Rev. Mr.	173	Utrecht	230
Still, Rev. C.	76		
Stillman, Rev. Dr.	149, 217		
Stockbridge, Mass.	42		
Stoddard, Rev. S.	38, 195		
Stone, Rev. Dr.	191	Vermont	81, 85, 371
St. George's, Del.	18, 19, 83, 141	Vernon, Mount	458
St. Louis	424, 455	Virginia	22, 28, 61, 74, 138, 204, 206,
St. Mary's	211		280, 293, 308, 339, 361, 388, 415
Strawbridge, Rev. Mr.	82		
Strong, Rev. Dr.	79, 123		
———, Rev. Mr.	163		
Sullivan, General	203		
Summerfield, Rev. John	184, 400	W., Mr.	431
Sunday, Rev. John	134	Wabash	409
Symington, Mrs.	161	Waddell, Rev. Dr.	155, 317
		Walker, Rev. J.	204
		———, Rev. Mr.	387
		Ward, Bishop	276
		Washington	418, 451, 458, 463
Taylor, Rev. Dr. N. W.	237	———, N. Y.	441
———, Rev. E. T.	76, 106	Waters, Mr.	182
Teetotaller, a staunch	386	Waubon, Indian chief	179
Tennent, Rev. G.	166, 453	Welch, Rev. Dr.	131
———, Rev. W.	54, 59, 117, 118, 120,	Wells, Rev. S. T.	391
	265, 360	Wesley, Rev. J.	315
Tennessee	358, 453	West, Rev. Dr.	42
Texas	282	Westminster, Vt.	371
Tinsley, Rev. D.	204	Whitefield, Rev. G.	83, 118, 135, 163,
Todd, Rev. Dr	357		196, 264, 337, 339, 449
Tom, poor	54	Whitman, Deacon J.	75

	PAGE	
Wickford	191	Worcester, Rev. Mr.
Willard, Rev. Mr.	154	Wrentham, Mass.
Willey, Rev. Mr.	72	Wykoff, Mr.
Williams, Rev. W.	217	Wyman, Deacon
Williamsburg, Va.	256	Wyoming, N. Y.
Wiltshire, town of	212	
Winder, Mr.	84	
Winthrop, Governor	111	
Wirt, Hon. Mr.	155, 317	
Wisner, Rev. Dr.	444	
Witherspoon, Mr.	19	Yale College
———. ———, Rev. Dr.	383	Yarmouth
Woburn, Mass.	396	York, Me.

THE END.

ANNOUNCEMENT.

The Editor of this work respectfully announces that he has in preparation a series of volumes, uniform in size and price with "The Clergy of America;" the publication of which may be expected at as early a period as may comport with the care demanded in their preparation by their importance. The following list will show the varied character, and give a general idea of the contents of the series; but probably it does not furnish the order in which they will be issued.

THE PULPIT OF AMERICA:—Facts relating to its occupants, incidents, and results, in the United States. A companion to "The Clergy of America."

THE LITERATURE OF AMERICA:—Anecdotes of its history, authors, curiosities, and influence, in the United States.

THE LADIES OF AMERICA:—Anecdotes illustrative of the female character in the United States.

ANNOUNCEMENT.

THE GENTLEMEN OF AMERICA:—Anecdotes illustrative of the character of professional and other members of general society in the United States.

THE YOUNG PEOPLE OF AMERICA:—Anecdotes illustrative of juvenile character in the United States.

www.ingramcontent.com/pod-product-compliance
Lightning Source LLC
Chambersburg PA
CBHW051855300426
44117CB00006B/403